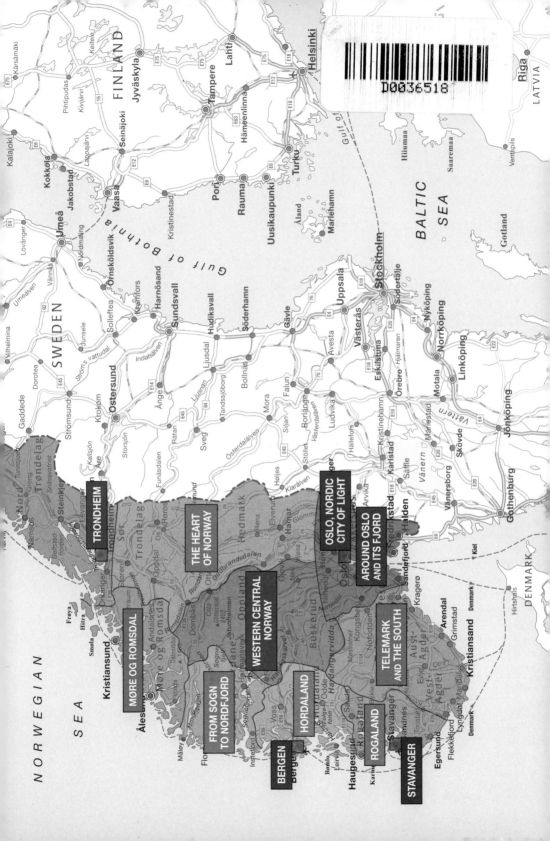

NORWAY

⊙ Walking Eye App

YOUR FREE DESTINATION CONTENT AND EBOOK AVAILABLE THROUGH THE WALKING EYE APP

Your guide now includes a free eBook and destination content for your chosen destination, all for the same great price as before. Simply download the Walking Eye App from the App Store or Google Play to access your free eBook and destination content.

HOW THE WALKING EYE APP WORKS

Through the Walking Eye App, you can purchase a range of eBooks and destination content. However, when you buy this book, you can download the corresponding eBook and destination content for free. Just see below in the grey panels where to find your free content and then scan the QR code at the bottom of this page.

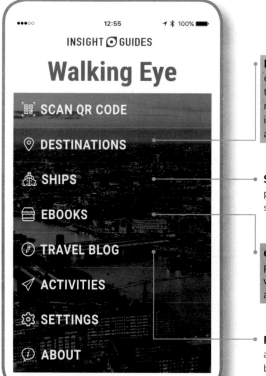

Destinations: Download your corresponding essential destination content from here, featuring recommended sights and attractions, restaurants, hotels and an A–Z of practical information, all for free. Other destinations are available for purchase.

Ships: Interested in ship reviews? Find independent reviews of river and ocean ships in this section, all available for purchase.

eBooks: You can download your free accompanying digital version of this guide here. You will also find a whole range of other eBooks, all available for purchase.

Free access to travel-related blog articles about different destinations, updated on a daily basis.

HOW THE DESTINATION CONTENT WORKS

Each destination includes a short introduction, an A–Z of practical information and recommended points of interest, split into 4 different categories:
- Highlights
- Accommodation
- Eating out
- What to do

You can view the location of every point of interest and save it by adding it to your Favourites. In the 'Around Me' section you can view all the points of interest within 5km.

HOW THE EBOOKS WORK

The eBooks are provided in EPUB file format. Please note that you will need an eBook reader installed on your device to open the file. Many devices come with this as standard, but you may still need to install one manually from Google Play.

The eBook content is identical to the content in the printed guide.

HOW TO DOWNLOAD THE WALKING EYE APP

1. Download the Walking Eye App from the App Store or Google Play.
2. Open the app and select the scanning function from the main menu.
3. Scan the QR code on this page – you will then be asked a security question to verify ownership of the book.
4. Once this has been verified, you will see your eBook and destination content in the purchased ebook and destination sections, where you will be able to download them.

Other destination apps and eBooks are available for purchase separately or are free with the purchase of the Insight Guide book.

CONTENTS

Travel Tips

TRANSPORT

A – Z

LANGUAGE

FURTHER READING

Maps

Inside front cover Norway
Inside back cover Oslo

LEGEND

⌕ Insight on
◙ Photo Story

THE BEST OF NORWAY: TOP ATTRACTIONS

△ **Preikestolen**. The route up to Preikestolen, or Pulpit Rock, is Norway's most popular hike, and with good reason. The views are stunning, but vertigo-sufferers should steer clear. See page 196.

▽ **Oslo**. Norway's capital is a vibrant city, with child-friendly museums, great dining and shopping, and a stunning opera house. See page 139.

△ **Tromsø**. The gateway to the far north, Tromsø has great museums and a beautiful cathedral, and appeals to adventurous types curious about the Arctic. See page 282.

▽ **Hardangervidda National Park**. Europe's largest mountainous plateau and a popular hiking destination in summer. See page 175.

△ **Bergen**. Norway's second city sits on a craggy shoreline on the west coast surrounded by islands. It's rich in history and sights, so allow a couple of days to make the most of its museums, galleries and restaurants. See page 217.

◁ **Trondheim**. Norway's third-largest city is still its historical and religious capital. Seen here is a monument to Olav Tryggvason, the city's founder. See page 255.

▽ **The fjords**. Norway's most spectacular attraction: each has its own character and appeal – this is Geirangerfjord, to many the most beautiful. See page 245.

△ **Lofoten**. Its dramatic island scenery with rugged peaks and white sand beaches, and its traditional fishing industry make Lofoten well worth the trip north. See page 275.

▽ **North Cape**. This is Continental Europe's northern-most tip and the last frontier. See page 287.

▽ **Røros**. The Unesco World Heritage Site is a beautifully preserved old mining town famed for its turf-roofed wooden buildings and its church. See page 170.

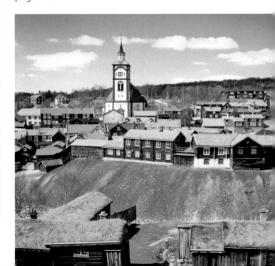

THE BEST OF NORWAY: EDITOR'S CHOICE

Lysefjord, Rogaland.

BEST FJORDS (FROM NORTH TO SOUTH)

Geirangerfjord. A Unesco World Heritage Site, Geirangerfjord is famous for its emerald waters and stunning waterfalls; it is arguably the most beautiful of the Norwegian fjords. See page 245.

Sognefjord. Norway's deepest and longest fjord, and one of its most spectacular. Here you'll find the Urnes stave church and the Norwegian Glacier Museum. The spectacular Flåm railway ends in Aurland on Sognefjord, and is a must too. See page 235.

Nærøyfjord. An arm of Sognefjord, and only 250 metres (820ft) across at its narrowest, the peaceful "Narrow fjord" is another Unesco World Heritage Site. The fjord, which sometimes freezes over in winter, is popular with kayakers in summer. See page 238.

Hardangerfjord. Visit this fjord in spring, when the many orchards are in full bloom, or in summer to gorge on the delicious *moreller* (black cherries), then call by the manor house of Baroniet Rosendal, and the excellent folk museum at Utne. See page 206.

Lysefjord. Barren and windswept, Lysefjord is home to Preikestolen, a huge block of granite jutting out 600 metres (2,000ft) above sea level, and Kjerag, a mighty boulder precariously stuck between two mountain walls. A popular destination for extreme-sport enthusiasts and hikers. See page 195.

BEST ARCHITECTURE

Oslo Opera House. This striking building in white granite and glass has made its mark on the Oslo waterfront since opening in 2008, and is now one of the capital's top attractions. See page 139.

Ålesund. When this town burned to the ground in January 1904 it was rebuilt in the *Jugendstil* style and today hosts a superb concentration of Art Nouveau buildings. See page 244.

Stave churches. There are 28 stave churches in Norway, two of the most striking being the church at Urnes, which is on the Unesco World Heritage list, and the Heddal stave church in Telemark, the largest. See pages 189 and 237.

Hamsun Centre, Nordland. With its grassy roof and black wood exterior, the Hamsun Centre towers over the island of Hamarøy, where the novelist Knut Hamsun spent his childhood. See page 280.

Sami Parliament, Finnmark. An outstanding exercise in modern architecture, with a design blending Sami culture and building traditions with modern technology. See pages 84 and 289.

Hallingdal stave church.

BEST OUTDOOR PURSUITS

Hiking. Norway is a hikers' paradise, and opportunities abound all over the country, with Jotunheimen and Hardangervidda among the most popular walking haunts. See page 93.

Whale-watching. Between May and September off the coast of Nordland and in the Lofoten Islands, you don't need too much luck to spot minke whales, orca and even sperm whales. See page 279.

Northern lights. There is nothing quite like witnessing the northern lights (aurora borealis), one of nature's most breathtaking spectacles.

Visible almost anywhere north of the Arctic Circle in winter when the skies are clear. See page 273.

Hurtigruten. The Norwegian coastal voyage from Bergen to Kirkenes has been recognised as one of the best cruises in the world – it's an ideal way to experience the drama of Norway's extraordinary coastline. See page 229.

Cross-country skiing. Come winter, Norway becomes one of Europe's best winter-sport destinations. Cross-country here reigns supreme, with thousands of kilometres of prepared tracks. See page 96.

Cross-country skiing.

BEST MUSEUMS AND GALLERIES

National Gallery, Oslo. A great introduction to Norwegian art, focusing on the late 18th century to the early 20th, with works by artists such as Christian Krogh and J.C. Dahl well represented. See page 145.

Viking Ship Museum, Oslo. Three carefully restored Viking ships and hundreds of artefacts draw the crowds to this ever-popular museum in Bygdøy. See page 152.

Maihaugen, Lillehammer. One of the best folk museums in the country, with 200 buildings,

wonderful handicraft and folk art, and activities for children year-round. See page 168.

Norwegian Petroleum Museum, Stavanger. A highly interactive, educational museum that will delight both grown-ups and children visiting the oil capital of Norway. See page 203.

KODE, Bergen. One of the largest arts, crafts and design museum complexes in Scandinavia, with a 50,000-strong collection spread out over four locations. See page 226.

BEST HISTORIC SIGHTS

Nidaros Cathedral, Trondheim. Norway's oldest cathedral, and the resting place of St Olav, the king who brought Christianity to Norway. See page 256.

Old Town, Fredrikstad. Scandinavia's best-preserved fortress town. Quaint, cobblestoned streets and period wooden buildings. See page 160.

Akershus Fortress, Oslo. The pride of Norway's capital, perched on a bluff overlooking the

harbour and fjord, this 1,000-year-old complex is a must. See page 141.

Røros. This perfectly preserved old mining town, with its 300-year-old wooden houses, is a remarkable survivor of the industrial past. Some mines are open for tours. See page 170.

Håkonshallen, Bergen. Norway's royal family still holds events at this legendary spot on the Bergen waterfront. See page 221.

The northern lights over Kvaløya.

Breathtakingly beautiful
Geirangerfjord.

West Norway Museum of
Decorative Art, Bergen.

Rorvik, capital of the Vikna
island group.

NORTHERN CONTRASTS

Norway rewards the visitor with a beguiling mix of tradition and modern convenience, spectacular nature and city delights.

Alpine landscape.

Norway is a land of contrasts: majestic mountains tower above mysterious fjords; harsh winters are relieved by often glorious summers; and long polar nights give way to the radiant midnight sun. One of the oldest civilisations in Europe has become one of its youngest nations. The rapacious Vikings have turned into global peacemakers. It is a country where Grieg and Ibsen compete with Eurovision and American sitcoms; where environmental concerns challenge over-consumption. Norway has urban excitement and rural tranquillity: shopping malls and Toyotas rub shoulders with compass and rucksack; high technology parallels tradition.

A thriving offshore oil industry has brought prosperity and, as a consequence, social habits are changing rapidly. Though, in a society where the divorce rate is high and cohabitation the norm, the home and family remain important. Politically, democracy and debate pervade all levels of society. Murray's *Handbook for Travellers in Norway* described the Norwegians in 1874 thus: "Great patriotism and hospitality are two of the leading characteristics of the Norwegians; they are often cold and reserved, and combine great simplicity of manner with firmness and kindness. 'Deeds, not words' is their motto" – 136 years later, little has changed.

Lindesnes Lighthouse.

UNEXPECTED PLEASURES

Most people are pleasantly surprised when they visit Norway. Not only are the people friendly (with many speaking fluent English), the scenery is even more breathtaking in reality than any guidebook could ever hope to inspire. The architecture too is stunning – from numerous Unesco-listed stave churches and entire *Jugendstil* cities like Ålesund to recent ultramodern designs in Oslo and Bergen. Add to this the fact that communications and services are efficient, and that it is safe to go out at night, and you have all the ingredients for an enjoyable stay. As for prices, Norway can be eyewateringly expensive, so budgeting for your trip is a must (see page 311). But Norway's spectacular nature is free – another reason to make the most of its best playground: the great outdoors.

Geirangerfjord, a Unesco World Heritage Site.

AN UNTAMED LAND

Throughout history, Norway's difficult topography has been both a challenge and a blessing for the country's inhabitants. It has also played a significant part in shaping the Norwegian character.

From the thousand islands and skerries of the Skagerrak in the south to the sparsely vegetated Arctic tundra landscapes of the far north, from the dense forests of eastern Norway to the deep fjords in the west of the country, Norway's landscape is amazingly varied.

Covering the western and northern part of the Scandinavian peninsula, Norway (together with the Svalbard archipelago and Jan Mayen island) spreads over 385,155 sq km (150,000 sq miles), an area almost as big as California. Stretching 1,750km (1,090 miles) from south to north, the country is unevenly distributed in width, with the bulk of the landmass south of Trondheim. At its narrowest point near Narvik, it is only 6km (4 miles) wide.

One of Norway's remote outposts, and home to the polar bear, is the Svalbard archipelago, 600km (370 miles) north of the mainland. First used as a whaling base, then mined for its coal, Svalbard today lives from tourism and research.

STRIKING LANDSCAPES AND SEASCAPES

Peaks and plateaux dominate the landscape in many places. Norway is one of Europe's most mountainous countries, with four-fifths of the landmass at an altitude over 150 metres (500ft). The highest summit, Galdhøpiggen in Jotunheimen (literally "Home of the giants"), culminates at 2,469 metres (8,100ft). The vast majority of Norway's highest peaks are concentrated in this area. Some of mainland Europe's largest glaciers can also

Summer scene in Eidsbugarde, Jotenheimen.

be found in Norway – at 487 sq km (188 sq miles), Jostedalsbreen is the biggest of them all. Elsewhere, forests cover 23 percent of the territory, and cultivated land a meagre 3 percent, with the rest being lakes, bog, marshes and uncultivated land.

The bulk of the population is concentrated along the coast, and inland in the many valleys carved by glaciers during the last Ice Age – the same ones that formed Norway's many fjords. One of the largest valleys is the 230km- (143-mile) long Gudbrandsdal, which stretches from Lillehammer in the south to Dovre in the north, and is a main traffic axis on the road from Oslo to Trondheim. South of Gudbrandsdal is Mjøsa, Norway's largest lake.

Another of Norway's striking features is its coastline, the world's most rugged, and Europe's longest, with a length of 25,000km (15,500 miles) – and that's taking into account only the mainland and fjords. Add in the outlying islands (around 200,000 are scattered along the coast of Norway) and it stretches to over 83,000km (51,500 miles).

FJORDS: THE SOUL OF NORWAY

Norway's long coastline is punctuated by fjords all the way from Oslo in the southeast to the

The rugged Lofoten Islands, lying off Norway's northwest coast, have since pre-Viking times been the centre for the country's cod-fishing industry, which is still thriving today.

Arctic north. The most dramatic are those found along the west coast, with steep mountain walls rising up from the water, and small farms clinging to every ledge and hectare of green. The

The Lysefjord, to the east of Stavanger.

⊘ VITAL STATISTICS

Highest mountain: Galdhøpiggen
Longest river: Glomma
Largest lake: Mjøsa
Largest glacier (on mainland Norway):
Jostedalsbreen, 487 sq km (188 sq miles)
Town receiving the most precipitation: Bergen
Population density: 16 people per sq km
(41 per sq mile)
Natural resources: oil, gas, iron, copper, fish, timber, hydropower
Land boundaries: Sweden (1,619km/1,006 miles), Finland (727km/452 miles), Russia (196km/122 miles)

fjords are beautiful, timeless, and everyone's idea of the soul of Norway.

The western fjords begin at Stavanger in the south, now Norway's oil capital, not far from Preikestolen (Pulpit Rock), the great slab of rock standing a dizzying 600 metres (2,000ft) above Lysefjord. They stretch north to Hardangerfjord, one of the largest in the country and an early favourite, where the old traditions of music and storytelling influenced travellers such as the 19th-century composer Edvard Grieg.

Further north along the coast lies the port of Bergen, known as the gateway to the fjords; then Sognefjord (the longest and deepest fjord) and Nordfjord, in an area of glaciers, lakes and mountain massifs; Storfjord, parts of which bite far into the land; and, finally, the calm of the Geiranger, arguably the prettiest fjord of them all.

HUMAN GEOGRAPHY

The country's topography has shaped the Norwegian character: Norwegians have had to adapt to the difficult lay of the land and fight the elements to harness nature's bounty.

The fjords gave Norway its great seafaring tradition. For the early Vikings, who travelled to Scotland, Iceland and the rest of Europe, as much as for the modern traveller who chooses a

local fishing industry, going back 1,200 years to the first exports of stockfish to elsewhere in Europe during the Viking age. More recently, it was the discovery of oil and gas in the North Sea which fuelled (literally) the huge economic boom that has seen Norway change from being a relatively poor country into one of the world's richest.

On land it was the cold winters with heavy snowfalls and the harsh terrain separating isolated valley communities that led Norwegians to invent skiing, and then to excel at it. To this day the saying goes that Norwegians are born

Climbing the glacier at Jostedal.

Ski sailing in a storm, Hardangervidda.

Hardangervidda, a popular hiking destination in the southwest, is Norway's largest national park. It is home to wild reindeer, arctic fox and snowy owl. The park doubled as Planet Hoth in the Star Wars film The Empire Strikes Back.

ship as the most comfortable way to experience this magnificent coastline, the sea has provided the link. Today 15 percent of Norwegian households own one or more boats, and sailing is one of the nation's favourite pastimes.

The proximity of seas teeming with fish has also been a key factor in the development of the

with skis on their feet, and anyone visiting Norway in winter will wonder whether to take this literally, such is the passion of Norwegians for winter sports.

When the snow melts, the mountains remain, and come summer Norwegians like hiking almost as much as they like cross-country skiing. The Jotunheimen, with its high peaks, has attracted serious mountaineers ever since the first tourists came to Norway in the 19th century, and the Hardangervidda, Europe's largest mountainous plateau, comes a close second among Norway's favourite places for hiking. Explorers Roald Amundsen and Fridtjof Nansen used the Hardangervidda to plan and prepare their polar expeditions.

NORTHERN LIGHTS AND MIDNIGHT SUN

Norway's climate is temperate along the coast, much milder in fact than its latitude would suggest. This is because the country benefits from the influence of the North Atlantic Current, warmed by the Gulf Stream, which keeps temperatures milder than they would otherwise be. Inland, winters can be harsh. Røros is one of the coldest places in Norway – record temperatures of –50°C (–58°F) have been registered here in winter, the coldest south of Finnmark. About one-third of Norway lies within

In summer, days are noticeably longer throughout the country, but the midnight sun can only be observed above the Arctic Circle. It is a big attraction, drawing many tourists to Arctic Norway and the North Cape every year.

the Arctic Circle. During the long winter nights it is not unusual for the northern lights (aurora borealis) to be visible in many places – a beautiful

Reindeer graze by Porsangerfjord.

Flowers in the Vesterålen Islands.

⊘ GEIRANGERFJORD

The famed Geirangerfjord and its surrounding area were in 2005 added to Unesco's World Heritage List, which came as no surprise to the locals. It's a magical place, narrow and far from the open sea, with waterfalls crashing down steep mountain sides. Today, Geirangerfjord is the second-most important cruise centre in the country. Its popularity comes at a price, with up to 100 ships visiting the fjord in summer, causing air pollution concerns. Efforts are being made to protect this environmentally sensitive area to prevent it from being damaged by the thousands of visitors arriving by ship and car every year.

natural phenomenon that brightens up the skies of Northern Norway from October to April.

FAUNA AND FLORA

The country stretches over many latitudes and, due to its varied topography and climate, it has a greater variety of habitats than almost any other European country. As a result it possesses a very rich fauna and flora – as many as 60,000 species have been registered (see page 89).

Vegetation varies considerably, although the most common tree species are pine, spruce and birch. Timber is one of the country's main resources, providing paper for printing. Mosses and lichens are found in local forests, and heather and berry bushes, most notably blueberry, are also abundant.

Spectacular northern lights display.

DECISIVE DATES

STONE AGE TO BRONZE AGE

10,000 years ago
The first hunter-gatherers appear in the territory of what is now Norway, following the retreat of the great ice sheets.

5,000–6,000 years ago
Growth of agriculture around Oslofjord.

Rock art.

1500–500 BC
Evidence of Bronze Age burial mounds and Iron Age workings.

ROMAN AGE

AD 1–400
Burial sites indicate links with countries to the south. Latin-based runic letters appear.

AD 793
Norwegian Vikings loot English monastery of Lindisfarne, and raid, trade with and colonise parts of Western Europe.

VIKING AGE (AD 800–1030)

840–66
Vikings found Dublin (840), sack Paris (861) and control most of England by 866.

872
King Harald Hårfagre wins battle at Hafrsfjord, Stavanger.

1001
Sagas relate that Leiv Eiriksson discovers Vinland (America).

1028
King Canute of Denmark invades Norway.

1030
King Olav killed at the Battle of Stiklestad. Christianity arrives through trade with Europe.

1050–66
Harald Hardråde founds Oslo (1048). His defeat at the Battle of Stamford Bridge, England, in 1066, ends the Viking Age.

MIDDLE AGES

1100
The first bishoprics include Nidaros (Trondheim) in 1152.

1130
Civil wars last until 1227. The population grows, towns

Viking expedition.

develop and farmers change from freeholders to tenants.

1299–1343
Oslo becomes capital during the reign of Håkon V. Royal marriages produce a Norwegian-Swedish monarchy.

1349
Black Death reduces the population by 50 percent to about 180,000.

1380
Olav, son of Håkon VI, becomes king of Denmark and Norway.

1397
Trinity Sunday: union of the three crowns is formalised in Kalmar, Sweden.

UNION WITH DENMARK

1536
Norway loses its independence to the Danes.

1537
Reformation of the Norwegian Church imposed by Denmark.

1624
Oslo burns to the ground.

1660
Introduction of absolute rule under Frederik III. In the 1660s the population reaches 440,000; 900,000 by 1801.

1807–14
Norway and Denmark ally with France in Napoleonic Wars; resulting blockade causes shipping and timber exports to collapse and famine to spread.

UNION WITH SWEDEN
1814
January: Secession from Denmark. 17 May: Norwegian constitution is formally adopted at Eidsvoll. 10 October: Treaty of Kiel places Norway in a union with Sweden.

1825
Mass migration to the US begins.

1850–99
The first railway line (1854), the first trade union (1872) and the first political parties (1884) are set up. Norwegian folkloric arts flourish with Grieg's music, Munch's paintings and Ibsen's dramas.

1905
August: national referendum ends union with Sweden.

INDEPENDENCE
1905
18 November: Storting (Parliament) elects Prince Carl of Denmark to be King (Haakon VII) of Norway.

1913
Universal suffrage is granted to women.

1920
Norway joins the League of Nations.

1939–45
Norway proclaims neutrality in World War II, but German forces invade in 1940. On 7 June 1945, King Haakon returns from exile. Birth of the social-welfare state.

1957
Haakon VII dies; Olav V is crowned king.

1960s
The start of oil exploration in the North Sea, leading to new-found wealth for Norway over the following decades.

1972 and 1994
Norway votes against EU membership.

1991
King Olav V is succeeded by Harald V.

1994
Winter Olympics in Lillehammer.

2000
Oslo celebrates its 1,000-year anniversary.

2006
Centre-left government led by prime minister Jens Stoltenberg of the Labour Party takes office. It is re-elected in 2009.

2008
The new Opera House opens on Oslo's waterfront.

2009
Norway is named best country to live in by a United Nations report. It ranks first again in 2013 and 2015.

Erna Solberg.

2010
New Holmenkollen ski jump opens in Oslo.

2011
Deadly terrorist attacks by right-wing extremist Anders Breivik on government buildings in Oslo and a Labour Party youth camp on the island of Utoya.

2013
The Conservative Party wins elections. Erna Solberg becomes Norway's second woman Prime Minister.

2016
The Norwegian Lutheran Church allows gay couples to marry in church. Construction of the fence along the border with Russia starts. Record number of illegal immigrant deportations.

2017
Erna Solberg and her right-wing coalition government are given another four-year mandate.

The Gokstad ship, Viking Ship Museum, Oslo.

BEGINNINGS

For two centuries the Vikings terrorised large parts of Europe, travelling far and wide in search of land, wealth and trade.

Life in Norway has been influenced to an extraordinary degree by the terrain and the weather. The original inhabitants hugged the coastal areas which, warmed by the Gulf Stream, made life more bearable. With the gradual recession of the last Ice Age about 12,000 years ago, the hunters and fishermen inched northwards, but again only along the coast because the interior remained inhospitable.

The thaw was followed by mild weather, unknown before or since. Around 500 BC, however, just as iron was beginning to replace bronze and the Athenians were getting ready to build the Parthenon, the climate inexplicably deteriorated. The impact of suddenly colder, wetter weather was dramatic.

TAKING A STEP BACK

During the preceding Bronze Age considerable progress had been made in weapons, ornaments and utensils made out of metal imported from Britain and Continental Europe. These developments were thrown into reverse by the climate change and the population declined.

Survival in the new Ice Age demanded cultural adjustments. Men, who until then had usually worn a kind of belted cloak, pulled on underwear and trousers. Instead of a semi-nomadic existence, all had to settle on farms in order to secure winter fodder and shelter livestock. People and animals occupied opposite ends of the same house, an unhygienic but necessary form of early central heating.

In common with most of Europe, Norway was again struck by the weather in the 14th century. The economic decline that followed was exacerbated terribly by the Black Death. The resulting acute shortage of labour led to

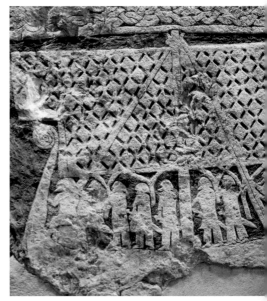

Runestone depicting the ship of Odin carrying the souls of the warrior heroes dead in battle to the Afterworld.

the collapse of the aristocratic estates and the number of knights in Norway dropped from 270 to 60.

THE PEOPLE

But who were these people? The recorded history of Norway begins remarkably late, in about AD 800, and the archaeological pointers towards specific events in earlier times are comparatively scanty. The ancient world had curious opinions about the northerners: one, advanced by Pomponius Mela, was that, living on birds' eggs, the people had hoofed feet, and ears so large that they covered their bodies, thereby dispensing with the need for clothing.

Another, Greek in origin and containing an element of truth, had the territory populated by Hyperboreans, a jolly race who lived in forests

> Rock drawings from the Bronze Age show boats that were capable of carrying 30 men (although not yet with sails), warriors on horseback and either two- or four-wheeled carts drawn by horses or oxen.

Runestone from the Frederikssund Viking Settlement.

and sang and danced their way to incredible longevity. When tired of life, they feasted, bedecked themselves with flowers and threw themselves off cliffs. Norwegians continue to live longer than many Europeans, and they remain energetic to the end. It is one thing for a foreigner struggling on skis to be overtaken by a blasé six-year-old, quite another if the speed demon is a venerable grandmother. Lieutenant W.H. Breton, a 19th-century tourist, was amazed by reports of a man who married at 113 and lived until he was 146. Another visitor commented on four peasants who were the principal dancers at an entertainment for King Christian VI: all of them were over 100. One Derwent Conway, in 1820, asked a 74-year-old in Telemark for the

secret of his robust health. Pouring himself a fifth glass of home-made corn brandy, he replied that it was due to this excellent drink.

NEW BLOOD

That the original inhabitants of Norway received infusions of new blood, probably from the east, is indicated by artefacts which have given their name to their respective cultures: Funnel-Beaker, Battle-Axe and Boat-Axe peoples. Changing burial practices are another reliable sign of influential immigration.

It was once thought that the Sami (Lapps of Finnmark) were the original inhabitants. With their ethnic features and short stature, they were very different from the familiar Scandinavian stereotype. However, it seems theirs was a relatively recent migration from Siberia, long after European types had moved in. The great majority of Norwegians are directly descended from the people who were occupying their territory long before 3000 BC, the date customarily taken as the beginning of Western civilisation.

Like a Nordic Rip van Winkle, Norway slept through the millennium in which Greece and then Rome flourished, although the runic alphabet did appear around the 3rd century AD. It was Latin in origin but dispensed with the curved Latin letters because, perhaps, straight lines were easier to cut into wood, stone and metal, as runic inscriptions invariably were.

Norway was ignored by the civilised world until the late 8th century. Nowhere in Pliny the Elder, Tacitus, Ptolemy or any of the celebrated descriptions of the then known world are the Norwegian people mentioned by name. Even the term "Scandinavia" is a misreading of a text by Pliny, who referred to the unknown land beyond Jutland as *Scatinavia*.

DEVELOPMENT IN SECRET

The outside world's ignorance did not mean that nothing was happening locally. The evolution of ship design was the most potent such development. Although the Phoenicians had undertaken stupendous voyages very much earlier, they routinely stayed within sight of land. The Norwegians were working on vessels capable of crossing oceans.

The Gokstad ship, found in a burial mound near Sandefjord in 1880, was a masterpiece.

Made out of oak planks, it was 25 metres (82ft) long and 5 metres (16ft) wide. It had a mast and 16 pairs of oars. The crew handled one oar each, which left enough room for an equal number of marines. The *styrbord* or rudder, which hung on the right (hence, starboard) side, could be raised for fast beaching. A modern replica crossed the Atlantic in just four weeks. These ships represented a menacing mobility, and when the Norwegians took their unsuspecting neighbours to the south by surprise, they were able to do so with stunning efficiency.

and the year after they arrived in southern Wales and Ireland with more than 100 ships. They were driven off by King Maredudd, and that, together with the resistance they had encountered in England, persuaded them, for a period of 40 years, to turn their attention to softer targets in Ireland.

There are various theories about the origin of the name "Viking", but there was no doubt among their victims in the 9th and 10th centuries that it was synonymous with the term "pirate" or "sea robber". This is further confused

Ancient rock carvings (petroglyphs) of longboats in Østfold.

The Norwegians introduced themselves to the rest of the world with deceptive tranquillity. The *Anglo-Saxon Chronicle* of 787 contains the laconic entry: "In this year King Breohtric married King Offa's daughter Eadburge. And in his days came the first three ships of the Northmen from Hereoalande" (known today as Hordaland, on Norway's west coast).

THE VIKINGS APPEAR

In 793 the Vikings plundered the monastery of Lindisfarne, off the northeast coast of England near the Scottish border and one of the great sanctuaries of the Western Christian Church. The next year they attacked the monastery of Jarrow further down the coast in Northumbria,

The verdict of one Arthurian romance is that the Vikings were "wild and savage and had not in them the love of God nor their neighbours".

by the tendency in English chronicles to call all Vikings "Danes", while many were actually "Northmen", "Norsemen" or, in present terminology, Norwegians. By contrast, in the records of other European countries, Norwegians take all the credit (or blame) for what was usually the work of Danes. Swedish Vikings were busy, too, but they tended to direct their attentions overland via Russia.

Serious outside interest in the geography and demography of Norway began with King Alfred the Great of England, who had every reason to

Some slaves, such as captured craftsmen, were prized, as were young women with whom masters could replenish the labour pool. Unlike in Sweden, the child of a Norwegian master and slave woman remained a slave.

A confrontation from the Frithiof Saga by E. Tégnér, illustrated by Knut Ekwall.

wonder about people who had become painful tormentors. His source was Ottar, a Norwegian chieftain from Hålogaland, at the same time as Alfred was waging war with other Viking chieftains. Ottar told the king that Norway was a very long and narrow country, full of rocks and mountains. The only places that could be pastured or ploughed were those close to the sea; the inhabitants kept sheep and swine and bred tame deer, which they called reindeer.

In reality, the Vikings were land-hungry adventurers for whom rich and undefended coastal abbeys were irresistible business opportunities. They had no scruples about violating holy ground; on the contrary, they saw Christianity as a heretical threat to their own heathen beliefs.

TRUCULENT POPULATION

While Christians put their faith in the sign of the cross, the Vikings trusted the hammer of Thor the Thunderer, defender of heaven against giants, men against monsters and themselves from the "Followers of the White Cross", as they called Christians. Small Viking raiding parties faced with a large and truculent population found that a reputation for uncompromising destruction and cruelty served their purposes well, encouraging the enemy to flee rather than put up a fight. Viking victory celebrations included the proven intimidatory tactic of drinking out of the skulls of fallen enemies.

The Vikings weren't all rape and pillage. Their managerial talents are evident in the way they controlled territory that they had occupied and their artistic streak is manifest in the finely worked ornaments recovered from excavated ships. In the early 18th century, Baron de Montesquieu praised them as an army of free men in an age when armies were usually press-ganged.

The historian Snorri Sturluson is disarmingly indifferent to the Vikings' darker side. The royal pretender Harald Gille is summarised as "friendly, jovial, playful, unassuming, generous, accommodating and easily led". This overlooks the grisly fact, which Sturluson himself recounts, that he blinded and castrated a rival, hanged a bishop and died drunk in the arms of his mistress with his wife standing by.

THE PROFITS OF PIRACY

The reason sometimes given for the sudden explosion of Viking activity beyond Scandinavia is that it was the result of another explosion, that of population because of uniform polygamy. Overpopulation was certainly the case in western Norway where agricultural land was so scarce. All sons, legitimate and otherwise, were entitled to equal shares of their father's inheritance, and as political power and social standing were invested in property, the aristocracy were reluctant to carve land up into small parcels. The surfeit of sons were thus encouraged to seek a fortune abroad.

Women and children often accompanied the men, but they were usually settled in fortified camps while the men "harried". Occasionally the women did join in the mayhem and one of them – an Amazon who rose to command her own army in Ireland – was acclaimed as the fearsome Red Maiden.

When the Vikings came across unoccupied land or, as in the Orkneys, rendered it so by annihilating the natives, they were keen to settle it. If that proved to be impractical, a raid might at least produce some slaves who could either be sold or put to good use at home. When piracy could not be made to pay, the Vikings were willing to engage in conventional trade. Profits from

obliged, however, to step in and rescue the last one left alive.

PROTECTION MONEY

The renewed Viking campaigns were launched from the west coast of Norway, from strongholds on the Scottish islands or from the Norwegian kingdom in Ireland, centred on a castle built in Dublin in 841 by Torgisl. The Vikings were overlords rather than settlers in Ireland, although some intermarried. Norway might still have overseas territories today if a Danish king, as we shall

A fleet of Danish longboats suffers defeat by King Alfred the Great's navy at Swanage in Dorset, England, 878 AD.

piracy and trade generated in Norway the nucleus of a merchant class which complemented the traditional structure of aristocratic earls, free men and thralls (or slaves). The pecking order was reflected in western Norway by *wergild*, a system which stipulated the compensation due in the event of murder. A slave was worth half the value of an ordinary peasant and a quarter of that of a landowner, who in turn was worth only a quarter of a chieftain and one-eighth of a king.

Slaves must have been worked hard, because there was a provision in law which absolved owners of guilt if a slave died through exhaustion or ill-treatment. Owners were permitted, when slaves died, to throw their children into an open grave to die from exposure. They were

⊘ PERMISSIVE ATTITUDES

Viking women made an impression abroad in a way that hints at the emancipated attitudes ascribed to them in the 20th century. In 844 a poet appointed to the court of a Norwegian king ruling in Dublin became enchanted by the queen. While keen to further their acquaintance, he was alarmed at the prospect of the king finding out. The queen reassured him that "it is not customary with us to be jealous. Our women stay with their husbands only as long as they please, and leave them whenever they choose." She seems not to have added that Viking husbands reciprocated in kind. Viking men traded wives or gave them away if they bored or displeased them.

see, had not mortgaged the Orkney and Shetland Islands to raise money for his daughter's dowry.

The Viking raids into Europe were conducted like annual summer holidays, and year after

---

The Viking kingdom on the Isle of Man lasted until 1263, when it was sold to Alexander III of Scotland along with the Western Isles. Remains of Viking forts can still be seen.

---

year the fleets grew larger. An alarmed Charlemagne threw up military posts along his northern borders to guard against them. The defence of Paris against the Vikings was led by Charles the Bald. The city was attacked in 857 and sacked in 861. Charlemagne offered one Viking band 1,360kg (3,000lb) of silver to go and fight some of their compatriots instead of him. In 885 they were back, and it cost a further 318kg (700lb) of silver to get rid of them.

The most enduring Viking presence in France was in Normandy, which was named after them

Painting of a Viking selling a slave girl to a Persian merchant.

⊘ THE VIKINGS IN BRITAIN

The Vikings attacked the British Isles in earnest from 834. The most spectacular campaign was in 851 when they sailed 350 ships up the Thames, stopping off to capture Canterbury before storming London, only to be turned back by Ethelwulf at the Battle of Aclea. By 866 most of England was under their control, with only Wessex, ruled by Alfred the Great, staying independent. After the initial success of a winter campaign in 878, the Vikings were defeated by Alfred, but continued to rule large parts of England from a kingdom based in York. All further territorial ambitions were curtailed with the arrival of William the Conqueror in 1066.

("Norman" is derived from "Norse-Men"). Over the years the Viking armies on the Continent grew to massive proportions and were not finally driven off until 891, by the German emperor Arnulf. Although geographical proximity recommended the British Isles, Vikings were active wherever the pickings looked good. At one point they laid siege to Lisbon, and they penetrated the Mediterranean as far as Constantinople. Nor did they restrict their territorial ambitions to Continental Europe. Vikings sailed west to Iceland, Greenland and eventually to the American continent. As many as 20,000 Norwegians emigrated to Iceland; by the latter half of the 10th century there were no fewer than 39 petty kingdoms established there.

Viking swords.

One of the oldest stave churches, Borgund.

KINGS AND CHRISTIANITY

Constant battles for the throne and the arrival of Christianity in a stubbornly pagan land were the unlikely precursors to Norway's "Period of Greatness".

With Snorri Sturluson, Norwegian history begins to speak for itself instead of relying on outsiders who observed or passed on fantastic tales about the land and its people. Sturluson's epic *Heimskringla (Sagas of the Norse Kings)* is a work of genius.

He visited Norway only twice, but, working on his remote saga island of Iceland, he compiled a huge corpus of information beginning in prehistory and continuing until 1177 (two years before he was born), by which time the Vikings had been tamed, Christianity had taken hold in Norway and the country had endured a century of civil war.

AMUSING TALE

Although Sturluson was himself a foreigner, he drew on the oral history of the skalds at the courts of the Norwegian kings. He was obviously a discriminating historian, although never one to exclude an amusing tale because he did not believe it. There are no fewer than 2,000 names

Harald Hårfagre (c.1200).

> Sturluson's unlucky recompense for recording early Norwegian history in his famous sagas was to be put to death by the King of Norway's men in 1241.

of persons and places in his saga, and he gives his readers a vivid sense of what was happening, as it were, at home.

Sturluson introduces the Norwegian royal line in the person of Halvdan the Black, a king troubled by his inability to dream. He consulted Torleiv the Wise, who said he had suffered from the same complaint and had cured it by sleeping in a pigsty. The king followed his example "and

then it always happened that he dreamed".

Halvdan was descended from the Swedish Ynglinger family, who ruled in Uppsala. His branch had moved to Norway about a century before the Viking period, when the concept of Norway as an entity existed only in the term *Norovegr*, or North Way, the coastal stretch from Vestfold to Hålogaland.

A king dreaming in a pigsty no doubt belongs to mythology rather than history, but Halvdan was real enough. The Oseberg ship unearthed in Vestfold in 1904 proved to be that in which his mother, a Danish princess, was buried. When Halvdan died, his body was chopped up so that the pieces could be more widely distributed to bring good luck to the recipients.

FEMALE DEMANDS

Halvdan's son, known as Harald Hårfagre (Fair Hair), was to become the first ruler of a united Norway. It was said of this subsequent unification that he was put up to it by a woman whom he wished to take to bed. Her reply to his proposition, conveyed by messengers, was that size does count and she could not possibly "waste her maidenhood" on a man who ruled over a kingdom that compared so unfavourably in extent with those in Denmark and Sweden. His messengers nervously reported her comment

The monument at Hafrsfjord, where Harald Hårfagre first united Norway.

but were relieved by the philosophical way in which he took it: "She has reminded me of those things", he said, "which it now seems strange I have not thought of before."

Harald advanced north from Vestfold to improve his conjugal prospects. He made contact with the powerful Earl Håkon, whose interests extended south from Trøndelag, the region surrounding what was eventually to become Trondheim. The cold facts, never as interesting as Sturluson's version, are that Harald and Håkon saw the mutual benefits of trade but first had to suppress unruly Viking bands along the coast who would have disrupted it.

> When King Håkon attempted to introduce Christianity and urged his people to fast on the seventh day, they devised ploys to trick him into breaking his fast by eating horse flesh or making him drink a toast to their pagan gods.

FRIENDSHIP WITH ENGLAND

Harald needed assistance and set the precedent for cooperation between the Norwegian and English thrones by turning to Athelstan, King of England. As a pledge of friendship, accompanied by some mutual chicanery, he initiated what was to become another quite common practice: he sent his infant son Håkon to be fostered at Athelstan's court.

Harald's campaigns sent many of his dispossessed opponents into exile in Iceland, Shetland, the Orkney Islands and the Hebrides. The decisive battle took place AD 872 at Hafrsfjord, near present-day Stavanger, in southwestern Norway. The victory made him, Sturluson says, the first king of the Norwegians, and also won him the postponed hand of the "large-minded maid", who proceeded to bear him five children. As a love story, however, the conclusion is not completely satisfactory. Sturluson writes: "They say that when he took Ragnhild the Mighty... he had divorced himself from nine other women."

TOO MANY CHILDREN

The awesome number of royal progeny was to prove a constant source of contention in the matter of choosing a successor.

The English chronicler Roger of Hoveden wrote: "It is the custom of the kingdom of Norway... that everyone who is recognised to be the son of any King of Norway, even though he be a bastard and born of a serving wench, can claim for himself as great a right to the kingdom of Norway as the son of a wedded king and one born of a free woman. And so fighting goes on incessantly between them..."

Harald Hårfagre's umpteenth son, but the only one by Ragnhild, was the wretched Eirik Bloodaxe, who advanced his succession in AD 933 by murdering all but one of his legitimate half-brothers. The exception was Håkon, the boy who had been fostered by King Athelstan. Eirik had none of his father's authority, and the united kingdom degenerated into squabbling petty kingdoms ruled by various of Harald's bastard sons. On Håkon's return from England, Eirik was forced to flee in the opposite direction, ending up as King of Northumberland.

FIRST CHRISTIAN

Håkon den Gode (the Good) was more successful than Eirik at holding hostile factions together. Before he died (about AD 960), he was acknowledged as king over the whole coastal area from Oslo to Hålogaland. He was a notable reformer of law and defence; he was also the first Norwegian Christian king, having been baptised while in England. He imported an English bishop and missionaries with a view to converting his countrymen; but that wasn't easy. Nowhere was resistance to Christianity more forcibly expressed than in Trondheim, which was then against any form of imposed authority, whether by Håkon or anyone else. Håkon urged people to "believe in one God, Christ, the son of Mary, and give up all blood offerings... and fast

Nineteenth-century painting of Håkon the Good, by Peter Nicolai Arbo.

⊘ PAGAN SIGNS

Even when Christianity was finally adopted in Norway, much of the old religion lingered on. The early Christian clergy ignored papal injunctions about celibacy, and the locals took a while to accept such unfamiliar ideas as original sin and immaculate conception. Some 13th-century runic inscriptions uncovered in Bergen show little Christian influence; one even appeals to a valkyrie. The medieval stave churches are reminders of an earlier faith, resembling nothing if not the keel of a Viking ship. They are adorned with dragon heads and scenes from heathen mythology. In the 19th century, many such churches were destroyed, victims of the extreme puritanical movement in Norway known as Pietism.

every seventh day". From the audience "there was straight away a mighty uproar".

MISSIONARIES' FATE

Håkon's imported missionaries despaired. Their targets would not deviate from drinking to pagan gods morning, noon and night. They were concerned, too, that their potential parishioners would drink themselves into extinction; by instructing them in the cultivation of fruit and vegetables, they hoped to persuade them to observe a healthier diet.

In the end the missionaries realised that pious sobriety was unattainable. The best they could hope for was to have the toasts in honour of Christian saints rather than pagan gods. They provided a long list of saints' names, and it seems that some of their parishioners were content to drink to them with undiminished frequency and pleasure.

The missionaries had less luck in suppressing traditions like blood sacrifices (usually animals but occasionally humans). In Trondheim the uncompromising response to the message they preached was to send out four ships looking for tiresome missionaries: they "slew three priests and burned three churches; they then went home".

On the military front, Håkon was under constant threat from Eirik Bloodaxe's avenging sons changed through a chance meeting in the Scilly Isles, where he was resting after some strenuous atrocities. A wise old man took him to one side and explained the True Path. Transformed overnight, Olav returned to England "and now went about peacefully, for England was a Christian country and he was also a Christian".

He was not so peaceful when converting his compatriots at home. It is said that those who opposed him "he dealt with hard; some he slew, some he maimed and some he drove away from the land".

King Canute and his queen Aelfgifu.

coming over from Northumberland. In defeat they turned to their uncle, the Danish king Harald Bluetooth, who wanted to regain old Danish territories at the mouth of Oslofjord. At a decisive battle in 960 Håkon was defeated and killed, paving the way for about 25 years of Danish rule, starting with 10 years under Eirik's son Harald II Gråfell.

UNLIKELY CONVERT

For its next champion, Christianity had to wait for Olav Tryggvason, later King Olav I (AD 995–1000) and a monument in Norwegian history. Sturluson says he was a great sportsman who could walk on the oars along the outside of a ship, "smote equally well with both hands" and could hurl two spears at a time. His personality

Olav Tryggvason was unlucky in love. In proposing marriage to the wealthy Queen Sigrid of Sweden, he insisted she would first have to be baptised. She refused, and Olav hit her with a glove. "That may well be thy death," she observed: so it proved.

She was a crafty enemy. Her wealth attracted a string of proposals from minor kings, but King Swein Forkbeard of Denmark, son of Harald Bluetooth, was her choice. As soon as they were married she talked her husband into an alliance with the Swedish King Olav the Tax Gatherer against Norway. A great sea battle ensued, at the climax of which Olav I, who was being assisted by King Boleslav of Poland, was forced to jump overboard. He was never seen again and

By the age of 12, Olav Tryggvason (the future King Olav I) was a full-blooded Viking, cruising the Baltic in command of five longships and later moving west to terrorise the English coast.

the victors, including the gratified queen, divided the spoils among themselves.

FIRST SAINT

The man who would soon restore Norway's integrity had, like Olav Tryggvason, embarked on a naval career at 12. Olav Haraldson, later St Olav, was in England when the same Swein Forkbeard landed his forces and was responsible for the then King of England, Ethelred, being castigated evermore as "the Unready".

Olav allied himself with Ethelred in an anti-Danish war which came to a head at London Bridge across the River Thames. The Danish forces were seemingly impregnable on their fortified bridge, but they reckoned without Olav's sturdy Vikings. Having fastened ropes to the piles under the bridge, they heaved at the oars and brought the whole thing down. Several churches in England are still dedicated to St Olav for this remarkable feat.

A FORMIDABLE ENEMY

Olav laid the foundations of the Church, even in ever-rebellious Trøndelag, but antagonised many potential rivals, none more than the expansionist King Canute of Denmark and England, who invaded Norway in 1028 with overwhelming forces. Olav fled to Kiev until he learned that the earl whom Canute had appointed to rule Norway was dead. He returned to regain his kingdom but miscalculated his level of support in Trøndelag and was killed at the Battle of Stiklestad in 1030.

Olav was elevated to sainthood and his body was originally placed in the church of St Clement in Trondheim. In spite of his insensitive missionary zeal, the memory of Olav kept alive the notion of a united and independent Norway through the troubled centuries ahead.

King Canute's kingdom fell apart after his death, the Scandinavian component re-forming into three distinct and generally hostile

kingdoms. Norway was later ruled by Magnus I and then by Harald Hardråde.

NOBLE MERCENARY

Harald was typical of the young nobles who were forced to look abroad to enrich themselves. He signed up as a Varangian mercenary for the Byzantine emperor in Constantinople and saw service in Syria, Armenia, Palestine, Sicily and Africa. He was an enterprising warrior. During one siege he faked his own funeral and, emulating the Trojan Horse, his men persuaded the townspeople to open the

Norse marauders at Clonmacnoise, Ireland.

gates to admit his coffin which, they promised, would work powerful magic to their benefit.

All of this was immensely profitable because the mercenaries were entitled to keep as much treasure from captured palaces as they could grab with both hands.

Harald consolidated the kingdom of Norway. Troubled as Norwegian kings invariably were by the people of Trøndelag and its capital, Trondheim, he founded Oslo in 1048 as a counterbalance.

He provided the town with a patron saint, Hallvard, whose main claim to sainthood is the reputed refusal of his body to sink after being thrown into a fjord with a stone tied around the neck.

DEFEAT IN ENGLAND

As King Canute's sovereignty over England (1017–35) was still within living memory, it was possibly inevitable that a confident Harald would develop similar ambitions. In any case, there had been so much toing and froing between the west coast of Norway and Britain that the affinities between them were as close, or closer, than those between scattered settlements in Norway. Harald therefore probably felt he was exercising a natural right in his invasion of England. His approach was from the north but his army was stopped at Stamford Bridge, in present-day North Yorkshire. Some historians argue that the English army's rush north to meet Harald weakened its ability to resist William the Conqueror when his forces crossed the Channel.

After Harald's death in this abortive conquest of England, he was succeeded by his sons Magnus and Olav the Peaceful. The latter founded the towns of Bergen and Stavanger before being succeeded by his son – yet another Magnus, but in this instance unforgettably "the Bareleg" – after visiting Scotland

The Ring of Brodgar, Viking remains on the Orkney Islands off the northeastern tip of Scotland.

⊘ HANSEATIC HERITAGE

Norway became almost totally reliant on the Lübeck merchants as trade with the Baltic burgeoned in the course of the 13th century. The merchants grew ever more powerful, and the trade privilege they were granted in 1278 provided them with concessions beyond those enjoyed by native Norwegians. For instance, they were allowed to buy property in Bergen and settle there. If their demands were not met, all they had to do was simply threaten to cut off corn supplies. It was clear that dependence on imported food risked costing the country its independence.

(which he dearly wanted to annex), he took to wearing a kilt.

The death of Magnus produced the familiar pattern of multiple and competing heirs, in this case three simultaneously acclaimed kings who were all minors. One died young, Sigurd went off to the Holy Land to earn his title, "the Crusader", and Øystein mixed Viking raids with improvements to fisheries, harbours and roads and the establishment of monasteries. Sigurd had the throne to himself after Øystein's death, though he continued to be confronted by the complicated rules of succession throughout his reign.

Such rivalries to occupy the Norwegian throne were incessant. There were brilliant interludes under a king like Sverre, but more often than

King Magnus the Lawmender introduced the first set of secular laws in the Western world. His law-making extended to his court, which was an unusually polite affair, with prescribed rules relating to court etiquette.

not the succession was a squabble between the powers behind official contestants, who might be children not yet six years old. With the stability of Håkon IV's 46-year reign and that of his son, Magnus the Lawmender, however, Norway achieved its 13th-century "Period of Greatness".

CULTURAL AWAKENING

Money was spent on cathedrals and churches, the arts flourished and Norwegians assiduously studied and followed European fashions. This cultural awakening was to some extent through the creation of a wealthy upper class and the consolidation of state and Church. It was not so beneficial for the peasants; riches were not evenly spread, and the number of independent farmers dropped significantly as they defaulted on mortgages, leaving the Church and big landowners free to repossess their land.

Norway's overseas empire contributed to a sense of greatness. Jämtland in Sweden was Norwegian, as were the Orkney and Shetland Islands. In 1262 Iceland accepted Norwegian sovereignty, as did Greenland. It was the period, too, which saw the growth of towns like Bergen with a rich trade in dried fish from the north. Foreign trade, to begin with, was mainly with Britain, but it then veered towards the Baltic coast, especially Lübeck and the merchants of the Hanseatic League. The Germans had plenty of corn but a shortage of fish; a perfect trade balance with Norway.

THE BLACK DEATH

A galley arriving in Sicily from the Far East in October 1347 brought the Black Death to Europe. Within a couple of years, a third of the European population was dead. The plague was carried north to Bergen in 1349 in the hold of an English ship. The effect on isolated Norwegian farming communities, especially, was catastrophic: farms which had been painfully

created in conditions difficult at the best of times were reduced to waste.

The estates generating the wealth which was the necessary platform for general economic development could not be maintained while labourers dropped dead. The nobles who survived were reduced to scratching a living out of the land like everyone else. The effect of *force majeure* acting as a social leveller assumed a pattern in Norwegian history which cannot be discounted in explaining the easygoing classlessness which remains today.

Carved viking stone at Borg Museum, Lofoten Islands.

The decimation of the nobility removed the impetus behind the normally turbulent activity around the Norwegian throne. Unchallenged, two successive kings sat out long peaceful reigns, a foretaste of the comparative stability about to be foisted on Scandinavia in the late 14th century through the cunning manipulation of Margareta, widow of King Håkon, the "Lady King", who first persuaded the Danes to accept as king her son Olav, then aged five. With mother active behind the scenes, Olav also took over the crown of Norway at 10, and inherited the claim of the dispossessed Folkung dynasty in Sweden. He died suddenly at 17, and Margareta found a suitable substitute in Erik of Pomerania, her five-year-old nephew.

THE 400-YEAR SLEEP

A long spell under the control of its more powerful neighbours brought Norway mixed fortunes and, ultimately, something to celebrate – a constitution.

Sweden's Kalmar Castle, where the Kalmar Union was formalised.

The union of the three crowns was formalised at a coronation in the Swedish town of Kalmar, close to the then border with Denmark. The date, appropriately, was Trinity Sunday, 1397. The coronation was performed by the Danish and Swedish archbishops; Norway was represented by the Bishop of Orkney.

Although there may have been an attempt to draft a constitution which would have united the three realms for ever under a single king, the rules of succession that were adopted left a gaping loophole. Erik of Pomerania was given full rights to dispose of the crown as he saw fit, a recipe for reversion to the old royal uncertainties after his death. In the event, the union collapsed during his lifetime. His greatest difficulty was paying for the court and administration in Copenhagen. The united crown had no significant estates of its own; the nobility did and was comparatively well off, but it was not inclined to surrender its wealth.

HANSEATIC BLOCKADE

While taking steps to undermine the authority of the nobility, Erik also tried to squeeze the Hanseatic merchants for money. Their response included an attack on Copenhagen, where they were seen off by 200 examples of a new invention, the cannon. He was less successful when the merchants retaliated with a blockade. Those hardest hit were the nobility and wealthy merchants who, holding Erik responsible for their misfortune, conspired to dethrone him. Erik retreated to the island of

Gotland in the hope that they would change their minds. Norway would have done so, but the Danish nobles wanted to make a fresh start. The invitation went to Christian of Oldenburg, who thereupon rose from the title of count in an obscure part of Germany to found a dynasty which was to last for more than four centuries. Sweden resisted the choice, but Norway went along with it.

Christian I was almost as short of money as Erik had been. His attempts to make up shortfalls were notoriously at the expense of Norway, the weaker partner. Expected to hand over 60,000 guilders as a dowry for his daughter Margaret's marriage to the heir to the Scottish throne, he mortgaged the Orkney Islands to Scotland for 50,000. When the time came for the wedding, he was still 8,000 guilders short, and so mortgaged Shetland as well. To put 8,000 guilders into perspective, he spent three times that on a trip to Rome a few years later, having borrowed the money from the Hanseatics. The Scots gloated over the deal; not merely the trifling price, but that Margaret "deemed it a greater thing to be queen in Scotland than daughter of a king who wears three crowns".

TREACHEROUS MURDER

Norway's resentment at such exploitation eventually boiled over. At the turn of the 16th century, Knut Alvsson, a Swedish-Norwegian nobleman, led an uprising that created a potentially independent state stretching from Oslo to Bergen. Danish troops were sent to put a stop to it. The outcome, however, was thoroughly dishonourable. Alvsson had established himself in Akershus Castle in Oslo. He was invited to negotiate under a flag of truce and promptly murdered. In the poem *At Akershus*, Ibsen called his death a blow to Norway's heart. Norwegian resentment at the treatment meted out to Alvsson was exacerbated by punitive taxes, imposed to pay for Christian II of Denmark's wars with the restless Swedes. Norwegians were not sorry to see him toppled and bundled off into exile, but they were not ready to extend a welcome to his successor, Frederik I.

Norway was nominally Roman Catholic, and there was little interest in the forces of the Reformation which lay behind the tussle for the Danish throne. The country did not have an urban bourgeoisie, who elsewhere were the first to adopt Lutheranism. The Reformation, when it reached Norway, was the first of the great European cultural movements that had any real impact on the country. Feudalism passed it by (never a Norwegian knight in armour rescuing damsels in distress), as did the Renaissance. Most of rural Norway remained in the past, Christianity providing only a veneer on what were fundamentally old pagan ways.

A NEW LEADER

It was at this point that a new Norwegian leader emerged: Olav Engelbrektsson, the Archbishop of Trondheim (or Nidaros, as it was then known). Olav raised an army with a view to getting Chris-

Queen Margaret.

European movements had little effect on Norway before the Reformation. Its peasant culture was deeply conservative, not to say backward, so much so that many scholars classify Norway as "medieval" until the early 16th century.

---

tian II back. The exiled king was able to muster a fleet with Dutch help and in 1531 set sail for Oslo. A storm scattered the fleet so that only a small part of it went into action against Akershus Castle. The attack was futile. Christian was captured and imprisoned, and the Norwegians were forced to acclaim Frederik I as their king.

Christian II was still in prison when Frederik died and was replaced by Christian III, a Protestant. He rounded up the Danish bishops and then ordered the Archbishopric of Trondheim to be abolished, if

The legacy of the zealous Pietism that arrived in Norway in the 18th century can still be felt today, especially when it comes to attitudes towards alcohol.

Wooden church in Torpo.

necessary by force. Olav thought of resisting but, having weighed up the likely repercussions, fled to the Netherlands.

Any further hope of Norwegian independence was quashed by Christian III's 1536 edict demoting the country to the status of a Danish province: "And it shall henceforth neither be nor be called a kingdom in itself." The humbled status was intended to last in perpetuity; in the event it lasted for less than 300 years, culminating not in independence but in takeover by Sweden in 1814 after Norway had become a coveted prize bobbing between its more powerful neighbours.

The loss of political sovereignty under Denmark could not obliterate Norway's separate identity at once. People went on speaking the same language as before and local administration retained many traditional features, but the creeping effects of the Reformation, and Christian III's determination to "Danicise" Norway, could not be postponed for ever.

VALUABLE ASSETS

The Norwegian economy began to recover from its long decline, partly as the result of vast shoals of herring which appeared off the coast and partly because of the invention of the water-driven saw, which made exploitation of the timber forests lucrative.

Christian IV was far more positive about Norway than his predecessors. He visited the country at least 30 times, making a special trip on learning of the discovery of silver at what is now Kongsberg. He supervised the founding of the town, hence the name, which translates as "King's Mountain". He founded and attached his name to Kristiansand, as he did "Christiania" to the new city built on the site where the former Oslo had burned down in 1624. Christian ran the country as if it were a private company. He cracked down on the Hanseatic traders, making them take Norwegian citizenship, if they had not already done so of their own accord, or leave. Foreigners from other parts were encouraged to bring to Norway their skills, enterprise and, best of all, their money. Under his encouragement, former trading posts became towns in places like Drammen, Moss, Larvik, Mandal and Arendal.

The Norwegians did not always receive these foreigners with uncritical joy. In 1700, for example, a simple fight between two men in Arendal escalated into a brawl which pitched all 900 resident foreigners against everyone else. It lasted a week. Nevertheless, a population which had been reduced by the Black Death to something like 180,000 picked up under Christian's energetic policies, reaching 440,000 in 1665 and nearly 900,000 by 1801.

Not all of Christian IV's successors shared his delicate touch with regard to Norwegian sensibilities. There were periods when the Danish crown was autocratically absolute, and respite depended on having an independently minded *Stattholder*, the crown agent with responsibility for Norway. Ulrik Frederik Gyldenløve, the illegitimate son of Frederik III, conscientiously protected his Norwegian charges. He intervened to save peasants from the more rapacious taxes sought by Copenhagen, and he built up the Norwegian armed forces so that at Kvistrum in 1677 they were able to humiliate a far larger force of Swedes.

HELLFIRE AND BRIMSTONE

As Norway belatedly shed the mantle of medievalism and got to grips with Protestantism, it adopted the faith as zealously as it had once defended paganism. The rural areas, especially, embraced Pietism, real hellfire-and-brimstone stuff which persuaded peasants that their austere existence was actually abominably frivolous. Gripped by a kind of manic fundamentalism, they despised their folk culture and, particularly in the 19th century when Pietism was still going strong, were encouraged to tear down the ornately carved, wooden stave churches. Confirmation and attendance at church on Sunday were made compulsory. Looking around them, the Pietists were appalled by the realisation that in their midst, or at least within the national boundaries, there were still heathens. On the other hand, when a liberal wind blew in Copenhagen, it was also felt in Norway. For example,

Christian VI and family.

⊘ THE DANISH INFLUENCE

By the 1530s Norway was being ruled by a Danish Protestant king, Christian III, whose influence, together with the imposition of the Reformation, was beginning to be felt among the population. Most of the new Protestant clergy were Danes. The revised version of the Bible was in Danish and so were the hymns. Official jobs were invariably given to Danes, who conducted them in the Danish language and reported back to Copenhagen. Danish noblemen also took over possessions as officers of the law in Norway, conducting (yet again) proceedings in their native Danish.

With the spread of schooling and therefore literacy by means of books imported from Denmark (the first printing press was late in arriving in Norway), the anomaly arose of people speaking one language among themselves but reading, albeit with characteristic Norwegian pronunciation, writing and conducting all official business in another. The result was a hybrid Dano-Norwegian and the genesis of a language dispute which has not been settled to this day (see page 72).

Norway won a measure of Danish respect in the latter's frequent wars with Sweden, in which the Norwegian contingents acquitted themselves well. Denmark began to realise that Norway could only be governed in its own way. Sweden was peering enviously over Denmark's shoulder at Norway. If Denmark alienated Norway too much, the country might accept a more attractive offer of union with Sweden.

when Christian VII went mad the affairs of state fell into the hands of his physician, a German named Johann Friedrich Struensee. He believed in unrestricted trade and freedom of the press.

Norway was gratified to see the abolition of a trading system which placed an artificially low value on Norwegian iron imported into Denmark, whereas Danish corn exports to Norway were sold at whatever the market would bear. Correcting the imbalance helped, but prospects of additional economic reforms ended abruptly when it was discovered that Struensee had been having an affair with Caroline Mathilde, wife of his deranged patient, and was executed.

NELSON ATTACKS

Coexistence between Denmark and Norway was traumatised from the unlikely quarter of Napoleon Bonaparte. Britain had fallen out with Denmark (and hence Norway) over the Danish alliance with Prussia and Russia. A total of 149 Danish and Norwegian vessels were seized in British ports; in response, a Danish force

The British defeat the Danish, First Battle of Copenhagen.

⊘ ONE-MAN ENLIGHTENMENT

Against a backdrop of Pietism and the death penalty for sexual irregularity, one of the first rays of the Enlightenment shone through in the person of Ludvig Holberg. Born in Bergen, he later became a resident of Copenhagen; he was a playwright, historian and satirist (what's more, in Latin) who, according to the historian T.K. Derry, "in his own generation had no obvious superior in range of intellect except Voltaire". Holberg's impressive output included 26 plays for the newly founded Copenhagen Theatre between 1722 and 1727. It is a pithy comment on the difficulty of drawing a line between Norwegian and Danish history that both countries now claim Holberg as their own.

marched into Hamburg and appropriated British property worth £15 million.

The British naval commander Horatio Nelson moved on Copenhagen with a powerful fleet. Danish and Norwegian crews manning a line of blockships put up a spirited defence, and after a six-hour battle Nelson urged the Danish crown prince regent to capitulate, failing which he would have to destroy the blockships "without having the power to save the brave Danes who have defended them". The prince agreed.

A few years later Napoleon insisted that Denmark-Norway join his Continental System and close their ports to British ships. A large British fleet demanded the handing-over of the Danish Navy, which Napoleon sorely needed after losing his at Trafalgar, and when this met with refusal, Copenhagen was bombarded with at least 14,000 rounds over three days. British troops occupied the capital for six weeks, after which they went home with the Danish fleet. The enormity of such an attack on what was a neutral country put Denmark and Norway firmly into Napoleon's camp, a position that required them to join him in attacking Sweden.

The division thus rendered between Sweden and Denmark was bound to have serious consequences. The inevitable began in 1810 when

BATTLE FOR THE THRONE

Christian Frederik was not going to surrender Norway without a struggle. He entertained the idea of getting himself popularly acclaimed as king (he thought his chances best in Trondheim) but the feeling among the population at large was that the Danish line had renounced its sovereignty and the Norwegians were now entitled to choose their own king.

In April 1814, an assembly of 37 farmers, 16 businessmen and 59 bureaucrats met in Eidsvoll to decide what that future should be. The con-

Christian Frederik of Denmark inspects his troops.

Sweden's King Karl XIII appointed as his heir (of all people, considering the events that had just passed) Jean-Baptiste Bernadotte, one of Napoleon's marshals. Bernadotte improved his Swedish credentials by changing his name to Karl Johan and succeeded to the throne in 1818.

Karl Johan conceived a plan whereby Russia and Britain would support Swedish claims on Norway. They agreed, with the result that Norwegian ports were blockaded to secure a "voluntary" union with Sweden. The Danish crown prince, Christian Frederik, tried to rally Norwegian loyalty. In the end, the decision did not rest in either Norwegian or Danish hands. Union between Sweden and Norway was imposed by the Peace of Kiel (following Napoleon's defeat at Leipzig) in 1814.

On 17 May 1814 Norway became a "free, independent and an indivisible realm" as stated in the new constitution, but it would take 91 years for these words to become a reality.

stitution they prepared was signed on 17 May, today Norway's national day. On the same day a new king was elected; it was the tenacious Christian Frederik. Sweden would have none of it. The Norwegians fought well in a one-sided contest but Christian Frederik soon had to sue for peace. Karl Johan stepped forward to occupy his double throne.

Map of Sweden, Norway and Finland in 1817.

UNION WITH SWEDEN

Through such artists as Ibsen, Grieg and Munch, the voice of an increasingly restless and independent-minded Norway could be heard beyond its own borders.

Divorce from Denmark was followed by a quarrel over the division of joint assets and liabilities. The assets were Iceland, Greenland and the Faroes, which Norway claimed were Norwegian colonies long before marriage with Denmark. The liabilities were the Danish-Norwegian national debt.

Who owed what? The Norwegian position was not only that Denmark alone should shoulder the burden, but that compensation was due to Norway for centuries of exploitation. Assuming powers granted under the Treaty of Kiel in 1814, which had brought about the union with Sweden, Karl Johan declared that Norway would pay off some of the debt. The matter of the colonies was not finally resolved until 1931, when the International Court at The Hague found in favour of Denmark.

TWO KINGDOMS

Friction between Karl Johan and the Norwegian half of his kingdom was present right from the start: he envisaged a gradual merging of the two kingdoms, while Norway was determined to consolidate the independence ratified by the 1814 constitution.

A constitutional battle took place over a bill to abolish all noble titles and privileges. Again and again the Norwegian Storting (Parliament) presented the bill and the king refused to sanction it. The constitution said he could refuse a bill only twice; the third time it automatically became law. Karl Johan objected strongly to this limitation on his authority, which did not exist in Sweden. A fundamental principle was at stake and the dispute was not to be resolved easily. Indeed, it remained the biggest bone of contention for the life of the union and, as much as anything else, was the cause of its eventual dissolution.

King Karl Johan XIV.

Norwegian pride was prickly. Merchant ships could fly the Norwegian flag close to home, but not in waters notoriously under the sway of North African pirates. Sweden had bought off the pirates, but the immunity extended only to the Swedish flag; if Norwegians wanted to take advantage of the immunity, then they had to switch flags.

Sweden's dogged refusal to allow Norway its own diplomatic and consular representation abroad was not only an insult but a practical handicap, because the Norwegian merchant fleet was well on its way to becoming, by 1880, the third-largest in the world. Its far-flung crews wanted and needed a purely Norwegian diplomatic service.

THE GREAT EXODUS

Poverty and lack of prospects at home pushed many Norwegians to emigrate to America and settle in the Midwest.

One thousand years after the first Norwegian Vikings turned their longships towards the west, pushing out as far as North America, a second wave of Norwegians began to cast their eyes in the same direction. The motives of these new emigrants were similar – lack of opportunity and poverty – but they had none of the warlike excitement of the earlier exodus. These

Norwegian emigrants on board SS Hero en route to America.

new "Vikings" sought a place where they could work and prosper in peace rather than a place for exploration and conquest.

Yet the first emigrant boat, the 16-metre (54ft) sloop *Restauration*, crammed full with 52 crew and passengers, must have been scarcely more seaworthy than the superbly built longships. But these early "sloopers", who sailed from Stavanger in July 1825, were idealistic and highly motivated. The leader, Lars Larsen Geilane, was a Quaker, and there were members of the religious Haugeans sect among the crew. Their intention to found a classless society where they could follow their own religion had been further encouraged when the previous year another Norwegian pioneer, Cleng Peerson, returned with

reports of the promised land. The *Restauration* reached New York in October of the same year, and these farming people, mostly from Rogaland, lost no time in settling on land bought for them by Cleng Peerson at Kendall on the shores of Lake Ontario.

When the *Restauration* left in 1825, Norway's population was only 1 million, yet the next three generations sent 750,000 Norwegians to North America, reflecting a population increase at home rather than an emptying of the Norwegian countryside, though early industrialists began to campaign against such a dribbling away of potential labour. The main motive among the second and later waves of country people was good land and good farming prospects rather than religious or political repression. To be an *odelsbonde*, who owned his own land, was to be a free man and the goal of every Norwegian peasant. The American merchant fleets were also eager to make use of skilful Norwegian seamen.

The newcomers prospered, and regular letters home, reports and Norwegian visitors from the New World increased the fever. The letters were printed in newspapers all over the country, and one or two Midwestern American states began to use agents to encourage emigration.

By the middle of the 1830s new emigrants and some of the original "sloopers" had moved on to Illinois. Forty years later, their numbers had increased to more than 12,500. The 1862 Homestead Law, which granted land to immigrants, turned the early trickle into a steady flow, and Cleng Peerson founded Norwegian settlements in Iowa.

For many patriotic Norwegians it became *de rigueur* to help the expansion. The violinist Ole Bull had a well-intentioned but crashing failure with a planned settlement, "Oleana", in Pennsylvania. He was too far from his Norwegian farming roots. The soil was ungrateful, communications impossible, and Bull lost more than US$40,000.

Later, Norwegians also settled in Canada, but by the 1930s emigration had dwindled to a trickle. Yet the Norwegian influence was strong in the places where they settled. Today, the overt "Norwegianness" may have gone, but anyone who doubts it still exists need only read Garrison Keillor's winsome tales of life around Lake Wobegon.

> *The Norwegian peasant farmer was portrayed as the salt of the earth. The farmers' grip on the national heartstrings and purse has never been relinquished.*

OSLO ONCE AGAIN

Karl Johan was adept at making a timely concession to court popularity, and the welcome he received on visiting Christiania in 1838 was

carried the banner of separatism and rallied against the royal veto. Its leader, Johan Sverdrup, was a lawyer who worked at creating an alliance between urban radicals and wealthy farmers. Their interests were too divergent, however, and the party split, leaving room for the strong labour movement that characterised most of the 20th century. It dawned on poorer farmers and peasants, who had previously let the land-owning and merchant classes get on with government, that their special interests, especially a reduction in taxes, could be advanced only if they too

Women in traditional costume c.1890.

probably sincere, as was the public grief when he died six years later. Although changing Christiania's name back to Oslo obliterated a Danish memory, the capital was, and is, content to leave its main street named after Karl Johan.

OSKAR'S CONCESSIONS

Karl Johan's successor, Oskar I, immediately tried to placate Norway through gestures such as his title which, locally, was changed to King of Norway and Sweden, rather than vice versa. He also agreed to the introduction of a new flag which gave equal prominence to the Swedish and Norwegian colours.

Norwegian politics in the 19th century were dominated at first by the Venstre Party, which

became involved in the political process. They were assisted by a general mood in the country of national romanticism, a Nordic adaptation of the French philosopher Rousseau's belief in the nobility of savages.

EMIGRATION TO THE NEW WORLD

Putting peasants on a pedestal did not ameliorate the hard facts of life. Emigration to the United States began in 1825, although statistics reveal the irony that emigration was highest when the economic conditions at home were good, and lowest when they were bad. Perhaps it was a case of being too poor in the lean times to pay the fare.

In 1882 a record 29,000 Norwegians left, and by 1910 there were more than 400,000 people of Norwegian birth in the United States, their numbers growing right the way through to World War I.

THE ARTS FLOURISH

The rise of nationalism throughout Europe produced in Norway an unprecedented, and subsequently unequalled, flowering of the arts. Henrik Ibsen (1828–1906) and Alexander Kielland (1849–1906), giants among an extraordinarily talented assortment of writers – not forgetting composers, such as Edvard Grieg (1843–1907), and the painter Edvard Munch (1863–1944) – presented the world with a clearer insight into Norway than was available from the bestselling romantic writers.

The violin virtuoso Ole Bull was also caught up in his country's rising tide of romantic nationalism, and was another active promoter of Norwegian culture, helping revive old Norwegian folk songs and co-founding Det Norske Theater in Bergen, the first theatre in which actors spoke Norwegian, rather than Danish.

Bust of the playwright Henrik Ibsen.

King Oskar II.

⊘ HENRIK IBSEN

Henrik Johan Ibsen was born in Skien in Telemark (see page 188) and was apprenticed at an early age to a chemist. His first poems, with titles such as *Resignation, Doubt* and *The Corpse's Ball*, give a clue to the majestic gloom – punctuated by delicious wit – of his later writing.

After working in the theatre in Bergen, he joined the Christiania Norske Theater in Oslo, which had been founded to promote Norwegian theatre. He fared miserably, with one failure after another, poor health and no money. In the depths of depression he began to question the deplorable position of the artist in Norwegian society, and that, ironically, put him on the road to better things. *The Pretenders*, first performed in 1864, was a success and helped him to obtain a travelling scholarship. He went abroad, first to Italy, and did not live in Norway again for another 27 years.

The plays for which he is best remembered include *Pillars of Society*, which broke new ground in dealing with the humbug of a small provincial town. Ibsen touched on subjects that audiences were not ready for. According to the *Daily Telegraph* in London, the first overseas production of *Ghosts* was "positively abominable... a dirty act done publicly, a [lavatory] with all its doors and windows open... gross, almost putrid indecorum... crapulous stuff". George Bernard Shaw, however, summarised Ibsen's importance to the English theatre with: "The Norman Conquest was a mere nothing compared with the Norwegian Conquest."

CREATIVE AGITATORS

Henrik Ibsen and others such as the playwright and novelist Bjørnstjerne Bjørnson (1832–1910) were leading lights in agitation against Danish domination in the arts. They demanded, for example, that Danish actors should no longer be employed on the Norwegian stage, and Bjørnson in particular championed efforts to revive the Norwegian language.

While the Norwegian element in the work of the great playwright Ludvig Holberg in the previous century could hardly be told apart from the Dan-

effectively have lapsed. It would then revert to the Storting, which would choose a new king. The Storting agreed to this plan.

Oskar was hurt and the Swedish government outraged. Neither would have been placated by a plebiscite which showed 368,208 in favour of breaking away from Sweden and only 184 against. The "compromise" reached in 1905 was a surrender to Norwegian demands: Oskar's abdication and Norway's independence. The king's parting shot was that no member of his house would be allowed to accept the vacated throne even if

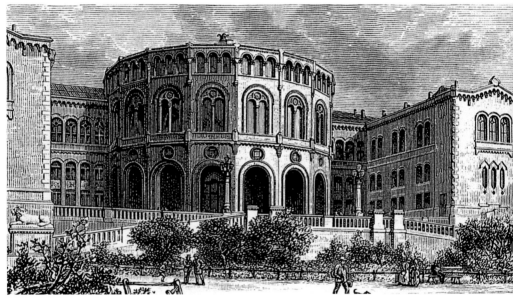

An early drawing of Oslo's Storting (Parliament).

ish, there was no ambiguity about Ibsen's contribution. As a curious footnote, Ibsen once wrote to a friend in England saying that "there are very strong traces in me of Scotch descent. But this is only a feeling – perhaps only a wish that it were so."

BATTLE OF WILLS

Ibsen's strong sense of national identity was mirrored in the political events swirling around him. Problems within the union with Sweden came to a head in 1905 over the lengthy dispute about diplomatic representation. The government wanted its own consular service; King Oskar II refused.

The government then argued that, if it resigned and the king was unable to obtain an alternative government, his royal power would

According to George Bernard Shaw, Ibsen's influence in England "is almost equal to the influence which three revolutions, six crusades, a couple of foreign invasions and an earthquake would produce".

it were offered. This was only in part petulance. Oskar was privately convinced that an independent Norway was bound to collapse and whoever was then king would thus be discredited. When that happened, an unsullied member of his house would, of course, be standing by to answer the call. The call never came.

AN INDEPENDENT, MODERN COUNTRY

Invaded by Germany, then caught up in the Cold War,
Norway has passed through difficult times to emerge
as an international peace-broker.

The prime minister who led Norway to independence was Christian Michelsen, a Bergen solicitor who founded one of the biggest shipping companies in Norway and was by 1903 a member of the government. In the meantime, he had formed a breakaway group in Bergen of "liberals" from the radical left. Michelsen's initial modest aim was to settle the issue of whether Norway should have its own consuls abroad, which would finally destroy the union with Sweden; but by 1904 he was warning the Swedes not to assume that if negotiations failed this time, they could be resumed.

MICHELSEN AT THE HELM

Michelsen had recognised the way Norwegian public opinion was running and the support the cause was getting from such famous Norwegians as the explorer Fridtjof Nansen (who later became Norwegian Ambassador in London) and the writer Bjørnstjerne Bjørnson. Soon Michelsen was heading a cabinet that included ministers from a wide range of parties and of many shades of opinion.

NO FOREIGN POLICY

In the long years of struggle, Bjørnson had claimed that "the foreign policy of Norway should be to have no foreign policy", and immediately after independence, the aim of all parties was to avoid entanglement in the affairs of the Great Powers. But, despite Norway's determined neutrality, World War I had the ironic effect of throwing it and Sweden back into one another's arms. "A new union, not of the old sort, but a union of heartfelt understanding," was the Swedish king's description, "to maintain the neutrality of the respective kingdoms in relation to all the belligerent powers."

King Haakon VII.

Norway did well out of its neutrality, at least for the first two years of the war. Germany was willing to pay top prices for all the fish Norway could supply, which attracted British attention and led to a secret agreement, backed by the threat to cut off supplies of British oil and coal, under which Britain itself would buy most of the fish. Norway, in return, would not export vital copper pyrites to Germany, but otherwise it was free to trade with both sides.

Those lucky enough to get a share of this trade, and of the domestic black market, flaunted their overnight fortunes in such a way that workers on fixed wages, which were forever falling behind rampant inflation, became rebellious. Employers retaliated with lockouts, and the government was forced to introduce compulsory arbitration.

WARTIME LOSSES

German submarine warfare put a damper on profiteering. Most of the Norwegian merchant fleet was under charter to Britain, and by the end of the war half of it, together with 2,000 crew members, was lost. In absolute terms only Britain lost more of its shipping. The intervention of the United States also made matters worse. The Americans demanded big cuts in trade with Germany before agreeing to make supplies available to Norway.

At the end of World War I the neutral countries had little say in deciding the terms of peace. Despite its heavy maritime losses the Norwegian Merchant Navy received no compensation in the shape of ships from the confiscated German Navy, and it was another 10 years before injured seamen

Devised by Fridtjof Nansen, the Nansen "passport" offered those people who had been made stateless by World War I a means of official identification.

King Haakon, Queen Maud and Crown Prince Olaf in 1913.

⊘ NANSEN AND THE LEAGUE

During World War I the Scandinavian monarchs met to discuss and set up committees to review the position of neutral countries when hostilities ceased. Under Fridtjof Nansen, polar explorer turned diplomat, Norway formed an Association for the League of Nations and drafted a potential constitution. But, as the war ended, the Great Powers were not inclined to take much notice of mere neutrals. Instead, they themselves laid down the rules and allowed the neutral countries just two months after the League was founded to seek membership.

Norway, temperamentally against alliances, was fiercely divided, and it was not until 1920 that the Storting finally voted for membership of the League of Nations.

This was Norway's first real move into internationalism. In fact, 16 of the Storting's 20 votes against membership of the League had come from the steadily growing Labour Party, which at the time took most of its principles and goals from the ideas behind the Russian Revolution.

Nansen, who had been so influential in the struggle for Norwegian independence, now had international links to the US, the Soviet Union and elsewhere, and became active in the League, particularly in the slow repatriation of nearly half a million prisoners-of-war from Russia. Later, he donated his own Nobel Peace Prize money for similar work for Russian and Armenian refugees. He was still working on this at the time of his death in 1930.

and the families of those killed received any form of compensation from the German government.

THE RISE OF LABOUR

By 1921 conditions had deteriorated into a full-blown economic depression, with more than a million tonnes of shipping laid up, free-spending local authorities in difficulty and, unthinkably to Norwegians, one of the biggest banks going bankrupt in spite of receiving secret state support.

Storms and controversies over prohibition caused the downfall of three different

The struggle for Narvik, 1941.

cabinets. The steadily growing Labour Party became more radical in its beliefs, and passed a resolution reserving the right to use "revolutionary action in the struggle for the economic liberation of the working classes". The point having been made, militancy declined and by the end of the decade the party had turned its attention back to parliamentary rule. In the 1927 elections, it became the biggest party in the Storting.

The Wall Street crash of 1929 compounded the economic misery. A third of all trade unionists were already out of work when employers tried to reduce wages which, in spite of nearly a decade of economic turmoil, were still very high compared to most European countries.

A lockout at Norsk Hydro produced not only the most notorious incident in the history of Norwegian industrial relations (police and troops fighting demonstrators), but also the rise to prominence of a figure as shameful in Norwegian memory as anyone since Eirik Bloodaxe. The defence minister who ordered in the troops was Vidkun Quisling, and he was soon accusing Labour of plotting an armed revolution.

By 1933, the economic crisis was so bad that the unlikely alliance of the Labour Party with the Agrarian (Farmers') Party put a Labour prime minister into power. He was Johan Nygaardsvold, who had had lengthy experience in the Storting. He was prime minister from 1935 and had a direct responsibility for creating employment. By 1939, the average day's wage had risen by 15 percent.

PRECARIOUS NEUTRALITY

When World War II broke out in September 1939 Norway proclaimed immediate neutrality, but had taken almost no precautions to defend itself. Perhaps Nygaardsvold was too immersed in his economic renaissance. He remained prime minister until 1945, but in the recriminations and resultant inquiry that followed the end of the war, he was deemed partly to blame for not having made adequate preparations when the threat of conflict loomed.

The first warning signs came from the Allied side, with Britain complaining that its ships were being sunk by Germany in Norwegian territorial waters. Also, German ships were being given free access to strategic iron ore from the port of Narvik. The ancient Norwegian fleet was in no position to keep territorial waters neutral, so the British suggested mining them.

The dilemma was highlighted by the *Altmark* affair. The *Altmark*, an auxiliary to the battleship *Graf Spee*, was on its way to Germany with 300 captured British seamen when it sought refuge in Norwegian waters near Egersund. The British Royal Navy was alerted to its presence and charged into the fjord to rescue the men while two small Norwegian vessels looked on, making vain protests. The Norwegian government complained to Britain about violation of its neutrality. The British government asked why Norway had been unable to prevent German abuse of its neutral waters, and Germany posed the same question, but the other way round.

INVASION BY SEA

Britain unilaterally began laying mines along the Norwegian coastline and, on the very day Norway lodged a protest – 8 April 1940 – German forces were on the high seas bound for Norway. Once the invasion was under way, the German minister in Oslo sent a note to say

minister. The government, which had moved itself from Oslo to Trysil, repeatedly refused to comply, and its defiance was repaid with a German bombing attack on the meeting place.

HELP FROM THE ALLIES

Norway's only hope against such lopsided odds lay in the Allies. From Britain's point of view, Narvik was the key because of the iron-ore traffic. The British Royal Navy went into action against German naval units in the area and destroyed them. A combined force of Nor-

The traitor Vidkun Quisling with Heinrich Himmler in Berlin.

that Germany was only occupying a few strategic points to keep the British out.

At last the Norwegian government woke up to what was going on. The German heavy cruiser *Blücher* was sunk by the Oscarsborg fortress in the Oslo fjord near Drøbak, and two creaking Norwegian destroyers boldly took on a much larger German force at Narvik.

The Storting granted the government full powers "to take whatever decisions might be necessary to ensure the best interests of the country", the point on which many a debate would later hinge. On 10 April the Germans showed their hand. Quisling, whose National Unity Party commanded all of 1.8 percent of the electorate, was their choice as new prime

Max Manus (1914–96) was a Norwegian Resistance fighter who earned fame as a saboteur during World War II. His life became the subject of a film of the same name that was a huge box-office success.

wegians, British, French and Poles fought to regain control of the city itself and on 28 May succeeded in doing so.

Earlier, on 14 and 15 April, other Allied troops had landed near Trondheim. They were joined by small Norwegian units. They put up a plucky fight but, practically without any air cover

THE HEROES OF TELEMARK

The Norwegian Resistance fought the Nazis during World War II, but it was the Heroes of Telemark who captured the people's imagination.

The most celebrated act of resistance in Norway during World War II was the sabotage of the Vemork heavy-water plant at Rjukan, in Telemark, in February 1943. No visitor to Rjukan, dwarfed and darkened by mountains all round, could fail to be awed by the audacity of the saboteurs. More impor-

Kirk Douglas in the film The Heroes of Telemark.

tantly, the production of heavy water in the plant, if it had not been stopped, could conceivably have aided the German development of an atomic bomb.

OPERATION "FRESHMAN"

The operation, named "Freshman", was planned for a joint force of Norwegian volunteers on the ground and British commandos transported in two towed gliders. It ended disastrously when both gliders and one of the aircraft towing them crashed 160km (100 miles) from Rjukan.

OPERATION "GUNNERSIDE"

The next attempt was an all-Norwegian affair. "Gunnerside", the code name for six men who had

been trained in Scotland, parachuted onto a frozen lake where they were supposed to join up with "Swallow", an advance party on the ground. The first person they bumped into was a reindeer-hunter. He was released, somewhat bewildered, with food and money on the promise that he would reveal nothing.

Once the parties had linked up, they skied to the ridge above Rjukan for the perilous descent on foot. They slithered down, up to their waists in snow. Just after midnight, the covering party took up positions while the six-man demolition team cut a chain on the gates and crept forward to the basement of the concrete building where the most vital equipment and the heavy-water storage tanks were located. All wore British uniforms and agreed that no lights would be carried; weapons would be unloaded to avoid the accidental discharge of arms, and anyone captured would take his own life.

As the basement was locked, the best way in appeared to be a funnel carrying cables and piping. Two of the men went through it. The solitary Norwegian guard was astonished, but agreed to lead them to vital components.

"I had placed half the charges in position when there was a crash of broken glass behind me," one of the pair wrote later. The other members of the team, not realising that their leaders had managed to get in, had decided to smash in through a window. With the rest of the charges laid, the six began a rapid withdrawal. They were nonplussed by the cooperative guard who, understandably getting out as well while the going was good, implored to be let in again. He had forgotten his glasses! The request was granted, but the delay meant that the party had only gone a few yards when there was what members later variously and incompatibly described as "a cataclysmic explosion" and "a tiny, insignificant pop".

Five members of the parachute team reached Sweden after a 400km (250-mile) journey on skis in indescribably difficult conditions; the sixth stayed on in the area for another year before eventually he was able to escape. In due course he turned up in Britain, reporting for further duties.

against the Luftwaffe, took a pasting from above. Towns where there was a British presence were bombed to ruin: Åndalsnes, Namsos, Steinkjer and Mosjøen.

During World War II, the old Viking character could be seen in the number of small boats that regularly made the crossing between Shetland and Norway, keeping links open with the exiled king and government in Britain.

The fight for Norway was overshadowed by the German steamroller in Western Europe and, with what were seen to be greater needs there, the Allied forces withdrew, leaving Norway alone.

The king and government, evacuated to the north and ready to fight on, decided to decamp to Britain; on 7 June 1940 they boarded a British cruiser.

REPRISALS BEGIN

A Nazi, Josef Terboven, was despatched to Norway as Reichskommissar. Quisling was appalled; he had expected to be appointed Führer, in which capacity he would then conclude peace with Germany and mobilise Norwegian forces on its side.

Terboven had little time for Quisling, but the latter had friends in Berlin who arranged to have him appointed "minister president". As such, Quisling ordered all children between the ages of 10 and 18 to join his version of the Hitler Youth. His plans for the Nazification of the civil service, courts, all professional bodies and trade unions were in every instance fiercely rejected. Resistance met with grim reprisals. Two trade union leaders, Viggo Hansteen and Rolf Wickstrøm, were shot; the rector of Oslo University was arrested. A steady flow of prisoners, including 1,300 uncooperative teachers, arrived at Grini, the prison camp established outside Oslo.

German tanks invade Norway in 1940.

⊘ AN OFF-THE-SHELF MONARCHY

Imported from Denmark in 1905, Norway's popular monarchy has passed through a number of trials on its way to acceptance by the nation. The various monarchs, from Haakon VII to the current king, Harald V, have managed to win their people's heart with their unassuming manner and their love of sport. Olav V, although born in England, proved he felt at home in Norway by winning prizes on the Holmenkollen ski jump (as daunting a test of Norwegian authenticity as could be), and Harald V has made a name for himself as a competitive sailor, something that went down well in a nation of seafarers.

King Harald married a commoner, Sonja Haraldsen (the current Queen Sonja), and Crown Prince Haakon did the same in 2001 when he controversially married an unwed mother and former waitress, Mette-Marit Tjessem Høiby. Like his father, Haakon chose to "marry the girl he loves rather than love the girl he marries".

In 2002, Princess Märtha Louise also married a commoner, author Ari Behn, reinforcing, once again, the national unity symbolised by the royal family.

Like the flag and the 17th of May celebrations, the Norwegian monarchy symbolises independence from the life under the rule of first Denmark and then Sweden. What often appears to be fervent nationalism is, in fact, no more than national pride and a desire to hold on to a hard-earned self-determination.

The most summary reprisals were meted out to members of the military underground, Milorg, a nucleus of survivors of the 1940 fighting augmented by volunteers and armed by clandestine shipments from Britain.

Telavåg, a village near Bergen, was razed to the ground when the Germans discovered it to be an assembly point for a clandestine ferry service known as the "Shetland Bus", which operated between Norway and Britain. The village men were deported to Germany, the women and children interned. A group of 18

May 1945. The gates of Grini were thrown open and thousands streamed out to join what was undoubtedly the biggest street party ever held in Oslo. It was still going strong a week later when Crown Prince Olav returned, five years to the day after his reluctant departure.

Cleaning up after the war concentrated on Quisling's prosecution. Charges were brought against 50,000 people, many for petty crimes rather than full-scale collaboration. The courts were not considered unduly harsh, perhaps sensing that participation in Quisling's so-called

Members of the exiled government return to Norway at the end of the war.

men waiting in Ålesund for the trip to Britain were found and shot.

CELEBRATION PARTY

The final chapter of the occupation was played out by German troops retreating from Finland through Finnmark in northern Norway. They adopted a scorched-earth policy which utterly destroyed many towns and villages. The inhabitants were herded into fishing boats to find their own way to the south.

The Germans were still very strong in Norway while their forces elsewhere capitulated – the army alone numbered 350,000. Fears that the whole country might be put to the torch were laid to rest only when they surrendered on 7

⊘ PEACEKEEPERS

In 1945 Norway was one of the founding signatories of the United Nations, and a former Norwegian foreign minister, Trygve Lie, became its first secretary-general. Lie held the office during the first hopeful years and continued to do so into the Korean War, in which United Nations troops took an active fighting role for the first and last time. Norway provided and staffed a field hospital in Korea. Since then some 32,000 Norwegians have worn a UN blue beret. Norway has continued its commitment to internationalism and peace, notably as broker in the 1993 Israeli-Palestinian peace proposals. It concentrates on human rights, humanitarian help and environmental issues.

"NS" would remain a stigma. Some 25 collaborators were executed, including Quisling and two of his ministers.

After that necessary purging, Norway's most pressing needs were to replace what had been destroyed during the war, and to modernise and expand industry and the economy. The whole of northern Norway had been so heavily devastated that in some cases areas of hasty rebuilding are only today being replaced, and many of the small northern towns still have an austere anonymity about them.

RISING STANDARDS

Fast economic expansion and many crash programmes led to large-scale investment and over-employment, but it provided a rising standard of living that climbed faster and further than that of most countries in Europe. By the early 1960s Norway used more electricity per head than any other country in the world, and only three people in every thousand in remote areas had no supply. The merchant marine had made good its wartime shipping losses by 1949 and tonnage tripled within 15 years.

As NATO's most northeasterly outpost, with a short 196km (122-mile) border with Russia, Norway inevitably walked a tightrope between the superpowers.

Then fortunes changed quickly when oil was found in the North Sea, and by the 1970s Norway was almost overwhelmed by the riches it was receiving from the oil industry.

All this went along with over 20 years of socialist government, which introduced comprehensive social-welfare services, Scandinavian-style, and much state control of industry. But this was no far-left Labour Party in the style of its post-World War I predecessors, and many shared its belief in an equal society and care for all. In keeping with similar parties in Sweden and Denmark, post-war Norwegian socialism had been middle-of-the-road, led first by Einar Gerhardsen, who had been a prominent Resistance worker, then Oscar Torp, and Trygve Bratteli.

In recent years, the best-known Norwegian prime minister, ranking high in international esteem, has been Gro Harlem Brundtland. She was appointed prime minister for the first time in 1981. That tenure was short, lasting only until a conservative-led victory at the polls that autumn; but at 41 she was the youngest person ever to hold the office, and the first woman. In total, she held the post for more than 10 years before stepping down in 1996. In 1998 she became Director-General of the World Health Organization. In 2001, a

Oslo's Nobel Peace Center.

☉ WHEN TRAGEDY BRINGS UNITY

On 22 July 2011, a car bomb exploded outside government offices in Oslo, killing nine people. It was the work of right-wing extremist Anders Breivik, who then made his way to the offshore island of Utoya. There, where the youth wing of Norway's ruling Labour Party was holding its annual summer camp, he slaughtered 69 teenagers and injured 115.

Norway's most lethal attack since World War II shook this peaceful nation to the core. But far from stimulating calls for greater security at the expense of individual liberties, the atrocity brought out the best in most Norwegians. After a fair and open trial, Breivik was sentenced to a minimum of 21 years in prison.

new centre-right coalition won the national election, followed by a centre-left coalition in 2006, This centre-left "red-green" coalition was led by Jens Stoltenberg (Labour Party), who was re-elected for a second mandate

> *In 2001, Norway signed the Schengen Agreement allowing citizens of other Schengen countries to travel without the need for passports.*

Gro Harlem Brundtland served three terms as Norway's prime minister.

in September 2009. In late 2013, reflecting a more general European lurch to the right, the Conservative Party won elections for the first time in more than two decades and Erna Solberg became Norway's 28th prime minister and the second woman to hold that office. In September 2017, she and her right-wing coalition were re-elected for a second mandate.

MAINTAINING INDEPENDENCE

In recent years Norway has been planning for the future, often ambitiously. The state's investment in big road-building projects is one example. Nothing has deterred Norwegian engineers from tackling the harsh terrain,

whether it's digging the longest tunnel in the world, the Laerdal Tunnel (see page 238), or building bridges (no fewer than eight) along Atlanterhavsveien (the Atlantic Road).

Oslo has been making international headlines of late, and attracting visitors with a mix of inspiring new architecture (see page 120), a growing number of music events and festivals, revamped shopping and dining, but also for altogether more tragic reasons, when in July 2011 Anders Breivik went on a killing spree, killing 9 people in the capital and a further 69 on the nearby island of Utoya (see box).

Gordon Ramsay officiating as guest of honour at the Gladmat festival in Stavanger in 2010, and President Barack Obama's visit in January for the awarding of the Nobel Peace Prize ceremony, are telltale signs that Norway now wants to play with the big boys.

NEW CHALLENGES

But Norwegians have also started thinking about new challenges lying ahead, such as what to do now the oil is running out; issues related to the environment have often been at the forefront of the debate, as with the proposed drilling for oil off the coast of the Lofoten Islands, or the building of high-power electric cable lines in the Hardangerfjord area. Both are areas of outstanding beauty, and popular tourist destinations, and the debate continues to divide.

Oslo's leftist city government wants to ban private cars from the city centre by 2019 as part of a plan to slash greenhouse gas emissions. If it is successful, it will be the first major European city to do so, paving the way for others to follow suit.

The ongoing migrant crisis has also affected Norway. And in 2016, following Sweden and Denmark's lead, Norway opted to reinstate border controls and implemented a crackdown on illegal immigration, reporting a record number of illegal immigrants in 2016. The same year construction started on a controversial fence along a section of the Russian border in order to curb the migrant influx.

And as Russia flexes its muscles in the Arctic Circle, Norway has also deployed troops to its Finnmark border with Russia, as part of a plan to strengthen its defence.

BLACK GOLD

The discovery of oil and gas in the North Sea has made Norway rich, but resources won't last and plans are being made for the future.

It became clear in the 1970s that vast oil and gas riches lay beneath the ocean floor off the Norwegian coast, and yet the full extent of these resources is still being determined today. Current estimates predict that without major new oil discoveries oil production will gradually decline, but as a major gas exporter Norway can count on a longer perspective.

It all started in 1962 when, prompted by a gas find off Holland, the American Phillips oil company acquired the right to explore in Norwegian waters. Other companies soon followed. After clarification of legal problems and territorial rights with Denmark and Britain, drilling started in earnest in 1966. Four years later, Phillips announced the discovery of a giant oil field, Ekofisk. The 1970s saw a series of major discoveries: French ELF found Frigg; American Mobil found the world's largest offshore oilfield, Statfjord; Shell confirmed the giant Troll gas field off Bergen. The Norwegians learned quickly, and two Norwegian oil companies joined the fray. The state-owned Statoil discovered Gullfaks, and the semi-nationalised Norsk Hydro became the operator at Oseberg.

Oil production at the Ekofisk field started modestly from a floating rig in 1971. Permanent installations and a pipeline to Teesside in northeast England were commissioned in 1975. By the end of the 1970s Norway had built a gas-processing plant at Kårstø, near Stavanger, and was exporting dry gas to the rest of Continental Europe, and the Norwegian shipbuilding industry was entering a golden age as far as contracts were concerned.

After several years of discussing production levels, and with low oil prices, the offshore industry was finally forced into a 3 percent production cut, with the hope that this would help oil prices rise once again.

International terrorism and wars later sent oil prices skyrocketing, fuelling a new exploration boom that focused attention on the Barents Sea. Norwegian companies were keen to team up with Russian oil interests in the development of the Stockman field, while massive investment was also made in the Snow White field and its ground facilities at Hammerfest. Today, the big question is whether or not to look for oil off the coast of the Lofoten Islands, an area of stunning natural beauty and a popular tourist destination.

The Norwegian state has three sources of revenue from its offshore industry: taxes and duties levied on the oil companies; the state's direct economic involvement; and share dividends from its ownership stakes in Statoil and Norsk Hydro. Since the late 1990s, much of Norway's oil revenue has been stashed into what initially was called the state's Oil Investment Fund

Oil drilling platform.

(now the Government's Pension Fund). By 2006, its value equalled that of all the real estate on Manhattan, and it had become a serious player in international stock and bond markets. The Norwegian Ministry of Finance predicted that by the end of 2019 the value of the fund would be – hold on to your hat – NOK6 *trillion* (US1 *trillion*). The money is earmarked for future pension demands, a key concern in a country that is among the most expensive in the world.

A very high proportion of Norway's formidable supplies of oil and gas is exported. Cannily, Norwegians are investing heavily in solar power, heat pumps and wind energy, sending fossil fuels elsewhere and aiming to keep their country clean and ever environmentally more pure.

Skiing is a way of life in Norway.

WHO ARE THE NORWEGIANS?

Ask a visitor what defines a Norwegian and you might get a general description of a Scandinavian. While some of the stereotypes ring true, differences abound.

One character in a Hans Christian Andersen story proclaims: "I'm a Norwegian. And when I say I'm Norwegian, I think I've said enough. I'm as firm in my foundations as the ancient mountains of old Norway... It thrills me to the marrow to think what I am, and let my thoughts ring out in words of granite."

Andersen was, of course, a Dane, and he was teasing the Norwegians, as their Scandinavian neighbours are apt to do. In much the same way as Italians are satirically reduced to being tearful opera and ice-cream fiends, and Frenchmen become obtuse philosophers in garlic necklaces, so the typical Norwegian has often been portrayed as a simple, stubborn peasant who needs a comforting pat on the head.

Naturally, Norwegians see themselves rather differently. A Gallup poll once asked 200 people from each of 12 countries to rank themselves in terms of culture, food, living standards, beauty, *joie de vivre* and national pride. The Norwegians gave themselves top marks in virtually every category.

GENEROUS HOSPITALITY

The Norwegian character is, of course, far more complex than Andersen would allow or Gallup could measure. It is sometimes said that Norwegians are xenophobic. While this may be an exaggeration, it is often the case that they do not accept outside criticism. Yet the hospitality shown towards foreign visitors far exceeds the demands of mere good manners. An English visitor arriving late was whisked off spontaneously to a wedding party in Oslo. As the only foreigner among 200 guests, he was disarmed when the bride's father, advised of his surprise presence, gave away his daughter in English. Although the younger Norwegian guests were, as usual, fluent

National pride at the Holmenkollen ski jump.

in English, some older ones were left in the dark, but they thoroughly approved of the gesture.

A WELCOME CANDLE

Other signs of welcome are given without thinking. A visitor in the house is the signal for lighting candles, probably a throwback to the days when, compounded by the long hours of winter darkness, houses shuttered against the cold were rather gloomy. Most of Norway's population was thinly scattered across a vast landscape in a patchwork of tiny communities, so visitors invariably arrived after a long and exhausting journey, sometimes on skis. The assumption was that they arrived hungry, and restorative food and drink still appear as if by magic.

TEN COMMANDMENTS (JANTE LAW)

The more enigmatic aspects of the Norwegian psyche – including the Nordic gloom which descends after a drink too many – have been famously scrutinised by native Henrik Ibsen. He was brought up in small communities and, during a long exile, turned his critical eye on the experience. One of the themes running through his writings is the double-edged nature of life in such a community: mutual support in adversity weighed against a suffocating lack of privacy.

can trace an unbroken line of descent from people who inhabited their territory in prehistoric times, a homogeneity whose origins predate the beginnings of Western civilisation in the Aegean.

Yet the present state of Norway was reconstituted only in 1905, which makes it younger than many of the junior members in the United Nations, themselves pasted together by the imperial powers in the 19th century. Having been relegated to a back seat in Scandinavian affairs for hundreds of years, these distant descendants of the illustrious Vikings need

Part of a multicultural society in Bergen, the second-largest city in Norway.

Norwegian elders.

The lesser-known Aksel Sandemose wrote Ten Commandments (Jante Law) for village life, the essence being humility bordering on self-abasement. They included: "You must not think that you are worth anything; you must not think that you are better than anyone else; you must not think yourself capable of anything worthwhile; and you must not think that you are in any way exceptional."

Jingoistic chest-pounding of the sort noted by Hans Christian Andersen is derived to some extent from Norway's peculiar position as both one of the oldest, if not the oldest, nation in Europe and at the same time one of the youngest. It is the oldest in the sense that the Norwegians

> *Peer Gynt, Ibsen's (anti-) hero, is seen as a satire of the Norwegian character, displaying weaknesses such as self-delusion. The play's popularity says much about Norwegians' ability to laugh at themselves.*

to pinch themselves – or blow a trumpet – as if they nervously expect to find that their independence was a cruel dream.

FREE TO SHOW THE FLAG

Well-deserved national pride makes Norwegians ardent flag-wavers. This could be construed as a rude gesture to the Swedes who, under the union, decided when, where and how the Norwegian colours were to be shown in foreign waters, relegating them to a mere patch on a much larger Swedish flag. The flag flown on Norwegian ships was, like separate consular representation and the establishment of a national bank, a perennial bone of contention before independence.

Many houses have flagpoles and every home possesses a flag which is hoisted on the slightest pretext, if only to indicate that the owner is in residence.

Their dignity as a sovereign state is not to be trivialised. The Swedish king who reluctantly oversaw Norway's independence predicted that bureaucratic incompetence would soon have Norwegians begging to be returned to the fold. The response, even now, is a reluctance to admit (to outsiders) that they are capable of making a mistake.

Paraglider flying the national flag.

⦿ A MULTICULTURAL SOCIETY

Norway is an increasingly multicultural society. As of 2017, there were almost 725,000 immigrants and nearly 159,000 children born from immigrant couples living in Norway. Together they represent 16.8 percent of Norway's population. Oslo has the largest proportion of immigrants (33 percent), with over 217,000 people. Poles now outnumber Swedes as the largest immigrant group in Norway, followed by Somalis, Lithuanians, Pakistanis and Iraqis in that order.

Until the 1960s, immigration to Norway had mainly consisted of Europeans and people from other Nordic countries. The first labour migrants arrived from Pakistan in the 1960s, followed in the 1970s by Thai, Filipino and Russian women who had married Norwegian men, and refugees from developing countries such as Chile and Vietnam. The mid-1980s saw an increase in asylum-seekers from countries such as Iran and Sri Lanka, joined by war refugees from the Balkans in the 1990s and later from Iraq, Somalia and Afghanistan. Today, it's mainly Eastern Europeans.

The arrival of these immigrants has not been without its challenges (the debate about Muslim women wearing the hijab, for example, has received extensive coverage and in 2017 the government announced its plan to outlaw it in all educational institutions), but it has also been a force for change and, as a result, Norway is a more tolerant society. Their influence can also be felt in the media, on the cultural scene and in the culinary diversity on offer.

LANGUAGE

Did you know that Norway has three official languages? This has created problems over the years as well as enriching the cultural scene.

Bokmål? Nynorsk? Sami? Language was a burning issue in Norwegian politics until the 1950s, even causing a prime minister to resign in 1912. The long-running controversy started as a form of agitation against Danish rule, throughout which Danish was the language of the civil service, schools and the Church. Long after the

Fortunately you don't need to know Norwegian to get by, as most Norwegians speak English.

Reformation the revised Bible was available only in Danish. Denmark got its first printing press in 1480 but Norway had to wait until 1643, so books were imported and in Danish. When reading aloud, Norwegians modified standard Danish through the use of their own pronunciation and intonation, eventually producing the hybrid known as *bokmål* (book language).

The 19th-century nationalists saw it as fundamentally Danish and wanted a national language that was authentically Norwegian. Unfortunately, there was no single Norwegian substitute. In a land that stretches from Baltic to Barents Seas, where land communications were difficult, especially in the north, and communities small, there was – and still is – a profusion of dialects.

The early language reformers – including Ivar Aasen and Knut Knudsen, the latter a schoolmaster driven by his pupils' frustration in trying to decipher Danish spelling – concentrated on developing a composite. They worked on what became known as *landsmål* or *nynorsk*, but their efforts were not unreservedly welcomed. Danish was the language of society and the theatre, and if Norwegian had to be spoken, a "Danicised" pronunciation was fashionable. These tendencies eroded as intellectuals like Ibsen lent respectability to the campaign for the revival of a purely Norwegian language.

In 1929 *bokmål* and *nynorsk* were recognised as dual official languages, the hope being that they would drift towards a blend to be known as *samnorsk*. Progress towards *samnorsk* was given a nudge in the 1950s with a proposal to have school textbooks converted into it. There was such an outcry, however, that the government backed down. Subsequent policy has been to treat the two languages even-handedly, still hoping that they will one day converge. But *nynorsk* is today used by only about 15 percent of Norwegian primary school children. As a language based on rural culture, *nynorsk* suffered because of 20th-century urbanisation, and today, in spite of attempts to shore it up through radio and television, it is losing ground to *bokmål*, although *nynorsk* literature remains popular.

Educated speech is distinctly that of the southeast, although that does not prevent country-dwellers on a visit to the capital, say, from laying on their regional accents thick for effect. The Bergensere, at the heart of the *nynorsk* area, are certainly proud of their individualistic tongue.

This said, the two rival versions of Norwegian essentially concern how to write the language. In their everyday dealings, people speak uninhibitedly with the accent and/or dialect of their home region. A bookish issue arguably but one that can arouse great passion.

The third language, *Sami* (Northern Sami, the most widely spoken of the Sami languages), is used by nearly 25,000 people in Scandinavia, most of whom live in Finnmark and Troms in northern Norway (see page 81). Sami is a member of a quite different language family and belongs to the Finno-Ugrian group, sharing a close affinity with Finnish and Estonian and a looser link with Hungarian. Nowadays, most Sami are equally at home in their mother tongue and Norwegian too.

As long as authority was vested in foreigners, Norwegians did not regard it too highly. On assuming it themselves, authority took on the aura of divine right before which loyal citizens should willingly prostrate themselves. Norwegian history is full of swings from one extreme to another. Pagans who held out against Christianity until a surprisingly late date became, and in some cases remain, doggedly fundamentalist after seeing the light. And a nation once thought in danger of drinking itself to death has by no means buried the bottle, even

The klem, a typically Norwegian embrace that consists of putting your arms round someone while simultaneously touching cheeks, but not kissing, is reserved for good friends, and is a common way of showing one's affection.

for "please". The only thing remotely unruly in Norwegian manners occurs in the busy streets of Oslo. People jostle each other with

Women are more economically independent in Norway than in most other European countries.

if alcohol consumption is now kept mainly for the weekend and Norwegians are adopting more Continental customs – wine sales are up, hard liquor down.

FRIENDSHIPS WORTH FORGING

While drinking customs are becoming a little more moderate, there's no question that Norwegians become less reserved after a skål or two. Foreigners moving to Norway discover quickly that sober Norwegians aren't big on small talk. They are, however, open and considerate people. And they are polite, too, even if they do not say *takk* (thank you) as frequently as English-speaking people, and if there is no word in their language

⊘ WOMEN'S EQUALITY

Norway's main strategy in achieving gender equality has been to strengthen women's economic independence through increasing their labour market participation, with a welfare system ensuring childcare and parental leave for all. Today, the percentage of women in the workforce is among the highest in Europe. Norway was the first country to appoint a Gender Equality Ombudsman, and its governments have always had a high proportion of women ministers. Women increasingly occupy top positions in business (40 percent of board members in public limited companies are women), but at grassroots level there are still more women than men in low-paid employment.

impunity, as they tend to do in most big cities the world over: don't be offended if you don't get an apology after someone bumps into you – as long as it's gentle. Of more concern are the mad darts people make across streets, without regard for traffic lights.

Although young people tend to be a lot less formal than their parents, Norwegians do still go about life with some surprisingly rigid rules of behaviour. And everyone, young or old, likes to dress up, and finds an excuse to do so for any occasion – 17 May being the biggest one.

Society tends to place a high value on family and long-term friends.

A language instructor at the University of Oslo claimed that "Norwegians are like a Thermos bottle, hard and cold on the outside, but nice and warm once you open them up". Society is very closely tied to family and long-term friends from school days. Many do not feel inclined to extend their relationships to outsiders, and establishing friendships can take time. Once formed, genuine friendship is taken very seriously.

A GENEROUS PEOPLE

The Norwegians' penchant for sharing their wealth is also legendary, both at home and abroad. Many Norwegians say they pay their high taxes with pleasure, firmly believing that no

one should be too rich or too poor, while their generosity in donating money to worthy causes and international relief efforts leads all other countries on a per-capita basis.

Norwegians can also be remarkably generous where they might be expected to be most possessive. There is little alarm about the predatory impact of, say, satellite television on a language which hardly exists outside Norway. Far from resenting visitors who presume to address them in a foreign tongue, Norwegians positively relish the challenge, usually responding with fluency. Confidence in the hardiness of their language is curiously at odds with its historical background.

> Norwegians are great hand-shakers. Strangers meeting always shake hands and exchange names. When meeting casual acquaintances, you shake hands as you arrive and leave.

AUTONOMY AND SELF-SUFFICIENCY

The regional fragmentation at the heart of the language debate extends to most facets of cultural and economic life. While Norway has since Viking times been a single nation, it has been a confederation of many parts. Norway can be divided north–south, east–west, or a dozen different ways. Like the Renaissance, the Industrial Revolution hardly intruded, so there was not the rapid urbanisation that occurred elsewhere. Trondheim, Bergen and Oslo were towns rather than cities. A later creation, Stavanger owed its existence to the arrival of vast shoals of herring, which were the basis of jobs and trade. Most of Norway remained rooted in subsistence agriculture.

Rural families tended to be isolated and self-sufficient. Their lives depended on agriculture, and the land was not good enough to support more than a family or two in a single valley. Separated from their neighbours by mountains, which were easier to cross in winter (on skis) than in summer, they effectively lived in different worlds. There were hardly any villages where tradesmen could be found and paid in cash. The versatile family managed on its own, a resourcefulness which still runs in the blood.

NORWAY AND ITS NEIGHBOURS

While outsiders talk about "Scandinavians", there are marked differences between Norwegians and their neighbours.

If you walked into a room and met three Scandinavians, it would be hard to tell which was the Norwegian, which the Dane and which the Swede. They look alike, have similar interests and seem to speak the same language, even if the accent is somewhat different.

The written languages, all based on Old Norse, are so similar they are generally understood by all, and SAS, the airline shared by the three countries, allows its crews to use their own language. This works well when a crew is Norwegian, but less well with Danes and Swedes, who sometimes find each other incomprehensible.

This Scandinavian family is often taken to include Finland, though the Finns are of a different race with a language related to Hungarian. In any event, all four countries are part of the Nordic group, which includes Iceland, the Faroes, Greenland and the Åland Islands in the Gulf of Bothnia.

Like all families, Scandinavians have the usual squabbles and false images of one another that come out of close proximity. To other Scandinavians, Norwegians are "blue-eyed" or naive, often the butt of innocuous jokes, yet both Swedes and Danes are astonished to learn that similar jokes are told by Norwegians against them. The family analogy continues in that the Danes tend to look on Norway as a younger brother, with all that that implies.

Sweden, with which Norway shares a 1,700km (1,000-mile) border, is often looked on by Norway (and to a lesser extent by Denmark) as an elder brother, with allegations of arrogance and insensitivity from the smaller countries and a tendency for the larger to think it "knows best". But since Norway discovered oil in 1969, the big-brother attitude has taken a knock, and left Sweden looking at Norway with a degree of wonder and envy. The image of Norway as the junior partner is partly due to the fact that, after 500 years ruled first by Denmark and then Sweden, the present Norwegian state is just over a century old, though Norway has been a nation for as long as any Scandinavian country.

Norway's only non-Nordic neighbour is Russia. The two countries coexist with scarcely any friction on Spitsbergen (Svalbard), the remote northern islands, best known for coal, bird- and plant-life, and the sealers and whalers of former days.

In the days of the Soviet Union they were at odds over their joint border in the far northern Barents Sea. Norway favoured a border on the median line equidistant between the two countries, but their Russian neighbours wanted to adopt a sector principle, giving them control of larger fish areas and oil reserves. In 2010, the two countries agreed on a line straight

King Harald of Norway takes his visitor King Carl Gustav of Sweden on a walk of Tromsø.

through the grey zone that had been a bone of contention since the 1970s.

During World War II, when only Sweden was neutral, the Scandinavian countries did their best to help one another, although neither Norway nor Sweden has yet managed to forget that Sweden allowed German troops to pass through its country on their way to attack Norway. Many Finnish children left for homes in Sweden, and that country also became an escape route from Norway. At the end of the war, Norway, Denmark and Iceland joined NATO, Sweden remained non-aligned, and Finland (in an uneasy position between the Eastern and Western Blocs) declared itself neutral.

EPIC EXPLORERS

Whether because of exile, scientific exploration or wanting to be the first, Norwegian explorers have travelled the world from the North to South Poles.

Although exploration is most often associated in modern times with rocket journeys into space, the names of at least two Norwegian explorers are as evocative now as at the time of their epic achievements: Roald Amundsen (1861–1930) is for ever remembered as the man who beat Captain Scott to the South Pole, and Thor Heyerdahl (1914–2002) for the *Kon-Tiki* expedition.

Their fame steals some of the limelight which ought to be apportioned to a much larger cast of intrepid Norwegians, beginning with Bjarni Herjulfsson who, in 986, lost his way while sailing from Iceland to Greenland and ended up, according to an ancient saga, as the first European to sight the American continent.

EARLY MIGRATIONS

A 19th-century Norwegian explorer, Fridtjof Nansen (1861–1930), set the pattern for the investigation of human migration. He established his reputation in 1888 with a hazardous crossing of Greenland from east to west. A few years later he was excited by the discovery near the southern tip of Greenland of some wreckage whose origins were traced to the New Siberian Islands. How had it got there?

Nansen determined to find out. His vessel, *Fram*, was designed to lift herself under the crushing pressure of the drift ice in the Arctic Ocean. She was set adrift off the New Siberian Islands in September 1893 and, two years later, emerged near Spitsbergen – but without Nansen. He had left the ship in charge of his second-in-command in a heroic but vain attempt to reach the North Pole with dog-drawn sledges. He and his companion survived a winter in Franz Josef Land, living in an ice hut and eating whatever they could shoot. They reached

Roald Amundsen.

safety on practically the same day as *Fram*, and Nansen's six volumes of findings are the basis of the science of oceanography.

The purpose of the 1947 *Kon-Tiki* expedition was to test a theory about the origins of the Polynesian people and culture. Heyerdahl demonstrated that a balsawood raft set adrift off the coast of Peru could eventually – it took him about four months – reach the Tuamotu Archipelago 8,000km (5,000 miles) to the west. In the 1960s he successfully conducted a similar experiment – the *Ra* expedition – to discover whether West African voyagers using rafts may have reached the West Indies before Columbus. Although accepted scientific opinion gives little credence to Heyerdahl's theories, his *Kon-Tiki* adventure and the account he wrote of his epic journey enthused a generation.

VIKING EXPLORERS

The father of Norwegian exploration is Erik the Red, a man who seems to have had a liking for slaughter. In the 10th century he was banished from Norway to Iceland for murder, and then from Iceland for several more killings. Unwelcome anywhere, he sailed west with a shipload of livestock and discovered the world's largest island – a lump of ice, more than 3km (2 miles) thick in

find out for himself what it was all about. His 35-man expedition left Greenland about the year 1000. According to legend, they landed first at

Liv Arnesen (born 1953) was the first woman to reach the South Pole alone in 1994, and Monika Kristensen (born 1950) led a South Pole expedition in 1986–7, following in the footsteps of Roald Amundsen.

Thor Heyerdahl's Ra under construction in Egypt.

places. A keen angler, Erik was so engrossed by the excellent catches to be had in summer that he neglected to collect enough animal fodder for the winter. His livestock starved to death. He resolved to risk violation of his ostracism to collect replacements from Iceland and to persuade others to join him on his return.

Erik trumpeted his new-found land with the zeal of an unprincipled estate agent. It was so wonderful, he said, that he had decided to call it Greenland. By 985 he had acquired animals and enticed enough colonisers to fill 25 ships, of which 14 reached their destination.

It was in one of the settlements founded by Erik the Red that his son, Leiv, having heard Bjarni Herjulfsson's strange tale, prepared to

"Markland", a wooded region on the coast of Labrador, and then continued south to "Vinland".

An inscription on a map probably drawn by a monk in Basel in 1440 describes Leiv Eiriksson's discovery of "a new land, extremely fertile, and even having vines… a truly vast and very rich land". Attempts to settle the land were defeated by the hostile natives.

RACE FOR THE POLE

Roald Amundsen had served a rigorous apprenticeship for his famous assault on the South Pole, which came about as a last-minute change of plan. Although he had taken part in a Belgian expedition to Antarctica, his first interest was the Arctic. He was stuck for two years off King

William Island in a seal-hunting boat, *Gjøa*, and applied his time to studying the Inuit inhabitants and making reckonings on the magnetic pole.

Amundsen knew about Captain Scott's ambitions to reach the South Pole, but he himself was more concerned with reaching the North. Nevertheless, faced with the shattering news that Robert Peary had pipped him to the post in the north, in 1910 he secretly went south instead in Nansen's old ship, *Fram*. But not until he reached Madeira did he let anyone know what his intentions were. Amundsen decided to dispense with all scientific work in his sprint to the South Pole. Scott had a head start but discovered too late that his Siberian ponies were useless in the conditions. He and his team had to pull their sledges. Amundsen took a shorter, rougher route and had the benefit of dog teams. In the event, he beat Scott by a month.

The dispirited English team perished on their return, and this unlucky fate took some of the lustre off Amundsen's feat. At last, though, the director of London's Royal Geographical Society, which had backed Scott, paid tribute to Amundsen's effort as "the most successful polar journey on record".

Liv Arnesen, the first woman to ski alone and unsupported to the South Pole, on Christmas morning, 1994.

⊘ AMERICAN PROOF

The discovery of America by Christopher Columbus in 1492, a significant landmark in world history, was not contested for several centuries. The Italian explorer, however, was not the first European to set foot on the American continent – the Vikings had got there first, as it turned out.

The existence of "Vinland" was known to Adam of Bremen, a chronicler in the 1070s, and to writers of the sagas, but it was through archaeology that Eiriksson's discovery of America is put virtually beyond doubt. Excavations on the site of a Greenland farm belonging to a member of the Vinland expedition produced a lump of anthracite, which is unobtainable in Greenland but plentiful in Rhode Island.

The case was strengthened in 1960 by Helge Ingstad, who thought about the likely landing place on the American continent of an expedition from Greenland. This made geographical sense since the sea channel between Greenland and Canada is a mere 26km (16 miles) wide at its most narrow point. He backed a hunch and at L'Anse aux Meadows, on the northern tip of Newfoundland, discovered that six buildings had once stood on the site. Carbon dating proved they were medieval, and the archaeological remains left no doubt that the occupants had been Norsemen.

The Norse colonies in Greenland were wiped out by the late 15th century due to malnutrition and competition for resources with the native Inuit. Barely a few years, the European population of the Americas was to explode...

The Sami have preserved their traditional way of life.

THE SAMI: PEOPLE OF FOUR NATIONS

Behind the popular image of the Sami with their colourful costumes and large herds of reindeer lies a rich, complex culture that is an important part of modern Norway.

The Sami (or Lapps, as they are sometimes called despite its derogatory overtones) have lived in Norway from time immemorial. Traces of their presence stretch back more than 8,000 years. The name Sami comes from the Sami *sápmi*, denoting both the people themselves and their traditional territory. Samiland extends from Idre in Sweden, and adjacent areas in Norway, south to Engerdal in Hedmark; to the north and east it stretches to Utsjoki in Finland, Varanger in Norway and on to the Kola peninsula in Russia. It covers a larger area than Norway and Denmark combined, and the population is cautiously estimated at 70,000, of which around 45,000 live in Norway, mainly in Finnmark.

Norwegian Sami divide roughly into three groups. The Mountain Sami are the most widespread, ranging from Varanger to Femunden. They live mainly by breeding reindeer. The

Sami woman in traditional costume.

> *Reindeer-herding is at the heart of Sami culture and influences all aspects of life, including the concept of time – the Sami people count eight seasons, related to the annual behavioural pattern of their reindeer.*

River Sami live around the waterways in the interior of Finnmark and have turned to agriculture and animal husbandry, though hunting, fishing and berry-picking still add to their income. The third group, the Sea Sami, is the largest, making a living from fishing and farming in a lifestyle that differs little from that of other northern Norwegians.

ANCIENT CULTURE

The Sami people have been particularly successful in conserving their rich cultural heritage and many unique traditions. Not the least important is the Sami language, which derives from the Finno-Ugric branch of the Uralic family and is closely related to the Baltic Sea-Finnish languages.

From ancient times, the sea has been of great importance as an abundant source of fish, and of seal to provide the Sami with valuable hides. Walruses, with their precious tusks, were also highly prized, particularly by the Sami craftspeople who produced all sorts of tools and utensils including needles, buttons, spoons, cups and a variety of musical instruments.

NOMADIC LIFESTYLE

Samiland is a mighty land, rich in lakes, rivers, small streams, grandiose mountains and boundless hills, which in some places reach as far as the Atlantic coast. Besides fishing, hunting also used to be important, and there was much game, big and small. Squirrels, martens, foxes, even bears were all hunted, but the most important animal was – and to a certain extent still is – the reindeer. About 10 percent of Norway's landmass is used for reindeer-grazing (mostly in Finnmark). While the economic value of this industry is minor on a national scale, it is important both financially and culturally to the Sami, with about 40 percent of the population living from herding reindeer.

Very few of the truly nomadic Sami people are left. Most Sami have settled down in the sense that they have a permanent address but move with their herds to the high ground in the summer. During late summer and in the autumn the reindeer are driven down to the woods near the foot of the summer mountain pastures where there is plenty of lichen. There they stay during

Sami women in the colourful traditional dress.

⊘ SINFUL SINGING

Of great importance when trying to get inside the world of the Sami people is to understand the importance of the *yoik*, a kind of primitive singing comparable with unaccompanied humming or melodic scanning. To outsiders, it is particularly difficult to grasp since the words can be isolated or subordinated to melody and rhythm, followed by long sentences of meaningless syllables, such as *voia-voia*, *ala ala*, or *lu-lu-lu*.

The *yoik* probably originated as a way of keeping reindeer quiet and at the same time frightened wild animals away. But it is also used as entertainment, when people are gathered together. In Finnmark, *yoiking* has grown strong, and each Sami has his own personal melody. Traditionally, a young Sami boy will compose his own *yoik* for the girl he is courting. However, today a suitable *yoik* can be composed to order for almost any occasion.

Like many other Sami traditions, the *yoik* was forbidden by the missionary Christians. At a time when the only decent song was a hymn, the *yoik* was seen as sinful, a relic of pre-Christian mythology, its mumbling, buzzing tones suggesting a throwback to pagan rituals. Indeed, as late as the 1950s, *yoiking* was forbidden in Sami schools. But a *yoik* can't be burned like a trolldrum. Many of the old melodies are still alive, handed down from one generation to the next.

winter, roaming in freedom until the spring when it is time once more to move up the mountain to the high slopes, now covered with succulent, nourishing vegetation.

Famous artists of Sami descent include actress Renée Zellweger (her Norwegian-born mother's family originally came from Lapland) and singer Joni Mitchell, whose paternal grandparents also emigrated from Norway.

BRILLIANT COLOURS

Perhaps the vivid colours of the land all around them have been a source of inspiration for the traditional Sami costume. In days gone by, this dress was for daily use; now it is kept for festivals, weddings, funerals and other important occasions. Easter is *the* big feast, particularly in Kautokeino, with traditional reindeer racing and other events. Then the richly ribboned skirts and frocks, with red their most outstanding colour, are fetched from drawers and chests.

There are no bounds to this richness and colour, which makes a magnificent sight. With these lavish dresses go jewellery in silver, exquisitely worked into neckchains and elegant pendants. Another speciality is pewter embroidery, in which very thin threads of pewter are sewn in ingenious patterns on fine bracelets or on bags made of reindeer hide.

THE OLD RELIGION

Like many other people living in close contact with nature, the Sami had, and still have, a religion related to shamanism, in which nature and its forces are of the greatest importance. Beaive (the Sun) and Mannu (the Moon) were the supreme gods; next came Horagalles, the god of thunderstorms. Under these main gods there were many lesser gods and spirit beings, who ruled over fertility and over wild animals and the hunt, as well as over lakes and their fishes and other inhabitants. There were evil spirits as well. One was Rota or Ruta, the demon of illness and death; another was the Devil himself, Fuadno. In many areas Sami religion was related to Norse mythology: Horagalles corresponding to the Norse god of Thunder, Thor.

Christianity did its best to combat and extinguish this popular belief and Swedish Laestadianism did much to destroy the Sami religion. Many of the ceremonial "troll-drums", of great importance in Sami culture but anathema to the would-be missionaries, were burned. The most effective Christian missionary was King Christian IV. He travelled to Finnmark around the turn of the 17th century and in 1609 introduced the death penalty for Sami who refused to give up their traditional faith. He followed this with an order to build the first Christian church in Varanger. To go

Coastal Heritage Centre in Foldalbruket, on the Arctic coast.

to church regularly was, nevertheless, impossible for many of the nomadic Sami, who had to travel over mountains and vast lakes. It was the great festivals which gathered the Sami together and so it is today, with New Year, Easter, Lady Day, and the spring and autumn equinoxes.

LANGUAGE REVIVAL

Traditionally, Sami culture possessed an extensive oral "literature", including a vast number and variety of legends and fairytales, many of which were written down earlier last century by J.K. Ovigstad in his *Sami Fairytales and Legends*. This literature also includes a distinctive form of poetry designed to accompany the traditional

Sami "song" or *yoik*. In the first half of the 20th century, it was government policy to encourage the "Norwegianisation" of the Sami people and their language. This led to the irony that one of the greatest writers of Sami descent, Mario Aikio from Karasjok, wrote only in Norwegian, though today a number of younger writers are once again using the Sami language.

As has happened with many minority languages in recent times, Norway now has a policy of encouraging the Sami language. In Sami areas, it is taught from the start of schooling,

Sami singer Mari Boine.

and Sami people can pursue higher education in their own language in various establishments such as the universities of Oslo and Tromsø, and their own teachers' training college in Alta. There is also a Sami TV channel, and several Sami radio stations.

TOWARDS HOME RULE

The Norwegian Sami have also fought for political control over their own affairs and for the preservation of their way of life, which has continued to be eroded by the opening up of the northern areas through improved roads and other forms of communication.

The establishment of national parks, for example, can lead to the protection of wild animals that prey on the reindeer herds, and Sami people have been successful in gaining compensation for reindeer-grazing areas and recognition of the right to hunt and fish. Sami have also succeeded in curtailing some electricity development projects that would have flooded whole districts and jeopardised the local reindeer economy.

Today, the Sami people have their own Sameting (Parliament), based in Karasjok, which was opened in 1989 with great ceremony. Parliament is an elected body, and to vote you must have

> The Sami singer Mari Boine, whose music is rooted in the Sami heritage, is known all over Europe, and her success has brought new life to Sami music and culture.

a grandparent speaking the Sami language or "feel that you are a Sami". Further progress was made in 1990 when Norway ratified the ILO Convention, which dealt with the rights of indigenous and tribal peoples.

The Sameting deals with all matters pertinent to the Sami people and has gradually been given more autonomy. It has developed a plan of action for Sami coastal and fjord areas, an agricultural plan, and has participated in a Sami fisheries committee. In addition, it has endeavoured to boost local employment (in which tourism is playing an increasingly important role). Nordic cooperation is also a central part of its activities. The Sami parliaments in Norway, Sweden and Finland collaborate through a special parliamentary council.

In the summer of 2006, the people of Finnmark finally won the right to administer their own lands. Crown Prince Haakon and several government ministers travelled north for celebrations marking a new law that shifts power from the state to the Sameting and local county councils. It was the biggest land transfer in Norway's history, encompassing an area the size of Denmark that is rich in natural resources. Local Sami, who had long made it clear they wanted their share of the area's potential wealth, are also keen on their share of offshore oil and gas riches from the Barents Sea.

The Mountain Sami live mainly by breeding reindeer.

📷 FOLKLORE: SAGAS AND FOLKTALES

Among the treasures of Norwegian heritage is its rich legacy of legends and sagas. This form of popular storytelling is an important part of the national psyche.

The Norwegian word for folktale, *eventyr*, crops up as early as the 12th century in the form *ævintyr*, borrowed from the Latin word *adventura*, meaning event or strange occurrence. These folktales were imaginative stories passed from one storyteller to another, and depicted relationships expressed in fantastic and symbolic terms. Narrators were often clergymen who used folklore as a moralistic vehicle. The folktale style was, above all, objective; however fantastic the subject, the narrative was always believable.

COUNTRY LEGENDS

A constant topic in Norwegian legend is its landscape. Many of the stories connected with the sea involved mythical creatures, the best known of which are the Lake Mjøsa monster and Draugen, the personification of all who have died at sea. In lakes and rivers lives the sprite Nøkken (Nixie). Many mythical creatures inhabit the mountains and forests, and tales about landmarks supposedly created by trolls exist all over the country. Marks said to have been left by trolls show their size, such as the Giant Cut (Jutulhogget) in Østerdal.

A 13th-century legend tells how two warriors carried the infant King Håkon to safety from rebel factions trying to claim the throne.

The Völsunga saga involves Odin punishing the Valkyrie Brunnhilde for disobedience.

The Oseberg ship, formerly used for sailing and as a burial vessel, dates from c. AD 815–20.

Forest Troll by Theodor Kittelsen, 1890.

The Golden Age of Literature

On 17 May 1814, after almost 400 years of Danish rule, Norway signed the constitution at Eidsvoll. This event heralded a revival of the Norwegian language. Per Christen Asbjørnsen (1812–55) and Jørgen Moe (1818–82) were part of this "golden age". Inspired by the German Brothers Grimm and Norwegian Andreas Faye, who published *Norske Sagn (Norwegian Legends)* in 1833, Asbjørnsen and Moe began compiling the first collection of Norwegian folktales, *Norske Huldre-Eventyr og Folkesagn (Norwegian Ghost Stories and Folk Legends)*. Their first volume appeared in 1845, the second edition in 1852. Asbjørnsen went on to publish an illustrated version, commissioning some of the best Norwegian painters of the time, including Erik Werenskiold and Theodor Kittelsen. Asbjørnsen and Moe's collections have become classic Norwegian folktales; Kittelsen and Werenskiold's illustrations have given the troll its visual image.

A pair of harness mounts from Gotland known as Odin's Birds, with exaggerated beak and talons.

Julenissen (Norway's Santa Claus, second from right) is said to live in Drøbak.

The rock carvings at Hjemmeluft, in the far north, date back as far as 6,000 years ago.

Halibut-fishing off the coast.

WILD NORWAY

Aside from the stunning scenery and the many outdoor activities, spotting wild animals in their natural habitat often features high on a traveller's agenda. While some of the rarer species might remain elusive, you don't need to venture far off the main road to find others.

You may be unlikely to spot one of Norway's last remaining brown bears unless you travel all the way to Øvre Pasvik National Park, on the border with Finland and Russia, and although wolves are present in parts of the country, mainly in the east and south, few visitors ever see them.

Elk, "the king of the forest", can be found throughout Norway, except in the very far north, where reindeer, which are herded by the Sami people, take over. Despite liberal hunting quotas, the elk thrives in Norway, and the current population averages 120,000.

Only males, known as bulls, have antlers, which they drop after the mating season each year to conserve energy for the winter. Your best chance to spot one is in summer, when they come out of the forest to eat ripe crops before the harvest.

MOUNTAIN RESIDENT

Other mammals of note include lynx, wolverine, deer, hare, beaver, otter, fox, lemming and the fascinating musk ox, a survivor of the last Ice Age and once close to extinction. It was imported into Norway from Greenland in 1932, and since then there has been a herd in the Dovre National Park (see page 173), one of only a handful of places in the world where you'll be able to see it.

Norway's national parks offer one of the best ways to spot wildlife. Rondane, a four-hour drive north from Oslo, is home to wolverine, marten and lynx, as well as a small population of bears, while golden eagles circle overhead.

Norway is the world's largest producer of Atlantic salmon, seen here leaping up a waterfall.

This mountain giant, famed for its thick coat and the male's pungent odour (to attract females during the mating season), feeds on grasses, reeds and moss, and can withstand particularly hostile climate conditions.

ENDANGERED SPECIES

For many, however, it is the Arctic animals that are the most fascinating. Sadly they are often the most endangered too, as is the case with the cute Arctic fox (in 2016, 40 litters were recorded in the whole of Norway, from which at least 60 cubs were born), and the polar bear, Europe's largest predator, is only found in Norway's northerly archipelago of Svalbard, which is increasingly threatened by the melting of the polar ice cap.

Safaris are organised throughout the country to give animal-lovers a chance to see the local fauna at close range, whether it's a bird-watching and photography trip to popular birding colonies, a king-crab safari in Kirkenes, or a whale-watching boat tour off the coast of the Lofoten or Vesterålen islands, where orca, minke and sperm whales are often spotted (see page 279).

Fishing is a national pastime, whether saltwater angling on the coast or freshwater angling

Norway was, as early as 1974, one of the first countries to ratify the Ramsar Convention, an international treaty whose aim is the conservation of wetlands. Ramsar areas are good places to observe wading birds.

on the lakes and the rivers – some of which are favoured by Atlantic salmon for spawning. (For more on fishing, see page 103.)

Husky dogs.

Elk can reach up to 2.1 metres (7ft) high at the shoulder.

⊘ UNDER THREAT: THE RED LIST

The Norwegian *Red List* is a record of the country's threatened species. Currently 4,438 species feature on the list – 23 percent of which are mammals and 20 percent are birds (seabirds especially). Fungi (with 353 species) and beetles (230 species) feature heavily, as well as butterflies and moths (430 species).

The highest concentration of threatened species can be found in forest and woodland, closely followed by agricultural landscapes (*kulturlandskap*), which is perhaps hardly surprising – increased agricultural activity and forestry destroy habitats, as do the building of roads and houses. Pollution and

climate change also form important pressures on biological diversity.

Most recently revised in 2015, the *Red List* was compiled by 24 teams of experts who assessed a total of 20,915 species in mainland Norway, on Svalbard and in Norwegian seas. The list helps to draw attention to threatened species not only at a national level, but also among regional and local authorities. The aim is to make sure species do not disappear from the country and to maintain viable and healthy plant and animal communities. The *Red List* also has an important role to play in long-term planning and environmental protection.

A BIRD-WATCHER'S PARADISE

Snowy owls, golden eagles, puffins, wild swans and many more species thrive in Norway's pristine coastal, mountain and wetland habitats.

Some 470 bird species are found in Norway, 260 of which regularly breed here, making it a great country for bird-watching year-round. Witness the impressive capercaillie mating display every spring in the deep forests in eastern Norway, or spot wild swans, geese, ducks and other waders resting in wetlands and marshes up and down the country during the great migration. Jæren, south of Stavanger, is one of the largest such areas, but there are others scattered around the country, the Ramsar sites being the best (see page 90).

With such a lengthy coastline, opportunities to observe seabirds in their natural habitat are many, whether in the Hvaler Archipelago in the south or in the rock cliffs around North Cape – and all the stretch of west coast in between.

The Femundsmarka National Park, southeast of Røros on the Swedish border, is a good place to spot falcons, while white-tailed eagles, the largest raptor in Scandinavia, can be found along the Nordland coast. Golden eagles inhabit mountainous areas. Norway also counts four different owl species, including the pretty snowy owl (known as the Arctic owl or the great white owl in North America).

SEABIRD COLONIES

The islands of Runde and Røst are both famed for their huge seabird colonies. Hundreds of thousands of birds nest on Runde, off the Ålesund coast, between February and August every year, including huge colonies of puffins, but you will also see kittiwakes, fulmars, shags, skuas, razorbills and guillemots here, making this one of the best bird sanctuaries in northern Europe. Gannets are also present – indeed the colony at Rundebranden is the biggest and oldest in Norway, one of only about 40 gannet colonies in the world.

The steep and towering islands of Røst, at the very southern tip of the Lofoten Archipelago, are home to the largest number of nesting birds in all of Norway, with approximately one-quarter of the country's seabird population. Boat trips to both Runde and Røst are available.

You don't need to head as far as northern Norway to experience the thrill of thousands upon thousands of seabirds. Especially during the spring migration, Jaeren, just south of Stavanger, is a prime site for observing waders, grebes, divers and other wildfowl.

Gulls shadow a fish shoal by the fishing village of Havøysund, north of Hammerfest.

ARCTIC SPECIES

If you're heading north in the summer, the Varanger peninsula in Finnmark is another compulsory stop, where you will see true Arctic species such as eiders (including the rare Steller's eider), guillemots, red-throated pipits, northern hawk owls, Siberian jays and great grey owls, among other species. The rare osprey can also be seen in the nearby Øvre Pasvik National Park.

Yet further north, Svalbard is another great place to observe puffins, purple sandpipers, little auks, kittiwakes, fulmars and Brünnich's guillemots. Most of the birds on Svalbard are migratory birds, and the Svalbard rock ptarmigan is the only species not to leave the archipelago in winter.

Tackling a frozen waterfall.

AN OUTDOOR LIFE

In Norway you are free to roam, through forest or over mountain; but wherever you end up, however remote, you can rely on the homely comforts of a *hytte*.

As a nation, Norwegians are quite at home in their wild, unspoilt country, and have a great feeling for its mountains. Composer Edvard Grieg, who did much to capture the Norwegian landscape in his music, wrote with passion of the Jotunheimen range in central Norway: "When I contemplate the possibility of a future visit to the mountains, I shudder with joy and expectation, as if it were a matter of hearing Beethoven's Tenth Symphony." There are higher, more remote, more exotically named countries with arguably more photographically stunning landscapes, yet few can claim a population so attuned to its great outdoors.

One Norwegian in four counts outdoor recreation as a first pastime, and Norwegians excel at sports evolved from outdoor pursuits such as cross-country running or skiing, orienteering and cycling. Everyone takes part: urbanite and ruralist, commoner and king tramp the terrain, year-round. Foreign visitors, unaware of this,

Hiking in Nordfjord.

> "There is no such thing as bad weather, only bad clothing" – goes a popular Norwegian saying, and only extreme conditions prevent Norwegians from enjoying the great outdoors.

often find the mass migration to the open air unnerving, especially if they arrive on business at Easter or during July, the prime times of the year for moor and mountain, sea and shore.

FREE TO ROAM

Centuries of that view evolved into one of the country's shortest laws – the *allemannsretten*, or right of access for all, made official with the 1957 Outdoor Recreations Act. It states succinctly that: "At any time of the year, outlying property may be crossed on foot, with consideration and due caution." The few restraints imposed are for environmental or safety reasons. Camping isn't permitted in the immediate watersheds of drinking-water reservoirs, and fires are forbidden during summer dry spells that can turn forests to tinder.

This liking for untethered roaming seems an integral part of the national character. Among the country's real-life heroes are Fridtjof Nansen and Roald Amundsen, towering figures of polar exploration around the turn of the 20th century, and Thor Heyerdahl, probably the most widely known Norwegian abroad.

MORGEDAL AND TELEMARK REVIVAL

It was in this mountainous region of southern Norway that skiing was honed into an art form and winter sports were born.

Morgedal, in the southern county of Telemark, is a hamlet that long remained an entry only found in history books pored over by scholars of the sport of skiing. Today, that has all changed because of a reawakening of interest in the style of skiing called Telemark, which evolved in Morgedal.

In cross-country skiing the heel is raised.

In the mid-19th century, there were even fewer people than the 168,000 who live in Telemark today. They were a hardy breed of woodsmen, small farmers, hunters and traders, who fashioned their own implements, including the skis they needed to get about on winter snows. Morgedal is in the mountains, so the ski-makers there sought designs that would perform well in the surrounding rugged terrain, both in everyday winter skiing and for impromptu sporting meetings.

Among the most visionary in the mid-1800s was Sondre Norheim, a young tenant farmer. He excelled

not only in village ski meetings, but also in ski-making skills.

Norheim devised bindings (devices that hold ski boots to skis) that were firm and were the first to give the feet control over the skis. He also gave the skis what is known as "sidecut", the slight hourglass profile of a ski seen from above. Sidecut is what enables skis to run true and turn easily.

Norheim and his fellow Morgedal skiers used the new designs to perfect new skiing manoeuvres, including ways of turning and stopping on snow, and ways of landing from airborne flights off snow-covered rooftops and natural outcrops. Their fame spread and, by 1868, Norheim and his farmers from Telemark were ready to show off their new skills. He led them on skis for the 180km (112-mile) journey from Morgedal to Christiania (now Oslo), where the city crowds turned out to greet and applaud the peasant skiers and their miraculous new techniques. This led to the start of the big ski-jumping contest at Husaby near Oslo in 1879, where 10,000 spectators led by the king cheered the skiing pioneers from Telemark. Around the same time, the Telemark skiers established the world's first ski school in Oslo.

While Telemark skiing originally meant a bent-knee stance with one ski trailing, in modern Telemark skiing, the heel is free to lift up from the ski, and turns are steered, with one ski trailing and at an angle to the other. From the side, the manoeuvre looks like a genuflection in motion. Although competitive Telemark ski races are now held on packed slopes, as are Alpine ski races, true Telemark skiing is a throwback to the skiing of Sondre Norheim's time. The rebirth of the Telemark turn has revived another old skiing practice – ski-athlon – in which competitors must ski-jump, ski through a slalom course, and undertake a cross-country ski race, all on the same pair of skis.

The name is new, but the combination of manoeuvres dates to the times when the men from Morgedal first mastered the ski-jumping meets in Christiania some 130 years ago. A ski-jumping performance required the competitor to jump through the air, come to a stop after landing, ski back uphill to the top of the ski jump, and jump again before finishing.

Encounters with nature thread the fabric of everyday life. A family returning from an autumn hike to collect wild mushrooms will drop into a public mushroom check station to verify their edibility. In the winter, city-dwellers heading for a ski tour in a nearby forest look for the snow report on the same website they checked the previous summer for the water temperatures at local bathing areas.

Norwegian kindergartens and day-care centres are usually small buildings attached to extensive outdoor playgrounds, designed for day-long activity. Only in extreme weather,

Well-marked walking trails connect the lodges that stand at crossroads on networks so extensive that DNT's trail marker, a red painted letter "T" on cairns, is synonymous with serious walking. When winter snows cover the cairns, poles in the snow serve the same purpose.

The bulk of the trails and lodges are conveniently in the middle of the triangle bounded by the cities of Oslo, Bergen and Trondheim. A central entry point is Finse, situated above the timberline at 1,200 metres (4,000ft). Finse's main street is the station platform; there are no cars

Norway is a hiker's paradise.

defined in most places as below −10°C (14°F), do the kids stay indoors. Yet Norwegians see no valour in doing battle with nature. As the British polar exploration chronicler Roland Huntford pointed out, that's more the British psyche: Norwegians are much more likely to meet nature on its own terms and seek or make their own comfort wherever they go.

FOLLOWING THE RED "T"

Supreme on that scale are the *hytter* run by Den Norske Turistforening (DNT), called "the Norwegian Trekking Association" in English (www.dnt.no). Even the simplest cabins put to rest any thought of a hut, while the larger ones make the title ludicrous.

⊘ HOME FROM HOME IN A HYTTE

In a country where winter days are short and nasty weather can crop up any time, comfort translates to secure shelter. A quarter of households own a holiday home, or *hytte*. The word *hytte* translates as "hut", but a *hytte* is by no means a rough structure; most are well-appointed small wooden houses. Indeed, *hytter* in parts of the country sell for as much as other houses. A few, particularly in remote locations, do not have running water and therefore feature a *utedo* (outside toilet). For those without a *hytte* of their own, clubs and associations often own one, and one of the standard business perks is liberal use of the company *hytte*.

because there are no roads. When a train has gone and the last passengers have left, Finse returns to normal, a speck in a seemingly infinite expanse of rock, ice and snow.

A few hundred metres from Finse railway station is the DNT *hytte*, with its 109 bunk beds in one- to five-person rooms, hot showers, a staffed dining room serving three meals a day, a snack bar and three lounges. Other DNT lodges are still larger: Gjendesheim in Jotunheimen has 129 bunks. The DNT also has unstaffed self-service accommodation. Here you can prepare

> *So ethereal yet so accessible is Finse that it was chosen as a location for the space adventure film The Empire Strikes Back, the sequel to Star Wars.*

30,000km (18,600 miles) – three times the distance between Norway and Australia – of marked ski trails wind their way through unspoiled scenery. Cross-country skiing in the mountains may be enjoyed up until May, although Easter usually

The most adventurous of skiers won't be disappointed.

your own food or purchase from a pantry. You pay upon leaving, by putting money in a box on the wall. The honour system works well.

SKIING

Skis have been a source of benefit and pleasure to Norwegians for thousands of years, with much local community life in winter dependent on skis. In the 19th century skiing evolved into a mass sport, urged on by the Morgedal pioneer Sondre Norheim. The first skiing competitions were arranged in the mid-1880s – the term "slalom" originated in Morgedal from the Norwegian words *sla*, meaning slope or hill, and *låm*, depicting the track down it. Norwegians have practically unlimited access to skiing and skating facilities. About

marks the end of the season. The winter darkness is no obstacle, with some 2,500 illuminated tracks providing for a bit of serious exercise after work.

Alpine skiing has gradually increased in popularity in Norway. Though by no means as universal as cross-country skiing, most communities have a locally prepared piste. Major ski resorts include Trysil in Hedmark, Hemsedal and Geilo in Buskerud, Voss in Hordaland (which is a year-round resort) and, of course, Lillehammer in Oppland, the location of the 1994 Winter Olympics. Ski jumping has again surged in popularity in recent years. There are some 600 ski jumps in Norway.

In the absence of snow, there is always skating or ice hockey. In winter, municipalities up and down the country convert sports fields and playgrounds into ice rinks by getting the local fire brigade to spray them with water. These are then used for ice hockey and speed skating. When the fjords freeze over, whole families take Sunday "walks" on skates among the rocks and islets.

OUTDOORS IN REACH

In travelling time, even the remote wilderness areas are close to the bulk of the population: the wilderness itself is still closer. Oslomarka, just outside the capital, is a vast area of forests set aside for outdoor recreation. Likewise, Bergen

has its Vidden, Trondheim its Bymarka, Tromsø its Tromsdalen. No Norwegian city is without nearby natural surprises. But to Norwegians, who are as likely to shoulder rucksacks as to carry a briefcase, that's no surprise.

The Rodøy Man, a 4,000-year-old rock carving in Nordland, is evidence that skiing in Norway dates back to the Stone Age.

Hytten in Nusfjord.

⊘ ACCESSIBLE MOUNTAINEERING

To the north of Finse lie the Jotunheimen Mountains, the range that took its name from Norse mythology, literally "Home of the Giants". The name is appropriate: peaks jut a kilometre and more skywards from lake-studded, moraine-strewn flats, all above the timberline. Nonetheless, even the loftiest of the Jotunheimen peaks, Galdhøpiggen and Glittertind, which are the highest in northern Europe with summits more than 2,400 metres (7,900ft) high, rank low on the international scale of noteworthy mountains where sheer altitude, not challenge, is the main criterion. Though this fact has led to relative anonymity – few Norwegian peaks appear in the classic mountaineering literature – it does mean that you can

ascend the equivalent of the Matterhorn or Mont Blanc without having to cope with the problems of altitude.

Most Jotunheimen trails meander from 900–1,200 metres (3,000–4,000ft) above sea level, and there are few or no acclimatisation problems at that height.

Some of the glaciers that hewed the Norwegian landscape left offspring. One, Jostedalsbreen (the Jostedal glacier), is the largest on mainland Europe. Jostedalsbreen and its siblings throughout the country are the places to see crampon-shod parties wielding ice axes from spring until autumn. Contact with the ice that shaped their land is currently the Norwegians' fastest-growing wilderness recreation, and many centres organise specialist courses.

SPORTING PASSIONS

To Norwegians, sport is almost a religion, permeating every aspect of life all year round, and there is room for everyone, from Olympic champions to Sunday goalkeepers.

Put the question "Are you a skier?" at almost any social gathering anywhere in Europe, and you could expect a few positive responses and perhaps a lecture or two on the virtues of the sport. Put the same question to someone you meet on a Sunday afternoon at one of the ski-trail lodges in Norway, which you can only reach on skis, and the answers will be quite different: "No, I'm a bank clerk"; "Who me? Never dream of it!"

A WAY OF LIFE

Why the disparity? The answer lies in a tradition that has woven sport deeply into the fabric of Norwegian life. It is even reflected in the language. While English has just one word, "sport", Norwegian has two: *sport* and *idrett.* The Norwegian *sport* is the umbrella word that covers all sporting events, so that a sports journalist in Norway plies exactly the same trade as his or her foreign counterpart. The word *idrett* is reserved for events in which the limits in performance are determined by the capabilities of the human body. Horseriding is not *idrett,* while scuba-diving is. There is a further nuance: *aktiv* (active) means a person currently competing in a sport classified as *idrett.*

This explains why, when you ask skiing Norwegians "Are you a skier?", you have asked if they currently compete in the sport. Ask often enough, and you unearth the astonishing fact that one Norwegian in three is *aktiv.*

MAD ABOUT SPORT

This amazing statistic reflects the high priority Norwegians give to sport. Oslo has numerous statues of living Norwegians in sporting poses: a statue of King Olav V skiing, near the Holmenkollen ski jump, one of marathon runner Grete Waitz running, of course, at the marathon gate

A family bike ride.

of Bislett Stadium, and statues of speed-skater Oscar Mathisen and figure-skater Sonja Henie near the Frogner Park Stadium. All new high-rise flats are obliged by law to include "sports gear storage rooms".

Within the Ministry of Church and Education there is a department for "Youth and *Idrett*". City newspapers vie with each other for sales on the strengths of their sports sections, and almost 15 percent of the Norwegian Broadcasting Corporation's output is devoted to sports. So pervasive is sport that visitors sometimes ask "Where is the flash, the excitement?"

The answer is that the pinnacles are there, as high and sometimes higher than elsewhere, but the surrounding plateau of sporting achievement is so high that it makes the peaks appear less prominent.

Norges Idrettsforbund (NIF), the Norwegian Confederation of Sports, is the umbrella organisation for 55 separate national sports federations with, in total, more than 2.2 million registered memberships (that's considerably more than one in three Norwegians, young or old!). It spotlights this fact in its motto "Sport for All", and the pinnacles are grouped and designated "elite". So, for the Confederation and its member associations, competitive sport is both egalitarian and elitist.

Handball is a favourite team sport in Norway, with the women's national team scooping a gold in the 2008 and 2012 Olympic Games, a bronze in the 2016 Olympics, and winning the 2008, 2010, 2014 and 2016 European Championships.

INTERNATIONAL COMPETITION

From the broad base of people for whom sport is a major leisure-time activity come the elite,

Norway tops the gold medal world count at Winter Olympics.

⊘ THE WINTER OLYMPICS

It might have a population of only 5.2 million, but Norway has won the most medals in the history of the Winter Olympics. A fair reward, you might say, for a country that invented and honed a good number of the events. Its tally to date is a whopping 329 medals, well ahead of the United States in second position with 282, and Germany with 209. Norway has won a total of 118 gold medals in the Winter Olympics, again ahead of the US and Germany (96 and 78 respectively).

In terms of gold medals, the best games to date for Norway were at Salt Lake City in 2002, when the country scooped an impressive 13 gold medals out of the 25 medals they brought home. The most successful games overall were at Lillehammer in 1994, when Norway, which was competing on home turf, beat all the other participating countries and topped the table with a remarkable 26 medals, 10 of which were gold.

Norwegians also did well in the 2014 Winter Olympics in Sochi, coming second in the medals table behind the hosts, Russia, and bringing home 26 medals – 11 gold, five silver and ten bronze. Cross-country skiers were once more making headlines, with national heroine Marit Bjørgen repeating her 2010 Vancouver success and scooping three golds.

competitors who enter the many national championships and represent Norway in international sports meetings. The results speak for themselves. For a country with such a small population, Norway has always been disproportionately strong in sports.

Traditionally, Norwegian competitive prowess has been in winter sports and in sailing, but Norwegians have also won international medals in a wide range of other events. Such pervasiveness and prowess have their price. The annual turnover in sports, excluding the sports equipment sector,

Norwegians love their football.

is more than NOK1,560 million (£150 million), and sports are supported through many channels: the NIF receives a major chunk of its revenue from the government, and sport receives one-third of the profits of the state-run football pools and the national lottery. The 5,000-odd clubs use extra-curricular activities, such as bingo and local lotteries, to raise up to 40 percent of their income.

FOOTBALL

As in other European countries, football (soccer) is the biggest sport in Norway, with more than 1,800 clubs and over 280,000 players. The national team had its golden age in the 1990s, when Norway twice reached the World Cup finals and even beat Brazil. A number of Norwegian players have become famous

> *Wherever you go in Norway, you are besieged by young people selling lottery tickets to support the local sports club.*

internationally, among them Ole Gunnar Solskjær (ex-Manchester United) and John Arne Riise (ex-Liverpool). Now both retired, Joshua King is Norway's shining star in the Premier League..

Women's football is also big in Norway, with some 110,000 registered members. There are 12 clubs playing in the top division, and another 12 in the first division (each football club in Norway, has both a men's and women's team).

The country also hosts the Norway Cup – the world's largest football tournament for children and young people – held every year in the first week of August. The tournament, which dates back to 1972, attracted some 32,000 participants in 2016, with 2,199 teams from over 50 countries.

WINTER SPORTS

Number two in the statistics and, its supporters contend, spiritually number one, is the country's traditional stalwart, skiing, with more than 1,500 clubs and a total membership of more than 200,000. Together, the five skiing disciplines – cross-country, Alpine, ski jumping, biathlon (a cross-country skiing and rifle-shooting combination event), and combined (ski jumping followed by a cross-country competition) – receive as much funding as football.

GRASSROOTS SUPPORT

The backbone of Norwegian sports is, of course, people's involvement. A great deal of work on sports facilities is local and voluntary – and that includes raising funds, too. One persistent reminder of this involvement is the seeming ubiquity of sports facilities and sports instruction. There are 10,000–12,000 sports centres in Norway, from the most modest local football field to major stadiums and indoor halls.

In summer and autumn, these centres are hatcheries for future football and track-and-field athletic talents. In winter, their iced surfaces swarm with figure and speed skaters and serve as mini-arenas for ice hockey and *bandy,* a related sport played with a ball instead of a puck, to rules more closely resembling those of field hockey.

THE GREAT SKI JUMP

No Norwegian icon enjoys quite the same status in the heart of the population as the Holmenkollen ski jump, the nation's top jumping hill.

The Holmenkollen Ski Festival is the oldest in the world, taking place in March and attended by 1 million people each year. At the climax on Holmenkollen Sunday, more than 50,000 people gather at this famous ski-jump hill to watch ski jumping in the country that invented it. Although the Nordic skiing competitions (cross-country and ski jumping) and the newer events attract top competitors eager for World Cup points, Holmenkollen is much more than yet another international winter competition. This is very much a citizens' festival, a chance for ordinary Norwegians and visitors to take part in the events.

The idea of sitting or strolling as a spectator all day in the middle of a Norwegian winter might sound like the best way of catching a cold, but the excitement is high. Wrapped in boots, anoraks, gloves and hat, with the necessary extra of a warm cushion to sit on, you need no more than a regular quick coffee, best laced with aquavit, to keep out the cold.

Norway was the first country to introduce ski competitions when Norwegian soldiers began to compete as early as 1767, and the first civilian event took place in 1843 at Tromsø. By the 1880s, the Norwegian Society for the Promotion of Skiing already held a winter competition and in 1892, this transferred to Holmenkollen. That year, the longest ski jump was 22 metres (72ft). Today, it is 141 metres (463ft).

In the very first days the competitors were all Norwegians, but even by 1903 Swedes had arrived, and were soon joined by French and German skiers. Since World War II, foreigners from most skiing countries have taken part. Women first competed in 1947, when Alpine skiing events were introduced, but they weren't admitted to the cross-country race until 1954.

The fact that women are still not able to take part in the ski-jumping competition, because there are allegedly too few athletes to compete at this level, is an issue that periodically makes the headlines in Norway, and this is likely to change in the next few years.

Norway's King Olav V, a first-class sportsman, made his debut on the Holmenkollen jump in 1922, and was a faithful spectator for nearly 70 years. His son, King Harald, has inherited this keen interest in the sport. Norwegian members of parliament – fitter perhaps than their counterparts elsewhere – and local politicians, also take part. On Children's Day more than 5,000 children swarm into the arena for events to mark the end of the season at the children's ski school, and the Holmenkollen March attracts around 7,000 to 8,000

Holmenkollen ski jump.

people, many just ordinary skiers, to ski either 21 or 42km (13 or 26 miles) through the Nordmarka forest finishing beneath the jump.

The atmosphere of Holmenkollen Sunday is electric. They call it Norway's second national day, after Constitution Day on 17 May, and when the new ski jump opened in March 2010, thousands of Norwegians spent the night outside, braving the cold winter air to secure a good view of the action.

The huge crowd packed into the arena hushes as the first skier appears. Up there, on the top platform, he looks like a being from another world. The silence lasts until the tiny, bright figure takes off and, in a second, is flying through space with an ease that makes it look simple. Then, as skier follows skier in graceful arcs, a roar loud enough to cause an avalanche fills Holmenkollen.

FISHING: SPORT AND SUSTENANCE

Norway's fjords, rivers and coastline are a veritable anglers' paradise. And when it comes to eating fish, Norwegians have a dish for every occasion.

To Norwegians, fish is the standby staple. Even in modest markets, the variety of fish and fish products is amazing, and Norwegians look on a proper wet fish shop as an asset to a community. Fish is both humble fare and holiday cuisine. Fish balls in white sauce are the Norwegian dining-table stalwart, and steamed cod is a favourite for Sunday dinners. On festive occasions, herring in myriad forms takes its place with other delicacies such as *gravlaks* (cured salmon), *rakfisk* (half-fermented trout) and *lutefisk* (dried codfish marinated in a lye solution, a dish few foreigners appreciate).

AN ANGLER'S PARADISE

Angling in Norway is done both for the sport itself and as part of other outdoor pursuits. Fishing tackle is among the paraphernalia of camping trips, just as it is the prime equipment for avid anglers.

The long coastline is a mecca for saltwater angling, yet freshwater angling is the more popular pastime, and there are a quarter of a million fishable inland lakes and ponds. The most common of around 40 freshwater species are trout and char; in the northernmost parts, and in lakes and ponds at higher elevations, they are the only fish. Grayling and pike are more common in larger lakes and rivers in eastern and central areas. Local legends about lakes rich in pike hold that the fish are descended from stocks set out in the late 18th century by the ruling Danes.

Bream, whitefish, perch and carp are found in most lower lakes in the southern part of the country, as well as in eastern Finnmark in the far north. Reliable varieties in salt water

Fishing is hugely popular.

include cod, coalfish, haddock, whiting, halibut, herring and mackerel.

SALMON RIVERS

The stars on the angling scene are the Atlantic salmon and sea trout, related varieties which are both popular game and commercial fish. The commercial varieties now come largely from fish farms, but the game fish still swim the rivers until they are two to six years old, migrate to the sea, and then return to spawn in some 400 rivers. Norwegians argue about the best rivers, but five in the northern part of the country stand out – the Alta and Tana rivers in Finnmark, and the Gaula, Namsen and Orkla rivers in Trøndelag, all of which draw anglers from around the world. There, the sport is so popular that you have to apply for licences as much as a year in advance. Fly-fishing is also a favourite pastime.

GAINING A LICENCE

You need two types of angling licence to keep within the law. The first one is the annual *Fiskeravgift* (fishing fee) that helps to offset the costs of overseeing fishing and the aquatic environment (particularly adding lime to the water). The *Fiskeravgift* can be obtained at a post office and covers freshwater fish and crabs, but not

the most plausible ascribes it to Norway's location and topography. In the north, there are few insects large enough to use as bait, and worms are hard to find on rocky shores. Minnows and other live fish are prohibited as bait, primarily to curtail the spread of diseases. For the same reason, the transfer of live fish, water, or wet fishing boats or other equipment, from one watercourse to another is prohibited.

Just as winter does not deter Norwegians from walking (they switch to cross-country skis),

Freshwater angling is the most popular pastime.

salmon and sea trout. The latter two are, however, included in the annual fishing licence, which is usually twice the cost of the fishing fee. Fishing in sea water is free, whereas fishing in lakes and rivers requires a further local licence. Freshwater fishing licences come from the owners of the fishing rights, usually the property owners along the banks of a river or the shores of a lake, whether private persons or communities. These vary in price, and are valid for specific dates and periods. You can buy them from local hotels, sports shops or tourist offices.

BAITING THE HOOK

Even youngsters start fishing using artificial bait. Theories abound as to why this is so, but

The minimum permissible sizes for keeping caught fish are 25cm (9.75ins) in length for salmon, sea trout and sea char, and 30cm (11.75ins) for all other fish.

frozen lakes do not halt fishing. Ice fishing is a prime wintertime hobby, a simple and straightforward form of angling, which requires only a baited hand line or short pole and line, an icedrill, warm clothing, and patience. Ice anglers must hew holes in the ice by hand as motorised augers are prohibited. It's a sport for the hardy, but ice-angling contests are popular.

NATURE'S LARDER

Norway's culinary traditions have evolved from two key ingredients: its wild nature and its climate.

Magnificent landscapes and climatic contrasts have helped to create a natural larder from which Norwegians have helped themselves for centuries. Norway's long, varied coastline has provided ample opportunity for harvesting both "wild" and farm-raised fish; the slow ripening process of everything that grows during the light summer imparts an extraordinary aroma to berries, fruits and vegetables; and the animals that graze on the lush grass provide meat with a distinctive full flavour. Today foodstuffs from Norway such as apples, pears, cherries and strawberries, not to mention the famed smoked salmon and Jarlsberg cheese, are in demand well beyond its frontiers. Although eyebrows are raised when the nation's chefs win international awards (like Geir Skeie and Ørjan Johannessen being awarded the prestigious Bocuse d'Or in 2009 and 2015 respectively, for example), it is not the first time that foreigners have been impressed by Norway's fare.

Fresh prawns (reker) are a favourite among Norwegians, often served with white bread (loff), mayonnaise, lemon and an ice-cold pils.

PAPAL SURPRISE

When papal envoy Cardinal Wilhelm Sabina attended the coronation of King Håkon IV in Bergen in 1247, he arrived with apprehension, having been forewarned about the food. However, in his speech following the banquet he lavished praise on the meal he had been served. Sadly, the historical record of his speech makes no mention of the menu, but visitors to Norway in the 18th and 19th centuries speak highly of the salmon, fowl, game and strawberries with cream – treats which modern-day visitors may also experience.

The Bergen fish market is no longer the bustling hub it once was, but it's still a good place to pick up picnic food to eat on the waterfront – freshly boiled shrimps are popular.

Cloudberries (or multebær) are found in mountain marshlands in late summer/early autumn. Rich in vitamin C, multer is used as a jam, a liqueur and in desserts.

Popular brand of aquavit, Norway's favourite tipple.

Akevitt – The Water of Life

Akevitt (aquavit or "water of life") is the national spirit of Norway. The most famous aquavit, Løiten Linie, is matured through a 150-year-old process that includes a sea voyage in oak casks across the equator and back (each bottle carries details of its voyage on its label). This story originates from 1840, when the Norwegian ship *Preciosa* rounded Cape Horn; on board was aquavit, which the crew swore had improved in flavour.

Distilled from Norwegian potatoes, this blend of spirit, caraway and other herbs and spices is matured for several months in sherry casks. The result is a smooth spirit of about 45 percent proof by volume. Norwegians regard Linie as an accompaniment to pork *(ribbe)*; it also goes well with seafood and the Christmas *lutefisk* dish.

Klippfisk (dried, salted split cod) is a major Norwegian export.

Chanterelles are found in forests throughout the country from July to October, and are a delicious complement to reindeer and game.

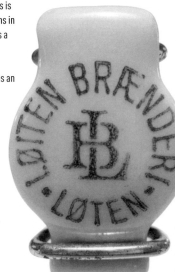

Logo of the Løten brewery in the Hamar region of Norway.

A Norwegian bride preparing the traditional dress for the ceremony, by Adolph Tidemand (1814-1876).

THE TRADITIONAL ARTS

Tradition is strong in Norway, especially when it comes to the folk arts; but to an inquisitive eye, that tradition contains some unexpected influences.

In AD 793 "dire portents appeared over Northumbria and sorely frightened the people. They consisted of immense whirlwinds and flashes of lightning, and fiery dragons were seen flying in the air. A great famine followed those signs, and a little after that in the same year, on 8 June, the ravages of heathen men miserably destroyed God's church on Lindisfarne, with plunder and slaughter."

So the *Anglo-Saxon Chronicle* documented the destruction of the monastery at Lindisfarne, now Holy Island, just south of Berwick-upon-

> *The Frognerseteren Restaurant, built in 1891 on a hillside overlooking Oslo and remodelled in 1909, is one of the best examples of the more modern dragon style of decorated wooden buildings.*

Tweed in Northumberland in the northeast of England. It was the first major impact on Christendom by the Vikings, the pagan men of the north who were to make their mark on European culture for the next three centuries. But in the end, it was a reciprocal cultural exchange. An early Viking king, Olav Haraldson, converted to Christianity, was baptised in Normandy, and returned to his homeland to introduce the faith. By the year 1030, when he fell in battle, he had firmly rooted Christianity in most areas as Norway's future religion.

Today, the legacy of the Vikings is neither blurred nor buried, but still highly visible in a myriad of forms, collectively termed the folk arts, which include woodcarving, rustic painting, national costumes and decorative painting.

Carving on Heddal stave church.

WOODCARVING

The Viking Age owed its very being to superior sea power. The Viking craft, or longships as they became known, were at once extremely seaworthy and boldly beautiful. They were clinker-built (overlapping planks held together with iron rivets) on long keel planks that swept up to a stem at either end. The Vikings carved elaborate decorations on the prows down to the waterline, often with dragon heads and figures. They also carved elaborate designs on everyday items, from the handles of implements to the lever of the aft-right mounted *styrbord*, or steering board.

On land, the details of buildings were similarly enhanced. Pillars were carved, not just at their capitals, but over their entire surfaces. There were ornate friezes, interior mouldings were decorated and gable ends became display points. Woodcarving was a highly developed art, executed primarily for, and partly by, the Viking aristocracy.

A PASSION FOR THE PAST

With the arrival of Christianity, medieval woodcarvers focused their attention on creating wonderfully ornate stave churches. At home, people decorated chairs, beds, tables, ladles, bowls and other household items with intricate carving.

Some of the best-preserved examples of the work of Norwegian medieval artisans are the carved portals, window surrounds and other details of farm buildings. The traditions survive to the present day, and the current nostalgia in home furnishings, nowhere better expressed than in the timber *hytte*, is not for the lavish designs of the courts of the past, but rather for peasant pieces of native spruce or pine, the more ornately carved the better. "Collecting old houses is something of a family mania," says one shipowner (the nearest Norway comes to

Grass-roofed houses in Torndelag Folk Museum, Trondheim.

⊘ STAVE CHURCHES

By the 12th century, Christianity had supplanted the Viking aristocracy as the prime patron of the arts, and the wooden *stavkirke* (stave church) became the foremost outlet of woodcarving as an art form. Around 1,000 of these magnificent structures were built in Norway, the majority in a 100-year period from 1150 to 1250, and 28 survive to this day, making them among the world's oldest wooden buildings.

Their ornately carved portals serve the same purpose as original book illumination in England. They form one of the country's "manuscripts". If you look closely, first, there are the animal heads of

Nordic mythology, documenting the remnants of the Viking Age; then the classical tendril of Christian art appears, springing from the jaws of a beast; and finally, tendrils and flowers assert themselves, sometimes solo and sometimes interwoven with other motifs, partly but not completely replacing the beasts.

Some of the best stave churches to visit include Heddal in Notodden, Telemark, which is the largest and best preserved, and Urnes in Luster, Sognefjord, which dates back to the first half of the 12th century. The church at Urnes, listed as a Unesco World Heritage Site, is believed to be the oldest of its kind.

an aristocracy). "My father, brother and I have been combing the back country for 40 years for handcrafted dwellings and objects, homesteads, barns, cabins and huts complete with their country beds, chests, baskets and cupboards. Each must be unique to its own valley and period."

Typical of the national mania for folk art, this family's collection began simply by bartering with valley farmers for small items, such as handcrafted butter and porridge *tine*. These colourful wooden caskets, often a first gift to a betrothed, form an unbroken tradition from Viking times to the present. Always highly decorated, the *tine* are still used by country lads to show off their carving and rose-painting skills.

ROSE PAINTING

Much as woodcarving evolved from the urge to decorate functional items, the art Norwegians call *rosemaling* or "rose painting" sprang from humble surroundings. The two were often used together: carved building details and household furnishings and implements were frequently painted, both as enhancement of, and in contrast to, the carved wood. The name misleads: roses appear only in a few of the traditional patterns; it would be more correct to term it "rustic painting", which denotes its agrarian roots, far removed from the cities.

True *rosemaling* is not limited to flowery designs, although variations of the tendril motif are its strongest themes. It also includes geometric figures, portraits, and even an occasional landscape.

The earliest decorations have survived less well than the carvings on which they were painted, so the beginnings of rose painting remain an enigma. The oldest surviving examples date from around 1700, centuries after the necessary paints were first available.

IMPORTED STYLES

Rose painting evolved and, in its own right, became a record of its times. The earlier rose paintings of interiors and household articles clearly show that the art of the Renaissance reached as far as the Norwegian countryside. The colours are the peasant stalwarts, blue, green, red and yellow, but the patterns are definitely imported.

The prosperity of the late 18th century brought more clerics and more functionaries to rural districts, and with the new professionals came their belongings, decorated household furnishings and implements. What the peas-

> *Rose painting survives today, like woodcarving, as a nostalgic link with the past, and throughout the country amateur rose painters keep that link alive.*

Rustic painting in Kvernes stave church in Møre og Romsdal.

ants saw they replicated as best they could in their own style.

Most were untutored, and the commonest way of learning the skills was either from travelling artists or from local practitioners. The relative isolation of the valleys, cut off from their neighbours by the high mountain ranges, meant that every valley became its own art centre for a particular style of painting.

Hallingdal farmers were partial to delicate S-curves applied to everything from walls to spoons and bowls. In affluent Gudbrandsdal, the locals carved their decorations into built-in benches and box beds. The most isolated districts, such as Setesdal, have a very simplified *rosemaling* tradition.

So individual were the styles, today's experts can identify the age and origin of almost any item with uncanny accuracy. Their knowledge is currently much in demand, as rose-painted period furniture commands the highest of prices for Norwegian antiques.

THE NATIONAL COSTUME

Norway's *bunad* is as colourful as the national costume of any country. It is not just worn by folk dancers or for fancy-dress parties, but is in regular use as formal attire at weddings,

Brooches compliment the traditional costume.

⊘ FOLK REVIVAL

In the mid-19th century, factory-made garments began to replace homespun products. As people moved from farm to town, the *bunad* (national costume) was heading for extinction. It was rescued by Hulda Garborg, a prominent author, who saw a need to preserve the rural traditions. In the late 1800s, she founded a folk dance group in Oslo. Folk dances should, she believed, be performed in folk costumes, which led her to compile the first anthology of *bunads*, published in 1903. It was a bestseller, and Garborg and one of her dancers, Klara Semb, succeeded in starting the folk dance movement and a *bunad* renaissance which continues to the present day.

official ceremonies and gatherings on national holidays. Many claim that the *bunad* is Europe's most often worn national costume.

The *bunad* is a throwback to the clothing of times past, and the word itself means simply "clothes". It has developed variations in style, cut, colouring and accessories according to locality and the skills and tastes of its makers. There were costumes for men, women and children, everyday *bunads* and dress *bunads*. As with rose painting, every area of the country had its own style.

Despite these differences, the *bunad* has common characteristics that identify the dress as Norwegian. Women's costumes characteristically have skirts or dresses of double-shuttle woven wool and bodices or jackets of similar or contrasting material worn over blouses with scarves. Sashes, purses, beautiful silver accessories and traditional shoes and stockings complete the costume. Men's *bunads* are essentially three-piece knickerbocker suits, with matching or contrasting waistcoats, white shirts, long socks and traditional shoes.

Although *bunads* are no longer daily wear, the number of known types and varieties is greater than ever. Some, like those from Setesdal, date back 300 years or more. Others, such as the costume from Bærum, a suburb of Oslo, have been designed in the past 40 or so years.

WHO SHOULD WEAR THE BUNAD?

Its current popularity is matched only by the range of opinions about how it should be worn. Traditionalists contend that a *bunad* from a particular district should be worn only by a person born and bred there. Moderates maintain that correct style outweighs the circumstances of the wearer's birth and upbringing, and the radicals view the *bunad* as a style to be copied piecemeal in modern clothes.

While the standard dark suit has, like in so many other countries, become the bastion of the Norwegian male wardrobe, women still face the dilemma of what to wear for formal occasions. In Norway, a *bunad* is always correct. It is timeless and may be passed on from generation to generation, while the traditional silver belt is often a gift from a parent to their son's wife.

Henrik Ibsen.

ART AND CULTURE

Norwegian artists, writers and musicians dug deep into the country's rural past in search of a new national identity.

The cultural scene in Norway has been experiencing a significant revival in the past few decades, fuelled in part by money from the oil boom. This new-found confidence was perhaps best illustrated with the opening of the stunning opera house on the Oslo waterfront in 2008, which put Oslo under the limelight, and Norway firmly on the international cultural map. For if until recently glittering gala soirées were the preserve of rare occasions such as the annual Nobel Prize award ceremony in Oslo Town Hall, things have since changed dramatically, with top events now taking place year-round throughout the country. Bergen hosts Scandinavia's largest annual cultural event, Festspillene, a huge showcase for art, music, theatre and dance in northern Europe; Stavanger was in 2008 named European Capital of Culture; and in spring 2010 Oslo welcomed tens of thousands of pop music fans to the Eurovision Song Contest, on top of an already charged music festival programme.

HOME-GROWN CULTURE

Historically, Norwegian culture is something far more fundamental – folksy, a reaction to foreign domination. As a political entity, Norway was established in 1905 after centuries of Danish and Swedish rule. All Norwegian "dialects" were forbidden by the Danes for official documents and communications. Such cultural imperialism was crushing to Norwegian self-esteem and national identity.

Ordinary Norwegians turned to rural tradition, folk costume and the old ways as a cultural refuge and repository of Norway's national personality. Culture with a capital "C" was something the overlords brought with them from foreign

In Ole Bull's villa on the island of Lysøen.

capitals. And it was something they took away with them when they left.

While politicians could elect a king and parliament, it fell to writers, musicians and artists to revive the national identity. They turned for inspiration to the traditions of those isolated valleys with their ancient farmsteads and their equally ancient verbal customs, telling heroic sagas about an expansive Norway of earlier days and of the greatness of native Viking lords.

Henrik Wergeland (1808–45), a richly talented poet and prose writer, became an early and passionate propagandist of this sort of Norwegian nationalism. Following the same call, artist J.C. Dahl (1788–1857) left his studio for the wilds of Norway's hinterland. His shimmering, majestic views of the mountains are major attractions at the National Gallery, which he helped to found in 1836.

On the dark side, the epoch's fears of isolation and rampant anxiety of the future inspired

A Doll's House and the much-loved Peer Gynt are among Henrik Ibsen's most famous plays. For more on Norway's influential playwright and cultural icon, see page 54.

Edvard Munch's Midsummer (1915).

the violent, emotionally charged style of painter Edvard Munch (1863–1944). Death and desolation are his recurring themes, most strongly expressed in The Scream (1893), The Kiss and The Vampire (both 1895). Munch's art has come so close to the national heart that his works have been enshrined in their own museum in Oslo as well as several rooms in the National Gallery.

Equally loud cries for freedom came from Henrik Ibsen (1828–1906), whose poetic drama Brand was a spirited indictment of Norwegian authority at home. It put Ibsen on the cultural map for the first time even outside Norway.

He was not the only one, at the close of the 19th century, to turn homewards for inspiration. Nobel laureate Knut Hamsun's (1859–1952) chilling novel Hunger (1890) is an exposé of the abuses of bourgeois Swedish rule. His masterpiece, The Growth of the Soil (1917), reflects a deep love of nature and concern for the effects of material conditions on the individual spirit, themes that still dominate Norwegian writing. Dramatist Bjørnstjerne Bjørnson (1832–1910) also helped promote home-grown themes and talent.

Even architects abandoned continental idioms to embrace a native "Viking Romanticism". They began building in heavy timber and turfed roofs. Eaves and gables sprouted carved and polychromed dragon heads, in an unabashed folkloric, wildly romantic style.

Works by major authors such as Amalie Skram (1847–1905) and Alexander Kielland (1849–1906), who abandoned a promising international career to write about old Norway, were front-page news in Oslo, Bergen and Trondheim. Critics and politicians publicly debated new works; plays became issues, even national causes. Literature became the smithy where the nation's identity was being forged.

POST-WAR ART

As with other cultural forms, Norwegian art began to drop its nationalist style after World War II. Gone (but certainly not forgotten) were the fairytale illustrations of Theodor Kittelsen (1857–1914) and morbid subject matter of Edvard Munch, and in came the modernists. Impressionism inspired such landscape artists as Gladys Nilssen Raknerud (1912–97) and Thorbjørn Lie-Jørgensen (1900–61); Expressionism found its place through the likes of Arne Ekeland (1908–94) and Rolf Nesch (1893–1975); and Abstract Expressionism appeared in the early 1960s through the work of Sigurd Winge (1909–70) and Jakob Weidemann (1923–2001). However, the old nationalist style continued well into the 1950s with such artists as Hjalmar Haalke (1892–1964) and Søren Steen Johnsen (1903–79), and the team responsible for the Oslo Rådhus murals.

There was also the inevitable reaction to the modernists. When Odd Nerdrum (born 1944) applied for a place at the National Academy of Fine Arts he submitted three works; two of these had been long-term projects, but he was selected on the basis of his third work, an abstract image thrown together the night before. With his scepticism towards the establishment and doubts about abstract art reinforced, the young Nerdrum turned to the great masters, in particular Rembrandt, in whom he saw "eternal tranquillity". However, his subject matter was always on the controversial side – *Amputation* (1974), *Hermaphrodite* (1976–81) – and it took until the late 1980s for the Norwegian public to catch on to his postmodern classicism.

There is growing interest in the moderns, which had hitherto been the domain of the avant-gardist Swedes. The focal point of the Norwegian art calendar is the Autumn Exhibition in Oslo, and the city's three main contemporary art galleries, which exhibit the works of national and international artists, have been growing in popularity in recent years.

Norway has a wealth of talent to continue the traditions of the prolific sculptor Gustav Vigeland (1869–1943). There are more 20th-century sculptures/statues per capita in Norway than in any other country in Europe.

Writer and nationalist Bjørnstjerne Bjørnson with his wife Karoline in 1908.

⊙ BJØRNSTJERNE BJØRNSON (1832–1910)

Dramatist, novelist and poet Bjørnstjerne Bjørnson is, together with Henrik Ibsen, Alexander Kielland and Jonas Lie, known as one of the Four Greats (*De Fire Store* in Norwegian), a term referring to the four most influential Norwegian writers of the late 19th century. Not as well known as Ibsen outside his homeland, Bjørnson is nonetheless widely acknowledged for having championed the Norwegian cause, working his entire life to free the Norwegian theatre from Danish influence.

While director of Bergen's Ole Bull Theatre (1857–9) and the Oslo Theatre a few years later, he commissioned new, saga-like dramas drawing on Norway's epic past, such as *Kong Sverre* (1861) and the trilogy about *Sigurd*

Slembe (1862). His efforts helped to revive Norwegian as a literary language.

He became poet laureate, and his poem *Yes, We Love this Land of Ours* became a rallying point in the struggle for political independence from Sweden. The poem is now the national anthem of Norway. Other works include his greatest plays, *Beyond One's Powers* I and II (1893, 1895).

Bjørnson, the son of a Norwegian pastor, was born in Kvikne in Österdalen. He was awarded the Nobel Prize for Literature in 1903, and his statue today stands proud outside the National Theatre in the capital, together with that of Henrik Ibsen, one of his fellow students at school in Christiania, as Oslo was then called.

NEW CONCERNS

The 1980s produced a sort of realistic novel, written in sociology textbook style, directly opposed to the older, bourgeois psychology novels, "a die-hard heritage from Hamsun, Cora Sandel and Torborg Nedreaas". Most readable among these "revolution" works are Dag Solstad's (b. 1941) trilogy about World War II, *Svik (Betrayal), Krig (War)* and *Brød og Våpen (Bread and Arms)*. This revival of social realism allowed an author such as Asbjørn Elden (1919–90) to produce essentially modern yet "back to our roots" sagas about the inconspicuous lives of ordinary people, such as his *Rundt Neste Sving (Around the Next Bend)*.

Women have come to the fore of Norwegian writing. Cecilie Løveid (b. 1951) and Kari Bøge (b. 1950) crashed onto the literary scene in the late 1970s with audacious, even shocking works. Ignoring male-dominated social realism, they picked apart purely female problems using "street language" and spoken modes of expression. Løveid's lyrically erotic *Sug (Suck)* rocked the staid Oslo critics but has brought her international recognition. Liv Køltzow's (b. 1945) third

> Norwegian movies Pathfinder, by Nils Gaup (1988), Petter Næss's Elling (2002) and Kon-Tiki (2012), by Joachim Rønning and Espen Sandberg, were all nominated for an Oscar. In 2008, Max Manus, about Norway's World War II saboteur, was also a big box-office success.

The novelist Liv Køltzow.

novel, *The Story of Eli*, explores sex roles in society. The 1990s saw a general literature boom. Whodunnits by Gunnar Staalesen, Jo Nesbø, Karin Fossum, Ingvar Ambjørnsen and Anne Holt are popular. The first prize, however, must go to a book on the history of philosophy written for adolescents: *Sophie's World* by Jostein Gaarder. He is the most famous Norwegian writer since Knut Hamsun.

LEADING THE WAY

If there is one area where Norwegians have the edge it is in furniture (consider Peter Opsvik's classic TrippTrapp chair for kids, for example) and architecture, which in recent years has responded to increasing demands for sustainable development.

Probably the most internationally renowned Norwegian architect was the "concrete poet" Sverre Fehn (1924–2009), whose main materials were concrete, wood, glass, and the Nordic light. In 1997, Fehn became the first Nordic architect to win the American Pritzker Architecture Prize, the "Nobel Prize" of architectural awards, and the award cited "a marvellous, lyrical and ingenious architectural form... both forceful and extremely rational". To see his work, visit the Norsk

⊘ OLE BULL (1810-80)

Born 200 years ago, "The Nordic Paganini", as Ole Bull was known, became a model for musicians and writers such as Grieg, Bjørnson and Ibsen. A virtuoso violinist and composer, famed for his charismatic personality and his way with the ladies as much as for his musical brio, Bull was Norway's first superstar, performing in front of adoring audiences in packed concert halls at home and abroad. He died, aged 70, on his island at Lysøen, near Bergen, and his funeral procession was one of the most spectacular in Norwegian history, with countless smaller boats following the ship carrying his body – a nation's fitting farewell to one of its beloved sons.

Bremuseet (Glacier Museum) in Fjærland, or the Norwegian Museum for Architecture in Oslo. Snøhetta is another architect firm that has now made a name for itself, most spectacularly with the new Opera House on the Oslo waterfront.

NORWAY'S PAGANINI

Norway has a long tradition in music. The skaldic poems of the Viking Age provide a medieval link to the music traditions of Central Europe; Gregorian chants used in the worship of St Olaf are very similar to the Parisian school of the 13th century.

Ludvig Mathias Lindeman's collection of Norwegian folk tunes. Many composers incorporated some element of folk music in their works.

With the end of the union with Sweden in 1905, Norwegian composers found the need to define a national identity, and reverted to the music of the Norwegian Middle Ages. Seeking inspiration in medieval poetry, German Romanticism and French Impressionism, David Monrad Johansen (1888–1970) tried to create a monumental kind of music based on musical archaisms. This national Romanticism continued until just after

Concert in Oslo.

While higher forms of music stagnated during the 450 years of Danish rule, folk music unfolded freely, encouraged by the ecclesiastical centres and travelling musicians of the time.

Norwegian music developed for the first time in the early 1800s, mainly as a result of the union with Sweden and the influence of the Royal Swedish Court, but also because of the international breakthrough made by violin virtuoso Ole Bull (1810–80).

The 1870s and 80s became known as the Golden Age of Norwegian music, with such prominent composers as Halfdan Kierulf (1815–68), Edvard Grieg and Johan Svendsen (1849–1911). Music took on a national flavour, urged on by Ole Bull's promotion of the Hardanger fiddle and

the war, when a new generation of composers went to study in Paris or the United States, consciously aware of the need to internationalise their musical language.

FESTIVALS

The Norwegians' yearning for culture is most explicit, however, in the myriad of annual festivals. There is a festival, big or small, to cater for every taste, from the northernmost jazz festival, in Svalbard, to the Notodden Blues Festival, the biggest of its kind in Norway, not to mention the Ice Music Festival in Geilo, where every instrument is carved out of local ice, or the Øya Festival in Oslo, one of Scandinavia's best-loved rock events.

📷 ARCHITECTURE

Visionary new projects are gracing the skyline, from the Opera House in Oslo to a seed bank in Svalbard, with wooden stave churches and a complete *Jugendstil* town along the way.

The stunning Oslo Opera House might be the best known, but is only one of many innovative and exciting new buildings to have appeared in Norway over the past two decades. From the new Holmenkollen ski jump in Oslo to the Global Seed Vault in Svalbard, the country is littered with such gems. There are hotels, like the glimmering steel-and-glass "Sail" in Molde, or the new Preikestolen Mountain Lodge, part of a project promoting environmentally-friendly timber technology in modern architecture; public and religious buildings, such as the Sami Parliament in Karasjok and the Arctic Cathedral in Tromsø; and, of course, museums and galleries, like the Petter Dass Museum and the new Hamsun Centre, both in Nordland, to name but a few.

It is not just about new buildings, though. The stave churches, which date back to the Middle Ages, are masterpieces in their own right, and the *stavkirke* at Urnes has been on the Unesco World Heritage list since 1979. Also on the list are Bryggen, the Hanseatic merchant houses in Bergen, and the old mining town of Røros, famed for its church and colourful wooden turf-roofed buildings. Nidarosdomen, Norway's oldest and largest cathedral in Trondheim, and the town of Ålesund, whose entire centre was rebuilt in the *Jugendstil* style after the town burned to the ground in 1904, are equally impressive.

Trondheim's cathedral has been an important pilgrimage destination since construction began in 1066. The cathedral houses the relics of St Olav, Norway's patron saint.

Trondheim's cathedral has been an important pilgrimage destination since construction began in 1066. The cathedral houses the relics of St Olav, Norway's patron saint.

Ålesund's town centre has an impressive 320 Art Nouveau (Jugendstil) buildings.

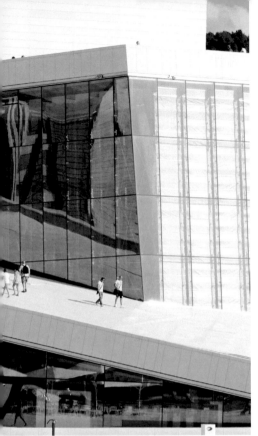

The spectacular Stegastein viewpoint.

National Tourist Routes Project

It all started in 1994, as a trial project aimed at improving the driving experience in Norway by offering motorists an alternative to the main roads. Routes were selected for their outstanding scenery and equally striking architectural features were constructed along the way. A special council was set up, a team of international architects assembled, and before you knew it really interesting buildings were beginning to pop up at the roadside.

The focus throughout has been on quality, and many of the 200 or so buildings and structures (most of them information centres, rest areas or observation platforms) have already won awards in their field. The jaw-dropping Stegastein viewpoint at Aurlandsvegen, a wood-and-glass platform jutting out 650 metres (2,133ft) high over the green waters of the fjord below, might be the most photographed, but there are many other striking structures.

This visionary project covers 1,850km (1,150 miles) in all. Every single one of the 18 routes selected is breathtaking in its beauty, both natural and enhanced by man. For striking images and details of each, go to www. nasjonaleturistveger.no.

Designed by Norwegian architect firm Snøhetta, Oslo Opera House has won several awards since its inauguration in 2008, including the prestigious Mies van der Rohe Prize.

The design of the Sami Parliament in Karasjok, Finnmark, was based on techniques and materials that reflected Sami culture and building traditions.

The intricately decorated wooden stave churches are an important, and unique, part of the Norwegian heritage. Dating back to the Middle Ages, as many as 28 stave churches survive today.

Fine dining in Norway is a luxury.

WHY DOES EVERYTHING COST SO MUCH?

Norway's high standard of living has its price, but the country is not as expensive as it used to be.

There's no getting away from it: Norway hits a visitor's wallet hard. The reason is very simple: thanks to oil and gas extraction, the country is mega-rich. That's fine if you're paid in krone and enjoying commensurately high wages, tough if you're from elsewhere. Today, some food items, such as coffee and butter, are generally less expensive than elsewhere but these are the exception rather than the rule. Visitors are often surprised at the relatively high prices for meat and, amazingly enough, fish. Staple vegetables are reasonable; exotic types, for which there is less demand, are expensive. Fruit follows the same pattern. You can find imported apples or tomatoes at normal European Union (EU) prices. To reduce costs, it's worth looking out for *lavpris* (low-price) shops.

Somewhat surprisingly, Norway produces a reasonable tomato crop, less because of sunshine and high temperatures and more because of encouragement from the Norwegian Ministry of Agriculture, which sees independence from other countries as its main aim. The tomatoes don't always have much taste though, and their price shoots up when imports are restricted.

"MADE IN NORWAY"

Norway's desire to be self-sufficient has blossomed in unusual areas. The farmers in some tiny valleys in the west of the country live in grand style because their tomatoes, cucumbers, Chinese cabbages or cattle are highly subsidised. Only 3 percent of the land is used for agriculture, so variety is essential. Cattle farmers are proud of their beef and pork, vegetable farmers praise their organically grown produce. Around 95 percent of the grain consumed is harvested in the country, and cattle is almost entirely reared for the domestic market.

Much of the farming is still in traditional style.

At 25 percent, VAT (known as MVA or "moms" in Norway) is one of the highest value-added taxes on goods in the world.

As far as foodstuffs are concerned, the logo "Made in Norway" is more an expression of a political principle than of exceptionally high quality. Things are changing though. The higher standard of living has stimulated a demand for a richly laid table. Admittedly, prices in Norwegian hotels are high – but so is the standard of the breakfast buffet. Anyone sampling a fully laden breakfast table can only start the day in a good mood: fruit juice, smoked salmon, pickled herring, fresh bread, fruit and muesli. This meal can easily get light eaters through the day and save them the expense of lunch.

TAXED TO THE HILT?

Not so long ago, it was fashionable to blame rich farmers and a false subsidy policy for high taxes. In reality these subsidies are cut each year and many smallholdings have been given up. Income is subject to 30–45 percent income

Fresh produce "Made in Norway".

> *To encourage Norwegians to recycle, the "money back" system is often used: a deposit of NOK 1 (pant) may be charged when buying bottles, either glass or plastic, and the money is refunded on return of the bottles.*

tax. In return, Norwegians enjoy generous social security, health insurance and pension payments, and even the Church is funded by the state.

Other state revenue comes from oil and gas sales as well as taxes on various luxury items – which explains the high prices for cars, alcohol and cigarettes. Luxury costs money, and Norwegians aren't supposed to enjoy luxury items – or at least they should do it in a different way.

The debate on cigarette and alcohol prices is an inevitable item in the annual budget discussions, and only two of the eight political parties in the Storting ever vote to reduce these taxes; the rest squeeze yet a little more out of them every year.

What is the reasoning behind these constant tax increases? The government insists that the treatment of alcohol and cigarette-related illnesses costs billions. And the budget discussions are also enlivened by the Christian Democratic Party, which rallies against these habits. Norwegians, however, have long learned to live with the link between vice and illness, and have stopped arguing about prices – these days they drink their beer in peace.

PAYING FOR THE ROADS

It's no exaggeration to claim that car drivers have financed their own infrastructure. Here, as with alcohol and tobacco, Norwegians believe in the principle of cause and effect, which is paid for through high car prices (Norway doesn't have its own car industry), a large tax on petrol and toll charges: if you want to drive through Oslo (and there are few ways to circumnavigate it), Bergen, Trondheim or Stavanger, you have to pay a toll.

The road system, on the other hand, has been considerably upgraded and now, with numerous bridges and tunnels (including under the sea), reaches the tiniest villages.

⊘ PRICE CHECK

Room for two in a mid-range hotel: NOK 1,500*

Campsite plot for the night: NOK 100–200

Main course in a mid-range restaurant: NOK 200–250

Hot dog in a kiosk: NOK 40

Glass of beer in a bar: NOK 80

Bottle of red wine in Vinmonopolet: NOK 130

Car rental per week: NOK 4,000; 1 litre petrol: NOK 15

Bus ticket: NOK 33; cinema ticket: NOK 120

1 litre milk: NOK 16; bread: NOK 23

Ice cream: NOK 22

Newspaper: NOK 25–35; paperback: NOK 160

Postcard: NOK 15; stamp (Europe): NOK 17

*All prices approximate at time of going to print.

TO DRINK OR NOT TO DRINK

From Viking mead-drinking sessions to 20th-century prohibition, the consumption of alcohol has always been a subject of heated debate.

The question of alcohol and its corollary, tee totalism, have long been burning issues in Norway. The climate is often blamed for Norwegian drinking. There may be some truth in this, since long winters used to put a premium on the art of preserving and storing food. Salt was the key, and it was consumed in such quantities that great thirst followed. At one time, the "normal" consumption of beer and mead was between 6 and 10 litres (10–18 pints) a day.

The 19th century produced a rash of travel books about Norway, and all of them drew attention to a weakness for drink. Even boys of 12 and 14 years, according to the Reverend R. Everest, indulged in the "odious vice", drinking quantities of brandy "that would have astonished an English coalman".

Today's statistics show that Norwegians actually consume less alcohol than almost any other European nation. And that beer and wine have supplanted harder spirits. But unreported numbers are higher: Norwegians like to travel and certainly buy the complete quota of duty-free items – understandably, given the sky-high price of spirits back in Norway, where a few amateur chemists still brew their own schnapps.

The situation was very different in the early 20th century. In 1917 the Norwegian government decided to prohibit the sale of alcohol. Large parts of the Norwegian population were struggling to feed themselves during World War I, so it seemed unreasonable to use grain and potatoes for the production of alcohol. Prohibition was only supposed to last as long as the war raged in Europe, but as it had worked well and helped to reduce social problems related to alcohol consumption, the Norwegians decided in a referendum in 1919 to keep it.

Interestingly, it was the prohibition issue that mobilised women politically. They came out in droves to vote for prohibition in 1919 because they had had enough of their drunken husbands spending their weekly wages on alcohol. But trouble with trade partners such as Spain, Portugal and France – who threatened to stop buying Norwegian fish if Norway stopped buying their wine – and widespread smuggling, led to the ban being lifted in 1926.

Until the late 1990s, the import and sale of wines and spirits was a state monopoly. Government buyers decided what was to be made available (and the price) in the chain of *Vinmonopolet* shops, as well as in most hotels and restaurants. It was said that by this act the Norwegian state had made itself the biggest single buyer of alcoholic drinks in the world, a painful irony for the numerous prohibitionists who were still beating the drum.

A glass of aquavit, Norway's spirit of choice.

In 1997, the Norwegian government made a major concession to the EU by deregulating the import, wholesale and distribution side of the market. This means that hotels, restaurants and bars may now do business with independent importers, although *Vinmonopolet* maintains its monopoly on retail sales.

One of the results of this, as visitors find out, is that drinks are freely available in major cities, albeit at numbing prices. Today, it is easier to be served a drink in Oslo at 2am than it is, say, in London. Laws affecting the sale of alcohol are decided at the *kommune* level (by town and rural councils), so outside the cities, and especially on the southwest-coast *bibelbeltet* (bible belt) it is a matter of luck whether a particular place is completely dry or not – although such conservative attitudes seem to be increasingly on the way out.

Old wooden houses at Bergen.

Reindeer herd in Finnmark.

Ålesund at dusk.

Awe-inspiring Trollfjord.

INTRODUCTION

A detailed guide to the entire country, with principal sights clearly cross-referenced by number to the maps.

'King Neptune' anoints passengers as they cross the Arctic Circle.

Norway is a long narrow strip of a country, stretching north from mainland Europe far into the Arctic. In the ancient capital of Trondheim, you are 500km (350 miles) from the modern capital of Oslo, but only a quarter of the way up the country's jagged coast. Oslo is as far from Monaco as it is from Nordkapp (North Cape), with Norway's northernmost outpost, the islands of Svalbard (Spitsbergen), several hundred kilometres further north. With a population of only 5.2 million, Norway has, above all else, space.

Yet travel is not difficult. From early times, the Norwegians (as Vikings) were magnificent sailors, and sea travel remains important through the Hurtigruten coastal express, plus smaller local ferries that link coastal communities and cut across fjords. On land, the Norwegians have connected even the most isolated settlements by building railways, roads and bridges across their fjords and by digging road tunnels deep into the mountains and under the sea.

The Atlantic Road in Møre og Romsdal.

The scenery is dramatic and the land changes constantly, from mountain to sea, fjord to forest. Oslo, Stavanger, Bergen, Trondheim and Tromsø are small, manageable cities that make good use of the surrounding countryside. Neither the Norwegian climate nor the people are as chilly as the northern latitudes might suggest. The Gulf Stream warms the western coastline so that the seas are ice-free all the year round, and the great distances between villages, towns and farms have encouraged an age-old tradition of hospitality.

In the 1970s, oil brought wealth to Norway, and now these deeply patriotic people enjoy one of the highest standards of living in the world. But money hasn't changed Norwegians' deep-rooted love of nature: they are first and foremost an outdoor people, living in a land where inhabitants and visitors alike can make the most of limitless space for walking, skiing, touring and breathing in the clear air. All things considered, Norway must rank as the ultimate active-holiday destination.

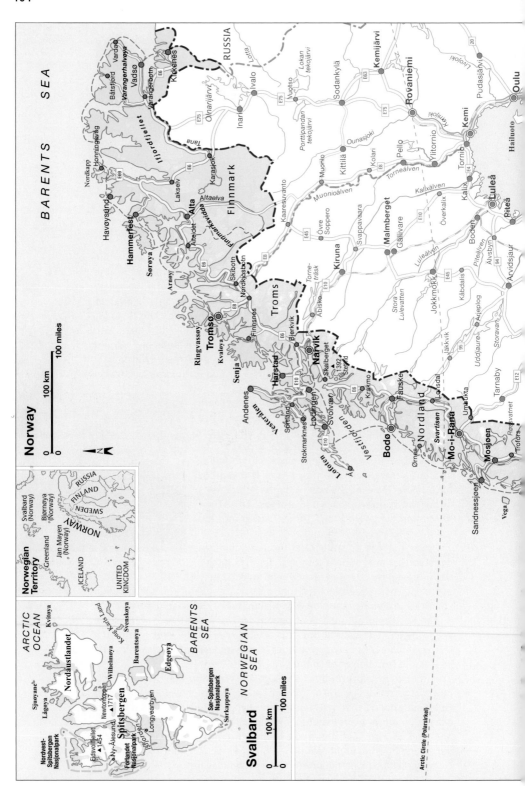

Norway

BARENTS SEA

Norwegian Territory

Svalbard (Norway)
Bjørnøya (Norway)
Greenland
Jan Mayen (Norway)

ARCTIC OCEAN
ICELAND
UNITED KINGDOM
RUSSIA
FINLAND
SWEDEN
NORWAY

Svalbard

ARCTIC OCEAN
Sjuøyane
Kvitøya
Kong Karls Land
Nordaustlandet
Wilhelmøya
Svenskøya
Barentsøya
Edgeøya
BARENTS SEA
Nordvest-Spitsbergen Nasjonalpark
Eidsvollfjellet ▲1454
Ny-Ålesund
Newtontoppen ▲1717
Spitsbergen
Forlandet Nasjonalpark
Isfjorden
Longyearbyen
NORWEGIAN SEA
Sør-Spitsbergen Nasjonalpark
Sørkappøya

Arctic Circle (Polarsirkel)

RUSSIA

Vardø
Vadsø
Varangerhalvøya
Båtsfjord
Varangerbotn
Kirkenes
Honningsvåg
Nordkapp
Nordkapp
Nordkinn
Havøysund
Hammerfest
Søroya
Arnøy
Kvaløya
Ringvassøy
Senja
Tromsø
Finnsnes
Skibotn
Nordkjosbotn
Alteidet
Alta
Altaelva
Lakselv
Karasjok
Karasjok
Finnmarksvidda
Finnmark
Ivalo
Inari
Olnarijärvi
Tana
Kaaresuvanto
Kautokeino
E6
E75
E75
Vuotso
Lokan tekojärvi
Lotta
Sodankylä
E63
Kemijärvi
Rovaniemi
Kemi
Oulu
Hailuoto
Pudasjärvi
Livojoki
Kemijoki
Ounasjoki
Portipahdan tekojärvi
Muonioälven
Muonio
Kittilä
Kolari
Pello
Ylitornio
Tornio
Kalix
Luleå
Piteå
E4
E8
Torneälven
Kallxälven
Överkalix
Boden
Älvsbyn
Piteälven
94
Arvidsjaur
Svappavaara
Malmberget
Gällivare
Kiruna
Kaaresuvanto
E10
E45
Övre Soppero
Torne-träsk
Abisko
E10
Stora Lulevatten
Luleälven
Jokkmokk
Kåbdalis
Jäkkvik
96
Uddjaure
Storavan
Tärnaby
E12
Troms
Bjerkvik
Narvik
Skalberget
1392 Stetind
Harstad
Vesterålen
Andenes
Stokmarknes
Lødingen
Sortland
Svolvær
Lofoten
Å
Vestfjorden
E6
Krakmo
Fauske
Bodø
Nordland
Saltfjellet
Svartisen
Mo-i-Rana
Mosjøen
Umbukta
Lovisdal
Røsvatnet
Trofors
Vega
Sandnessjøen
Ørnes
E10
Skalstugan
Skalberget
100 miles
100 km
N

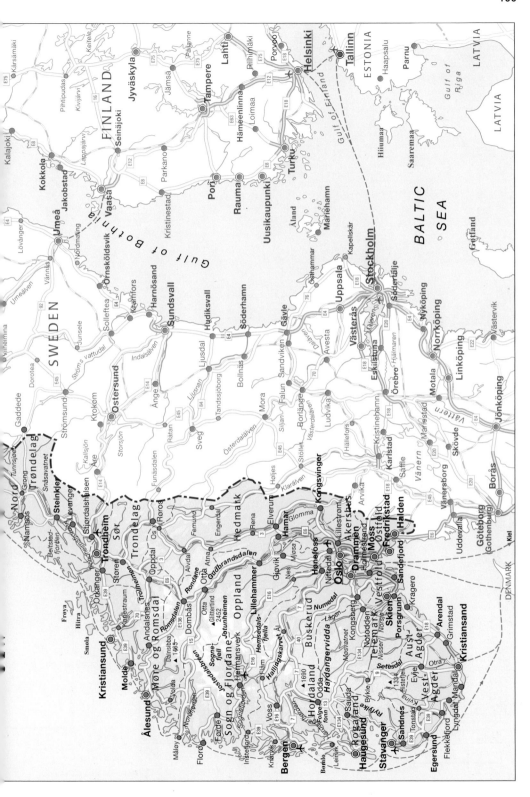

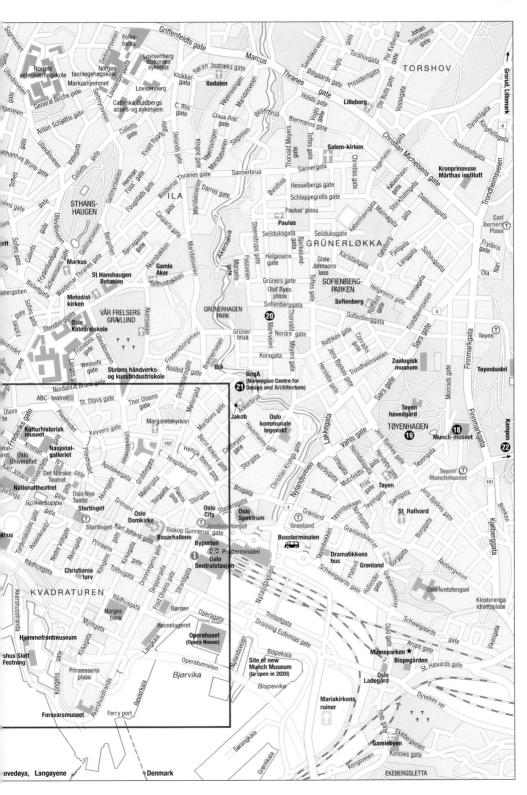

OSLO, NORDIC CITY OF LIGHT

With its idyllic setting, a multitude of galleries and museums and a magnificent Opera House overlooking the Oslofjord, the capital of Norway is a great introduction to the country.

Travellers to Norway once gave Oslo no more than a passing nod as they steamed through on their way to Bergen and the more spectacular scenery of the west-coast fjords. But if Oslo once lacked the vitality of Copenhagen or Stockholm, prompting Munch and many of his contemporaries to leave the country for the Continent, today the city bears little resemblance to its 1880s, or even 1980s self. The small capital by the fjord, which celebrated its 1,000th birthday in the year 2000, has come of age in quite a spectacular way, and its newfound confidence can be felt on every street corner.

ON THE WORLD STAGE

Oslo has a vibrant city centre, heaving with shoppers, visitors and businesspeople day and night. There's a stunning opera house, a revitalised waterfront area, world-class museums and, standing proud on the hills above the town, the world's most modern ski jump. An array of festivals draw big international names and music fans from far and wide, while top restaurants rival the best in the world. The list goes on...

Oslo ranks as one of the world's most expensive cities but, on the positive side, it has awoken to the attractions of city fun, and developed into a

Dining At Aker Brygge.

metropolis with a revitalised cultural life and a diverse and lively nightlife. Oslo's cultural renaissance in recent years has seen a remarkable creative outburst, often supported by infusions of money in the right places.

On the back of the oil boom came more money for the arts. Suddenly there was enough of a buzz at home to induce Norwegian artists-in-exile to return. And since the opening of the magnificent waterside **Opera House** ❶ (Operahuset; http://operaen.no) in Bjørvika, artistes have been lining up

⊙ Main Attractions
Opera House
National Gallery
Munch Museum
Holmenkollen Ski Jump
Norwegian Folk Museum

Maps on pages 136, 140

to perform here. This iconic landmark, designed to resemble a glacier floating in the harbour, has spearheaded the redevelopment of the entire downtown area around the central train station. It was designed by Norwegian architects Snøhetta, and the white marble and glass structure has won an array of prestigious architectural prizes and awards. An impressive 1.3 million people visited it in the first year of opening alone.

OSLO FROM THE WATER

Oslo, at the head of a fjord shaped like a swan's neck; is surrounded by low hills. Your initial impression will vary according to how you arrive. The ideal way is by boat, for then you get the most complete picture, though arriving by car from the south along the Mosseveien also offers some impressive views.

Your view from the fjord will be dominated by the **City Hall ②** (Rådhuset; www.rft.oslo.kommune.no; tel: 23 46 12 00; daily 9am–4pm, July–Aug until 6pm; free guided tours daily June–Aug at 10am, noon and 2pm). This large, mud-coloured building is topped by two square towers, known as the "goat's cheese" (geitost) because of its resemblance to blocks of Norwegian brown goat's cheese.

The courtyard is adorned with fantastic figures and symbols from Norwegian mythology; note the **astronomical clock**, the **Yggdrasill frieze**

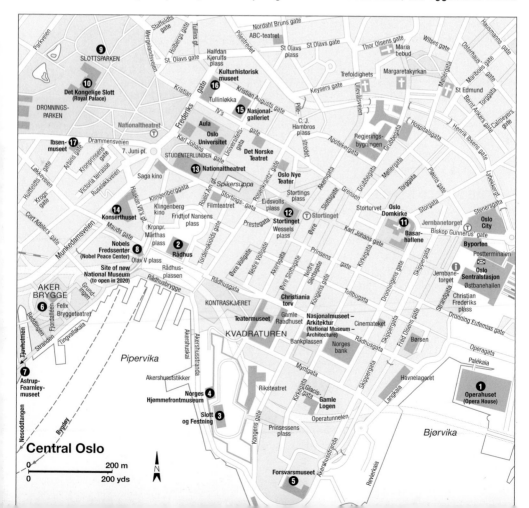

Central Oslo

by Dagfin Werenskiold and Dyre Vaas' **swan fountain**. The murals inside the main hall are based around more modern themes, and this is where the Nobel Peace Prize is awarded every year on 10 December. The south-facing clock, at 8 metres (30ft) in diameter, is one of the largest timepieces in Europe.

WAR AND PEACE

Walking south from the Rådhus along the fjord, you come to the medieval **Akershus Castle and Fortress** ❸ (Slott og Festning; tel: 23 09 39 17; castle May–Aug Mon–Sat 10am–4pm, Sun noon–4pm; Sept–Apr weekends only noon–5pm, grounds May–Sept 6am–9pm, Oct–Apr 7am–9pm; grounds free). Built originally in 1299, it helped to protect Christiania (as Oslo was called until 1925) from marauders. The Nazis took over Akershus during World War II and shot several Resistance fighters near the old magazine. When the war was over, the traitorous Norwegian chancellor, Quisling, was shot on the same spot.

The **Resistance Museum** ❹ (Norges Hjemmefrontmuseum; tel: 23 09 31 38; June–Aug Mon–Sat 10am–5pm, Sun 11am–5pm; Sept–May Mon–Fri 10am–4pm, Sat–Sun 11am–4pm) in the grounds illustrates the intense story of occupied Norway, while the **Armed Forces Museum** ❺ (Forsvarsmuseet; tel: 23 09 35 82; May–Aug daily 10am–5pm, Sept–Apr Tue–Sun 10am–4pm; free) covers Norwegian military and political history from the Vikings to the present day.

Thrusting up on the opposite side of the Pipervika inlet are the glass, chrome and neon buildings of **Aker Brygge** ❻. Centred around an open-air sculpture court, this renovated shipyard and harbour-side development is the setting for shopping arcades, trendy bars and restaurants, food stalls, theatres and galleries. It is also the venue for outdoor summer festivals. Buzzing with activity, this pedestrian area is hugely popular. On a hot summer day it's a pleasure to sit at one of the many outdoor terraces and watch life go by on the waterfront.

Oslo's Opera House.

A statue of Karl Johan XIV stands on the steps of Det Kongelige Slott, the Royal Palace.

West of Aker Brygge is the swanky newer development of Tjuvholmen, which also has its fair share of restaurants and expensive apartments as well as the swanky **Astrup Fearnley Museum of Modern Art** ❼ (Tjuvholmen; www.afmuseet.no; tel: 22 93 60 60; Tue–Wed and Fri noon–5pm, Thu until 7pm, Sat–Sun 11am–5pm), which moved in 2012 into splendid new waterside premises designed by renowned Italian architect Renzo Piano. In addition to its permanent collection, which features work by the likes of Olafur Eliasson, Damien Hirst, Jeff Koons, Charles Ray and Andy Warhol, it regularly mounts avant-garde temporary exhibitions.

Between Aker Brygge and City Hall is the **Nobel Peace Center** ❽ (Nobels Fredssenter, Rådhusplassen; www.nobel peacecenter.org; tel: 48 30 10 00; daily June–Aug 10am–6pm; closed Mon rest of the year). It illustrates the history of the prize and the lives of those who have won this honour. There are also temporary exhibitions on themes such as democracy, peace and conflict resolution. Housed in a renovated train

Nobel Peace Center.

station, it's an ultra-modern account of world affairs since the late 1800s. There are also changing temporary exhibitions and a popular café on site.

In summer, Oslo goes green. From the fjord approach you'll see the tops of the trees of the **Palace Gardens** ❾ (Slottsparken), and other parks that extend northwards beyond them to the wooded hills that are Oslo's backdrop. Your eye will surely be drawn to the impressive Holmenkollen ski jump on one of the city's highest hills (see page 101).

ROYAL AVENUE

Oslo city centre is large enough to be interesting yet compact enough to cover on foot. The main axis is **Karl Johans gate**, originally designed in 1826 by the royal architect H.D.F. Linstow. It was widened some 30 years later to become Oslo's equivalent of the Champs Elysées. Its western end merges into the broad avenue leading to the doors of the **Royal Palace** ❿ (Det Kongelige Slott; www.royalcourt. no; mid-June–mid-Aug by guided tour only, tickets available online at www.

ticketmaster.no and by phone, 81 53 31 33. If you haven't pre-booked, try your luck at the main entrance, where remaining tickets are sold on the day. Guided tours in English take place four times daily). The palace is the focal point of Norway's National Day celebrations on 17 May. Karl Johans gate runs eastwards to Jernbanetorget, the location of **Oslo S station** (Oslo Sentralstasjon). To the south, the centre extends to the fjord.

CATHEDRAL OF ART

Parallel to Karl Johans gate to the north is **Grensen**, another busy, shop-lined street. **Oslo Cathedral** ⓫ (Domkirke; tel: 23 62 90 10; Sat–Thu 10am–4pm, Fri 4pm–6am; free) dominates the Stortorvet (square) at the east end of Grensen. Completed in 1697, its exterior is of darkened brown brick, while inside artists of the 18th, 19th and 20th centuries have contributed to the cathedral's adornment. Features include stained-glass windows by Emmanuel Vigeland and ceiling paintings by Hugo Lous Mohrs that took over 14 years to complete and

are the largest of their kind in Norway. Look out for the massive bronze doors by artist Dagfin Werenskiold and original, intricate acanthus carving on the baroque altar panel, pulpit and front of the organ. Also, the silver altar piece by Italian sculptor Arrigo Minerbi, famous for his work on Milan Cathedral. Behind Domkirke is **Basarhallene** – a round, colonnaded market with food and handicraft stalls. Lille Grensen leads south to the **Parliament** ⓬ (Stortinget; tel: 23 31 35 96, www.stortinget.no; early July–early Aug guided tours Mon–Fri 10am, 1pm, Sept–Nov guided tours Sat 10am, 11.30am; free) on **Karl Johans** gate, from where **Eidsvollplass** spreads out in front of the Storting.

Every winter, Eidsvollplass is flooded to create a large, free, open-air ice rink, while in summer it's a popular lunchtime spot for nearby office workers, who come and sit by the fountains while enjoying their *matpakke* (packed lunch). Within **Studenterlunden**, the small park around the university, is the main university building, **Aula**, which is decorated with murals by Edvard Munch.

⊙ **Tip**

Fancy a ski? Oslo Vinterpark, only 20 minutes north of downtown Oslo, has 18 runs that are floodlit at night, 11 lifts, a terrain park, and more. Accessible by tram and bus from the city centre, it's open from early December to April (www.oslovinterpark.no).

Outside the National Theatre.

Norway's **National Theatre** (Nationaltheatret) stages a mix of classical drama and groundbreaking contemporary productions. It first opened its doors in 1899, and is flanked with statues of national icons Henrik Ibsen and Bjørnstjerne Bjørnson. It is just opposite Studenterlunden with Slottsparken immediately to the west.

MUSIC VENUES

The Oslo Philharmonic, whose home is the **Konserthuset** (tel: 23 11 31 11; see www.oslokonserthus.no for programme) on Munkedamsveien, performs with a dazzling sequence of guest conductors and soloists.

In addition to the classical music scene, the variety of music to be heard in Oslo's clubs and concert halls is vast, from world music to indie rock and black metal, and everything in between. International rock stars now regularly add Oslo to their world-tour calendar, and two of the best venues to see them are the **Oslo Spektrum**, Sonja Henies plass 2 (tel: 81 51 12 11; www.oslospektrum.no), and **Rockefeller**,

National Gallery.

Torggata 16 (tel: 22 20 32 32; www.rockefeller.no). The music festival calendar is a busy one, kicking off at Easter with the Inferno Metal Festival, while summer highlights include the Norwegian Wood Rock festival, held in Frognerbadet every June, and the Øya Festival, Oslo's largest rock festival, in August Oslo's international jazz and chamber music festivals also take place in August. Later in the year, the Ultima festival features contemporary music, while the World Music festival draws artists from far and wide.

CHRISTIAN'S TOWN

The need for space to accommodate all these new artistic ventures has also influenced the revival of neglected parts of Oslo. It has helped to breathe new life into **Christian IV's town** (Kvadraturen), a historic area bounded to the north by Rådhusgata and to the south by Akershus Slott, and characterised by old customs and shipping houses and grand open plazas. At one time this area was a haunt of prostitutes and their pursuers. The

district's history as a redoubtable part of Oslo is reflected in its former nickname, "Little Algeria" – see the painting in Engebret Café on Bankplassen, an artists' haunt since the early 1900s. **Gamle Logen** on Grev Wedels plass is now a serious concert venue, and there's also the **Cinemateket** (repertory film theatre) a few blocks away.

Worth a visit is the **National Museum for Architecture** (Nasjonalmuseet – Arkitektur, Bankplassen 3; tel: 21 98 21 82; www.nasjonalmuseet.no; Tue–Wed and Fri 11am–5pm, Thu until 7pm, Sat–Sun noon–5pm) where you will find models of some of Norway's most significant buildings, as well as exhibitions covering a range of related topics. The purpose-built pavilion housing the changing exhibitions was designed by Sverre Fehn, one of Norway's most acclaimed architects.

NEW NATIONAL MUSEUM

The **National Gallery** ⓯ (Nasjonalgalleriet, Universitetsgaten 13; tel: 21 98 20 00; www.nasjonalmuseet.no; Tue–Wed and Fri 10am–6pm, Thu until 7pm, Sat–Sun 11am–5pm; Thu free) will be a revelation for those who have never heard of any Norwegian artist apart from Edvard Munch. The sheer size, if not the content, of the forest and fjord paintings of the Romantic artist J.C. Dahl (1788–1857) will impress you. You'll also see the work of his prolific contemporaries Adolph Tidemand (1814–76) and Hans Frederik Gude (1825–1903). There is a wonderful series of etchings depicting barn dances, village scenes and festivities. The display of Impressionist works is excellent. And don't forget, of course, the Munch room, with the painter's most famous version of *The Scream* (*Skrika*, 1893).

From 2020, the collections of the National Gallery, the National Museum of Contemporary Art, the Museum of Decorative Arts and Design and the National Museum for Architecture will all be gathered under one roof, that of the new National Museum for Art, Architecture and Design which is being constructed on the site of the former

Berry picker.

⊘ WEEKENDS OUTDOORS

A typical city-dweller from Oslo spends huge amounts of time outdoors. In summer, people are likely to enjoy the outdoors after work; they might go swimming, berry-picking, walking, boating or simply cycling in the suburbs by the light of the evening sun. Norwegians treasure their space and contact with nature, and many people who work in Oslo live a fair distance from the city; in winter, this means they can quickly hit the floodlit slopes and cross-country ski trails after work.

Come the weekend, there is a widely followed pattern for the 48 hours. Friday night is usually a night out on the town. Saturday morning is for shopping, followed by gardening or watching football, and Saturday evening tends to be dinner or a party at someone's home. No matter how wild or calm the Saturday night, Sunday is *tur* day. The *tur* is a walk or ski tour, and a formidable tradition. Depending on a person's age, fitness and the number of accompanying children, the *tur* can be anything from a one- to six-hour affair. Some walks will include café stops in one of the 70-odd cabin lodges in the Nordmarka area of Oslo; if not, coffee and hot chocolate come along in a vacuum flask.

Then it's off home to change for an early dinner before heading to the cinema. And in no time at all, it's Monday morning...

Vestbanen train station. There is an information centre for the new National Museum called Mellomstasjonen in the station's main building (Mon–Fri noon–5pm, Sat–Sun 11am–4pm).

Behind the National Gallery is the **Historical Museum**  (Kulturhistorisk Museet, Frederiksgate 2; tel: 22 85 19 00; http://www.khm.uio.no; mid-May–mid-Aug Tue–Sun 10am–5pm; rest of the year 11am–4pm), which traces Norwegian history from the Stone Age to the present time. The museum contains Norway's largest collection of gold treasures from Viking times, and an interesting exhibit of Norwegian coins. Other exhibitions, both temporary and permanent, cover the Arctic, East Asia, Africa, Latin America and Ancient Egypt.

IBSEN AT HOME

West along Drammensveien from the National Gallery is the **Ibsen Museum**  (Ibsenmuseet, Arbins gate 1; tel: 22 12 35 50; http://ibsenmuseet.no; mid-May–mid-Sept daily 11am–6pm, rest of year Fri–Wed 11am–4pm, Thu until

The Ibsen Museum bookshop.

6pm), with guided tours (30 minutes, leaving on the hour) of the apartment where Henrik Ibsen lived from 1895 until his death in 1906.

For the technically minded, 8km (5 miles) to the north there is the **Norwegian Museum of Science and Technology** (Norsk Teknisk Museum, Kjelsåsveien 143; tel: 22 79 60 00; www.tekniskmuseum.no; 20 June–20 Aug daily 11am–6pm; rest of year Tue–Fri 9am–4pm, Sat–Sun 11am–6pm; suburban train, trams 11 or 12, buses 22, 25 and 54 to Kjelsås). It makes a great day out for children, with lots of hands-on exhibitions about energy, industry, transport and telecommunications. Nearby is a watermill that feeds the Akerselva River.

SHOWCASING MUNCH

The suggestions that follow focus on sights outside the centre of Oslo.

One of Norway's best-known museums is the **Munch Museum**  (Munchmuseet, Tøyengata 53; tel: 21 98 20 00; www.munchmuseet.no; daily early May–early Oct 10am–5pm, early Oct–early May until 4pm; T-bane

Tøyen/Munch-museet) in the east of the city. This is the largest collection of Munch's works in the world, each item donated by the artist himself, and the museum has proved too small to exhibit it all at once. So new premises, housing the collections of the Munch Museum and the former Stenersen Museum, are scheduled to open at Bjørvika, next to the Opera House, in 2020. The Stenersen collection was donated to the city by businessman and author Rolf Stenersen, an admirer of Edvard Munch. Until the new museum opens it is showcased as part of the Munch Museum's project "Munchmuseet on the Move".

The life of Edvard Munch (1863–1944) was a sickly one, and this is reflected in his paintings. He was a delicate child and both his mother and sister died at an early age from tuberculosis. Festive renderings of gypsy families and blazing autumn landscapes counterbalance canvases with gloomier themes. The famous The Scream (Skrika, 1893), stolen in 2004 but recovered two years later, is darkly riveting as is the Death of Marat series (Marats død, 1907) in which Munch portrays himself bleeding from gunshot wounds inflicted by an angry mistress.

After a series of breakdowns, Munch returned to Norway, having spent most of his adult artistic life in Paris and Berlin. He sought peace, but continued working, in his cottage at Åsgårdstrand in Vestfold.

The Munch Museum is flanked by parks. The one to the east contains the **Tøyenbadet** (public swimming pools), including a lido, water slide and saunas. To the west are **Tøyen Botanical Gardens** ⑲ (Tøyenhagen), with the Zoological, Mineralogical, Geological and Palaeontological Museums at its north end (all year). In September and early spring this is the site of Norway's largest traditional circus.

VIBRANT GRÜNERLØKKA

A few streets northwest of Munchmuseet, across Trondheimsveien, is the **Grünerløkka** district, a former working-class neighbourhood nowadays favoured by artists and writers. The

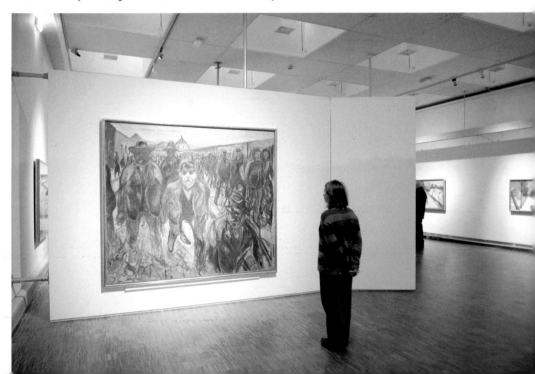

Inside the Munch Museum.

most interesting street in Grünerløkka is **Markveien** 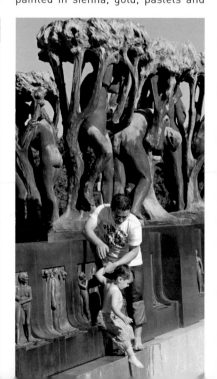, painted in muted pastel colours and lined with galleries and boutiques. Parallel to Markveien is Thorvald Meyers gate, with many restaurants and bars open until 3am. On long, warm summer nights, locals like to sit alfresco at one of the many terraces, and getting a table outside can prove tricky.

Continuing north on Markveien, you'll find a cross street called Grüners gate. From here up to Schleppergrells gate are some magnificent residential courtyards: peer inside for a look at tranquil urban living in Oslo.

FUTURISTIC DESIGN

Just to the southwest of Grünerløkka, across the Akerselva River, the **Norwegian Centre for Design and Architecture** (Haussmans gate 16; tel: 23 29 88 70; Aug Mon–Fri 8am–4pm, rest of year Mon, Tue and Fri 10am–5pm, Wed–Thu until 8pm, Sat–Sun noon–5pm; free) has taken up home in a restored transformer station next to Jakob's church. It presents the latest in Nordic

Cooling off at the Vigeland Sculpture Park.

contemporary design – furniture, lighting and graphics – with new exhibitions every couple of months, a shop selling choice items, and a restaurant.

MULTICULTURAL GRØNLAND

Southeast of Grünerløkka is one of Oslo's biggest ethnic commercial neighbourhoods, **Grønland** (T-bane to Grønland station). Pakistanis are in the majority but plenty of other cultures are represented in the shops and cafés. The **Grønland Basar**, at the corner of Tøyengata and Grønlandsleiret (Mon–Fri 10am–8pm, Sat until 6pm), offers everything from a halal butcher's shop to oriental sweets and Persian carpets. The former Grønland Police Station next door at Tøyenbekken 5 now houses the **Intercultural Museum** (tel: 22 05 28 30; Tue–Sun 11am–4pm, free), with exhibits on immigration, a gallery and a café.

Kampen, whose northern limit is Kampenparken (on the southeast side of Munchmuseet), is a district of attractive wooden houses brilliantly painted in sienna, gold, pastels and

⊙ OSLO'S NIGHTLIFE

Oslo's streets are tangibly alive, especially in summer: festivals come fast and furious, and the crowds at restaurants and cafés brim onto the pavement. The city's nightlife owes much to the extension of licensing hours to 3am.

The influx of immigrants has resulted in a wide variety of restaurants being opened, which complement the Norwegian and fish menus traditionally on offer. Other dining options include the more casual and often cheaper *kafé*, *gjæstgiveris*, pubs, *kros*, *bistros*, *spiseris* and *kafeterias*. Seattle-style coffee shops are also popular.

Bars and clubs are spread throughout the city, and range from underground to upmarket. The "in" scene can be identified by the queue out front, which will certainly not disperse until after 1am. Since eating and drinking in restaurants and bars is expensive, many people invite friends into their homes for "before" drinks *(vorspiel)*. Likewise, after a night on the town it is not unusual to invite friends back to polish off the remaining contents of the house bar *(nachspiel)*.

For concerts and special events, pick up a copy of *What's On in Oslo*, a free monthly brochure available from the tourist office.

vibrant blues. Some of the tranquil streets in lower Kampen are overhung by trees; look up, too, at the dormer windows above the street corners, hung with macramé and lace curtains.

VIGELAND'S VISION

West of the city centre is **Frogner Park** (Frognerparken) or **Vigeland Sculpture Park** ㉓ (Vigelandsparken; www. vigeland.museum.no; all year; free). The park, containing the life's work of Norwegian sculptor Gustav Vigeland (1869–1943), is a 40-minute walk from the centre. On foot, head northwest from the Royal Palace to Hegdehaugsveien, which becomes Bogstadsveien – a long, lively street of art galleries and enticing shops. Or simply hop on a bus (No. 20) or tram (No. 12) in the direction of Frogner. Any westbound T-bane from the Nationaltheatret stops at Majorstuen, the end of Bogstadveien, from where it is a short walk to the main entrance of the park.

Once inside the intricate wrought-iron gates, you'll see before you **Vigelandsbroen** (bridge), flanked by 58 bronze figures of men, women and children, including *Sinnataggen (Angry Boy)*. Next is *Fontenen (Fountain)*, six male figures raising a giant bowl. Vigeland was obsessed with the cycle of life, which he depicts here in 20 reliefs around the edge of the fountain pool.

Above the fountain, on a raised plateau, and surrounded by 36 groups of granite figures, is *Monolitten* ㉔, a great spire 17 metres (55ft) high composed of 121 figures sculpted from one solid block of Iddefjord granite. The last of the major sculptures, the *Livshjulet (Wheel of Life)* is a continuum of human figures that seem to perform an aerial ring dance.

The **Vigeland Museum** (Vigeland-museet; tel: 23 49 37 00; www.vigeland. museum.no; May–Aug Tue–Sun 10am–5pm, Sept–Apr Tue-Sun noon–4pm), containing the rest of Gustav Vigeland's work, is at the southern end of the park. He spent 40 years of his life designing and constructing the park, all financed by the taxpayer, something he reciprocated by donating all his works to the city.

Autumn colours at the Tøyen Botanical Gardens.

NOBEL'S PEACE PRIZE

Out of dynamite came peace: in his lifetime, Alfred Nobel amassed a great fortune which he left to endow the Nobel prizes.

One of life's great ironies is that the Swedish armaments manufacturer Alfred Nobel should have been the founder of the world's most prestigious prize for peace (www.nobelprize.org). Was it the realisation that his invention of dynamite in 1866, originally used for blasting tunnels and quarrying, had become a devastating weapon of war that led him to include the peace category alongside prizes for physics, chemistry, medicine and literature? Or was his conscience troubled by the thought that his great riches came from weapons of destruction? Then again, his motive may have been simply a tribute to Norwegians' reputation as workers for peace.

When he set up his trust fund, Nobel chose the Norwegian parliament (Storting) to make the peace award. It was a time when the near century-old union between Sweden and Norway was collapsing. Perhaps Nobel hoped that this might help to keep the two nations together. If this was his aim, he failed. The union was dissolved less than 10 years after his death in 1896, and Norway was already a year-old sovereign state at the first ceremonies in 1906.

Alfred Nobel (1833–96).

Except for the Peace Prize, the other categories are judged in Sweden and presented in Stockholm to those who, in Nobel's words, "shall have conferred the greatest benefit on mankind". The Nobel Peace Prize ceremony takes place in Oslo's City Hall (Rådhus) on 10 December every year.

Nobel's early instructions were that the Peace Prize should be used to award efforts to reduce the size of military forces and standing armies, but the prize broadened its remit to the promotion of peace in general. This vague brief can lead to controversy, as it did when the Israeli and Egyptian leaders, Menachem Begin and Anwar Sadat, received the Peace Prize jointly for their 1978 efforts to open up talks and communication between their two countries. Dr Henry Kissinger's award in 1972 also aroused controversy, particularly when his Vietnamese co-recipient, Le Duc Tho, turned down his award for their joint efforts in ending the Vietnam War.

However, few begrudged Nelson Mandela and F.W. de Klerk their joint award in 1993. There were no dissenters when the Red Cross received the prize in 1917 for its work amid the battlefield carnage of World War I. The explorer Fridtjof Nansen regarded the Nobel Peace Prize as the greatest of the tributes to his years as internationalist, humanitarian and head of the Norwegian delegation at the League of Nations.

Among the many other recipients were Martin Luther King, Dr Albert Schweitzer, Amnesty International, the Dalai Lama, Kofi Annan and US president Barack Obama, whose high profile and much publicised visit to Oslo to pick up his prize in 2009 contrasted with that of Mother Teresa, who 30 years earlier had accepted her award in her customary habit and sandals despite the Norwegian winter.

Prominent women who have been honoured include Betty Williams and Máiread Corrigan in 1976 after they campaigned for an end to military and paramilitary bloodshed in Northern Ireland. In 2011, the peace prize was awarded jointly to three outstanding campaigners for women's rights (Tawakkul Karman from Yemen, plus Ellen Johnson Sirleaf and Leymah Gbowee both from Liberia). In 2014, 17 yer-old Malala Yousafzai, a Pakistani activist for female education, became the youngest-ever Nobel Prize laureate.

Learn more about the Nobel Peace Prize at the Nobel Peace Center in Oslo (see page 142).

OSLO IN THE MAKING

Frogner Park also contains the **Oslo City Museum**  (Oslo Bymuseet; tel: 23 28 41 70; www.oslomuseum.no; Tue–Sun 11am–4pm; free), which traces the city's history. Founded in 1050 by Harald Hardråde, Oslo was originally bounded by the (now subterranean) Bjørvika, Alna and Hovin Rivers. It took another 250 years before it attained capital status during the reign of Håkon V (1299–1319) when the town had barely 3,000 inhabitants.

Following a great fire in 1624, which caused immense destruction, Christian IV decided to move the city settlements to where Akershus Festning (fortress) now stands, and the town became known as Christiania (Kvadraturen). What was the centre is now called **Christiania torv**, where in 1997 a statue of Christian IV's index finger was erected to commemorate the historic event.

With its strict grid plan, Christiania had little in common with medieval Oslo. The greatest change, however, has occurred over the past 150 years. In 1880, Christiania had 120,000 inhabitants; by 1910 the population had doubled. By popular consensus the town reverted to its original name of Oslo in 1925.

From 1945 to 1955, Oslo experienced a new period of growth, and surpassed the half-million mark in 1997. Today the city counts 658,000 inhabitants, and the greater Oslo area has about 1 million.

NORWAY'S NATIONAL JUMP

For the striking **Holmenkollen** ski jump and **Ski Museum** (Skimuseet; tel: 91 67 19 47; www.skiforeningen.no/en/holmenkollen; June–Aug 9am–8pm; Oct–Apr 10am–4pm; May and Sept 10am–5pm) take T-bane 1 to Holmenkollen. Although intrepid ski jumpers launch themselves from the top of the tower only in winter, this Oslo icon and Ski Museum merit a visit, whatever the season. It's the venue for the crowning event of the international ski-jump season on the second Sunday in March (see page 101).

Holmenkollen is a national symbol, as well as Norway's most popular attraction, bringing in more than a million visitors every year. The ultramodern jump, which was rebuilt for the Nordic World Championships in 2011, has an observation platform at the top of the tower (accessible by lift), which affords fantastic views of the city and beyond.

The Ski Museum, situated inside the jump itself, is a monument to "One Thousand Years of Skiing". Early skis and snowshoes are on display, as well as gear carried by such Norwegian explorers as Fridtjof Nansen, who crossed Greenland on skis. There is also a ski simulator, which recreates the thrill of a Holmenkollen jump. The same metro line to Holmenkollen (T-bane) ends at **Frognerseteren** (with a restaurant of the same name, famous for its home-made apple pie). The area is thickly forested and popular for walking and skiing. If you choose to go back to Holmenkollen on

⊙ Kids

Oslo's Reptile Park (Reptilpark, St Olavs gate 2; tel: 41 02 15 22; www.reptilpark.no; Apr–Aug daily 10am–6pm; rest of year Tue–Sun 10am–6pm) has over 50 different animal species, including snakes, iguanas, caimans, lizards, frogs and more. A good place to spend a rainy afternoon with the kids.

Holmenkollen ski jump.

foot, the walk is signposted and takes 15 to 20 minutes.

BYGONE DAYS ON BYGDØY

Oslo's city limits extend far down the flanks of the fjord. Just west of the harbour is the **Bygdøy peninsula**, where old Viking ships and the more recent explorer ships are kept, and where Norway's maritime past is commemorated (bus No. 30 or from May–early Oct boat from Rådhusbrygge 3 in front of City Hall).

Bygdøy is home to the **Viking Ship Museum** ㉗ (Vikingskipshuset; tel: 22 13 52 80; www.khm.uio.no; daily May–Sept 9am–6pm; Oct–Apr 10am–4pm), where the three best-preserved Viking ships found in Norway – the *Gokstad*, the *Oseberg* and the *Tune* – are displayed, together with other artefacts found at the sites. Each ship had been buried for over 1,000 years in royal burial mounds around the Oslofjord in accordance with Viking tradition.

The **Fram Museum** ㉘ (Frammuseet; tel: 23 28 29 50; www.frammuseum. no; daily June–Aug 9am–6pm, May and Sept 10am–6pm, Oct–Apr 10am–5pm), houses Fridtjof Nansen's polar sailing ship *Fram*. Launched in 1892, it was a remarkable vessel that sailed further north and further south than any other on three acclaimed polar expeditions.

Nearby, the **Kon-Tiki Museum** ㉙ (tel: 23 08 67 67; www.kon-tiki.no; daily June–Aug 9.30am–6pm; Mar–May and Sept–Oct 10am–5pm, Nov–Feb 10am–4pm), contains both the *Kon-Tiki* raft on which Thor Heyerdahl travelled from South America to Polynesia, and *Ra II*, an equally fragile-looking reed barque on which he sailed from Morocco to Barbados. There is also a collection of his Easter Island artefacts.

Almost opposite, the **Norwegian Maritime Museum** ㉚ (Norsk Sjøfartsmuseum; tel: 24 11 41 50; www. marmuseum.no; mid-May–mid-Sept daily 10am–5pm; mid-Sept–mid-May Tue–Sun 10am–4pm) presents the history of Norway as a seafaring and boatbuilding nation. It has a unique collection of vessels and maritime-themed paintings, countless models of ships, and a stunning panoramic film

Norwegian Maritime Museum.

that simulates a cruise along Norway's extraordinary coastline.

Also on Bygdøy is the **Norwegian Folk Museum** ③ (Norsk Folkemuseum; tel: 22 12 37 00; www.norskfolkemuseum.no/en; mid-May–mid-Sept daily 10am–6pm, rest of the year Mon–Fri 11am–3pm, Sat–Sun 11am–4pm). The Folk Museum, established in 1894, is an indoor/outdoor museum devoted largely to Norwegian rural culture. The collection of outdoor buildings, including a stave church from Hallingdal, gives a good idea of what old villages and agricultural settlements looked like. Other exhibits include Sami ethnography, a pharmacy museum, a delightfully quaint "colonial shop" (grocery) still in use, and a renovated Oslo building featuring apartments as they have evolved since the 1800s.

A 15-minute walk to the south brings you to **The Holocaust Center** ③ (Huk Aveny 56, bus No. 30; tel: 22 84 21 00; www.hlsenteret.no; mid-May–mid-Sept Mon–Fri 10am–6pm; rest of the year Mon–Fri 10am–4pm; Sat–Sun 11am–4pm). Housed in the mansion occupied by traitor Vidkun Quisling during World War II, the museum offers a permanent exhibition on the Holocaust and the tragic fate of Norwegian Jews, while serving as a centre for studies of the Holocaust and religious minorities.

EXPLORING THE OSLOFJORD

Most of the islands and peninsulas of Oslofjord are accessible by ferry from Aker Brygge quay or Vippetangen near Akershus Fortress. Many of the ferries are operated by the same public transit service that runs the bus and tram network, and the same tickets can be used. Mini-cruises of variable duration are also available.

At the tip of a hilly, wooded peninsula jutting from the east side of the fjord is **Nesoddtangen**. Local artists exhibit at **Hellviktangen Manor** ③ (May–Sept; weekends out of season), where a café serves coffee and waffles on Sundays. The house, which is surrounded by an apple orchard, gives directly onto the fjord.

At the Norwegian Folk Museum.

⊘ FERRY TO THE ISLANDS

Gressholmen is only 15 minutes by boat from Vippetangen (on the Akershus Fortress-side of the harbour, next to the DFDS and Stena terminals). One of the prettiest islands in the Oslofjord, it has a popular café and makes an ideal excursion for those who prefer a walk to a dip in the sea. As many as 160 species of birds have been spotted here. If it's a swim you fancy, **Hovedøya** is where many families head. It has one of the best sand beaches in the area, as well as fantastic views of the city. There are plenty of walking trails, too. Or you can venture further to **Langøyene**, the last island on the 94 ferry route, and the only one on which it is permitted to camp. There is a big grassy area and another fine sand beach here.

The island of Tjøme.

AROUND OSLO AND ITS FJORD

The charms of the Oslofjord may need some searching out, for this is Norway's industrial heartland, but it is rich in natural beauty and Viking history, and the surrounding area echoes to its pulse.

At dusk the islands of the fjord that leads to Oslo look like hunched prehistoric animals about to sink into a subaquatic sleep. In the colder months, the sky at sunset grows from lavender to purple while the islands turn slate-grey, then ominous and black. Summer sunsets bring twisted pink clouds underlit by a huge red sun that drops only briefly behind the fjord's western cliffs before rising again in the east.

Daytime along the 100km (60-mile) long fjord reveals a high concentration of industry down both the eastern and western sides. With Oslo at its head, the fjord is the capital's workhorse, its roads travelled by juggernauts with cargoes of timber and oil, its ports and waterways busy with yachts and barges. Outside its working ports, Oslofjord is a magnificent expanse of water, sprinkled liberally with islands, skerries, natural marinas and swimming beaches, and is a popular playground for Oslo residents.

THE LUNGS OF THE CITY

Akershus, **Vestfold** and **Østfold** are the three main counties to touch Oslofjord. Akershus county contains parts of the Oslo metropolitan area, the national Gardermoen Airport, plus a broad swathe of agricultural and forest land reaching to Sweden. At its northern limit lies the Mjøsa lake town

of Eidsvoll, where the Norwegian constitution was signed and the modern state born in 1814.

Østfold (east) and Vestfold (west) spread down from Oslo like a pair of lungs. Some of Scandinavia's oldest ruling families were found buried in Vestfold along with Viking ships loaded with booty, while Østfold is rich in ancient rock paintings and stone circles. Both counties contain towns of major historic significance: Fredrikstad and Halden in Østfold, two magnificent fortress towns, and Tønsberg

Main Attractions
Oslomarka
Drøbak
Hvaler Archipelago
Fredriksten Fort, Halden
Åsgårdstrand

Map on page 156

Hiking in Oslomarka.

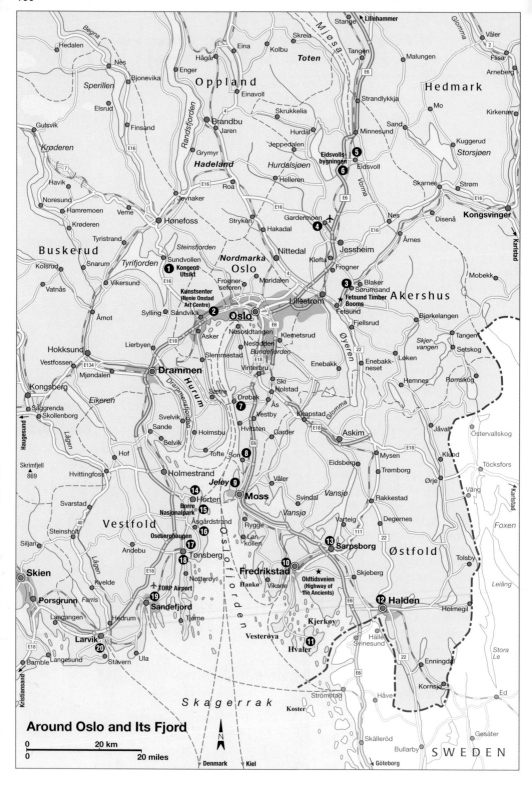

Around Oslo and Its Fjord

0   20 km
0   20 miles

N

Denmark   Kiel

in Vestfold, the oldest extant Scandinavian city, founded in 872. Remains of **Kaupang**, the oldest Nordic town yet discovered, were found a couple of kilometres from Tønsberg and are now in Oslo's Historical Museum (Kulturhistorisk Museet, see page 146). Corroboration of its early existence appeared in a world history by England's 9th-century monarch King Alfred the Great. All are accessible within a couple of hours from Oslo.

Despite its rich history and good travel links, the Oslofjord area doesn't get as many tourists as western Norway; the scenery isn't as dramatic. There are, however, more habitable islands than in any other fjord, many with sports centres and hotels offering everything from tennis to windsurfing and swimming. Inland, the sloping countryside is punctuated by forests, orchards and tilled fields and is ideal cycling country.

A TRAIL THROUGH AKERSHUS

There are fantastic walks in **Oslomarka** (the forests surrounding Oslo) accessible by bus, train or tram. By car you can explore further. If you're a fan of Norwegian rural architecture you will have your fill in outer Akershus. Take route E16 in a westerly direction towards Tyrifjorden and Sundvollen into the **Krokkleiva** district. The paths cross wooded hills 400–500 metres (1,300–1,600ft) high. The **King's View** ❶ (Kongens Utsikt) gives panoramic views across Steinsfjord and Tyrifjord.

Afterwards, rejoin the E16 northbound, direction Hønefoss. Leave it before Hønefoss, direction Jevnaker. There you can visit **Hadeland Glass Works** (Hadeland Glassverk; www.hadeland-glassverk.no; daily, all year) and the countryside of Hadeland. South of Highway 35 is a wilderness of pine marshland, secluded lakes, oak forests and stream-bordered fields. Road 4 south returns you to Oslo and the junction with the E6; northbound

it leads to Gjøvik on the western side of Lake Mjøsa.

The **Henie Onstad Art Centre** ❷ (Kunstsenter; tel: 67 80 48 80; http://henieonstadsanatorium.no; Tue–Sun 11am–5pm) at Høvikodden, about 10km (6 miles) west of Oslo on a headland jutting into the Oslofjord, contains over 4,000 20th-century works. Housed in a striking neo-expressionist building, and surrounded by a vast sculpture park, it is one of Norway's foremost contemporary art galleries, founded in 1968 by figure-skater and actress Sonja Henie and her husband.

AROUND EIDSVOLL

If you go east from the junction of Road 4 and the E6 along Road 170 you come to the small village of **Fetsund**, just past Lillestrøm, and the **Fetsund Timber Booms** (Fetsund Lenser; tel: 63 88 75 50; http://mia.no/fetsundlenser; exhibitions June–Aug Tue–Sun 11am–4pm; May and Sept Sat–Sun 11am–4pm; grounds free), a timber-floating centre celebrating the industrial activity on the banks of the Glomma River.

Shopping at Østfold.

The museum includes a nature trail, a nature centre (weekends only, all year) and boat trips to the North Øyeren Nature Reserve, a haven for migratory birds.

Heading northeast, a road to the left will bring you to **Sørumsand ❸**, where there is a narrow-gauge "Tertitten" railway (tel: 66 86 81 50; http://mia.no/tertitten; June–Sept departures Sun at 11am, 12.15pm, 1.30pm and 14.45pm). From here, Road 171 will bring you back to the E6. Travelling north you come to Jessheim near **Gardermoen ❹** and **Rakni's Mound** (Raknehaugen; all year), a 77-metre (253ft) diameter barrow, centre of an ancient kingdom.

Continuing in a northerly direction, at the southern end of Lake Mjøsa is **Eidsvoll ❺**, about 80km (50 miles) from Oslo. Eidsvoll is a lake town of old wooden houses and churches. Nearby, on the other side of the E6 at Eidsvoll Verk, is a national landmark: **Eidsvoll Memorial Building ❻** (Eidsvollsbygningen; tel: 63 92 22 10; www.eidsvoll1814.no; May–Aug daily 10am–5pm; Sept–Apr Tue–Fri 10am–3pm, Sat–Sun 11am–4pm), a mini-museum to the Norwegian constitution which includes the room where the document was signed. The nearby **Eidsvoll Museum** (Eidsvoll Bygdetun; tel: 63 93 66 34; http://mia.no/eidsvoll; June–Aug Tue–Sun noon–4pm) consists of a collection of 29 farm buildings (Eidsvoll Municipal Museum) and a World War II museum (The Occupation Museum), all set in beautiful countryside. Then tour Lake Mjøsa on the old paddle steamer *Skibladner* (tel: 61 14 40 80; www.skibladner.no; late June–mid-Aug Tue–Sun). The round trip takes 12 hours, with the halfway point at Lillehammer (see page 168).

FJORDSIDE DRØBAK

Heading south out of Oslo on the east side of the fjord, the quiet way to Fredrikstad is via the old **Mossveien**, which hugs the fjord as near as topography allows. Having taken the E6 or E18 out of the city, turn right off the main road at Vinterbru and head for the tip of Bundefjord. Take the road signposted

Halden lighthouse.

⊘ TREKKING IN OSLOMARKA

Oslo is surrounded by hills and forests known as *marka*. Larch, birch, pine, aspen and several deciduous species dominate; the colour contrast in autumn is worth a special trip. The Norwegian Trekking Association, Den Norske Turistforening (Youngstorget 1, Oslo; tel: 40 00 18 68; www.dnt.no; weekdays only) has maps of trails in these areas. Most walking trails double as cross-country skiing trails in winter, and many are floodlit. Access to the trails from the centre is easy via public transport. For **Grorud** and the **Lillomarka** area to the northeast, take either T-bane 5 or bus No. 30 from Jernbanetorget. Trails begin just west of the Grorud T-bane. Due north is **Grefsen**, along a suburban train line (information from Ruter at Oslo Sentralstasjon). Alternatively, take tram 11 and 12 (Grefsen/Kjelsås), or the bus to Grefsenkollen. **Maridalsvannet** is parkland with a lake fed by clear-water brooks. **Sognsvann**, the lake west of Maridalsvannet, is at the end of T-bane 5. The most heavily used trails start from Sognsvann and **Frognerseteren**.

For walks in the **Holmenkollen** area and the northwest part of Nordmarka, take T-bane 1 to Frognerseteren (not to be confused with Frognerparken) until the end of the line. In winter, you can rent a sled (*akebrett*) to hurtle down a 3km (2-mile) trail (the Corkscrew). All trails are signposted.

to Nesoddtangen and you will come across a signpost to **Drøbak** ❼.

The village of Drøbak was once a fishermen's settlement. Fishing vessels still arrive here and sell fresh prawns and fish on the quayside. Places of interest include the **Heritage Museum** (Follo Museum; tel: 64 93 66 36; Tue–Fri 10am–3pm, in summer also Sun noon–4pm), the small **Aquarium** (Akvarium; tel: 95 90 39 27; daily Apr–Aug 10am–6.30pm; Sept–Mar 10am–4pm) and **Oscarsborg Fortress** (Oscarsborg Festning; tel: 81 55 19 00; daily 7am–10.50pm; tours in summer) out in the fjord from where gunfire sunk the German cruiser *Blücher* in 1940 (guided boat trips from Drøbak's harbour).

Another point of pride is the cross-timbered **Drøbak Church** (Kirke) from 1776 (all year). The church has an elaborately carved model of a ship, a common piece of church decoration in seafaring towns. Rococo touches include wooden busts of Moses and Aaron. Gospel and jazz concerts are held here in summer. The road out

of Drøbak takes off just before the ferry terminal, from where small car ferries run every half-hour or so to the Hurum peninsula. The road runs through fertile farmland and forest, passing Hvitsten and continuing to **Son** ❽ (pronounced *soon*), a fetching artists' village hugging the edge of a sheltered sound. Son is a popular summer resort for boating enthusiasts. The surrounding countryside and shoreline here provided inspiration for the likes of Theodore Kittelsen and Edvard Munch.

The **Son Coastal Centre** (Son Kyst-kultursenter; tel: 40 02 09 30; mid-May–mid-Sept Tue–Sun noon–4pm) explains how this one-time Dutch freeport (the original name was Zoon) has thrived on timber, ice and fishing. The unusual elevated building at the edge of the marina is the last remaining fishing-net-drying structure in the Oslofjord.

SOUTH TO ØSTFOLD

Østfold is a long funnel through which Norwegians drive on their way to

> ⊙ **Kids**
>
> A few kilometres northeast of Drøbak is Tusenfryd, Norway's largest amusement park attracting almost half a million visitors a year. Get goose pimples at Nightmare, set in a haunted castle, where you are armed with a "revolver" to counter the fearsome tale which unfolds before your eyes.

Queen Sonja and King Harald at the celebration of the Constitutional Bicentenary in Eidsvoll.

cheaper shopping in Sweden. Despite its industrial towns such as Halden, Sarpsborg and Moss, Østfold is a thriving centre for outdoor pursuits: canoeing and cycling are popular, and the area is dotted with hiking and skiing centres. There are also golf courses, and the Mysen racetrack. The fjord's greatest draw card is **Galleri F15** (Tue–Sun 11am–5pm) **Jeløy** , on the Jeløy peninsula, with its fjord-side trails and stupendous lawns. Temporary exhibitions are held within this light-filled house. Its cafeteria is a favourite coffee pit stop. Down the coast is the royal enclave of **Hankø**, Norway's regatta centre. The summer home of Princess Martha Louise's grandfather is located here.

COBBLED FREDRIKSTAD

The **Old Town** (Gamlebyen) in **Fredrikstad** ⑩ is Scandinavia's best-preserved fortress town, dating from 1567. The cobbled streets of the Old Town were laid by prisoners; wooden stocks still face the former prison on the main square. Here you'll also find the former military barracks, now a school

(Gamlebyen was a garrison town until as recently as 2002), and a statue of Frederick II, the Danish king who founded the town. Other buildings of interest include the drawbridge, at the entrance to the town, the former arsenal (which today houses the tourist office and the museum) and the Provianthus, the Old Town's oldest building, whose walls are 4 metres (13ft) thick in places. From the leafy ramparts there is a good view over the Glomma River, and the moat that surrounds the fortress. Some of the 200 cannons that once defended the town are still in place. After browsing around an art gallery or two and exploring a few small boutiques, enjoy a cup of coffee or lunch in one of several little cafés.

The **Highway of the Ancients** (Oldtidsveien), along Rv110 between Fredrikstad and Skjeberg, is dotted with 3,000- to 4,000-year-old rock paintings (*helleristninger*) and burial sites such as the stone circles at **Hunn**.

HVALER MARINE HAVEN

Another great drive is the road to the island community of **Hvaler** ⑪, which

Oscarsborg Fortress.

crosses the water at some points. It ends at the charming village of Sjærhalden on **Kirkeøy**, where you'll find one of Norway's oldest stone churches, **Hvaler Kirke**, dating back to the Middle Ages. The population of Hvaler increases almost ten-fold in the summer, going from 3,700 permanent inhabitants to 30,000 between July and August. The outer part of the archipelago became Europe's first marine national park, jointly with its counterpart on the Swedish side of the border, when it opened in 2009.

Halden ⓬, situated south of Skjeberg and close by the Swedish border, is dominated by **Fredriksten Fort** (Festning; tel: 69 19 37 00; open access to fort; free; museum and tours mid–May–Aug daily 10am–5pm), a largely intact ruin with many of its buildings serving as small themed museums, including a historic pharmacy (1870), bakery and brewery. The streets below were laid out along the cannons' blast lines to give the fortress's defenders freedom to fire. Local residents famously torched

their town to drive out the Swedes in 1716, a heroic feat commemorated in the Norwegian national anthem. The views from the top of the fortress are stunning, and open-air concerts often take place here in summer. Between June and mid-August a passenger boat makes regular trips along the Halden Canal (one of only two inland waterway systems in Norway), navigating through the massive Brekke locks, the highest in Scandinavia, which rise to 26 metres (85ft).

Throughout Østfold, St Olav's Day (29 July) is celebrated with a great show of folk costumes, music and dance. One of the best displays is at the **Borgarsyssel Museum** (tel: 69 11 56 50; mid-June to mid-Aug daily noon–5pm, rest of the year shorter hours) in **Sarpsborg** ⓭, a town founded by St Olav himself in 1016.

ACROSS TO VESTFOLD

The Moss–Horten car ferry connects Østfold and Vestfold in less than an hour. There is much shared history between Østfold and Vestfold. It was

⊙ Where

Guidebooks on the *Highway of the Ancients*, the ancient sites along Rv110, are available at the tourist office at Kirkegaten 31B in Gamle Fredrikstad and in many local museums and bookshops.

Fredriksten Fort outbuilding.

⊘ Tip

If you're booked on a plane landing at Torp Airport, near Sandefjord, why not sample fjord life at Åsgårdstrand? Once home to Munch, the little town comes alive in summer with a festival, dance and music concerts, barbecues (the Wiener schnitzel barbecue is a favourite), and is a centre for boat trips.

the fast action of troops on both sides of the fjord that led to the sinking of the *Blücher*, scuppering Hitler's plans for an easy invasion.

The Norwegian **Naval Museum** (Marinemuseet; tel: 33 03 33 97; May–Sept daily noon–4pm; Oct–Apr Sun noon–4pm; free) at **Horten** ⓮ illustrates this event and many others in displays, including a full-size submarine that you can explore. There are also museums of photography and veteran cars in Horten (both all year).

Heading southwards, tranquil **Løvøy** island has a sombre medieval stone church. This was Viking country, and within **Borre National Park** ⓯ (Nasjonalpark), on the way to Tønsberg, are enormous turf-covered mounds concealing the graves of Viking kings. Borre also has an extensive network of trails, and the largest collection of Iron Age burial sites in Scandinavia.

MUNCH'S RETREAT

Keeping to the coastline along Road 311, you arrive at **Åsgårdstrand** ⓰, site of **Edvard Munch's House** (Munchs

Hus; tel: 48 22 92 98; www.munchshus.no; June–Aug Tue–Sun 11am–5pm; May and Sept Sat–Sun 11am–4pm), where the artist lived when he returned to Norway from abroad. Munch painted *Three Girls on a Bridge* here. Summer activities in Åsgårdstrand include a festival and boat trips, barbecues, and the Åsgårdstrand Festival. For more solitary pleasures, you can cycle, swim in the fjord, fish in Borre's lake, or watch the fishermen come in each afternoon with their catch.

VIKING BURIALS

Between Åsgårdstrand and Tønsberg is **Oseberg Burial Mound** ⓱ (Oseberghaugen; all year), the most important Viking site yet discovered. Oslo's Viking Ship Museum (Vikingskipshuset, see page 152) contains the finds, including the 20-metre (65ft) arch-ended wooden ship. Nowadays, only the mound itself, near Slagen church, remains.

Just to the south is history-rich **Tønsberg** ⓲, established in the 9th century and said to be Norway's oldest settlement. On the 65-metre (200ft)

Åsgårdstrand out of season.

high **Slottsfjellet** are the fortress remains and tower. The main street, Storgata, is flanked by Viking graves. These were excavated and incorporated, under glass, into the ground floor of the new library. Across the street are the walls of one of only two medieval round churches in Scandinavia. The most renowned king to hold court in Tønsberg was Håkon Håkonson IV (1240–63). The ruins of his court can be seen on Nordbyen.

To the south of Tønsberg, along the eastern side of the fjord, the islands of **Nøtterøy** and **Tjøme**, and the skerries, are popular summer hangouts. **Verdens Ende** (World's End) is, naturally, at the end – but for a few boulders – of the chain. The old lighthouse is an appealing simple stone structure.

On the other side of Tønsbergfjord lies **Sandefjord ⑲**, once the whaling capital of the world. The sea still dominates life here, and one of the main industries is marine paint production. The town centre is compact, and the venerable Kong Carl Hotel is one of its more handsome buildings. Near Badeparken are the former spa and the old town, along Thaulowsgate. Preståsen is the hilly park above it. Torp Airport is nearby.

Just outside Sandefjord is the **Gokstad Burial Site** (Gokstadhaugen; all year; free), in which the Gokstad ship, now in Oslo's Viking Ship Museum, was discovered in 1880. Beyond, the **Vesterøy** peninsula, a peaceful place for walking, cycling and boating. The film star Liv Ullmann's summer house is in the vicinity.

LARVIK WATERFRONT

Larvik ⑳ was home to two legendary boat-lovers: Thor Heyerdahl, and Scotsman Colin Archer, designer of the polar ship *Fram*. Archer's first house was at Tollerodden, on the fjord. At Larvik's back is the huge Lake Farris. **Mølland** beach with its sea-rounded pebbles, is one of many fine waterside spots around Larvik. Another is **Nevlunghavn**, an exquisite fishing cove tucked around the bay west of Stavern.

Inner Vestfold's rivers run with salmon and trout. **Brufoss** is a favourite anglers' haunt (accommodation and day licences available; tel: 33 12 99 20). In winter, this is a popular downhill ski district. In outer and inner Vestfold you will find a number of ceramic works which offer tours and, in common with Østfold, every little hamlet seems to have an art gallery.

FJORD PEOPLE'S PRIDE

People who live around Oslofjord may be the first to point out the area's shortcomings – smallish mountains, the stink of some pulp and paper plants – then the superlatives begin to flow. The birthplaces of the most intrepid explorers are here, as are the best sailing races, the warmest summers, the finest archaeological discoveries, the best drinking water, summer resorts... the hyperbole can go on...

Paradise beach Oslofjord.

THE HEART OF NORWAY

Away from Mjøsa and its lakeside towns, central
Norway extends east into the wilds around the old
copper-mining town of Rorøs, and north towards the
quintessentially Norwegian Dovre Mountains.

Norway's heartland is centred on the counties of Oppland and Hedmark. It has three main features: Lake Mjøsa, the country's largest lake; the great massif of Dovrefjell to the north; and the long, slanting valleys of Gudbrandsdalen and Østerdalen.

In this widest part of Norway, these great valleys lie straight and narrow from southeast to northwest, their rivers like veins cutting between the mountain ranges. Alongside the rivers are fertile farms, which climb up the valley sides to forests. Above the treeline stretch bare slopes of tussocky grass and rocks, a playground for skiers in winter and walkers, once the snows have melted away.

Despite Norway's extensive network of rural buses, it can be difficult to reach some of the more remote corners; but this region makes wonderful country for touring by car. Each new vista is more magnificent than the last as the road climbs, dips and circles. For some of the higher plateaux, it can be simpler and quicker to push further into the wilderness by local trains, which stop at small stations along the main line between Oslo and Trondheim – a route that is almost as spectacular as the famous Oslo–Bergen line in the west.

MJØSA AND MJØSABYEN

Lake Mjøsa ❶ also lies southeast to northwest some 160km (100 miles)

north of Oslo. One of the best ways to enjoy the lake and its surroundings is a trip on the old paddle steamer SS *Skibladner* (tel: 61 14 40 80; www.skibladner. no; late June–mid-Aug Tue–Sun). Built in 1856 as a continuation of Norway's first railway line between Oslo and Eidsvoll, she now plies the lake carrying tourists and is based in Gjøvik on the west side.

Around Mjøsa lies some of the most fertile agricultural land in Norway, and throughout the gently undulating countryside are large farms, encircled by thickly forested hills. Where Lake

⊙ Main Attractions
Lake Mjøsa
Lillehammer
Trysil
Rondane NP
Røros

Map on page 166

Lake Mjøsa.

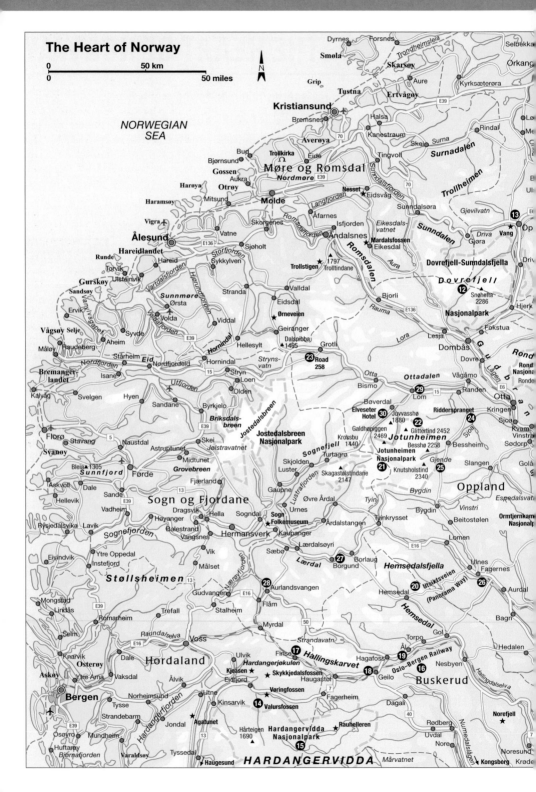

The Heart of Norway

0   50 km

0   50 miles

N

NORWEGIAN
SEA

Mjøsa is at its widest, some 17km (10 miles) across, is the attractive island of **Helgøya**. At its southern tip, the island has a burial mound, part of the historic Hovinsholm, a royal estate from Viking times until 1723.

Three main towns lie along the lake: Hamar and Lillehammer are on the eastern shore and Gjøvik on the west. A bridge across the lake about halfway between Hamar and Lillehammer links the towns into a larger unit called **Mjøsabyen.**

Hamar ❷ was the centre of Roman Catholicism in Norway in the Middle Ages and the seat of the bishop. It enjoyed great prosperity and had an impressive cathedral. The town's downfall came in 1537 when the Danes carried off the bishop, then 30 years later when the Swedes burned Hamar to the ground. Now the cathedral ruins at **Cathedral Point** (Domkirkeodden) are part of the **Hedmark Museum** (Hedmarksmuseet; tel: 62 54 27 00; www.hedmarksmuseet.no; mid-June–mid-Aug daily 10am–5pm, shorter hours rest of the year). They are enclosed in a superb glass structure designed by renowned Norwegian architect Sverre Fehn. There is also an **Emigration Museum** in Hamar (tel: 62 57 48 50; mid-June–mid-Aug Tue–Sat 10am–4pm, Sun noon–4pm, rest of the year Tue–Sat 9am–3pm) and the **Kirsten Flagstad Museum** (Kirsten Flagstadmuseet; tel: 62 53 32 77; mid-May–Aug Tue–Sun 11am–5pm, Sept–Oct Tue–Fri noon–3pm), the childhood home of opera star Kirsten Flagstad, who made her debut at New York's Metropolitan Opera in 1935.

Not until the 19th century and the coming of the railway did Hamar regain a measure of importance, this time as a railway junction with a locomotive-building works. The works have gone, but the **Norwegian Railway Museum** (Norsk Jernbanemuseet; tel: 62 51 31 60; www.norsk-jernbanemuseum.no; July–Aug daily 10am–5pm; June daily 11am–3pm, Sun until 4pm, Jan–May and Sept–Dec Tue–Sat 11am–3pm, Sun until 4pm), established in 1896, serves as a reminder. A highlight of this collection is the early steam engine *Caroline*, built by George Stephenson in 1861. There are regular excursions on a narrow-gauge railway.

The landmark Olympic **skating arena** (all year), in the style of a Viking ship, was built for the 1994 Winter Olympics, which were held in and around the Mjøsabyen towns. Seven of Norway's eight distilleries are located in the region. About 18km (11 miles) east of Hamar towards Elverum is the **Løten Brewery** (Brænderi; tel: 90 18 99 05; guided tours), which is famous for Løten aquavit. Løten is also the birthplace of artist Edvard Munch.

LILLEHAMMER WINTER SPORTS

The largest of the three Mjøsabyen towns is **Lillehammer ❸**, situated at the northern end of the lake where it narrows to become the Lågen River and crosses Gudbrandsdalen. Lillehammer is the main town in Gudbrandsdalen and was the site of the 1994 Winter Olympics. A downhill ski area on nearby **Hafjell** and 500km (300 miles) of cross-country skiing tracks were built for the occasion. Other facilities included an ice-hockey rink at Gjøvik, built inside a mountain,

Skier at Lillehammer.

Scandinavia's only artificially frozen bobsleigh and luge track (near Hunderfossen) and a ski-jumping arena over Lillehammer itself, all of which are still in use.

OPEN-AIR MAIHAUGEN

For summer visitors, the biggest attraction is Norway's remarkable open-air museum, **Maihaugen** (tel: 61 28 89 00; www.maihaugen.no; June–Aug daily 10am–5pm; Sept–May Tue–Sun 11am–4pm; guided tours throughout the day in summer, booking required at other times). Some 120 buildings, including a stave church and two farms, have been brought in to the 40-hectare (100-acre) site from all over Gudbrandsdalen. The museum was the life work of Anders Sandvig. A dentist by profession, he came to Lillehammer in 1885 suffering from tuberculosis and with a life expectancy of a mere two years. Could it have been his passion for the museum he founded in 1887 that kept him going? Whether or not, Sandvig lived for another 65 years and died in 1950. In addition to the buildings, which range from the medieval to the 19th century, Maihaugen has some 30,000 artefacts, the majority collected by Sandvig. In summer, there are regular demonstrations of rural skills and crafts.

ARTISTIC LIGHT

The quality of light in Lillehammer and its surroundings has attracted many artists to the area over the years. As a result, the town has an impressive art gallery, the **Lillehammer Art Museum** (Kunstmuseum; tel: 61 05 44 60; www.lillehammerartmuseum.com; daily 11am–5pm), which includes works by J.C. Dahl, Hans Gude, Adolph Tidemand, Christian Krohg, and Norway's most famous artist, Edvard Munch.

One of Lillehammer's most revered names is Danish-born Sigrid Undset, winner of the 1928 Nobel Prize for Literature, who took up residence in the town in 1919. "Bjerkebæk", **Sigrid Undset's home** (Sigrid Undsets hjem; tel: 61 25 94 00; late May–Aug daily 10am–5pm, Sept Sat–Sun 10am–5pm), was created from two wooden farmhouses which had been moved from Gudbrandsdalen. Her statue stands on Lillehammer's main shopping street.

Aulestad ❹ (tel: 61 22 41 10; late May–Aug daily 10am–5pm, Sept Sat–Sun 11am–4pm), about 11km (7 miles) northwest from Lillehammer, is the home of another notable Norwegian author and playwright, Bjørnstjerne Bjørnson (1832–1910; see page 117), one of the writers who inspired the nationalist movement in the 19th century. He wrote Norway's national anthem, *Ja, vi elsker dette landet (Yes, we love this land of ours)*, in 1870, promoted performances of Norwegian plays in preference to Danish works and won a Nobel Prize for Literature in 1903. His house is just as it was when he died.

Lillehammer also has a couple of treats for younger visitors. On the outskirts of the town is **Lilleputthammer** (www.lilleputthammer.no; July daily 9am–8pm, mid-June to end-June and Aug–Sept times vary so check online), with its quarter-scale version of Storgata, Lillehammer's main street, as it was in 1930. As you walk down the street, peer in the windows of the shops, some of which are open to the public. North of Lilllehammer, the popular **Hunderfossen Family Park** ❺ (Familiepark; tel: 61 27 55 30; www.hunderfossen.no; late June to mid-Aug daily 10am–6pm) features – wait for it – the world's largest fibreglass troll.

Nearby is the **Lillehammer Olympic bobsleigh and luge track**, built for the 1994 Winter Olympics, which offers dry runs for tourists during the summer (tel: 61 05 42 00; times vary).

ØSTERDALEN

To the east of Lake Mjøsa lies **Østerdalen**, which cuts through the mountains running roughly parallel with Gudbrandsdalen. In places the valley is narrow, with seemingly endless forests on either side, broken

Sledging at Lillehammer.

RØROS AND THE OLD COPPER COUNTRY

The copper-producing town of Røros, active until 1972, is now preserved in its entirety as a Unesco World Heritage Site.

Røros was the archetypal company town, with life and society revolving around the mining of copper. Isolated, exposed, nearly 600 metres (2,000ft) above sea level and surrounded by mountains and enduring winter cold, its existence was entirely due to the discovery of copper, which was first mined here over 300 years ago and was worked until 1972. The town was hardly beautiful, and slag heaps and the smelter provided the backdrop to the miners' houses. These were usually small and overcrowded, but many workers also possessed a small patch of land and one or two animals as a source of food.

Further away from smelter and slag lived those higher up the company pecking order – in the executive area. Røros escaped the fires which so often laid waste to the wooden buildings of many other Norwegian towns. Today, it has a unique townscape, and almost the entire older part of the town is preserved by law. Doors, windows and colour schemes all have to conform, buildings must be lived in, and there is strict control of advertising signs and notices. As a result, Røros is in a time warp, retaining much of

Røros' characteristic turf roofs are now preserved.

its mining-town atmosphere, and is on the Unesco World Heritage list (www.worldheritageroros.no).

The most noticeable feature in Røros is the stone church (Bergstadens Ziir; tel: 72 41 00 50; late June–mid-Aug Mon–Sat 10am–4pm, Sun 12.30–2.30pm, early June and mid-Aug–mid-Sept Mon–Sat 11am–1pm, rest of year Sat only 11am–1pm) – "the pride of the mining town" – which was dedicated in 1784 and replaced a wooden church built in 1650. The interior reflects the mining society, with paintings of clergymen and mining officials. Prayers were said every Sunday for the company and its directors.

The smelting works (smelthytta; tel: 72 40 61 70; www.rorosmuseet.no; all year; guided tours in English mid-June to mid-Aug daily 11am) were the heart of the copper-mining company and the focal point of the town. Its bell was rung at the start and end of each shift and is still in place today. The smelter has been restored as a museum: the exterior resembles the building as it was in 1889, but the interior is now given over to a series of exhibitions depicting life in the town, mining techniques in Europe in the 18th and 19th centuries, cultural features of southern Lapp society and aspects of Røros society and its environs. Small-scale models help to explain the production process.

One of the most interesting elements in the museum is the series of working models to one-tenth scale which demonstrate the arduous methods called for when the only power available was water, horses and human muscle. In the past it was usual to make such scale models to see if a new technique or piece of equipment would work, so today's replicas are following an old tradition.

Thirteen kilometres (8 miles) from Røros is the Olav Mine (Olavsgruva; tel: 72 40 61 70; mid-June to mid-Aug daily 10am–5pm, rest of year Sat only tour 3pm), which was opened as a mining museum in 1979. The guided tour takes visitors 50 metres (165ft) below ground. Until 1880, when dynamite was introduced, the miners used the heat from wood fires stacked against the rock face to crack the rock.

Back on the surface, the bare, bleak scenery surrounding the mine, even in the summer sun, somehow befits the wretched existence of those early miners.

occasionally by patches of farmland. The valley starts at **Elverum** ⑥ in the south and continues northwards for 250km (150 miles), becoming broader and more open further north. Throughout its length flows Norway's longest river, the **Glomma**, accompanied for much of its length by both the railway and the E3.

Elverum is one of the essential crossroads of Norway with routes splaying out to Hamar to the west, Kongsvinger to the south and Trysil to the northeast. It has the well-preserved **Terningen bastion**, built in 1673. Climb to the top of the water tower for a great view. The town's most famous episode is commemorated in a monument to the fierce battle fought in April 1940 which delayed the German Army for long enough to allow the king and members of the government to escape further north, then sail to Britain to continue the fight in exile.

Elverum has two major museums. The **Glomdal Museum** (tel: 62 41 91 00; mid-June–Aug daily 10am–5pm; rest of the year daily 10am–4pm), opened in 1911 on a large natural site, has 88 traditional rural buildings, brought in from Østerdalen and Solør. The indoor exhibition is divided into three sections – the farming year; transport and communication; and handwork and crafts – and shows what life was like in Østerdalen from 1870 to 1900. There is also a collection from the Neolithic age and Viking era, as well as an open-air theatre.

The **Norwegian Forestry Museum** (Norsk Skogmuseum; tel: 62 40 90 00; late June–mid-Aug daily 10am–5pm; rest of the year daily 10am–4pm) illustrates forestry, hunting and fishing. The main building also has exhibits related to geology and wildlife, and children usually head for the aquarium. The outdoor collection is mainly situated on the small island of Prestøya in the middle of the River Glomma.

SKIING AND MORE AT TRYSIL

To the northeast, **Trysil** ❼, in Hedmark near the Swedish border, is Norway's largest ski resort. In summer, the town is a centre for paragliding, rafting, canoe tours and mountain tours with pack dogs to carry your luggage.

North from Elverum along the E3 there are few places of any size or importance, but the whole of this area is well off the tourist track and ideal for exploration.

At **Koppang**, about halfway along the length of Østerdalen, you can take an alternative route north, along Road 30 past the long thin Storsjøen (lake), to rejoin the E3 at **Tynset**. Northwest of Tynset you come to Kvikne and near it the rectory at Bjørgan, the birthplace of Bjørnstjerne Bjørnson.

Alternatively, Road 219 turns west at **Atna**, some 30km (20 miles) north of Koppang, for a drive into the foothills of the wild and mountainous region of **Rondane**, where the peaks rise to 1,800 metres (6,000ft) high. At Enden, the road meets Road 27, which has taken the parallel route north

⊘ Tip

To learn more about the history of the Olympic Games, visit the Norwegian Olympic Museum in Håkons Hall, Lillehammer (Norges Olympiske Museum; tel: 61 05 76 50; https://ol. museum.no; June–Aug daily 10am–5pm; Sept–May Thu–Sun 11am–4pm).

Heading through the Østerdalen valley.

Peer Gynt, as depicted by P.N. Arboe.

from Ringebu. Called the **Rondevegen** N, this road climbs steeply from Gudbrandsdalen and offers superb views of the Rondane Mountains. It is well worth continuing from Enden to Folldal, past the great peaks that include Rondeslottet at 2,178 metres (7,144ft), with the **Rondane National Park** to the west. Established in 1962, this was Norway's first national park and offers a wide range of trails of varying difficulty.

Road 27 ascends to nearly 915 metres (3,000ft) before reaching **Folldal**, one of the highest permanently inhabited communities in Norway. The community's history began when copper was discovered hereabouts in the 18th century. Although the mine is no longer worked, the controlling company is still based here to serve a new mine at Hjerkinn about 30km (20 miles) away. The buildings of the former **Folldal Mine** (Folldal Gruver; tel: 62 49 05 05; all year) are now a museum, with train rides into the mine (mid-June–Aug daily 11am–6pm).

⊘ PEER GYNT COUNTRY

The 19th-century Norwegian folklorist Peter Abjørnsen walked the country gathering material for a book of local folk tales, *Norske Folkeeventyr*, which he published with his friend Bishop Jørgen Moe in 1844. One of Abjørnsen's characters was Peer (Per) Gynt, a legendary marksman, ski-runner and braggart, who was often economical with the truth yet had his gallant side, rescuing hapless dairymaids from trolls and taking on the Bøyg, a gigantic, worm-shaped troll. The character inspired the dramatist Henrik Ibsen – who believed that the legend was based upon fact, however distorted – to write the play *Peer Gynt* (1867) and Edvard Grieg to compose his *Peer Gynt* Suite No. 1 (1888). Today, the play is performed with Greig's music every August in the outdoor amphitheatre at **Gålåvatnet**, southwest of Vinstra. One of the so-called Gynt cottages serves as the tourist information office in Vinstra (tel: 61 29 53 76).

The character has also inspired the creation of a mountain route, the **Peer Gyntvegen**. Negotiable only in summer, it winds through Gudbrandsdalen. The 60km (37-mile) round trip is accessible from Vinstra, Harpefoss and Hundrop on the E6. Passing through Gålå, it reaches an altitude of over 900 metres (3,000ft) and presents a panorama of mountains and lakes – stark but appealing.

ALONG THE COPPER ROAD

From Folldal, if you head east you return to the Glomma River valley and the E3 at Alvdal. Along the way abandoned mine works indicate how important minerals were and, to some extent, still are to this area. North of Alvdal, rail, road and river head northeast, through Tolga and Os – which is the start of the **Kopperveien** (Copper Road) – before coming to the former copper-mining town of **Røros** N, a World Heritage Site east along Road 31.

Røros is also a junction for three roads that lead through an eastern wilderness with little habitation: Road 31 leads to the Swedish frontier, 45km (30 miles) to the east, past several lakes, some of them artificially dammed, that were dug to provide water for mining operations; Road 30 leads north to Ålen, which has a small open-air museum, then through the fast-flowing gorge of the Gaula River until the valley broadens out near Støren; the third road runs southwest to Femund Lake, Norway's third-largest, which offers good fishing.

GUDBRANDSDALEN

After Østerdalen, **Gudbrandsdalen** is the second-longest valley in Norway. The Lågen River runs its full length and the valley stretches for 140km (90 miles) northwest from Lillehammer to Dombås, the starting point for climbing trips into the Dovre rock formation. This huge plateau is popular with walkers, not least because it is framed by impressive peaks such as the **Snøhetta** (2,286 metres/7,498ft).

Perhaps because it was surrounded by mountains and relatively cut off from the wider world, the Gudbrandsdal valley has a long tradition of folk dancing and folk music. It is also famous for its woodcarving and rose painting, and you can find good craftwork to take home. North of Lillehammer at **Ringebu** N, you can visit the 13th-century **Ringebu stave church** (Stavkirke; late May–Aug). Built of tall upright timbers, it has a statue of St Lawrence, crucifixes and a baptismal font, all dating from medieval times.

VINSTRA FOLKTALES

Vinstra ⑪ is at the heart of what is known as "Peer Gynt country" after the legendary figure first written about by Peter Asbjørnsen in the 19th century, and then made famous by both Ibsen and Grieg. Scottish visitors may also want to stop at **Kringen** to see the memorial to a battle of 1612, when an army of Scottish mercenaries was defeated by local farmers. Despite – or perhaps because of – their defeat, the Scots (said to be Sinclairs) are recalled in the checked cloth used in one of the local costumes, which looks remarkably like Sinclair tartan.

DOVREFJELL

Travelling north from Vinstra, the E6 passes through Otta (where Road 15 heads west to the western fjords) on its way to Dombås. Here it turns northeast, accompanied by the railway, and climbs up and over **Dovrefjell ⑫**. The train stops at small stations such as Fokstua, Hjerkinn, Kongsvoll (with its excellent historic lodge) and Drivstua to disgorge walkers with boots, poles and backpacks.

The summit of Dovrefjell is at Hjerkinn, reputed to be the driest place in Norway, and for the rest of the way it is downhill across the **Dovre National Park** en route to Oppdal.

Oppdal ⑬ looks up towards the Dovre plateau, and to Trollheimen to the northwest. In winter it is a centre for skiing and in summer for walking, fishing, rafting and riding. The **cable car** takes walkers and skiers high above the village.

West of Oppdal, off Road 16, a small path leads to a peaceful place with trees and uneven mounds which indicate 758 graves dating back to the early Iron Age are Viking graves. This is **Vang**, once the centre of the community until the railway brought Oppdal to life.

Dovrefjell is one of only three places in the world where musk ox can be seen in the wild.

Stone church dominating the town of Røros.

Footbridge in Hardangervidda National Park.

WESTERN CENTRAL NORWAY

Whether on foot or by car, the peaks of Jotunheimen and the flat rocky expanse of the Hardanger plateau both mesmerise and stun the senses with their sheer size and magnificence.

Jotunheimen ("Home of the Giants"), which includes Norway's mightiest mountain range, and Hardangervidda (*vidde* means highland plateau) together form an extensive area of outstanding natural beauty. Centres of population are few, and places of interest are also thin on the ground, but of superb scenery – mountains, glaciers, lakes and rivers – there is an excess.

CROSSING HARDANGERVIDDA

Hardangervidda's great pull is its wide open spaces. On average 900 metres (3,000ft) above sea level, it lies south of Jotunheimen with three main valleys – Begnadalen, Hallingdalen and Numedalen – cutting across it. The centre of the plateau with its lakes and streams (a paradise for anglers) is the source of the mighty Hallingdal and Numedal Rivers. There are a number of magnificent waterfalls in the area, including **Vøringfossen** (see page 211) and **Valursfossen** ⑭, which drops 90 metres (300ft) into Hjelmodalen. To the south, Hardangervidda broadens out from Hallingskarvet, a rocky wall rising to a height of 1,700 metres (5,700ft).

Hardangervidda is Europe's largest mountain plateau, covering an area of 10,000 sq km (3,860 sq miles), nearly a third of which lies within the **Hardangervidda National Park** ⑮ (www.

hardangervidda.com). The flora and fauna of the plateau includes Arctic species and is hugely varied: several thousand reindeer roam freely, around 100 species of birds breed on these upland moors, and there are in excess of 500 different species of plants. Such abundance is due to the two distinct climates of Vidda – the gentle western coastal climate and the harsher inland climate of the east. There are tracks and trails galore, and isolated cabins provide basic overnight accommodation.

Map on page 166

Main Attractions
Hardangervidda NP
Jotunheimen NP
Borgund stave church
Aurlandsvangen
Sognefjellet Mountain
  Road

Aurland valley seen from the Norway in a Nutshell trip.

The **Oslo–Bergen railway line** N cuts across Hardangervidda, keeping Road 7 company as far as Haugastøl, where it goes north of the Hardangerjøkulen through **Finse** N (see page 178), Myrdal and Mjølfjell. The road takes a different course, heading southwest across the wide, empty landscape with distant views of mountains, passing lakes and streams, before making a dizzy descent to sea level via a series of tunnels to Eidfjord.

EXPLORE GEILO AND AROUND

Travelling northeast from Haugastøl, both road and railway are initially dominated by Hallingskarvet. The immediate surroundings become somewhat softer as you reach **Geilo** N, which has a good strategic position at the head of the Hallingdal valley and is the gateway to Hardangervidda. Though it lies at a height of 800 metres (2,650ft) above sea level, Geilo has grown into one of Norway's most popular winter sports resorts, with 20 lifts, three snow parks, 40 well-groomed downhill runs and 220km (135 miles) of cross-country

tracks. With its range of hotels, Geilo is also popular as a summer holiday centre and as a base for exploring the region by car (although the choice of roads is limited), on foot or horseback.

HOL'S RURAL HERITAGE

From Geilo, Road 40 goes southeast past **Hol Museum** (Hol Bygdemuseum; tel: 32 07 14 85; July–mid-Aug Tue–Sun 11am–4pm), a museum with a collection of traditional rural buildings, including the Mostugu (1750), the Hågåstugu (1806) and a mill from 1774. Road 40 continues along the eastern edge of Hardangervidda before it follows the Numedal valley to Kongsberg.

Road 7 continues northeast to Hagafoss, where **Road 50** turns off it towards Lake Strandavatn. It leads along the north side of the long, clear lake, which is bordered by a scattering of small mountain huts. The landscape soon changes, allowing a magnificent view, and a summer skiing centre is located nearby. Suddenly, the road begins to descend through a series of tunnels, including spirals, until the motorist is

The Bergen line, part of the Norway in a Nutshell trip.

⊘ THE BERGEN LINE

A vital link between Norway's two biggest cities, Bergen and Oslo, the Bergen line (Bergensbanen) was established in 1909 to connect the rail networks in the east and west of the country. As many as 15,000 men worked on this daring engineering project, laying tracks, building bridges and carving out over 180 tunnels. The final bill totalled NOK 50 million.

The line covers a distance of 496km (308 miles), but it is the stunning stretch across the Hardanger plateau that has made the railway famous and earned it a place among the Society of International Railway Travelers' top 25 trains in the world. A must for any rail enthusiast, the trip between Oslo and Bergen takes about eight hours. Trains run year-round, with several departures daily.

decanted into the Aurlands valley, which continues to the village of Aurlandsvangen at the head of Aurlandsfjord.

ART IN ÅL

After being separated by the waters of Strandfjord, Road 7 and the railway meet up at **Ål** ⑲, where the Norwegian-German artist Rolf Nesch (1893–1975) lived and worked for 25 years. The **Rolf Nesch Museum** (tel: 32 08 51 00; all year Mon–Fri 8am–4pm) contains the largest exhibition of his work in the country. **Torpo** has a stave church (June–Aug) which is the oldest building in Hallingdal. It dates back to the second half of the 12th century and has a splendid painted ceiling from the 13th century. The motifs include scenes from the life of St Margaret, to whom the church is dedicated.

Just past Gol, Road 7 turns south towards Nesbyen, site of Norway's oldest outdoor museum. Founded in 1899, the **Hallingdal Folkemuseum** (late June–mid-Aug) has 29 buildings, the earliest – Staveloftet – dating from 1330. All come from different parts of Hallingdal.

Some interiors are rose painted, and the exhibition building houses collections of furniture, textiles and weapons.

The two other roads leading from Gol both take the traveller through yet more attractive scenery. Road 52 goes northwest along the Hemsedal valley through Hemsedal, another winter sports centre, with 24 lifts, 50 runs, five snow parks and 212km (131 miles) of cross-country tracks. The church (Mon) has an altarpiece from 1715 and a painting of *The Last Supper* from 1716.

THE PANORAMA WAY

From Hemsedal a minor road goes past a small open-air museum near the village of Ulsåk and, further on, a private toll road winds its way across superb scenery to Ulnes on Road E16. This is the **Panorama Way** ⑳ (Utsiktsveien; summer only), a popular route which links the Hemsedal and Valdres valleys. Although narrow and rough in parts, it lives up to its name, threading its way between lakes and providing fine views of the Skogshorn, known as the "Queen of the Hemsedal".

⊙ Tip

Buskerud county has several stave churches worth visiting, in addition to the one at Torpo. South of Geilo, on Road 40 to Kongsberg, you will find *stavkirkes* dating from the 12th and 13th centuries at Uvdal, Nore, Rollag and Flesberg.

Winter in Finse.

⊙ Tip

One of the most popular day walks in the Jotunheimen is the hike to Besseggen, a mountain ridge between Lake Gjende and Bessvatnet in the eastern part of the massif, which affords spectacular views of the area. Maps and further details from the tourist information centres at Lom, Skjåk and Vågå.

JOTUNHEIMEN NATIONAL PARK

Jotunheimen was, in Norwegian mythology, the home of trolls and giants, and it is here that the mightiest mountains are to be found. In the east is the **Jotunheimen National Park ㉑**, which includes the two highest mountains in the country: Galdhøpiggen at 2,469 metres (8,098ft) and **Glittertind ㉒** 2,452 metres (8,043ft). In west Jotunheimen there is another range of crevassed mountains, the **Skagastøl-stindane** (2,000 metres/8,000ft).

The southern part of the Jotunheimen has some major lakes, including Gjende, with its greenish glacier water and flanked by impressive peaks. Other major lakes are Bygdin, Tyin and Vinstri, while glaciers add to the superb natural attractions. Opportunities for walking abound in the area, from day walks to longer treks, and the Jotunheimen is the number one destination for hiking in Norway. Try to go slightly off-season if you can, to avoid the crowds that flock here in summer.

The northern border of Jotunheimen is the Otta River valley, which acts as a natural boundary. From **Otta** in the east the river and Road 15 wend through fertile countryside, with farms and forests. Beyond Lom the scenery gradually changes as the lush, green countryside gives way to forests and rocky outcrops and the river grows more turbulent. Eventually, at the tree line, the scenery becomes bare and rather inhospitable.

INTO THE MOUNTAINS

Grotli, which consists of little more than a large roadside hotel, cafeteria and souvenir shop, marks the beginning of Lake Breidalsvatnet. Shortly afterwards, at Langevatnet, Road 63 turns off and becomes a spectacular mountain road that skirts Djupvatnet and then descends steeply to Geiranger. Road 15 continues on its course through 15 tunnels until it reaches Stryn on Innvikfjord. An alternative to Road 15 from Grotli is the old **Road 258 ㉓**. Some 26km (16 miles) long, it climbs to a height of 1,139

Jotunheimen National Park.

⊙ FINSE

South of Jotunheimen lies the hamlet of Finse, at 1,225 metres (4,000ft) the highest point on the Oslo–Bergen railway line. Its main street is the station platform, as there are neither cars nor roads. It's a small speck in a seemingly boundless expanse of snow and ice in winter, and a gateway to some of Norway's most beautiful wilderness.

Finse has the country's largest *hytta* (holiday lodge) for hikers and skiers, and a single hotel, Finse 1222 (www.finse1222.no) that gives out information about walks in the area. It is the starting point for two long-distance trail networks, stretching as the crow flies 225km (140 miles) north to the Jotunheimen and 100km (60 miles) south to Hardangervidda. In summer the region offers more than 5,000km (3,000 miles) of T-marked hiking trails. At Easter-time, 2,000km (1,240 miles) of ski trails are marked by poles in the snow.

metres (3,736ft). Although narrow and unsurfaced in parts, it makes for a thrilling journey.

Between Otta and Grotli only two roads go south, penetrating to the heart of Jotunheimen. Road 51, the most easterly, leaves the Otta–Grotli road at Randen and heads into the **Valdres** region. It starts by climbing into an area of upland pastures with a distant backdrop of mountains. A further climb to Darthus brings **Ridderspranget** ㉔ (Knight's Leap) close at hand, where the Sjoa River is channelled into a narrow gorge.

Lakes lie scattered across to the west, while beyond looms the peak of Glittertind. The most important stretch of water is **Lake Gjende** ㉕, long and narrow and curving slightly to the southwest. Beyond Bessheim there are more inspiring views, and this scenic feast continues for kilometre after kilometre.

Bygdin lies between two lakes: Lake Bygdin stretches like a long finger pointing to more distant mountains in the west; eastwards is the major expanse of Lake Vinstri. There are boat trips on several of the lakes, and Lake Bygdin has northern Europe's highest scheduled boat service, in waters 1,060 metres (3,477ft) above sea level.

THE HEART OF THE VALDRES

Between Bessheim and Bygdin the road reaches its highest point – 1,389 metres (4,557ft). From here it descends, first to the tree line, then to more gentle scenery at **Beitostølen**. This winter sports resort has nine lifts, 12 runs and more than 325km (200 miles) of cross-country tracks. It is a typical village of its kind with several hotels – very popular for cross-country skiing – and a school for disabled and blind skiers.

Fagernes ㉖ is at the heart of the Valdres area. Its main attraction is the large **Valdres Folk Museum** (Folkemuseum; www.valdresmusea.no; daily June and Aug 10am–4pm, July 10am–5pm, Sept–May Mon–Fri 10am–3pm), which features some 95 buildings built between 1200 and 1900. Of particular interest are a 16th-century tapestry, medieval chests, a collection of antique silver, folk-music instruments and hunting weapons. This area has several **stave churches**, including those at Hedalen, Reinli, Lomen, Høre, Øye, Hegge and Garmo. Fagernes is also the birthplace of *rakfisk*, one of Norway's strangest delicacies – brine-cured fish, usually trout or char, that has been left to ferment for several months before being eaten.

In one direction the E16 heads southeast through the Begnadal valley and eventually to Hønefoss. In the opposite direction the road goes west through more exciting scenery on the southern edge of Jotunheimen. At Tyinkrysset a road goes off to Øvre Årdal on Årdalsfjord while the E16 turns south, descending through forested scenery to **Borgund** ㉗. Borgund stave church (May–mid-June and mid-Aug–Sept 10am–5pm, mid-June–mid-Aug

Valdres Folk Museum.

Tip

If you are heading for Aurlandsvangen on the beautiful fjord of the same name, and are pressed for time, take the Lærdalstunnel rather than the mountain route. It is the longest road tunnel in the world at 24.5km (15 miles).

8am–8pm) is regarded as the most typical and best preserved in Norway. Built in 1150, it is dedicated to St Andrew.

A few kilometres past Lærdalsøyri, a minor road goes to **Aurlandsvangen** ㉘. It starts to climb almost immediately through lush scenery that gradually changes as the narrow road ascends higher and higher, unfolding a series of stunning panoramas until the summit at 1,305 metres (4,284ft). It then begins an increasingly steep descent to the village of Aurlandsvangen, offering breathtaking views from the heights over Aurlandsfjord several thousand feet above it. It is not for the fainthearted. Stop at the Stegastein viewpoint to take in the scenery before completing your descent towards Aurland.

ACROSS SOGNEFJELL

The second route south from the Otta–Grotli road is Road 55 from Lom to Lustrafjord, which is the part of Sognefjord furthest from the sea.

Sognefjellet is one of 18 National Tourist Roads in Norway, each one selected for its exceptional scenic beauty. What is more, this one was once named by *The Guardian* as one of 10 top bike rides in the world. **Lom** ㉙ is a typical Norwegian "junction" village with a couple of hotels, shops and garages, plus a fine stave church. The Stone Centre (Fossheim Steinsenter; July–mid Aug daily 10am–6pm, May–June and mid-Aug–Sept daily 10am–4pm) in Lom contains stones, rocks and gems from all over Norway, and it has a collection of minerals from Jotunheimen. The associated **Mountain Museum** (Norsk Fjellmuseum; mid-May–early Oct) focuses on mountain life throughout Norway.

From Lom, you drive through the placid Bøverdal valley, passing small farms and villages, then the view gradually changes as you gain height and the mountains come into sharp focus. At Galdesand there is a toll road to Juvashytta, which is the nearest point by car to the Galdhøpiggen mountain.

At 640 metres (2,100ft), **Elveseter** ㉚ (May–Sept) is one of Norway's most unusual hotels. The Elveseter family has owned the property for five generations, gradually converting it into a hotel but retaining many of the old buildings. The oldest is from 1640 and has survived as a wooden building because of the dry mountain air. The first visitors arrived in the 1880s. Later, the opening of the Sognefjell road in 1938 led to an expansion of tourism.

KROSSBU SUMMIT

The road continues its upward ascent past the isolated Jotunheimen Fjellstue to the summit at **Krossbu** at a height of 1,400 metres (4,590ft) amid superb mountain scenery. From there, make the steep descent to **Turtagrø**, where the hotel (which is about all there is to Turtagrø) is a popular base for walkers and climbers; continue the downward course to softer surroundings at Fortun and, a few miles on, to sea level, at the end of **Lustrafjord** at Skjolden.

Elveseter Hotel.

Boy Riding Bear in the sculpture gardens.

TELEMARK AND THE SOUTH

Norway's southern coastline is a magnet for summer visitors with its beaches and picturesque seaside towns. Inland, the scenery is starker and life in the mountain valleys lingers in the past.

As they are proverbially advised to do "when in Rome", visitors to Oslo – or, equally, to Stavanger and Kristiansand – could usefully do what the locals do for recreation. The choice is either mountains and lakes, in which case they steer a course for **Telemark**, or the sea, which draws them to **Aust-Agder** and **Vest-Agder**, jointly known as Sørlandet (south land).

Locals usually travel in their own cars, a definite advantage in trying to make the most of Telemark but not so necessary on the coast, along which it is possible to leapfrog from port to port on ferries, which are sufficiently frequent to permit an improvised itinerary.

Oslo, Kristiansand and Stavanger, the principal cities along the southern rim of Norway, have good connections, including flights, so they all serve as practical starting or finishing points for a visit to the region, and you can combine Telemark and Sørlandet on one of several bus tours. One from Oslo, for example, covers nearly 1,200km (750 miles) by road and ferry and lasts five days.

DESIGNED BY A KING

In 1639 King Christian IV of Denmark-Norway had the sort of whim which is the privilege of kings and very few others. He wanted to found a town and name it after himself.

Pedalling through the streets of Kristiansand.

In the event, the choice of the site where **Kristiansand** ❶ now stands was not entirely capricious. It was an admirable base from which to control the approaches to both the North Sea and the Baltic. The town had to be fortified, and much survives of the first of many forts to be built on the site, **Christiansholm Festning** (fortress; tel: 38 07 51 50; May–Sept 9am–9pm; free). Through nearly three turbulent centuries, however, none of the forts ever fired a gun in anger (not until 9 April 1940), and gradually Kristiansand changed

Map on page 184

Main Attractions
Kristiansand
Kristiansand Zoo
Grimstad
Telemark Canal
Heddal stave church

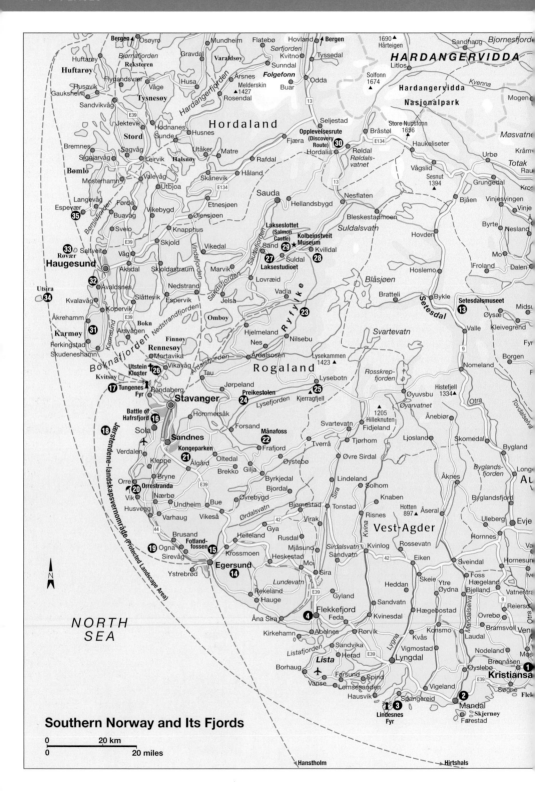

Southern Norway and Its Fjords

Bergen
Osøyro
Mundheim
Flatebø
Hovland
Bergen
1690 ▲
Hårteigen
Sandhaug
Bjørnesfjord

Huftarøy
Bjørnafjorden
Gravdal
Varaldsøy
Sørfjorden
Kvitno
Tyssedal

Huftarøy
Reksteren
Sunndal
Folgefonn
HARDANGERVIDDA

Flydandsvær
Våge
Husa
Arsnes
Melderskin
Buar
Odda
Solfonn
1674 ▲
Hardangervidda
Kvenna
Mogen

Gaukshein
Sandvikvåg
Tysnesøy
▲1427
Rosendal
13
Nasjonalpark
Litlos

Jektevik
Hodnanes
Husnes
Hordaland
Seljestad
Store Nupsfonn
1636
Møsvatne

Stord
Sunde
Husnes
Fjæra
Opplevelsesrute (Discovery Route)
Bråstøl
Haukeliseter
Urbø
Kråm

Bremnes
Sagvåg
Utåker
Matre
Hordalia
Røldal
Røldalsvatnet
Vågslid
Totak
Rau

Bømlo
Siggjarvåg
Leirvik
Halsnøy
Rafdal
13
Sesnut
1394
Grungedal
Kros

Mosterhamn
Valevåg
Utbjoa
Skånevik
Håland
Sauda
Nesflaten
Bjåen
Vinjesvingen
Vinje

Langevåg
Førde
Vikebygd
Etnesjøen
Hellandsbygd
Bleskestadmoen
Hovden
Byrte
Nesland

Espevær
Buavåg
Ølensjøen
Suldalsvatn
Mo

Svelo
Knapphus
Lakseslottet (Salmon Castle)
Kolbeinstveit Museum
Kvildal
Froland
Dalen

Rovær
Saltveit
Skjold
Vikedal
Sand
Suldal
Hoslemo

Haugesund
Våg
Aksdal
Skoldastraum
Marvik
Lakkestudioet
Blåsjøen
Bratteli
Bykle
Setesdalsmuseet

Utsira
Avaldsnes
Slåttevik
Espervik
Lovræd
Vadla
Setesdal
Øysæ
Midsu

Kvalavåg
Kopervik
Jelsa
Svartevatn
Valle
Kleivegrend

Åkrehamn
Bokn
Omboy
Hjelmeland
Ryfylke
Nomeland
Fyr

Karmøy
Arsvågen
Finnøy
Nes
Nilsebu
Rosskrepfjorden
Borgen

Ferkingstad
Rennesøy
Mortavika
Ardalsosen
Lysekammen
1423 ▲
Øyuvsbu
Histefjell
1334 ▲
Otra

Skudeneshamn
Utstein Kloster
Vikavåg
Tau
Rogaland
Lysebotn
Øyarvatnet
Fyr

Kvitsøy
Tungenes Fyr
Randaberg
Jørpeland
Preikestolen
Lysefjorden
Kjerragfjell
1205
Hilleknuten
Fidjeland
Ånebior
Bygland

Battle of Hafrsfjord
Stavanger
Hommersåk
Lysebotn
Svartevatn
Tjørhom
Ljosland
Skomedal
Byglandsfjorden
Long

Sola
Sandnes
Forsand
Månafoss
Frafjord
Tverrå
Øvre Sirdal
Åknes
Byglandsfjord
Au

Verdalen
Kongeparken
Oltedal
Øystebø
Lindeland
Solhom
Uleberg
Evje

Kleppe
Ålgård
Brekko
Gilja
Byrkjedal
Bjordal
Knaben
Hotten
897 ▲
Åseral
Hornnes

Bryne
Nærbø
Bue
Øvrebygd
Bjørnestad
Tonstad
Risnes
Vest-Agder
Foss
Hægeland
Bjelland
Vatnestrø

Orre
Orrestranda
Undheim
Vikeså
Ørdalsvatn
Virak
42
Eiken
Skeie
Ytre Øydna
9
Reiers

Vik
Varhaug
Gya
Rusdal
Mo
Sirdalsvatn
Kvinlog
Rossevatn
Sveindal
Ovrebø
Ven

Husvegg
Brusand
Helleland
Mjåsund
Sandvatn
42
Hæddan
Sandvatn
Hægebostad
Bramsvoll

Ogna
Fotlandfossen
Krossmoen
Heskestad
Sira
Gyland
Kvinesdal
Konsmo
Laudal

Sirevåg
Egersund
Flekkefjord
Feda
Rørvik
Kvås
Nodeland
Møs

Ystrebrød
Lundevatn
Rekeland
Åna Sira
Abelnes
Sandvika
Vigmostad
Lyngdal
Vigeland
Brønnåsen
Øyslebø
Kristiansa

NORTH
SEA
Hauge
Kirkehamn
Listafjorden
Herad
Lista
Farsund
Spind
Spangereid
Mandal
Kristiansa

Borhaug
Vanse
Lemesanden
Vigeland
Skjernøy
Søgne
Flek

Hausvik
Lindesnes Fyr
Mandal
Farestad

Southern Norway and Its Fjords

0 — 20 km
0 — 20 miles

Hanstholm
Hirtshals

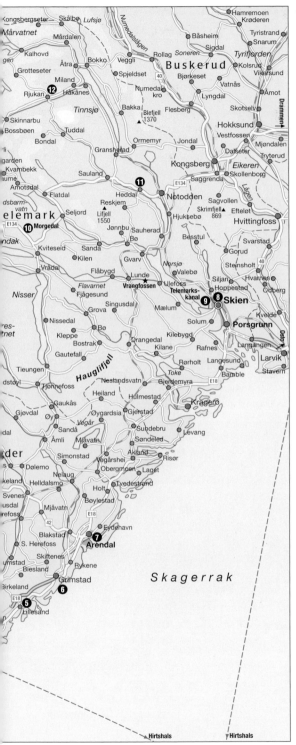

from being a military town to a trading and administrative centre.

Present-day **Kristiansand** is a pleasant city, laid out in a grid according to Christian IV's directive, and the sort of place that invites visitors simply to stroll about. The weather is more reliably sunny than anywhere else in Norway, the port and central market are always busy, the **Posebyen** is a picturesque quarter of old wooden houses, and one never has to look far for a spot to sit down and watch the world go by. "A total of more than 10,000 seats in cafés and restaurants" is the city's proud claim.

Kristiansand Zoo (Kristiansand Dyrepark; tel: 97 05 97 00; www.dyreparken.no; all year, times vary), which includes the miniature town of Kardemomme By, is the most visited family park in Norway. The fictional town, 11km (6.8 miles) east of Kristiansand, is modelled on a popular children's story by Torbjørn Egner. In addition to its large zoo there are water chutes and other attractions. The zoo itself contains 800 animals, including Scandinavian fauna such as wolves and elk, exotic wild animals such as lions and tigers, and even a few endangered species such as the red panda. There is also a large breeding ground for camels.

Just north of the city centre, the **Ravnedalen Park** is set in attractive, hilly grounds. The **Gimle Mansion** (Gimle Gård; tel: 38 10 26 80; mid-June–mid-Aug daily 11am–5pm; closed rest of the year) across the Otra River is a magnificent symbol of 19th-century Norwegian capitalism. It was built by a shipping tycoon, Bernt Holm, and remained in the family until it was bequeathed to the town and opened to the public in 1985.

Also worth visiting are the **Railway Museum** (Setesdalbanen), with its narrow-gauge steam railway (summer departures twice daily Sat and Sun, once Wed, tel: 38 15 64 82; www.setesdalsbanen.no), a short way north of the city, and southwest on the way to Mandal, the **Kristiansand Cannon Museum** (Kanonmuseum; tel: 38 08 50 90; www.vestagdermuseet.no/kristiansand; mid-June–mid-Aug Mon–Fri 10am–5pm, Sat–Sun noon–5pm), the highlight of which is a cannon built by the Germans in World War II to guard the Skagerrak. It is the world's second largest land-based cannon, weighs a whopping 337 tonnes, and its range extends halfway to Denmark.

WEST TO LINDESNES FYR

About 45km (28 miles) west of Kristiansand is **Mandal ❷**. A busy port long before Christian IV felt the urge to build Kristiansand, it later suffered from competition with King Christian's pet project. A 1799 traveller remarked that "the houses are jammed together so tightly that a careless pipe-smoker at any open window could spit into his neighbour's parlour." The point known as **Kastellet** is where a wealthy Dane, who once reached into his pocket to make a personal loan to the notoriously empty-pocketed King Frederik IV, installed a cannon to keep pirates away from his estate.

Another 40km (25 miles) west, the lighthouse at **Lindesnes Fyr ❸** (all year) marks the southernmost point of Norway, and in bad weather is buffeted by ferocious winds. The small islands 5km (3 miles) offshore feature in ancient Norse sagas as a refuge for Viking ships waiting for better weather before turning the corner into or out of the Skagerrak. **Farsund**, a little further west and once a haven for privateers, has been destroyed by fire so often that there is hardly a building still standing that predates the 20th century. Nevertheless, the houses of today are spruce, painted white and present a pleasing spectacle.

FLEKKEFJORD'S DUTCH TOWN

The region is rich in rock carvings and ancient sites including, near Vanse, the remains of nine Iron Age homes surrounded by 350 burial mounds. **Lomsesanden**, a popular beach on the Lista peninsula, is 10km (6 miles) of white sand. The last town before Vest Agder rises to meet Rogaland is the small port of **Flekkefjord ❹**, known for its Dutch Town (Hollenderbyen), a historic area with Dutch-style white houses lining narrow streets. Some of Norway's longest railway tunnels (there are 46 between Flekkefjord and Kristiansand) bore through this mountainous country, which is also renowned for several spectacular waterfalls, especially around Kvinesdal.

The small harbour at Mandal.

EAST TO GRIMSTAD

The principal centres along the coast east from Kristiansand are, in order, Lillesand, Grimstad, Arendal and Risør. **Lillesand ⑤**, apart from being a pretty holiday town with a pleasant selection of cafés and restaurants around the harbour, has a special place in Norwegian history as the centre of an 18th-century revolt led by a farmer named Lofthus, a Robin Hood figure who travelled to Copenhagen to confront the crown prince with a long list of grievances. On his return he collected a force of 2,000 men and caused panic among the Danish establishment in the coastal towns. The house where he was arrested still stands. The **Lillesand Town and Maritime Museum** (By og Sjøfart museum; tel: 46 81 75 10; mid-June–mid Aug Tue–Sun noon–4pm or by appointment) tells the whole story.

Grimstad ⑥ is indelibly associated with the playwright Henrik Ibsen. It was here that he served his apprenticeship to a chemist. Ibsen was an unhappy young man and Grimstad, though a pretty place, must have contributed (together with Skien, where he was born) to his searing exposure of goings-on in small Norwegian towns. His works caused a scandal at the time, but years have healed the wounds and he is commemorated in the **Ibsen House/ Grimstad Town Museum** (Bymuseum; tel: 37 25 01 68; mid-June–mid-Aug daily 11am–4pm or by appointment), which holds the largest collection of Ibsen memorabilia in Norway.

ARENDAL'S ISLAND SETTING

Arendal ⑦ was lucky to survive King Christian's plan to close it down and transfer the inhabitants to his pet project, Kristiansand. Arendal prospered in the 17th and 18th centuries as a conduit for timber shipments abroad, including much of the timber used for the rebuilding of London after the 1666 Great Fire. In 1863, Arendal itself was struck by fire, which consumed the houses on stilts that had earned it the nickname of "Little Venice". Overflowing onto a number of small islands, it retains its lovely setting.

One of its more unusual attractions is a museum meticulously created by

Ibsen House, Grimstad.

⊘ Tip

Feeling adventurous? Why not visit Norsjø Kabelpark (tel: 35 95 84 30; www.3norsjo-kabelpark.no) in Akkerhaugen (40km/ 25 miles north of Skien). It's one of Europe's best arenas for wake-boards, wake-skates and water-skiing. Open to all aged eight years and over. Tuition available.

unpaid volunteers out of the contents of a pottery factory that went out of business some years ago. It is located in the Regency-style Kløcker's House (1826) and the enthusiasm of the staff at the **Arendal Town Museum** (Kløck-ershus; tel: 37 02 59 25; Tue–Fri 10am–3pm, Sat 10am–2pm) is infectious. The **Town Hall** (Rådhus), previously the home of a merchant, is said to be one of the largest wooden buildings ever constructed in Norway.

Risør, the most easterly town in Aust Agder, was also threatened by the creation of Kristiansand. Its trad-ers were forced to maintain residen-cies in the new city, but they kept their links with their hometown. Mary Wol-lstonecraft, an English visitor in 1795, noted an addiction to tobacco. The men never took their pipes out of their mouths and absolutely refused to open a window. The women, she decided, dressed like "sailor girls in Hull or Portsmouth". Many of these women were probably Dutch, since it was fash-ionable among young seamen to bring wives back from the Netherlands, the

main trading partner. In Risør, as in other parts of Sørlandet, children may still be given distinctly Dutch names.

SKIEN, IBSEN'S BIRTHPLACE

The capital of Telemark is **Skien** ❽, the birthplace, in 1828, of Henrik Ibsen. His home, **Venstøp**, forms part of the **Tele-mark Museum** (Brekke Park; tel: 35 54 45 00; www.telemarkmuseum.no; May–Aug daily 11am–5pm) and has become a national shrine.

Skien, nowadays better known for its Ibsen connection, was famous in the past for producing stone projec-tiles for military slingshots. Another regional industry which prospered in the nearby village of Ulefoss until the late 19th century was the production of ice. Ice was easily transported along Telemark's natural waterways, which were later rationalised into a canal system, the **Telemarkskanal** ❾.

INLAND TELEMARK

Throughout Telemark one senses an older Norway lurking just beneath the surface. The higher areas were, until

M/S Victoria on the Telemark Canal.

⊘ TELEMARK CANAL

The Telemark Canal (Telemarkskanal), com-pleted in 1892, links lakes and waterways between **Skien** and **Dalen** at the foot of Hardangervidda. Eight sets of locks raise boats a total of 72 metres (225ft) up to Flåvatn, which in turn leads into Kviteseidvatn and Bandak, and on to Dalen, where travellers can check in at the historic Dalen Hotel. The canal cuts 105km (65 miles) into the interior and is now used by pleasure boats such as the M/S *Victoria*, M/S *Henrik Ibsen* and M/S *Telemarken*. The full voyage from Skien to Dalen takes around 12 hours (tel: 35 90 00 20; www.visittelemark.no/telemarkskanalen; operational May–Sept), but you can hop off at several intermediate ports. Attractions en route include the old lock-keepers' houses, smithies and saw-mills, and the Vrangfossen waterfall above Ulefoss, as well as places to stay.

recently, impenetrable except on skis, so travel in winter was actually easier than in summer. Isolated communities were not inclined to take orders from interfering outsiders and its people were described (in 1580) as "shameless bodies of the Devil whose chief delight is to kill bishops, priests, bailiffs and superiors – and who possess a large share of all original sin".

A finger of Telemark reaches out to the sea at Kragerø, not far from the mouth of the Oslofjord, but the province is associated in most minds with the inland terrain, which inspired an eccentric farmer named Sondre Norheim to turn the pedestrian business of plodding about in snow on two planks into the sport of skiing (see page 94). His discovery of the delights that could be achieved with planks that were properly shaped and had heel bindings made him overlook his domestic chores. The story goes that when he ran out of firewood in winter, he simply hacked off another piece of his house and put that to burn on the fire.

Morgedal ❿, where Norheim lived (he later emigrated to America)

deserves to be called the cradle of skiing, but it is now only one of dozens of skiing centres in the county. Norheim's statue is a feature of the **Norwegian Ski Museum** (Norsk Skieventyr; tel: 35 05 42 50; mid-June–mid-Aug daily 10am–6pm; times vary the rest of the year), near Kviteseidvatn.

HEDDAL STAVE CHURCH

Visitors with their own transport in Telemark can hardly go wrong: pick any of the winding roads that head inland and the scenery is bound to be breathtaking. For those who do not have a car, the waterways are a wonderful alternative: Skien is a good place to pick up boats going north through Sauherad to Notodden (schedules from Skien tourist office; tel: 35 90 55 20); roads 36 then 360 cover the same route.

West of Notodden, along Road 11, lies **Heddal ⓫** with its famous **stave church** (Stavkirke; tel: 35 01 39 90; www.heddal stavkirke.no; mid-May–mid-Sept 10am–5pm), the largest and most impressive in Norway. Built between 1147 and 1242, it has a richly carved doorway with animals

> ⊙ **Tip**
>
> Notodden Blues Festival takes place every year in August and is one of the most popular music festivals in Norway (www.bluesfest.no).

A romantic way to travel.

Inside the silver mine at Saggrenda, 50km (31 miles) east of Heddal on Road E134.

Heddal stave church.

and human faces. The Telemarkers are masters at expressing nature through art, and nowhere is this more evident than in the rose paintings in the Ramberg room of **Heddal Museum** (Heddal Bygdetun; tel: 35 02 08 40; farmhouses: mid-June–Aug 10am–5pm).

Further on, Road 37 branches off to the north past Lake Tinnsjø towards **Rjukan** ⓬. For a breathtaking alternative route, stay on the E134 to Sauland and turn north, through Tuddal, to drive past Gausta Toppen, one of Norway's landmark peaks. The stretch from Rjukan west to Rauland is also lovely and can be covered by public bus. Keep an eye open for highly decorative wooden houses and double-storey barns, with a ramp leading to the upper floor.

The attraction of Rjukan and nearby Vemork is now the **Norwegian Industrial Workers Museum** (Norsk Industriarbeidermuseum; tel: 35 09 90 00; mid-June–mid-Aug 10am–6pm, shorter hours rest of the year). Formerly a heavy-water plant, it was the target in 1943 of a daring sabotage attack by the Norwegian Resistance (see page 60).

Rjukan is generally rather gloomy because the sun is nearly always blocked off by surrounding mountains. On top of those mountains, though, another world of vast vistas opens up, and it is said that on a good day it is possible to see one-sixth of Norway. You can take northern Europe's oldest cable car, the **Krossobanen** (tel: 35 09 00 27; late June–mid-Oct daily 9am–8pm; times vary rest of the year) from Krosso to the top of Gvepseborg at 860 metres (2,800ft) for just such a view.

REMOTE SETESDAL

An alternative route inland is Road 9 from Kristiansand, which climbs up the Otra valley and runs north along **Byglandsfjorden** to **Setesdal**. Until modern times this area was very remote. The inhabitants sent their timber down to Arendal by pushing it into a river, which plunged 700 metres (2,300ft) over a distance of about 150km (90 miles). They preserved their own traditional way of life, including a distinct dialect, dress and cuisine, into the 20th century.

Setesdal is a haven for those in search of rural culture. The most famous dwelling is **Rygnestadtunet**, a 16th-century windowless tower of three storeys with an amazing collection of relics, such as leather hangings depicting St George's battle with the dragon.

The tower was built by Vond-Asmund who, on discovering that his fiancée was about to marry someone else, snatched her away from the wedding procession. From the upper floor of his fortress, he fired off arrows at anyone who approached, killing at least four people. Rygnestadtunet is part of the **Setesdalsmuseet** ⓭ (Heritage Museum; tel: 37 93 63 03; late June–mid-Aug daily 11am–5pm), 15km (9 miles) to the south.

You can also visit the Sommarland family park at Bø (tel: 35 06 16 00; http://sommarland.no; June–Aug, 10am–7pm most days), Scandinavia's largest waterpark.

Lindesnes Fyr (lighthouse) on the southernmost tip of Norway.

ROGALAND

This often overlooked corner of the country offers many delights, from the picturesque fishing harbour of Egersund to an eagle's-eye view over Lysefjord from the top of Pulpit Rock.

Many consider that Norway's fjord country begins at Hardangerfjord and the city of Bergen, and stretches north. But such a vision overlooks all the southern fjords and islands, where Norway first became a nation. Today this area of Rogaland is centred on Stavanger, the heart of Norway's international oil industry, and contains some of the fjord country's most spectacular natural sights: what a pity to miss enticing attractions such as **Preikestolen** (Pulpit Rock), a flat slab of rock swooping some 600 metres (2,000ft) up from Lysefjord, with its 360-degree view over *fjell* (mountain) and fjord.

Rogaland has the mildest climate in Norway and the beauty of the coast is unsurpassed, but the downside of such closeness to the sea is unexpected showers and a higher rainfall than elsewhere in much of Norway. In winter, thanks to the Gulf Stream, there is little snow, and the fertile fields of Jæren are green for most of the year.

STARTING IN THE SOUTH

By air, the way in is Stavanger's international airport at Sola, or you might come by express boat from Bergen in just under three hours. From the south, the main road is the E39, which crosses into Rogaland north of the old town of **Egersund** ⑭, now Norway's largest fishing harbour. There is also a coastal

route (the scenic Road 44), which hugs the coastline all the way north to Stavanger. At the southern corner of this route, small fjords bite into a rough, rocky coast and lead to green valleys and a myriad of shining lakes.

The best view of Egersund's sheltered harbour, where pleasure boats, both big and small, bob with the waves, is from the top of the lighthouse. The town itself has a fine **cruciform church** (mid-June to mid-Aug) from 1620 (renovated in the late 18th century) and the **Dalane Folk Museum** (tel: 51 46 14 10; June–Aug

◎ Main Attractions
Egersund
Jæren
Kongeparken
Pulpit Rock
Karmøy

Map on page 184

Egersund's cruciform church.

daily 11am–5pm, shorter hours rest of the year), which includes the **Egersund Fayance Museum** (same hours), which displays painted earthenware crockery, once the town's main industry).

Inland is the waterfall **Fotlandfossen ⓯**, and further north on the E39 you come to the southern end of **Ørsdalsvatn**. From here, Rogaland's last remaining inland waterway boat, *Ørsdølen*, sails the 20km (13 miles) to Vassbø at the far end of the narrow lake. Near there you can have a simple home-made meal before the boat returns. A few miles further on is Vikeså, where Road 503 to Byrkjedal runs north past **Gloppedalsura**, where the boulders are as big as houses.

VICTORY ON JÆREN'S FIELDS

Jæren, the flat and fertile country north of Egersund and Norway's main area for the production of meat, dairy products, poultry and eggs, was not always as peaceful as it is today. In AD 872, at Hafrsfjord, it was the scene of the **Battle of Hafrsfjord ⓰**, where King Harald Hårfagre (Fair Hair) won

his most important battle to unite the warring Norwegian kingdoms.

A narrow strip of coast some 70km (43 miles) long, from Raumen Island at the southern end to **Tungenes Fyr ⓱** (lighthouse; www.jaermuseet.no/tungenes fyr; mid-June–mid-Aug daily noon–4pm, shorter hours rest of the year) northwest of Stavanger, forms a Protected Landscape Area, **Jærstendene landskapsvernområde ⓲** (see page 203). It includes the scenic Jæren beaches and offshore islands. Raumen itself is one of eight bird sanctuaries where, at different times of the year, you can find turnstones, ringed plovers and knots taking a brief rest on the long flight to or from southern Europe or Africa; offshore are wintering eider and long-tailed ducks, and the islands provide nesting places for seabirds (often closed to visitors during the breeding season).

In the eight botanical reserves you can find such delights as the spearleaved fat hen saltbush, and the rare marsh orchid growing in the reserve near **Ogna ⓳**. There are also four geological sites and no less than 150

Kongeparken fun.

monuments listed and protected. But Jærstrendene is more than flora and fauna. Beaches with white-gold sand are popular picnic spots, and though the water can be chilly, this does not deter swimmers. **Orrestranda ⑳**, which stretches from Vik in the south to Reve in the north, is Norway's longest sand beach, and many come here in summer to watch the sun set below the horizon.

SANDNES BY BICYCLE

Sandnes on Sandfjord is Norway's "bicycle town", where the famous DBS bicycles are made and where you can hire bikes to explore the surrounding countryside. It is also home to one of Norway's largest shopping centres, Kvadrat (Mon–Fri 10am–8pm, Sat 10am–6pm). A delight for youngsters is **Kongeparken ㉑** (tel: 81 52 26 73; www.kongeparken.no; June–Aug daily 10am–6pm; May and Sept Sat–Sun only 10am–5pm), south of Sandnes at the little town of Ålgård; it's the biggest amusement park in the southwest of Norway. At 80 metres (260ft) long, Kongeparken's Gulliver is hard to miss.

Inside, Gulliver's body is full of unusual playthings. The park has Scandinavia's longest bobsleigh ride.

In many of the mountain areas around the fjords, waterfalls cascade hundreds of metres below. One of the most famous is **Månafoss ㉒** on the Frafjord, the innermost finger of the Høgsfjord, reached by Road 45 south from Ålgård to Gilja. At Gilja, turn down the steep road to Frafjord for a fantastic view of the water. There are directions to Månafoss in the car park at the foot of the mountain.

AWESOME LYSEFJORD

The **Ryfylke ㉓** area northeast of Stavanger is true fjord country, one of the least-known parts of Norway despite the drama of its scenery. In the south, due east of Stavanger, Ryfylke starts with **Lysefjord**, under Pulpit Rock, and stretches north past long narrow lakes that once were open fjords, until it reaches **Vindafjord**, **Saudafjord** and **Suldalsvatn**. Although he never saw it, Victor Hugo described Lysefjord in *The Toilers of the Sea* as "the most terrible

Wedged between two rocks, the famous Kjerragbolten offers a one-of-a-kind vantage point from which to view Lysefjord.

Breathtaking Preikestolen.

⊙ Tip

Allow some time to visit Flor og Fjære, with its lush exotic gardens and a restaurant surrounded by palm trees. You'll find Flor og Fjære on the island of Sør Hidle, 20 minutes by boat northeast from Stavanger. Tel: 51 11 00 00; www.florogfjare.no.

of all the corridor rocks in the sea". A walk through heather moor and scrubland brings you to the top of **Pulpit Rock** ㉔ (Preikestolen), a rock platform high above the fjord (see box).

From the village of Forsand at its mouth, Lysefjord is 40km (25 miles) long. At its innermost end is one of Europe's most remarkable feats of civil engineering: the road to the hydroelectric power station at **Lysebotn**, which is hidden hundreds of metres inside the mountain. This road, which seems to defy gravity, snakes up and down more than 750 metres (2,500ft), with 27 hairpin bends, and connects Lysebotn to Sirdal and Setesdal to the east along the Lyseveien. If you dare to keep your eyes open as the bus takes its dizzying route downwards, the view is magnificent.

Near the end of the fjord on the south side towers **Kjeragfjell** ㉕, an enormous granite mountain around 1,100 metres (3,550ft) high. Lie on your front and look down through the wedge cut out of the mountain plateau to the fjord below. To get there takes about two hours' walking from several spots along the

Lyseveien. Lysebotn has become a draw for extreme-sports daredevils in recent years, and Kjerag is a favoured spot with both base jumpers and climbers.

MUSIC ON MOSTERØY

The sheltered bay north of Stavanger, and the outer islands such as Karmøy, protect Ryfylke's inshore islands from the North Sea. Christianity flourished early here under the protection of the bishops of Stavanger, and the islands have many churches.

In summer, the 12th-century **Utstein Monastery** ㉖ (Utstein Kloster; tel: 51 72 00 50; mid-May–mid-Sept Mon–Sat 10am–4pm, Sun noon–5pm) on **Mosterøy** makes a beautiful setting for concerts which are mostly of classical music. It offers the traveller a refreshing break on the way from Stavanger to Boknafjord. The monastery's acoustics and the palpable sense of history give these concerts a very special atmosphere. The many **lighthouses** are not only landmarks for islanders and seafarers but make excellent bird-watching sites, as you spy cormorants and a variety of other seabirds on wave-washed rocks below. The waters around these peaceful islands are a sea kingdom for sailors of all kinds, with many yacht harbours. Most of the island grocers provide boat services, and it is easy to hire rowing boats and small craft with outboard engines.

SULDAL HIGHLANDS

Here fjords, lakes and rivers are rich in fish and fine for sailing and canoeing, and all these inland, eastern areas of Rogaland have good cross-country skiing tracks in winter as well as some fine Alpine slopes. Among the best holiday areas is the **Suldal district**, stretching from Sand on the Sandsfjord, along the Suldalslågen River – where the rushing waters have produced huge salmon (the largest so far weighed almost 44kg/97lb) – to the long, narrow Suldalsvatn. At the Sand end of Suldalslågen, **Laksestudioet** ㉗

⊙ PREIKESTOLEN: THE ROCK WITH A VIEW

The most famous mountain formation in the Lysefjord, east of Stavanger, is Pulpit Rock (Preikestolen), which protrudes about 30 metres (98ft) from the precipitous mountain that towers more than 600 metres (1,968ft) over the water below. Preikestolen is among the most famous tourist attractions in Norway, visited by some 120,000 people every year.

The trail to the top of Preikestolen, which starts near the stunning Preikestolen Mountain Lodge (fjellstue), climbs 350 metres (1,148ft) through somewhat uneven terrain, although the hike is accessible to most. On the way, look out for golden eagles, willow grouse, ptarmigan and other birds, as well as reindeer or even an elk if you are lucky. The hike takes two hours each way. Pack sturdy walking boots, warm clothing (the weather can change quickly, so even if you set off in sunny conditions, it might be foggy or windy by the time you reach the top) and some water. There are no railings near the steepest spots, so keep an eye on children, and walk as closely to the mountain wall as possible. The views from the top over the fjord are amazing, so allow enough time there before starting your descent.

Sightseeing boats leave from Stavanger for Lysefjord all year round to view Pulpit Rock from below.

(mid-June–mid-Aug daily 11am–7pm, mid-Aug–Sept Sat–Sun noon–4pm), is an observation studio, built under a waterfall, where visitors look through two large windows at the salmon resting before their next leap up the fish ladder on the way to their spawning grounds. Where river meets lake is **Kolbeinstveit Museum** (Rural Museum; tel: 52 79 93 04; mid-June–mid-Aug daily 11am–5pm), with the old Guggedalsloftet farm which dates back to the 13th century.

From Sand, a bus follows the path of the river to the giant **Kvilldal** ㉘ power station, opened in 1982 by King Olav, who chiselled his signature into the mountain side. On the way to this cavernous power station the bus stops at the **Lakseslottet** ㉙ (Salmon Castle) at Lindum, built by Lord Sibthorp in 1885 when the British "salmon lords" looked on a few weeks in Norway as part of the fishing season. River and lake still draw anglers, and the castle is a popular guesthouse.

From Stavanger and Jæren, ferries and express boats reach this fjord country and its islands, and it is easy to combine bus and ferry. Vindafjord, Saudafjord

and Suldalsvatn look up to 1,500-metre (5,000ft) peaks that lead the way to the great mountain plateau of Hardangervidda. In summer you can take the exciting **old mountain road** north from Sauda to Røldal; the new road has tunnels to keep it open all year. At Røldal, where there's a stave church, you pick up the **Discovery Route** ㉚ (Opplevelsesrute, E134), which has come over the Haukeli Mountains from Telemark, and you can continue north along it until it becomes Road 13 towards Odda.

EXPRESS BOAT TO KARMØY

The sea route north to Bergen is one of the most popular ways to see the northern coast. By taking an express boat (a cross between a catamaran and a hydrofoil) you can drop off at any of the harbour stops. **Karmøy** ㉛, the island at the south of the outer islands chain, is big enough to merit its own boat service, which goes to **Skudeneshavn** in the south, an idyllic old port with white wooden houses along narrow streets (tours from **Mælandsgården Museum**; June–Aug). The north of the island is

Typical "seahouses" in Skudeneshavn.

⊙ **Fact**

Following claims by the Norwegian film critic Pål Bang-Hansen that Marilyn Monroe's father was a Norwegian émigré from Haugesund, the town erected a statue on the quayside to the Hollywood goddess.

linked to the mainland just south of Haugesund, the first sizeable coastal town north of Stavanger.

Karmøy's known history dates back to saga times, when it was the "North-way" shipping lane that gave Norway its name. Harald Hårfagre made his home at **Avaldsnes**  after the battle at Hafrsfjord. Also here is **St Olaf's church** (kirke), which was built between 1248 and 1263 by King Håkon Håkonson and restored in 1922 as the parish church. Near its north walls stands St Mary's Sewing Needle, a strange 6.5-metre (21ft) high stone pillar leaning towards the church wall. Legend tells that the Day of Judgement will come when the pillar touches the wall; priests are said to have climbed the pillar in the dead of night to pare away the top to make sure that the day is not yet nigh.

On the west coast at **Ferkingstad** are historic boathouses with walls made of stone blocks 1.5 metres (5ft) thick. Further north on the west coast, outside the town hall at **Åkrehamn**, stand two stone pillars from the Iron Age. Crossing to the east coast, near the town of

Along Haugesund's waterfront.

Kopervik are burial hills and mounds and stone pillars. The largest burial mound, Doøa Hill, was restored in 1978 and, though it has not yet been fully excavated, it dates back to the Bronze Age. Further north, on the mainland side of the bridge to Haugesund, are the **Five Bad Virgins** (Dem Fem Dårlige Jomfruer), stone monuments some 2.5 metres (8ft) high, where excavations in 1901 revealed a Roman bowl dating from AD 300–400.

HAUGESUND AND THE ISLANDS

Haugesund has long been a centre for fishing, shipping and farming. Today its harbour is filled with pleasure boats. The town has also become a festival and congress centre, and plays host to the Sildajazz Festival and the Norwegian International Film Festival (both Aug) and Rockfest in June.

Numerous fjords and lakes cut into the roughly shaped peninsula, ideal for fishing, sailing, rowing, canoeing, diving and walking. A boat trip to the idyllic group of islands of **Røvær** ㉝, around 10km (6 miles) to the west, occupies a day and offers shore fishing, interesting flora and fauna and, in summer, a wharf-side café.

M/S *Utsira* (tel: 91 88 15 65 or 47 88 01 44) provides a daily service to the island of **Utsira** ㉞, familiar from European shipping forecasts and Norway's western outpost. The 90-minute voyage makes a wonderful tour for bird-watchers, as does the island itself. Fishing is also excellent, and Norwegian saltwater fishing is free to holders of a national licence (see page 103). Day licences for lakes and rivers are available: contact Haugesund Tourist Office, tel: 52 01 08 30.

To the north, **Espevær** ㉟, a fishing village situated at the mouth of Bømlafjorden River, is well endowed with heritage sites. The village itself is one of the best-preserved sites in Norway; there is a maritime and fisheries museum, as well as a bathing house.

Stavanger is intrinsically linked to the sea.

STAVANGER

Once the port from which thousands emigrated to the United States, today Stavanger attracts an international crowd – and cuisine – as the centre of Norway's thriving oil industry.

Strange though it may seem in a city which has devoted nearly 1,000 years to the sea, the best way to arrive in Stavanger is by overnight train from Oslo. As the dawn arrives, the train slips along the side of the fjord with black mountain peaks outlined on either side, past the huge latticework of oil rigs and drilling towers which have made Stavanger Norway's oil capital. Enormous though they are, they do not intrude on the landscape, the size and grandeur of mountain and fjord serving to dwarf even these industrial giants.

Stavanger benefitted across the centuries from the bounty of the sea. As one source of prosperity disappeared, another arose. Shipping, fishing and trading have taken the city's ships and people all over the world, and brought seamen to Stavanger, to give it an easy-going relationship with other nations. Today, Norway's fourth-largest city, European Capital of Culture in 2008, is as international as ever: nearly a tenth of its 130,000 inhabitants are foreigners.

INTERNATIONAL EATING

This international community has demanded high standards, and Stavanger has good restaurants, hotels, entertainment and a cosmopolitan atmosphere out of all proportion to its size. As well as restaurants specialising in good Norwegian food, there is a

Norwegian flags for sale at Stavanger's market.

choice of Indian, Italian, Greek, Portuguese, Mexican, Chinese and Japanese eateries. The city is also home to Scandinavia's largest food festival, **Gladmat**, which draws thousands of visitors every year in late July, and to the country's only gastronomic institute.

Restaurants, and particularly alcohol, are expensive in Norway, but a great many cafés, bars and pubs have sprung up, sometimes with live music, so going out needn't cost an arm and a leg. In the **fish market** on the quayside, where fresh prawns eaten on the spot are the

Main Attractions
Gladmat Festival
Norwegian Petroleum
  Museum
Old Stavanger
Norwegian Canning
  Museum
Stavanger Cathedral

Map on page 202

favourite buy, and at the **fruit and flower market** nearby, you will hear many languages, and in the heart of Stavanger's shopping streets behind the market almost all the assistants speak English.

Apart from the prosperity brought by oil, Stavanger is also the principal town and seat of government of Rogaland.

AN AMERICAN CONNECTION

In the 19th and early 20th centuries Stavanger was the exit port for Norway's extensive emigration programme to the United States (see page 52) – there are more Americans of Norwegian descent than there are Norwegians. Not surprisingly, therefore, the city is host to the **Norwegian Emigration Centre Ⓐ** (Det Norske Utvandrersenteret, Strandkaien 31; tel: 51 53 88 60; www. emigrationcenter.com), where Norway's emigration history is documented and commemorated. For a fee, genealogical researchers will even help you to find your Norwegian roots. At the time of writing, the museum was temporarily closed to visitors but the genealogy service is still operating online.

THE SMELL OF SARDINES

The *iddis* (the colloquial name, meaning sardine label, for a person from Stavanger) claims to be the oldest true Norwegian; the city was founded in 872 after the Battle of Hafrsfjord, which took place just south of town. Here, King Harald Hårfagre won his final battle to unite the kingdom.

When work began on Stavanger Cathedral (Domkirken) in 1125, Stavanger was simply a cluster of small wooden houses at the end of the narrow inlet called **Vågen**. It was chosen as the heart of the bishopric, nevertheless, because it was the only recognisable settlement along this southwestern coast. From then on Stavanger was to be the most important town in the area. It grew slowly; the population was only 2,000 at the start of the 19th century, but had jumped to 30,000 by 1900.

In the 18th and 19th centuries, the city depended on fishing and maritime trade, and faced the world with an unbroken row of wharves and warehouses dedicated to these industries. Around the 1870s, at a time when fishing and shipping were

Salt cod for sale at the market.

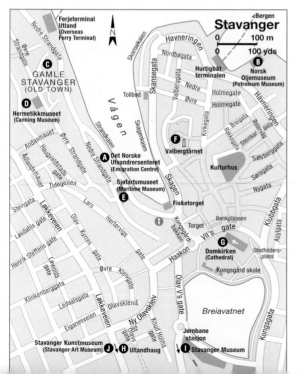

beginning to face decline, the fishermen turned their attention to brisling (small herring), which were cured and canned in the town and sent as Norwegian "sardines" all over the world.

At one time Stavanger had as many as 70 canneries, and nearly three-quarters of the population worked in the industry. In the first half of the 20th century, the smell of oily fish hung over the town and on every breath. But Stavanger never doubted the value of that smell. When, on a particularly malodorous day, a cheeky youngster wrinkled a disdainful nose, a mother would say: "Don't scorn it, that's the smell of money." It was, and Stavanger thrived on sardines until, after World War II, that all-pervasive tang began to fade along with the demand for sardines.

OFFSHORE OIL

For nearly 20 years, Stavanger knew difficult times. Then, in the late 1960s, came oil – once again the sea had provided. Visit the **Norwegian Petroleum Museum** ❸ (Norsk Oljemuseum, Kjeringholmen; tel: 51 93 93 00; www.norskolje. museum.no; June–Aug daily 10am–7pm, Sept–May Mon–Sat 10am–4pm, Sun 10am–6pm) by the harbour for an insight into this valuable source of energy. Here you will learn how petrol and gas were formed millions of years ago, and the history of its discovery in the North Sea in the late 1960s. You will also, with a range of models, films and interactive exhibits and experiments, get an insight into the technology used to harvest this source of energy, and the challenges it represents. You can find out what life on an offshore platform is like, and learn more about the way oil has influenced Norwegian society in recent decades. This modern, exciting and highly educational museum is one of the best in Norway, and a must-see in Stavanger. The Bolgen & Moi restaurant on the premises is also one of the best in town.

STREET OF MANY COLOURS

Round the corner from the Petroleum Museum, **Øvre Holmegate**, Stavanger's most colourful street, where all buildings have been painted in pastel hues, is a great place for a stroll and a bit of shopping. It is home to many

> **Ⓞ Tip**
>
> With much stamina and pinpoint planning you could take in all 10 sites of Stavanger Museum (www. museumstavanger.no) in one day for the price of a single ticket. Better perhaps to aim for the top five: Stavanger Museum itself, the Canning Museum, the Maritime Museum, the royal residence of Ledaal and the 19th-century manor house Breidablikk.

The Petroleum Museum.

> ## Ⓞ OUTDOOR ACTIVITIES
>
> Stavanger is on the doorstep of the *Jær-stendene landskapsvernområde*, a Protected Landscape Area which stretches 70km (43 miles) along the southern coast and its off-shore islands, with nature reserves (see page 194) and silver-sand beaches, ideal for swimming and picnicking. Sport is good year-round: swimming, sub-aqua diving, sailing, windsurfing and fishing. There is a hiking club, tennis and horse riding in Jær-stendene. In winter, the climate remains mild and the fields are rarely covered by snow; yet the good ski slopes are only an hour or so away.
>
> Stavanger also hosts the Sand Volleyball World Cup in late June–early July. The event attracts top beach volleyball players from around the world, who compete for medals, cash and Viking swords on courts set up around the harbour.

⊘ Eat

For a taste of old Stavanger, time your visit to the Norwegian Canning Museum for a day when the original ovens are lit and sample freshly smoked sardines straight from the fire (first Sun of every month and June–Aug Tue and Thu).

cosy cafés, the most famous of which is Sjokoladepiken (The Chocolate Girl) at No. 27), and small boutiques selling anything from funky retro fashion to second-hand books.

OLD STAVANGER

Many traces remain of the city's fluctuating fortunes over the years. **Old Stavanger ⊙** (Gamle Stavanger) is a preserved neighbourhood of more than 180 early 19th-century white wooden buildings looking down towards Vågen, with cobbled streets lit by old-fashioned streetlamps. But this is no museum. There may be a preservation order on the exteriors, and the owners take pride in keeping them in character, but the interiors have every comfort and gadget that modern Norwegians expect, and Gamle Stavanger is one of the most coveted areas in Norway in which to live.

Nor have the canning factories been lost. Many have been converted into modern offices, and a building that once canned sardines may now be the headquarters of an international oil company. One factory at Øvre Strandgate, in the old part of town near the harbour, has been preserved in its original state as the **Norwegian Canning Museum ⊙** (Norsk Hermetikkmuseet; tel: 51 84 27 00; mid-May–mid-Sept daily 10am–4pm; mid-Sept–mid-May Tue–Sun 11am–3pm). In the big open room with its curing ovens, the guides describe the life of the people who worked long hours at the intricate process of threading the sardines onto long rods, smoking, then packing them, almost all of it being done by hand.

Even nearer the harbour is the **Stavanger Maritime Museum ⊙** (Sjøfartsmuseet; tel: 51 84 27 00; mid-May–mid-Sept Mon–Wed and Fri–Sun 10am–4pm, Thu until 7pm; mid-Sept–mid-May Tue–Wed and Fri 11am–3pm, Thu until 7pm, Sat–Sun until 4pm) in one of the old mercantile houses on Nedre Strandgate, with its warehouses facing the sea. It traces the history of Stavanger's maritime links over the past 200 years. Today, large windows have replaced the warehouse doors, and you turn your head from the history behind you to the modern town outside. On the Nedre Strandgate side of the museum, away from the harbour, is a general store, its shelves stacked with the provisions that it would have held before World War II. Upstairs, where the owner lived, is an office just as it might have been when a crewman called in during the 1930s in search of a berth, or the skipper came to pay his respects. The apartment shows the comfortable life of a shipowner in the late 19th century.

On the other side of the harbour, facing the Maritime Museum, is the site of the original Viking settlement. The **Valberg Tower ⊙** (Valbergtårnet; tel: 90 72 63 94; mid-June–mid-Aug daily 10am–3pm, mid-Aug–Dec and Mar–mid-June first Sun of the month 11am–4pm), built in the early 1850s as a fire lookout, is the best point from which to get a view over the city. There is a small watchmen's museum on the first floor.

The nave of Stavanger Cathedral.

CENTRE OF WORSHIP

The heart of modern Stavanger is the area around **Breiavatnet**, the small lake in the middle of the city, near the oldest and biggest building, the 12th-century **Cathedral** G (Domkirken, Mon–Sat 11am–4pm, services every Sun at 11am). Construction began in 1125 by Bishop Reinald of Winchester in the Anglo-Norman style. It can claim with justification to be among the best-preserved medieval cathedrals in Europe. Alongside is the **Cathedral School**, built in 1758 on the 12th-century foundations of the Bishop's residence.

Inside this stone cathedral, the austere strength of the massive pillars contrasts with the elegant arches of the chancel and a tapestry by Frida Hansen (1927) in the vestibule. Both chancel and vestibule were rebuilt after 1272 in a style similar to the Scottish Gothic of the times, a reminder of Stavanger's international connections even in those early days.

ULLANDHAUG DISCOVERY

Even earlier than the cathedral is **Jernaldergarden**, the Iron Age farm at **Ullandhaug** H (tel: 51 83 26 00; http://am.uis.no/the-iron-age-farm; mid-June–mid-Aug daily 11am–4pm, mid-May–mid-June and mid-Aug–mid-Sept Sun 11am–4pm), about 2km (1.25 miles) southwest of the centre. Here archaeologists unearthed then reconstructed part of the farm to show three houses, parts of a cattle track and the original encircling stone wall from AD 350 and 550. This was a golden age in Norway, and the city's **Archaeological Museum** (Arkeologisk Museum, Peder Klows gate 30a; tel: 51 83 26 00; http://am.uis.no; June–Aug Mon–Fri 10am–4pm, Sat–Sun 11am–4pm, shorter hours rest of the year) showcases how people lived then.

From Ullandhaug, it is worth visiting the nearby **Botanical Garden** (Botanisk Hage; daily), which has a herb and perennial garden with more than 1,500 species from all over the world. Rogaland is rich in birds and fauna, and the

Stavanger Museum I (tel: 51 84 27 00; daily 10am–4pm) has an excellent exhibition, not only on Rogaland wildlife, but on cultural history, and the history of fishing (covering the industry and its creatures, including whales and seals).

LAKESIDE ART GALLERY

Last, but not least, the **Stavanger Art Museum** J (Stavanger Kunstmuseum, Henrik Ibsensgate 55; tel: 93 21 37 15; Tue–Wed and Fri–Sun 10am–4pm, Thu until 7pm), beautifully set in a park surrounding Lake Mosvannet, 3km (2 miles) south of Stavanger centre, has a good collection of Norwegian art ranging from 19th-century to contemporary. Of particular interest are the paintings by Lars Hertervig (1830–1902), who was born near Stavanger and whose haunting landscapes still have as strong an impact as they did when he painted them over a century ago. The museum houses the Halvdan Hafsten Collection, some 200 works by mid-20th century painters, making it a national centre for art from this period. Also here is the first of Antony Gormley's *Broken Column* figures that spread through town.

Learn all about the canning industry at the Norwegian Canning Museum.

⊘ ANTONY GORMLEY IN STAVANGER

Antony Gormley, the British sculptor known for his *Angel of the North* in England, has made his mark on Stavanger with **Broken Column** (2003). Twenty-three cast-iron figures have been strategically placed to give the appearance of an imaginary column stretching from the Stavanger Art Museum to the city's harbour. The figures are based on a casting of the sculptor's own body, and have been placed to reflect a broad perspective of people's life in the city, with the figure standing gazing out to sea on the fish market forming the cardinal point for all the other sculptures. The height of each sculpture (1.95 metres/6ft 5in) is the same as that of the sculptor himself. The first sculpture stands in its own room in Stavanger Art Museum, 41.41 metres (136ft) above sea level. The next sculpture on the line is in Mosvannparken at 39.46 metres (130ft) altitude (ie 41.41 minus 1.95 metres). The column of figures continues in this fashion down through the city until it reaches the sea. The last sculpture stands partly submerged on a rock beyond Natvigs Minde in Stavanger's harbour.

If you travel far enough north along Norway's coastline, you'll come across another of Gormley's haunting sculptures. Off Mo i Rana (see page 266), his lone *Havmannen (Man of the Sea)*, for ever up to its knees in water, gazes out across the ocean.

HORDALAND

An inspiration to generations of Norwegian artists, the mighty Hardangerfjord lies at the heart of this region, which mixes wild coasts with sheltered islands, and spring blossoms with fjord waters.

Map on page 208

Stretching a full 180km (110 miles) between the North Sea in the west and the reaches of the Hardanger plateau in the east, Hardangerfjord offers a variety of landscapes, from windswept islands and skerries at the ocean's edge to picturesque villages clinging to the hillsides further inland, not to mention mighty waterfalls in the mountains and majestic glaciers on the horizon. It's a place for outdoor pleasures; canoeing or kayaking on the main fjord or nudging into one or two of the myriad small inlets, walking the heights, cross-country skiing in season – or simply spreading a picnic and enjoying the freshest of fruits from the region's orchards.

Nobody has ever counted how many low islands, islets and skerries lie off the coast of Hordaland. Many of the inner islands around Bergen are linked by bridges and causeways in a pattern of islands and sea that seems all of a piece with the multitude of branched fjords, including the famous Hardangerfjord.

Hardangerfjord is also known for its orchards – the fruit-growing districts of Ulvik and Ullesvang are among Norway's largest, and Lofthus on Sørfjorden is home to a popular cherry festival.

EARLY CHRISTIANITY

The southwest district of **Sunnhordland** has islands, skerries, sounds and straits, good harbours and sheltered bays. Though the North Sea is its neighbour, the climate is surprisingly mild. The main islands are **Bømlo**, **Stord** and **Tysnesøy**, and even though they are close to the sea they have a variety of scenery.

Stord makes a good paddling-off point for sea canoeing, either from island to island, or into the mouth of the Hardanger. It is an "oil island", too, off which the gigantic outlines of oil platforms rear, some rising nearly 380 metres (1,250ft) out of the water.

The sagas tell that in 1024 St Olav first introduced Christianity to Norway

On a Norway in a Nutshell trip.

in these islands. Today, an annual outdoor performance (late May or early June; tel: 53 42 07 90) of the historical play *Mostraspelet*, held at **Mosterhamn ❶** on Bømlo, dramatises this ancient saga. Nearby is a stone cross erected in 1924 on the 900th anniversary of the arrival of Christianity, and Mosterhamn has the oldest **stone church** in Norway (May–Sept), built around 995–1100. The church bells bear images of St Olav.

SOUTHERN HARDANGERFJORD

The mouth of the Hardangerfjord is as beautiful as anywhere deeper into the fjord itself. Even so, Sunnhordaland generally tends to be overshadowed by the fame and drama of Hardangerfjord. Too many visitors travel through quickly on their way to other places. The discriminating know it deserves a longer look.

Leirvik on Stord is a good starting point, with short ferry connections to most of the surrounding islands and to the mainland. It is also the location of the **Sunnhordland Museum** (all year), which was established in 1913 as the local history museum.

To the south, the ferry to **Valevåg** puts you on the right track for **Ryvarden Fyr** (lighthouse; all year every Sun 11am–5pm, July to mid-Aug more frequently), sitting at the mouth of Bømlafjord, the home of the innovative composer Fartein Valen (1887–1952), where overnight stays can be arranged. There is also a museum, art gallery and café at nearby Møstrevåg.

To the east, a ferry to Sunde on the mainland brings you to where the cold waters of Hardangerfjord blend into the warmer tides from the west and the lovely 17th-century **Rosendal Barony** (Baroniet Rosendal; www.baroniet.no; mid-May–early Sept) in **Rosendal ❷**, the only one of its kind in Norway, which lost much of its aristocracy when the "occupying" Danes departed. The manor house was built in 1665 by Ludvig Rosenkrantz. He is buried in the nearby medieval Kvinnherad Kirke (church), snuggled into the shelter of a rock face and once owned by the barony. The barony today has a peaceful park and a large, carefully tended 300-year-old rose garden, and is held in trust by Oslo University. Throughout the summer there are art exhibitions, lunchtime concerts, and the **Rosendal Chamber Music Festival** (www.rosendal festival.com) is staged here in August.

Hardangerfjord is part of the Norwegian legend, the fjord that gave its name to Norway's national musical instrument, the eight-stringed Hardanger fiddle, and provided inspiration for the composer Edvard Grieg (1843–1907), the musician Ole Bull (1810–80) and, indirectly, for the 19th-century nationalist movement that eventually led to Norway's independence. Among these mountains and fjords, Grieg and Bull travelled on foot and horse, learning old melodies and dipping into centuries-old cultural traditions and folk customs.

POETIC ODYSSEY

Tourism came to the Hardanger district as early as the 1830s when the poet Henrik Wergeland (1808–45) wrote

Enjoying the water.

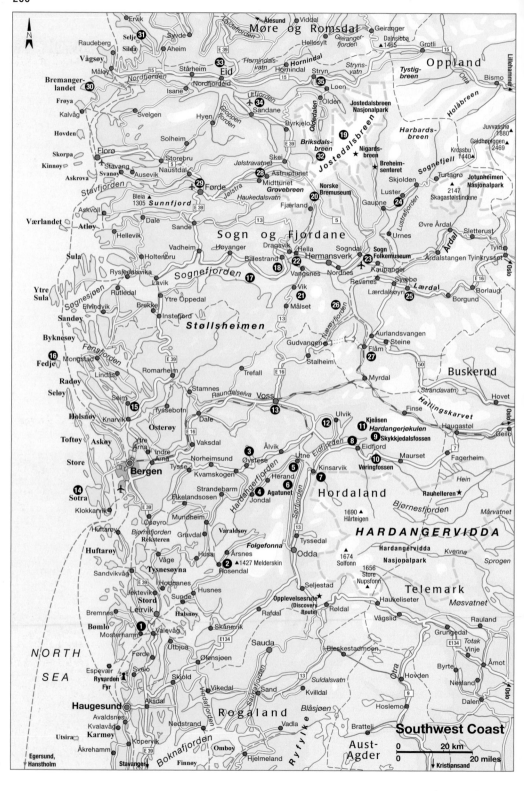

Southwest Coast

about "wonderful Hardanger", and foreign as well as Norwegian artists, scientists and other travellers began to arrive; first in a trickle, then in a flood when, 30 years later, the steamers began to run from Bergen or Stavanger. Like the visitors of today, they came to Hardanger for its waterfalls, the smaller fjords that lead almost to the Hardanger plateau, and for glaciers and mountains that rarely lose their snow caps, contrasted with orchards lining the fjord side. Nearly half a million fruit trees grow here, including plum, cherry, apple and pear, turning the fjord pink and white in spring as the blossom reflects in the deep, still water. At this time the waterfalls are in full spate, shooting over the sides of the mountains. The Hardanger has two of Norway's highest and best known: **Skykkjedalsfossen**, which falls 300 metres (1,000ft), and **Vøringfossen**, lower but famous for its beauty.

NORTHERN HARDANGERFJORD

Crossing by ferry to the north shore, Road 49 runs along the sunny side of Hardangerfjord towards the fjordside villages of **Norheimsund** and **Øystese** ❸. Alternatively, they can be reached through day or longer excursions from Bergen either by boat or road (E16 and then Road 11). Both of these villages offer excellent trips for exploring the fjords by car and ferry, and marked paths here and at **Kvamskogen** further inland make for safe walking. Take time out to visit the **Ingebrigt Vik Museum**, part of **Kunsthuset Kabuso** (www.kabuso.no; early June–Aug Tue–Sun 10am–5pm, shorter hours rest of the year) at Øystese, one of Norway's most distinctive museums, containing virtually all the works by the Norwegian sculptor of that name (1867–1927).

Not to be passed by is the **Hardanger Maritime Museum** (Hardanger Fartøyvernsenter; www.fartoyvern.no; May–Aug daily 10am–5pm) at Norheimsund, where conservationists patiently restore the wooden craft that made Norwegian boatbuilding famous. They range from small rowing boats to the centre's most prestigious restoration, the M/S *Mathilde*, a 22 metre (73ft)

The old fjord village of Utne.

⊙ Fact

Edvard Grieg used to visit a small *hytte* poised on the edge of Hardangerfjord near the village of Ullensvang where, with piano and writing desk at hand, he would compose surrounded by the beauty of the Norwegian fjords.

Hardanger yacht launched in 1884. This superb craft has regained her former splendour under the guidance of Kristian Djupevåg (who also restored Roald Amundsen's polar vessel, *Gjøa*), and it has the world's largest authentic yacht rigging. The *Mathilde* sleeps 25 passengers in bunks or hammocks and is available for cruises and day excursions, when she can take 50 people to sail fjord and sea, just as in earlier days.

ACROSS TO JONDAL

Ferries make the crossing from Tørvikbygd to **Jondal** ❹, on the south side of the fjord, and the entrance to the **Folgefonna Glacier** and **Folgefonna Summer Ski-Centre**. The safe but exciting 19km (12-mile) toll road to the new ski centre is clear from May to September. With snow at the centre for almost all of the year, there are three mobile ski lifts, Alpine and cross-country skiing tracks (you can hire all the equipment), a cafeteria and guided walks on the glacier.

Jondal itself has a school museum (tel: 55 66 85 31, guided tours), and

Hardanger Cathedral (late May–mid-June Tue–Fri 10am–2pm, mid-June–mid-Aug daily 10am–7pm). It was built in 1888 and is the largest church in the Hardanger region. Concerts are held in the church in July.

About 13km (8 miles) northeast at **Herand** you will find Bronze Age rock carvings and, at Herandsholmen, Hardanger's first guesthouse, which opened in 1754.

By now into the inner fjords, the road suddenly turns sharply southeast towards Utne village, part of Ullensvang *kommune*, which also includes both sides of Sørfjorden. When the fjords served as west Norway's main "roads", **Utne** ❺ was an important junction between east and west and had the first post and telegraph offices in Hardanger, in 1836 and 1876 respectively.

Two establishments in Utne which sum up Hardanger life over the past centuries are the **Hardanger Folk Museum** (Folkemuseum; www.hardangerfolkemuseum.no; May–Aug daily 10am–5pm, Sept–Apr Mon–Fri 10am–3pm), and the **Utne Hotel** (tel: 53 66 64

Local folk costume.

00; www.utnehotel.no), founded in 1722, the oldest hotel in Norway still in operation. Since 1787, five generations of the same family have owned the hotel. It first became famous internationally during the time of Torbjørg Utne (1812–1903), known with affection as Mor (Mother) Utne. Her picture hangs on the sitting-room wall. The family is represented today by her great granddaughter, Hildegun Aga Blokhus. It has always been a favourite spot for artists, who have donated many paintings, and the hotel also holds exhibitions of national costumes and embroidery.

Since it opened in 1911, the Hardanger Folkemuseum has collected old houses and farm buildings and has created a "cluster farm" as it would have been before the Norwegian agricultural reforms in the middle of the 19th century. Along the shore are old boathouses and a merchant's shop, which was in use in Utne until recently, and an orchard preserves many old varieties of fruit no longer cultivated around Hardangerfjord. Inside, the museum has a modern exhibition, rooms showing traditional crafts, local folk costumes and folk art and an example of the famous Hardanger fiddle along with a resident fiddle maker, and changing exhibitions on fjord themes.

AROUND SØRFJORD

Past Utne, the fjord-side road turns due south into the **Sørfjord**. For a magnificent view, stop at **Agatunet** ❻ (www.aga tunet.no; May–Aug 10am–5pm), the farm of a 13th-century local sheriff. From the Middle Ages to the recent past, Agatunet grew into a nine-family village with a hamlet of some 30 buildings. Today, the families no longer live there but the buildings have been preserved.

On the eastern side of Sørfjord, a short ferry ride away, is an amusement park, **Mikkelparken** (July daily 10.30am–6.30pm; late May–June and Aug Sat–Sun only 10.30am–6.30pm) at **Kinsarvik** ❼. A favourite with children,

it has a water chute, trampoline, a miniature zoo, a boating lake, and lends out surfboards, water mopeds and water skis. Kinsarvik was also part of the main east–west transport route, and its marketplace attracted merchants from both sides of Hardangervidda to exchange bog iron and furs for sea salt. The **stone church** is said to have been constructed by Scottish builders around 1160, and has a 17th-century pulpit painted by Peter Reimers. Until Utne church (kirke) was consecrated in 1896, Kinsarvik had for centuries drawn its congregation from all around the fjords, and many worshippers arrived in church boats.

DRAMATIC EIDFJORD

Heading northeast from Kinsarvik on the E13 and then Road 7, you will find one of the area's most beautiful stretches of water, **Eidfjord** ❽. It cuts far into the dramatic landscape, which includes the **Hardangerjøkulen** and, below it, **Skykkjedalsfossen** ❾, Norway's highest waterfall, and **Vøringfossen** ❿, which falls 180 metres (590ft) down into the wilds of Måbødalen. The path at the top

Vangskyrkja, a rare vestige of medieval Voss.

> ⊙ **Tip**

The Hardangervidda Nature Centre in Eidfjord is a good place to learn about the flora and fauna of Europe's largest mountainous plateau (tel: 53 67 40 00; www. hardangervidda.org).

overlooking the fall is not for vertigo sufferers. Alternatively, you can walk down to view this great outpouring from below, and fitness fanatics might welcome the challenge of the age-old packhorse track up Måbøfjell, with 1,500 steps and 125 bends. Look out for signs to the **Måbødalen Agricultural Landscape Museum** (Kulturlandskapsmuseum; tel: 53 67 35 00; all year; guided tours available), which provides a network of trails, all signposted and with information boards. The public barbecue areas make fabulous picnic stops.

Above tiny Simadalsfjord is a mountain farm, **Kjeåsen** ⓫, which claims to be the world's most isolated settlement. It lies like an eagle's nest 620 metres (2,000ft) on near-vertical rock above the distant waters of the fjord. Those feeling strong and brave can tackle the old path to the top and marvel how the villagers struggled up with their every need. For frailer spirits it is possible to reach Kjeåsen by car through a magnificent new tunnel. Inside the mountain is the **Sima Kraftverk** (Hydroelectric Power Station; daily July).

Crossing Eidfjorden at Brimnes you enter a farming and forestry district. Instead of taking the E13, take a right turn onto Road 572, which will bring you to **Ulvik** ⓬. Artists and other visitors have been coming here for many years, and the village has permanent exhibitions by artists such as Tit Mohr (born 1917) and Sigurd Undeland (1903–83). No one should miss the fine examples of **rose painting** in Ulvik's 19th-century church, created in 1923 by Lars Osa (1860–1958).

SPORTING VOSS

Continuing on in a loop back to the E13 you come to **Voss** ⓭, which lies next to a lake, **Vangsvatnet**, in the middle of rich farmland. The Voss *kommune* (district) makes full use of its surroundings to attract visitors. In summer they come for touring, fjord excursions, mountain walking, parachuting, hang-gliding and paragliding from **Hangurfjell**, and fishing and water sports on Vangsvatnet. In winter, Voss becomes one of the best centres in Norway for Alpine and cross-country skiing of the more energetic touring variety.

Traditional wedding at Voss led by a fiddler and toastmaster.

Voss is also a good place for mountain touring and sport fishing in the 500 or so lakes and innumerable mountain rivers and streams, with the Vosso River famous for the size of its salmon. Even in summer the high mountains call for boots or very strong shoes and plenty of extra clothes – temperatures drop quickly; this applies in all upland areas.

The top station of the **cable car** up Hangurfjell gives one of the best prospects of Voss in its bowl-shaped valley. Sipping a coffee on a sunny day on the platform outside the cafeteria, you may well spot a paraglider soaring into the sun and over the waters of Vagnsvatnet, way below.

At the time of writing the old cable car has ceased operating, to be replaced by a new one with a capacity of 1,300 passengers an hour, scheduled for the end of 2018. At the beginning of World War II, Voss was badly damaged by German bombing, and not much remains of the old town centre except the church, **Vangskyrkja** (June–Aug daily), which dates back to 1277. The interior has a colourfully painted ceiling liberally adorned with flying angels. Outside, a stone cross stands in a field south of the church. According to legend, it was raised two centuries before the church itself was built by the proselytising King Olav Haraldson. The church walls are 2 metres (7ft) thick, and the wooden octagonal steeple is unique in Norway.

Below Hangurfjell, about half an hour's walk above the town, is the **Voss Museum** (Folkemuseum; tel: 47 47 97 94; www.vossfolkemuseum.no; mid-May–Aug daily 10am–5pm, Sept–mid-May Mon–Fri 10am–3pm, Sun noon–3pm), a collection of 16 old wooden buildings standing in traditional form around a central courtyard. The houses date from 1500 to 1870 and contain implements and furniture in use until 1927. Yet somehow, despite the heavy farm work and meagre evening light, farm people like these managed to produce some beautiful embroidery, wood and other craft work.

ARTISTIC TRADITION

Voss, long a centre for artists and musicians, has several monuments erected in their memory. The 1957 Sivle monument marks the centenary of the birth of the author and poet Per Sivle (1857–1904), who grew up on the mountain farm of Sivle, in the great Stalheim Skleive (gorge); the monument behind Voss church commemorates three Bergslien artist brothers, Brynjulf, Nils and Knut; near Voss Fine Arts Society is a memorial to actor Lars Tvinde, born and bred on the farm of Tvinde, which lies below the Tvindefossen (a waterfall to the north of Voss); and on the same road the 1958 Sjur Helgeland Memorial commemorates another local fiddler and composer.

This artistic tradition continues, and Voss is one of the best places to hear the Hardanger fiddle and see folk dances performed in beautiful costumes. On the main street is a shop where you can see, or buy, the ornate silver belts and jewellery that go with the traditional Norwegian costume *(bunad)*. An international jazz festival is held in the town every April.

At Voss Folk Museum.

AROUND BERGEN AND NORTH

From Voss the E16 is the quickest way to Bergen. After an hour's drive to the long narrow island of **Sotra** , which shelters the city from the North Sea, you enter a different world. Sotra is a good base for sea canoeing in and out of its small offshore islands and rocks and, in good weather, as far as the open sea to combine canoeing with ocean fishing.

North of Bergen is a second island district, **Nordhordland**, that stretches as far north as Sognefjorden and includes the islands of Holsnøy, Radøy and Sandøy. At weekends, it is a favourite area for Bergensere who go sailing, swimming and fishing.

In Nordhordland the sea can be at its wildest, smashing against the western coast, yet the area has been inhabited for some 8,000 years. Håkon den Gode (the Good) is buried at **Seim** , near Knarvik (half an hour from Bergen by express boat). Another rare reminder of the Vikings is a beech wood, also at Seim, 1,000 years old and the northernmost beech wood in Europe.

Today, fish-farming is important to Nordhordland, which exports vast quantities of salmon and trout all over the world. Fish-farmers are also attempting to rear cod, halibut and other species and their farms are open to the public. There is good sea fishing for cod and coalfish, and special rosy-coloured trout thrive in many of the lakes. Diving and sub-aqua fishing are easy in these transparent waters. Oil is a modern industry in this widespread area, with the night gleam of the light from Mongstad signalling this large refinery.

PICNIC ON FEDJE

Most remote of all, and a target for sailing picnics and holidays, is the island of **Fedje** , an important navigation point for centuries with two 19th-century lighthouses still in use today. In these ever-changing waters, Norwegian sea laws insist that all ships must carry a Norwegian pilot, and tankers destined for Mongstad refinery are navigated from here through the unreliable waters. Stay overnight on Fedje in one of the guesthouses in Kræmmerholmen or in the Pensjonat or lighthouse there and enjoy this idyllic bird and flower habitat.

Kjosfossen waterfall.

⊘ NORWAY IN A NUTSHELL

If you have only a day to spare in this region, this tour which, but for its tagging on an island or two, might well be called "Hordaland in a Nutshell" covers many of the sights. It runs throughout the year and combines bus, ferry and train (see page 306).

The tour starts with a train journey from either Oslo or Bergen to Myrdal and can be done in a day in the summer months (in winter an overnight stop is necessary). From Myrdal it sets off on one of the steepest train journeys in the world, the 50-minute panoramic trip down 850 metres (2,800ft) of mountain gorge to the pretty village of Flåm, stopping – thanks to one of the five separate sets of brakes – for a photo opportunity at the torrent of Kjosfossen and to pick up passengers at one or two of the tiny stations.

The next leg is by ferry, which travels through Aurlandsfjord and Norway's narrowest fjord, Nærøyfjord, its rocky sides twice as high as the water is wide and now included on Unesco's World Heritage list. From here the journey continues on by bus to Voss, skirting around Oppheim Lake.

In summer the bus makes the hairpin ascent to the Stalheim Hotel. The hotel parapet looks down over the depths of the Stalheimskleive (gorge). A tortuous descent leads to the fjord.

BERGEN

With its relaxed atmosphere, stunning setting and vibrant cultural life, Bergen is an appealing mix of the cosmopolitan and the outdoors, with easy access to the western fjords.

There's always a sense of symmetry and order about a city built on hills. If it also stands on a peninsula and has a harbour at its heart, it is bound to be beautiful. Bergen, the capital of west Norway, ticks all these boxes. Built on seven hills, the city grew outwards from the coast and harbour in the quaintly named Puddefjord and spread across the steep slopes and over the bridges that link islands and headlands. Several world-class museums, an active cultural scene and the bustling fishing port complement the sheer beauty of the city and its surroundings.

Too many visitors allow only a day or even half a day for Bergen at the start and end of a visit to the western fjords, which doesn't give the city a chance. However, since the world-wide phenomenal success of Disney's animated movie *Frozen*, Bergen has experienced a boom in tourist numbers and there is now a new Disney Cruise Line route taking in Bergen and the fjord region. *Frozen* things aside, Bergen makes an ideal base for a fjord holiday, combining the cosmopolitan delights of the city with the splendid scenery of the fjords. Bergen has plenty to do and see, or you can simply spend some time just soaking up the atmosphere down by the busy harbour. But take an umbrella: Bergen may be one of the

prettiest towns in Norway, but it is also the wettest – on average it rains 220 days a year.

A VIEW FROM THE TOP

The best place to get a feel of the city's natural location is to take the funicular, **Fløibanen** Ⓐ (www.floibanen.no; daily every 15–30 minutes, 7.30am–11pm), that climbs more than 300 metres (1,000ft) in just eight minutes from the centre to **Fløyen**, high above Bergen. On the downward journey, you seem to be tipping headfirst into the city.

⊙ Main Attractions
Fløibanen
Hanseatic Museum
Old Bergen
Fish market
KODE Art Museums of Bergen

Map on page 218

Bergen's funicular railway on its way up to Fløyen.

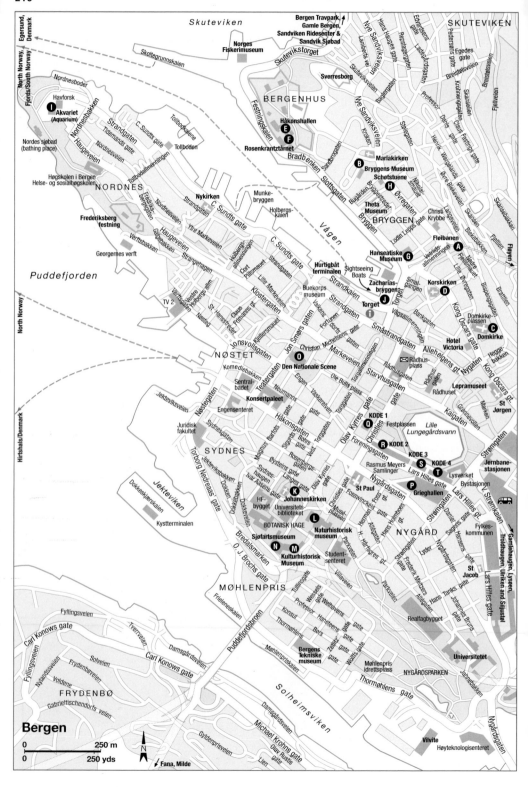

Skuteviken

Bergen Travpark,
Gamle Bergen,
Sandviken Ridesenter &
Sandvik Sjøbad

SKUTEVIKEN

Egersund,
Denmark
North Norway
Fjords/South Norway

Norges
Fiskerimuseum

Skutevikstorget

Sverresborg

BERGENHUS

Skoltegrunnskaien

Nordnesboder

Havforsk

Akvariet
(Aquarium)

Håkonshallen

E

F

Rosenkrantztårnet

Mariakirken

B

Bryggens Museum

Schøtstuene

H

Nordes sjøbad
(bathing place)

Tollbøden

Bradbenken

Høgskolen i Bergen
Helse- og sosialhøgskolen.

Theta
Museum

BRYGGEN

NORDNES

Nykirken

Munke-
bryggen

Holbergs-
kaien

Bryggen

Frederiksberg
festning

Vågen

Fløibanen

A

Georgernes verft

Hanseatiske
Museum

G

Puddefjorden

Hurtigbåt
terminalen

Sightseeing
Boats

Korskirken

D

TV 2

Buekorps
museum

Zacharias-
bryggen

North Norway

Torget

J

Domkirke-
plassen

Domkirke

C

NØSTET

Hotel
Victoria

Hirtshals/Denmark

Den Nationale Scene

Jekteviken

Rådhus-
plass

Lepramuseet

Rådhuset

St
Jørgen

Konsertpaleet

KODE 1

Q

Festplassen

Lille
Lungegårdsvann

SYDNES

Juridisk
fakultet

KODE 2

R

KODE 3

S

Jernbane-
stasjonen

Rasmus Meyers
Samlinger

KODE 4

T

Lysverket

Bystasjonen

Johanneskirken

K

St Paul

Grieghallen

HF-
bygget

Universitets-
biblioteket

L

NYGÅRD

BOTANISK HAGE

Naturhistorisk
museum

Fylkes-
kommunen

Gamlehaugen, Lysøen,
Troldhaugen, Ulriken and Siljustøl

Sjøfartsmuseum

N

M

St
Jacob

Kulturhistorisk
Museum

Student-
senteret

MØHLENPRIS

Realfagbygget

Bergens
Tekniske
museum

Møhlenpris
idrettsplass

NYGÅRDSPARKEN

Universitetet

FRYDENBØ

Solheimsviken

Bergen

0   250 m
0   250 yds

N

Fana, Milde

Vilvite
Høyteknologisenteret

At the top is the lovely old-fashioned building that houses Fløien Folker-estaurant, built in 1925. It marks the start of eight marked walking routes, the longest no more than around 4km (2.5 miles), that buck up and down steep hills, through woods and over open moor. There are several huts for shelter along the way.

A leisurely coffee or lunch on the veranda of the restaurant gives a chance also to drink in the superb view over hundreds of islands, many with small *hytter* (wooden cabins) and a couple of boats tied to a landing stage – many a Norwegian's dream for an ideal summer. All around are the mountains and hills that cradle the city – Fløifjellet, Damsgårdfjellet, Løvstakken, Sandviksfjellet, Rundemånnen, Blåmannen, and the highest of them all, **Ulriken** at around 640 metres (2,100ft) and reached by a cable car (tel: 53 64 36 43; http://ulriken643.no; daily 9am–9pm; the cable car might not operate on very windy days). The Ulriken mountain café is open when the cable car is running. There is a double-decker bus connection (peak season only) with the cable car from Torget, the site of the famous Bergen fish market.

A long tradition of international trade has made this city the most outgoing in Norway and, some say, given the Bergensere a jauntiness in their walk that hints at generations of sailors, quick wits, worldliness and a sense of their own worth. Bergensere are certain they are the best, reckoning that, although Oslo may now be the capital, it is historically a mere toddler compared with their city.

OLAV KYRRE'S CITY

King Olav Kyrre is credited with founding Bergen in 1070 at Torget. But long before, the site, with its perfect natural harbour and sheltered fjords, was a home for small communities that depended on the sea. During the 13th century, Bergen became the first capital of a united Norway, and a great ecclesiastical centre, with a cathedral, 20 churches and chapels, five monasteries and two hospitals for the poor. Bergen lost its capital status to Oslo during the Middle Ages, but still dwarfed the new capital. In medieval times, it was the biggest city in the Nordic countries and, until 1830, the largest in Norway. Today, with a population of around 278,000, it is roughly half the size of Oslo.

Much of this early size and success came when Bergen was chosen as the northern hub of the medieval German Hanseatic League. Their trading base on the north side of **Vågen** became the powerhouse of all trade on the northwest Norwegian coast. But the Hansa began to grow too powerful all over Scandinavia and, at last, Norway broke the tie that kept the west in thraldom.

THE PERILS OF FIRE AND WAR

As in all wooden cities, fire has swept through Bergen on many occasions, often devastating it. The result is that the oldest surviving buildings are built

Serving as the starting point for numerous tours and cruises, Bergen is known as the "gateway to the fjords".

Bergen's harbour.

The Hanseatic Museum illustrates Bergen's history.

of stone, and the present streets, following the last fire in 1916 when a gale fanned the flames to an inferno, are wide and designed as fire breaks.

During World War II, Bergen was a centre of the Resistance movement, and many young people from the town took the perilous route out to the Shetland Islands. One group, with members aged 19–22, escaped to Scotland and returned with radio equipment to establish contact with exiled Norwegian authorities in England. The actions of the movement are commemorated by the **Theta Museum** in Bryggen (tel: 55 55 20 80; June–Aug Tue, Sat, Sun 2–4pm). Yet the major disaster of this unhappy period came not directly from war but through accident caused by war. In 1944 a Dutch ammunition ship in the harbour blew up, damaging many of the oldest buildings on the northern promontory, including Håkonshallen and Rosenkrantztårnet. Anti-German feelings ran high at that time. The famous Tyskebryggen (or "German Quay", named after Hansa merchants) has been shortened to simply **Bryggen**.

STARTING WITH THE PAST

The earliest archaeological remains are in **Bryggens Museum** Ⓑ (tel: 55 30 80 30; www.bymuseet.no; mid-May–Aug daily 10am–4pm; Sept–mid-May Mon–Fri 11am–3pm, Sat–Sun noon–4pm), past the Hansa houses on the north side of the harbour. The museum contains the medieval remains uncovered during archaeological digs between 1955 and 1972. There are also many artefacts and re-creations of medieval rooms. Together it gives a picture of the time when Bergen was a small fishing and sailing community that clung to the shallow slopes above the shore.

Nearby is the oldest building still in use, **St Mary's Church** (Mariakirken; tel: 55 31 59 60; July–mid-Sept Mon–Fri 9am–4pm), built in the early years of the 12th century and justly proud of its rich Baroque pulpit. The only other medieval churches to survive periodic fires are the present **Bergen Cathedral** Ⓒ (Domkirke; tel: 55 31 58 75; closed for restoration), once dedicated to St Olav and rebuilt five times owing to

fire, and the **Church of the Holy Cross D** (Korskirken; daily Mon–Fri 11am–4pm), most of it now in the Renaissance style of the 17th century. The last two are relatively close to the harbour.

MEDIEVAL HÅKONSHALLEN

Holmen was the site of **Bergenhus**, the old timber-built royal palace used when Bergen first became a capital. At a time of much building in the 13th century, it was converted to a fortified stronghold of stone, and the restored remains are close to where the original cathedral and bishop's residence stood.

There are two particularly notable buildings: **Håkonshallen E** (tel: 55 30 80 30; www.bymuseet.no; mid-May–mid-Sept daily 10am–4pm; mid-Sept–mid-May daily noon–3pm), built by King Håkon Håkonsson between 1247 and 1261. The largest secular medieval building still standing in Norway, it was used for the wedding of King Magnus Lagabøte (the Lawmaker), who was Håkon's son and co-ruler; and **Rosenkrantztårnet F** (tower; tel: 55 58 80 50; www.bymuseet.no; mid-May–mid-Sept

daily 9am–4pm; Sept–mid-May Sun only noon–3pm). This tower was the work of a Danish governor of Bergenhus, Erik Rosenkrantz, who grafted it onto Håkon's original "Keep of the Sea" in the 1560s. You can buy a discounted joint ticket for Håkonshallen and the tower, and guided tours in English and Norwegian start every half-hour.

When both buildings were badly damaged in the 1944 explosion, Norwegian historians took the opportunity to reconstruct them as closely to the originals as possible. Today, Håkonshallen makes a magnificent concert hall, while Rosenkrantztårnet is now a museum, with permanent as well as special exhibitions.

BRYGGEN'S HANSA HOUSES

In summer, guides from Bryggens Museum conduct tours through the row of Hansa houses that line **Bryggen**. These homes and warehouses were all built after the great fire of 1702, which destroyed many buildings, and they are on the Unesco World Heritage list. One key to understanding the Hansa way of

⏱ Where

For accommodation, tours and brochures, you will find the Tourist Information Office in a striking building at Strandkaien 3, near the Fish Market (tel: 55 55 20 00; June–Aug daily 8.30am–10pm, May and Sept 9am–8pm, Oct–Apr Mon–Sat 9am–4pm).

Bryggen on the quayside.

> ⊙ **Tip**

Buy a *Bergen Kortet* (card), valid for 24, 48 or 72 hours, and enjoy free admission to many museums, free travel on city buses and on the funicular to Mount Fløyen, plus numerous discounts. Available from the Tourist Information Office and hotels.

life is a visit to the **Hanseatic Museum**  (Hanseatiske Museum; http://hanseatiskemuseum.museumvest.no; tel: 55 54 46 90; daily May and Sept 10am–5pm, June–Aug 9am–6pm, Oct–Apr 11am–3pm), furnished in the style of the time when the merchant had his accounting room within the main office on the first floor. This small room enabled him to keep an eye on the liquor room next door. The adjoining room, decorated with a "royal cod", distinguished by a bump on its head and said to bring luck, served as dining and sitting room for merchants and apprentices. On the floor above are the apprentices' tiny box beds, one above the other. The sleeping quarters were cramped, but importantly retained heat. Although apprentices generally were merchants' sons, sent to learn their business with a colleague, they were locked into their "prisons" at night.

As a fire precaution – all too often in vain – no heating was allowed in these Hansa houses so the Germans must have suffered torments of cold in the biting damp of a Bergen winter.

Bryggen's characteristic wooden carvings.

No wonder that **Schøtstuene** (http://hanseatiskemuseum.museumvest.no; tel: 55 54 46 90; daily May and Sept 10am–5pm, June–Aug 10am–6pm, Oct–Apr Sun 11am–3pm), the assembly rooms nearby, were so popular during winter when trade was slack and few ships were in the harbour. The long central table held both beer jugs and the Bible, exemplifying the two religions of the Hansa. In a drawer was the cane used to discipline the apprentices who had their schooling there. The "rules of the club" adorn one wall, written in Low German (old northern dialect).

OLD BERGEN

At Elsesro, further out along the coast road, past Bergenshus and the North Sea quay, is **Old Bergen** (Gamle Bergen; tel: 55 30 80 30; www.bymuseet.no; mid-May–Aug 9am–4pm, early May and early Sept 10am–3pm; guided tours only, every hour), one of the finest open-air museums in Scandinavia. Here there is a collection of 40 wooden buildings from the 18th and 19th centuries, the interiors decorated to show different styles. Along the cobbled streets, guides in traditional red calf-length costumes and black shawls lead tours, which range from the French Empire splendour of the official's drawing room to the tiny house where the seamstress plied her diligent needle in the 1860s. Nearby is the popular **Sandvik Sjøbad** (bathing area), which looks out over Byfjorden to the city.

SHIPS, SHARKS AND MORE

Back along Vågen, a short ferry trip from below Rosenkrantztårnet to the Nordnes peninsula gives a good opportunity to view the beautiful lines of the sailing ship *Lehmkuhl*, which trains youngsters in sailing techniques and gleams with polished brass. A short walk towards Nordnes point reveals another castle, **Fredriksberg** (no visitors), and further north is **Nordnes sjøbad**, which includes a heated outdoor pool.

Here, too, you will find **Bergen Aquarium ❶** (Akvariet; tel: 55 55 71 71; www.akvariet.no; May–Aug daily 9am–6pm; Sept–Apr Mon–Wed and Fri 10am–4pm, Thu and Sat–Sun until 6pm; penguins' feeding time at 11am, seal show at 1pm). The aquarium, now more than 50 years old, might be showing its age a bit, but it remains the largest aquarium in Norway and one of the main attractions in Bergen, and is particularly popular with children. The penguins and the seals steal the show, but here you will also find the largest collection of crocodiles in Norway, plus snakes, reptiles and fish aplenty, as well as a shark tunnel, where sharks swim right over your head.

FISH MARKET SPECTACLE

Early each weekday morning, **Torget ❶** is the site of Bergen's fish, fruit and flower market. Customers engage the fishermen in serious conversation about the day's catch, watched by an interested circle, and the stalls sell *gravlaks* (cured salmon), lobster and *klippfisk* (dried cod). This busy scene is the heart of Bergen,

where people linger to watch the transactions or peer into the boats tied up at the quay after a night's fishing.

Just south of the fish market is **Torgalmenningen**, housing many of the city's best shops and departments stores. The most striking of these is **Sundt**, built in the Scandinavian Funkis style, popular in the late 1920s and 1930s in Norway (the building dates from 1938). The square also holds the **Sailors' Monument**. Carved figures march round the base of this memorial dedicated to all Norwegian sailors who lost their lives at sea.

Just up the hill from the fish market, in another historic quarter of the city, is the **Old Town Hall** (Gamle Rådhuset). Originally built as a private house in 1558, it was presented to the town in 1562 and served the city for several centuries until, in 1974, the city administration moved to an inelegant highrise modern block.

MUSEUM CLUSTER

Bergen is a good walking city and, if you fix your eye on the tall steeple of

At the fish market.

The composer Edvard Grieg (1843–1907).

View from the top of Fløyen.

St John's Church (Johanneskirken; mid-June–late Aug Mon–Fri 10am–4pm; rest of the year shorter hours; free), a short walk up Vesl Torggate from Torgalmenningen takes you to the top of **Sydneshaugen**, near the university area and the site of a clutch of museums: the **Natural History Museum** (Naturhistorisk Museum; tel: 55 58 29 20; www.uib.no; closed for restoration until 2019) standing in the lush **Botanisk Hage** (Botanic Garden), with its tropical greenhouse; the **Cultural History Museum** (Kulturhistorisk Museum; www.khm.uio.no; daily mid-May–mid-Sept 10am–5pm, mid-Sept–mid-May 11am–4pm), where you can learn more about stave churches and religion in Norway, among other things; and the **Maritime Museum** (Sjøfartsmuseum; tel: 55 54 96 00; daily mid-May–Aug Mon–Fri 10am–4pm, Sat–Sun 11am–4pm, Sept–mid-May 11am–3pm), which traces the history of this seafaring area from the Old Norse period to the present day.

The university area consists of beautiful merchants' villas from the turn of the 20th century, and is where the Arctic explorer Fridtjof Nansen spent the early years of his career. Vilhelm Bjerknes, the father of weather forecasting, also lived here for a time.

FAMOUS NAMES

It is not surprising that this lively city, with its close European links, should have been the birthplace of many famous people. It was also a strong base for 19th-century nationalism which culminated in 1905, when Norway gained its independence from Sweden. The prime minister at the time was Christian Michelsen, whose home **Gamlehaugen** (tel: 55 11 29 00; June–Aug Tue, Thu and Sat–Sun noon–3pm, English tour at noon; gardens all year) at Fjøsanger is now the residence of the king when he is in Bergen.

DRAMA AND MUSIC

Nationalism had strong roots in the 19th-century revival of Norwegian culture, led by the playwright Henrik Ibsen, the violinist Ole Bull, the composer Edvard Grieg and writers such as Bjørnstjerne Bjørnson. Though Ibsen and Bjørnson were not natives of

west Norway, Bjørnson was for a time director of Bergen's **National Theatre** ❻ (Den Nationale Scene) founded by Ole Bull in 1850, and Bjørnson's statue stands on the steps in front.

The virtuoso violinist Ole Bull's contribution to Norwegian culture was a consequence of his wanderings in the villages of west Norway and the great Jotunheim mountain plateau east of the fjord country. Here he collected many old folk melodies which were played on the Hardanger fiddle, the area's traditional instrument. Later, Grieg transcribed some of these folk tunes for piano, saving them from being lost. He also founded Norway's National Theatre and hired a young Henrik Ibsen as a writer.

GRIEG'S SUMMER RETREAT

Every year, thousands of visitors come to look round Grieg's summer home at **Troldhaugen** (tel: 55 92 29 92; www. griegmuseum.no; daily May–Sept 9am–6pm; Oct–Apr 10am–4pm) some 8km (5 miles) south of Bergen, where Grieg found the peace to compose in his *hytte* (holiday lodge).

The house is just as Grieg left it; his manuscripts are scattered around and even his piano is in working order in the comfortable drawing room. In the past, this room was the venue for many musical evenings; today, if you are lucky, the curator will play some of Grieg's music for you. The size of the room inevitably limited the capacity of the audience, and in 1985 Troldhaugen opened a special **Chamber Music Hall** seating 200, with a turf roof and built into the hillside so that it is barely visible among the tall trees. The floor-to-ceiling windows behind the stage provide the audience with a lovely view of the composer's *hytte* and Lake Nordås. The latest addition is the **Edvard Grieg Museum** close to the concert hall and villa.

Troldhaugen is a wonderful setting for a concert and a continuation of the summer evening tradition when Grieg and his wife, Nina Hagerup, a Danish

singer, would entertain their friends in the quiet garden outside the drawing room. Any bus for the Fana district goes to Hopsbroen, then a 15-minute walk leads to Troldhaugen; many city excursions also include Troldhaugen.

OLE BULL'S ISLAND

Ole Bull built his home on the island of **Lysøen** (tel: 56 30 90 77; www.lysoen.no; mid-May–Aug daily 11am–4pm; Sept Sun only 11am–4pm) in 1873, when his fame had long spread throughout and beyond Norway. Bull turned the island into a park with woodland and walking routes, and the house itself is unlike any other in the country. Made of traditional Norwegian wood, the decorated and screened balcony and the pointed arches of the windows on the front of the building have an almost Moorish flavour, and the tower topped by a minaret is reminiscent of St Basil's in Moscow's Red Square.

To reach Lysøen, take the bus marked "Lysefjordruta" (No. 566/567) from bus station gate 19 or 20. The ride takes 50 minutes and stops at Buena Kai. Then take the Ole Bull ferry, which leaves

The National Theatre.

at 11am, noon, 1pm, 2pm and 3pm. By car, take road 553 and head south in the direction of Fana.

It's a good idea to combine your visit to Lysøen with a stop on the way at **Lysekloster**, where the ruins of a 12th-century Cistercian abbey, a daughter monastery of Fountains Abbey in Yorkshire, England, can be seen.

COMPOSER'S HOME

Dedicated music-lovers could also check out **Siljustøl** (tel: 55 13 60 00; early May–late Aug Sun only noon–4pm), the home of Harald Sæverud, at Rådal on the way to the airport. Sæverud (1897–1992) was the most important Norwegian composer of the 20th century, and he himself designed part of the interior of his unusual home, built in wood and natural stone.

GRIEGHALLEN CONCERT HALL

Perhaps in part as a result of the fame of people such as Bull and Grieg, Bergen has a lively artistic and cultural life – hence it was honoured as one of the European Cities of Culture in 2000. The

Bergen International Festival (Festspillene; www.fib.no), held each year in late May–early June, attracts international artists and thousands of visitors. At the end of the 1970s, the festival led to the building of a new concert hall, **Grieghallen ℗**, with marvellous acoustics. The outside of the building looks remarkably like that of a concert grand piano, perhaps as a tribute to the composer whose name it bears. This is the heart of the 12-day festival, but the whole city is involved, with events in Håkonshallen, Troldhaugen, Lysøen and Mariakirken.

ARTISTIC ENCLAVE

Bergen boasts one of the largest art, craft and design museum complexes in the Nordic countries: **KODE, Art Museums of Bergen** (tel: 53 00 97 04; www.kodebergen.no). KODE is centred around **Lille Lungegårdsvann**, the octagonal lake in the middle of the park, not far from the statues of Edvard Grieg and of Ole Bull playing his violin, and near Grieghallen. The collection of around 50,000 art objects is spread over four sites, all within easy walking distance of each other. **KODE 1 ℚ** (Nordahl Bruns gate 9; mid-May–mid-Sept daily 11am–5pm, mid-Sept–mid-May Tue–Fri 11am–4pm, Sat–Sun 11am–5pm) showcases the works of the former Permanenten – West Norway Museum of Decorative Art featuring furniture, textiles, ceramics, glass and silver, as well as Norway's largest collection of Chinese art. **KODE 2 ℝ** (Rasmus Meyers Allé 3; same times as KODE 1) focuses on contemporary art and **KODE 3 Ⓢ** (Rasmus Meyers Allé 7; mid-May–mid-Sept daily 10am–6pm, mid-Sept–mid-May Tue–Fri 11am–4pm, Sat–Sun 11am–5pm) displays the Rasmus Meyers paintings collection and the Munch collection. Finally, **KODE 4 Ⓣ** (Rasmus Meyers Allé 9; same times as KODE 1) has art collections ranging from the 14th century to the present day and also houses the Children's Art Museum.

Kode 4 Museum.

DESIGN AND CRAFT

Bergen shops often offer opportunities to see traditional crafts. Best known is **Husfliden** (on Vågsallmenningen 3), which has richly decorated traditional Norwegian costumes (*bunader*), textiles and woodwork, including the famous *rosemaling* (rose painting). For Norwegian glass, try Bergen's **Glasmagasin** at Torgallmenningen 8.

OPEN-AIR PERFORMANCES

From mid-June to late August the open-air stages at Lille Lungegårdsvann and Torgalmenningen are used almost daily for music and dance performances. Folk dancing and music from rural Norway are particularly popular with the Bergensere and visitors alike. The Bergen Philharmonic Orchestra and the Bergen Philharmonic Youth Orchestra give free summer concerts at Torgalmenningen.

OUTDOOR CITY

The most popular pastime is sailing. Not far behind are sea fishing and swimming. Or you could simply take a fjord cruise. The boats depart daily from the fish market, and offer three-hour trips in the nearby fjords (www.rodne.no, tel: 51 89 52 70; all year). The hills above Bergen, just 10 minutes away from the centre, are ideal for walking, and **Sandviken Ridesenter**, not far from the Gamle Bergen Museum, organises horse-riding tours.

For something different, try a racing evening at **Travpark** (Thu from 5.30pm; tel: 55 39 68 00) at Åsane, around 16km (10 miles) from the city (bus 285). The atmosphere is electric as the "trotting" horses and their drivers race round the track.

Apart from the gardens at Troldhaugen and Lysøen, the Norwegian Arboretum at **Milde** (tel: 55 58 72 50; www.uib.no/en/arboretet; daily all year; free), founded in 1971, has shrubs and trees from many parts of the world, and this pretty area along the shore has rocky gorges, hills and a small lake. The nearby Fanafjord also provides good swimming. It is about 23km (14 miles) south of Bergen. To get there take bus 525 to Mildevågen, and then a 15-minute walk to the arboretum.

In Ole Bull's home on Lysøen.

⊘ SCIENCE IN ACTION

Bergen is a big university town and, as such, knowledge is at the centre of much of what's going on here. Another museum worth mentioning, therefore, is *Vilvite*, the Bergen Science Centre (Thormøhlensgate 51; tel: 55 59 45 00; www.vilvite.no; Tue–Fri 9am–3pm, Sat–Sun 10am–5pm, late June–mid-Aug daily 10am–5pm), which is found south of Nygårdsparken.

The name Vilvite means "Want to know", and the centre, which contains 75 interactive displays, installations and experiments, aims to make science and technology fun, encouraging visitors to be curious about their environment, and how things around them work. It is a big draw with children of all ages; the older (and more adventurous) ones can enjoy a thrilling ride in the G-Force, the only of its kind in Europe.

THE MOST BEAUTIFUL VOYAGE

This is one of the great sea journeys of the world: from Bergen to the end of Norway and back again, the vessels plying the Hurtigruten route are mail boats, freight ships and passenger liners in one.

The ship slips out of **Bergen's** hill-ringed harbour at 10.30pm, day in, day out, all year round. In winter, it has been dark for hours, and passengers linger no longer than to wave goodbye to the lights of the city before scuttling below to the warmth of saloon and cabin. In summer, by contrast, the deck is crowded as the ship sweeps out towards the fjord, leaving behind the small houses where the Hansa merchants once lived.

The coastal express heads north through Byfjord and Hjeltefjord, past the islands of **Askøy** and **Holsnøy** for the open sea, at the start of a trip of 1,250 nautical miles round North Cape (Nordkapp) and then to Kirkenes near the Russian border, crossing the Arctic Circle en route.

Nowadays, this coastal voyage is, for most visitors, simply an entrancing cruise but it meant – and still means – much more to Norwegians. From earliest times, this long, beautiful coast has been the main link in Norway for communication and trade. Indeed until quite recently the sea was the sole means of transport between isolated shore-hugging communities in the far north. The western and northern Norwegians once regarded Scotland and Iceland as being easier to reach than the region around present-day Oslo. Even in winter the last petering out of the Gulf Stream

Taking the Hurtigruten.

keeps the seaways around the coast of Norway open year round.

THE SWIFT ROUTE

The first steamship, the *Prinds Gustav*, set out from Trondheim to Tromsø in 1838. In time, other steamers began to journey between the coastal towns, and in 1893 a local steamship company, Vesteraalens Dampskibsselskab, opened the Hurtigruten (literally "swift route") between Trondheim and Hammerfest, in the far northwest. As the line extended to Bergen and Kirkenes,

⊙ **Main Attractions**
Ålesund
Trondheim
Lofoten Islands
Tromsø
North Cape

⊙
Map on page 230

The Hurtigruten

```
0        100 km
0        100 miles
```
— · — route of the Hurtigruten

several shipowners became involved. Following various mergers, the last two companies running the fleet merged to form Hurtigruten Group in 2006. Today the group operates 14 ships. Of these, 11 constantly ply the Hurtigruten route (the Norwegian Coastal Voyage),while the remaining three operate as cruise ships in the Antarctic, Svalbard , Greenland and the Baltic. It also owns several fast-ferry routes in Norway, and other travel-related products. A round trip from Bergen to Kirkenes takes 11 days. The Hurtigruten could scarcely be more flexible. You can hop on and off at any port, travel one-way only, take a shorter trip – or even enjoy a single leg of the journey.

The Hurtigruten makes 34 ports of call along the ever-changing coast, some at places no bigger than a handful of houses around the harbour, with local people waiting on the quayside to collect a car or a container or to greet friends who have hopped a short distance between small towns where the alternative is a long, difficult drive.

From October to May the first stop for going ashore is **Ålesund 1**. It has all the natural design of a town built round a harbour. Following a disastrous fire in 1904, much of the centre was rebuilt in Art Nouveau style, the buildings carefully preserved and painted in bright colours. Between April and September the ship makes a detour to take in the scenic splendour of Geirangerfjord.

The next main stop is **Trondheim 2**, further north along a magnificent coast with 87 peaks, snow-capped for much of the year. When Trondheim was the ancient capital of Norway, it was called Nidaros, and **Nidarosdomen** (cathedral) is a national shrine; it contains a memorial to King Olav Haraldsson, who became St Olav after his death at the Battle of Stiklestad. The Trondheim stop is long enough for a morning tour of this historic city, with its busy harbours and bays, and wide streets lined with wooden houses and old warehouses. From May to September, the tour also visits the Ringve Music Museum .

Early next morning, as the ship steams north again, it crosses the **Arctic Circle ❸** (Polarsirkel) and sails into "the land of the midnight sun". From April to September passengers can board a smaller vessel at Grønøy to navigate the narrow Hollandsfjord inland. The tour then alights at the foot of the spectacular Svartisen, Norway's second-largest glacier. At the Arctic Circle crossing, "King Neptune" joins the celebrations on board to award Arctic Circle certificates.

HAMSUN'S NORDLAND

On its way to the **Lofoten Islands ❹**, the ship enters Nordland, the territory of one of Norway's most famous writers, Knut Hamsun. Hamsun named the old trading centre of **Kjerringøy** "Siri-lund" in his novels, which describe the lives of northern fishing and trading families around the early 1900s.

On deck, as the ship weaves in and out of the islands, bird-watchers may be reluctant to go below in case they miss one of the numerous seabird colonies, the congregations of colour-ful exotic ducks in winter harbours and comical little puffins by the thousand.

Between **Svolvær** and **Stokmarknes**, the ship makes a brief detour (in sum-mer, weather permitting) into **Trollfjord**, something no big cruise liner could do because the sheer faces of rock and scree press close in this narrow fjord. In winter, ice makes entry impossible, but instead there is the endless fasci-nation of the **aurora borealis** (northern lights) – sometimes white spears, at other times a blue-green or multicol-oured aura dancing across the sky. By now, the ship has the high mountains of fjord country far behind in its wake but, during the brief light of a winter day, the low slanting sun picks out the white cones of snow-covered hills.

WATCHING THE SEASONS GO BY

In spring and autumn, the 11-day jour-ney feels like a voyage through the seasons. Leave Bergen in May, when

⊘ **Tip**

A novel by Knut Hamsun, particularly *The Wayfarers*, is a good accompaniment to a voyage that illuminates his characters and their thinking, and gives an insight into life in these northern lands today.

Many snow-capped peaks can be seen from Molde.

⊙ **Fact**

Returning south to Trømso in summer, there is time for a midnight excursion by cable car to the summit of Mount Storsteinen. At 410 metres (1,350ft) above sea level, there is a wonderful sunlit view of coast and country.

the fjord valleys are brilliant with blossom, and the hills and mountains of the north will still be white as snow flurries scurry across the fjords and mountains. The return journey is the reverse: just as the north is beginning to slip out of its winter grip, the swift Norwegian summer marches north and will have already reached Bergen and the mountains around it, and it might even be warm enough to lie out in a sheltered corner of the deck.

The northern city of **Tromsø** ➎, set on an island in a rugged landscape, has a relaxed cosmopolitan atmosphere reflected in its numerous restaurants and street cafés. It has the most bars per capita in Norway, with a bustling nightlife. Among the stops are **Tromsø Museum** and the **Arctic Cathedral** (Ishavskatedralen), which has the largest stained-glass window in Europe.

Into Finnmark the ship sails past a coast of scoured hills and watercourses with forests along the valleys, to **Hammerfest**, Norway's most northerly town, then slips through the Margerøy Sound to Honningsvåg, from where you can take an excursion by bus to **North Cape** ➏ (Nordkapp) – a highlight of any visit to Norway.

As it rounds North Cape, the Hurtigruten turns to the east, across the very top of Norway, heading for **Kirkenes** ➐, 5km (3 miles) from the **Russian border**. Along the coast, place names begin to show Sami and Finnish origins. Kirkenes itself has a frontier feel. The street signs are in both Norwegian and Cyrillic and you'll hear Russian spoken. Here you can join a king-crab safari in summer, where donning a survival suit you will jump (and float) in the Barents Sea to watch the day's catch being hauled on board – before sampling the crabs' delicious flesh at a specially prepared meal; or opt to go dog-sledging or snowmobiling in winter instead.

NOWHERE MISSED

Heading south, after visiting Tromsø, the vessel takes in a brief sightseeing tour at Harstad in order to visit, among other sites, **Trondenes Church**, the world's northernmost medieval church. After a visit to Trondheim, passengers take in a short tour of the beautiful coastal fishing town of Kristiansund, then arrive at Molde to experience the panoramic views of the Romsdal fjord and the Romsdal Alps. On the way south, the ship stops by day at the places it visited when northbound passengers were fast asleep below decks, so nowhere is missed. Nor is it generally a rough voyage: the Hurtigruten hugs the coast or weaves in and out of islands that shelter the ship from the excesses of the Atlantic Ocean and the Norwegian Sea.

With the ever-increasing tourist traffic, the emphasis on delivering supplies to distant traders is changing, and Hurtigruten is now offering cruise-orientated packages and even side trips into the Geirangerfjord. For booking and information visit www.hurtigruten.com or, in the UK, tel: 020 8846 2666/020 3131 2281.

Commemorative plaques at the North Cape.

Along the Hurtigruten route.

Fjord scene.

FROM SOGN TO NORDFJORD

You sense the presence of the last Ice Age strongly here, in the shape of the great Jostedal Glacier, and Norway's deepest fjord; but humans have also left their mark, most impressively in the form of stave churches.

From a seat in one of the small planes that somehow contrive to land on the narrow strips along the fjords or the tiny green patches between the mountains, it looks an impossible territory. Yet the land that runs from Sognefjord in the south to Nordfjord to the north has all the features that made the country famous: Norway's longest and deepest fjord, mainland Europe's largest glacier and Jotunheimen, Scandinavia's greatest mountain massif.

The large *fylke* (county) of Sogn og Fjordane lies between a zigzag coastline drawn by the waters of the North Sea and the start of Jotunheimen's heights. Narrow fingers of water push inland from the main fjords to reach far into the mountains, and waterfalls tumble from the heights into the fjord below. The force of all this water feeds hydroelectric power stations tucked away inside the mountains. Aluminium plants also make use of the spouting waterfalls to generate power and, among other things, produce the road barriers for many of Europe's mountain roads.

In the past, fjord, mountain and valley could be near impassable in winter. Today, travel is made easier thanks to the network of ferries, tunnels and bridges. From Bergen, an express boat (a catamaran with water-jet engines) reaches deep inland as far as Sogndal on Sognefjord.

DEEPEST SOGNEFJORD

At 205km (120 miles) long and 1,300 metres (4,260ft) deep, **Sognefjord** ⑰ is unmatched anywhere in the world. After wealthy British visitors first came here for the fishing in the 19th century, royalty too endorsed the fjord's delights. As crown prince, Edward VII came from Britain in 1898, and Kaiser Wilhelm II was on holiday in Sogn when he learned of the assassination of the Archduke at Sarajevo which triggered World War I.

In spring, the fjord's scenery is pink and white with umbrellas of fruit

Main Attractions
Jostedal Glacier
Norwegian Glacier
  Museum
Urnes stave church
Nærøyfjord
Briksdal Glacier

Map on page 208

Watching a cruise go by on Sognefjord.

Tip

In summer, guides from the Jostedalsbreen National Park Centre, 20km (12 miles) east of Stryn, lead tours and glacier explorations to different offshoots of the great Jostedal (tel: 57 68 32 50; www.jostedal.com).

blossom in orchards and gardens. In the warm summer days, far above the fjord, cattle and sheep cling to the small grass plateaux around the mountain farms or *seter* where once women and young girls spent the summer making cheese. The majority of the 113,000 people in the county still make their living by farming or fishing, forestry or fruit-growing.

On both sides of the fjord small villages cling to every square metre of land, each with its own atmosphere. **Balestrand** ⑱ has been a favourite since the 19th century and has an English church, St Olav's, founded by one of those fearless Victorian Englishwomen who travelled the world. The Kviknes Hotel was built in the 19th century too, and is one of Norway's largest family-run hotels (it's been in the family since 1877). German artists from the Düsseldorf Academy were also quick to appreciate the beauty of Sognefjord, and built Swiss-style houses, decorated with dragon heads in deference to their hosts' Viking past. The area is renowned for its mild climate and lush vegetation;

St Olav's church in Balestrand.

across a small neck of water at **Drags-vik**, a pastor-botanist planted exotic trees which thrive in the sheltered bay.

JOSTEDAL ICE SPECTACLE

A narrow side-fjord leads to the little community of **Fjærland** (road connections here were not completed until 1986), a dairy-farming centre near the two southernmost offshoots of the great **Jostedal Glacier** ⑲ (Jostedalsbreen), mainland Europe's largest glacier. Nestling nearby on a large, flat esker deposited thousands of years ago is the **Norwegian Glacier Museum** ⑳ (Norsk Bremuseum; tel: 57 69 32 88; www.bre.museum.no; daily June–Aug 9am–7pm; Apr–May and Sept–Oct 10am–4pm). This environmentally aware, high-tech place offers an excellent 20-minute presentation about the Jostedalsbreen glacier and also Our Fragile Planet, a multi-media experience that takes visitors from the moment of creation to our world today, and our over-exploitation of its resources. From a distance, the concrete-and-glass building designed by

Norwegian architect Sverre Fehn could be an extension of the glacier itself.

Tiny Fjærland is Norway's equivalent of the Welsh town of Hay-on-Wye, with a string of second-hand bookshops selling titles in a variety of languages from wooden sheds alongside the picturesque fjord. Open from May to September (daily 10am–6pm).

FERRY TO VANGSNES

The ferry from Dragsvik runs to **Vangsnes** on the south side. From there, it is only a few kilometres to **Vik** ㉑ and the 12th-century **Hopperstad stave church** (Stavkirke; mid-May–Sept 10am–5pm), with dragon heads on the outside and rich decorations within. Vik also has a stone church, **Hove Kirke** (mid-June to mid-Aug Wed–Sun 11am–4pm), only 20 years younger than Hopperstad. On the way back, stop at the statue of the heroic Norwegian Viking figure Fritjof den Frøkne (Fritjof the Courageous), in Vangsnes, a gift from Kaiser Wilhelm II in 1913.

HEAD OF THE FJORD

Going east from Balestrand, a short crossing takes you to **Hella** ㉒ and past the glistening arc of **Kvinnafoss** (Lady's Waterfall) close to the main road. At the head of the fjord, **Sogndal** is the centre for trade and administration in an area of forestry and farming. The pretty little town swells during term time because it is also a centre for education, with university colleges and Norway's oldest folk high school. To the north, farms are dotted along Sognadalen's narrow lake.

Kaupanger stave church (mid-June to mid-Aug daily 10am–5pm), a little further along Road 5, was built in the 12th century; its plain dark-wood exterior has been restored, and there are organ recitals in summer. **Sogn Folk Museum** ㉓ (Folkemuseum; tel: 57 67 82 06; www.dhs.museum.no; daily June–Aug 10am–5pm, May and Sept 10am–3pm, Oct–Apr Mon–Fri 10am–3pm) was set up in 1909 as a living museum

with animals, including 35 houses and farm buildings. There are sometimes folk music and dancing performances.

Standing tall beside the fjord at **Nordnes** is a stone to mark the Battle of Fimreite in June 1184. That was when King Sverre and his peasant Birkebeiner (so called because of their birch-bark footwear) defeated King Magnus Erlingsson and the nobility, a turning point in Norwegian history.

URNES STAVE CHURCH

In **Luster** ㉔, to the northeast of Sogndal, is **Urnes stave church** (Stavkirke; tel: 57 67 88 40; www.sognefjord.no; May–Sept daily 10.30am–5.45pm). If you only manage to visit one of Norway's splendid stave churches, make it this one. Deservedly a Unesco World Heritage Site, it's also reputed to be Norway's oldest place of worship. Entry includes a particularly informative 45-minute tour in English.

Also within easy reach is **Nigardsbreen**, yet another icy tongue from Jostedal Glacier, where one of the delights is a boat trip over the ice-cold, cloudy green waters of a glacier lake.

Urnes stave church.

Inside the Jostedal Glacier.

South of Sogndal, Sognefjord ends in the two most easterly fjords leading to Årdal and Lærdalsøyri, lovely valleys with mountain farms and plenty of opportunities for walking, climbing, or fishing in upland lakes and streams. The **Norwegian Wild Salmon Centre** (Norsk Villakssenter; tel: 57 66 67 71; www.norsk-villakssenter.no; daily June–Aug 10am–8pm; May and Sept noon–8pm) at **Lærdalsøyri** 25 shows an excellent 20-minute film about the life cycle of salmon. Visitors can watch salmon and sea trout through viewing windows. Lærdal's one-time importance as an east–west trading route is evident in Old (Gamle) Lærdalsøyri, an area of restored 18th- and 19th-century listed buildings.

Aurlandvangen, Flåm and Gudvangen lie along the innermost recesses of the fjord, which stretch south from the main fjord like an upside-down "Y". **Nærøyfjord** 26 to the west is the narrowest in Europe and also a World Heritage Site. On it, you can take what is perhaps the most dramatic boat trip in west Norway, where the mountains press so close that you wonder if the boat will squeeze through. Nærøyfjord is also a popular venue for kayakers.

MOUNTAIN CLIMB BY RAIL

A trip on the **mountain railway** 27 from Flåm to Myrdal is one of the world's great train journeys, as the track spirals up the steep mountain gorge (see page 214). A masterpiece of Norwegian engineering, this 20km (12-mile) -long stretch, which is among the world's steepest, runs from Myrdal to Aurlandsfjord some 800 metres (2,620ft) below, clinging to the mountainside at a vertiginous angle, and passing through no fewer than 20 tunnels on the way.

NORTH TO FØRDE

If, instead of heading inland from Balestrand, you turn northwest, following Road 5-13 towards Førde and the coast, you come to **Jølstravatnet**, one of the region's many lakes that feed into the fjords in the west.

On the south side lies the farm **Astruptunet** 28 (tel: 57 72 67 82; mid-May to mid-Sept), home for the last 14 years of his life of the artist Nikolai

Lærdalsøyri's well-preserved 18th- and 19th-century houses.

Astrup (1880–1928), who found themes for his art in the local landscape. Astruptunet is just as it was during the painter's life, though the barn has been replaced by a new art gallery with a permanent exhibition.

Flowing from Jølstravatnet, the River Jølstra, said to be one of the best salmon rivers in the area, drops hundreds of metres by the time it reaches **Førde ㉙** on Førdefjord. Nearby is the main **Sunnfjord Museum** (tel: 57 72 12 20; July–mid-Aug Mon–Fri 10am–6pm, Sat–Sun noon–5pm; rest of the year shorter hours), a collection of 25 restored buildings, 17 of which are reconstructed as a mid-19th century farmstead.

ALONG THE COAST

The best view of Sunnfjord's many islands is from the high peaks in the east, though the coast itself is far from flat. **Bleia** rises straight from the north side of Førdefjord to more than 1,300 metres (4,300ft), the summit of the Sunnfjord Alps, and many of the islands have high peaks. These islands stretch the length of the coast, from Fensfjord and the island of Sandøy, north to Vestkapp (West Cape) where the Hurtigruten turns northeast to its next stop at Ålesund.

In **Florø**, the only community in this large county big enough to be called a town is the **Sogn og Fjordane Coastal Museum** (Kystmuseet; tel: 57 74 22 33; www.kyst.museum.no; mid-June–mid-Aug Mon–Fri 11am–6pm, Sat–Sun noon–4pm; rest of the year Mon–Fri 10am–3pm, Sun noon–3pm). It has a fine collection of old boats displayed in three modern buildings and a section on the petroleum industry. This most westerly town had its birth in the herring industry, which flourished in the middle of the 19th century. Today, it still depends on the sea for fish, while oil- and gas fields away to the west have turned Florø into something of an oil town.

OFFSHORE SIGHTS

There are many places to see: rock carvings at **Ausevik**, southeast of Florø; the nearby island of **Svanøy** with the ancient stone cross of St Olav, covered in runic inscriptions, a manor with a mature garden and magnificent trees;

Nærøyfjord.

a Romanesque medieval church on **Kinnøy**, where the Kinna drama *Songen ved det store djup (The Song of the Great Deep)*, is performed by local people, and draws thousands to the island each June.

To the north of Fløro, at the mouth of Nordfjord, is the island of **Bremangerlandet**  with its **Vingen carvings**, which are even older than Ausevik's and illustrate the lives of the fishing-settlers of Nordfjord. Further north, the village of **Måløy on Vågsøy** is one of Norway's largest fishing and trading ports, and at Raudeberg fish of all kinds are salted and dried. Måløy features the Allied Monument, a 6-metre (20ft) high granite obelisk raised in memory of 52 Allied soldiers who died during a raid on Måløy in 1941.

North of Vågsøy and Raudeberg is **Silda**, a tiny island for sea-anglers, divers and bird-watchers. It has only a handful of permanent inhabitants, no cars and, on an islet in the middle of the harbour, a restored fish-salting works that serves a feast of seafoods. On the nearby island of **Selje** are the medieval ruins of **St Sunneva Monastery**

(Kloster). The northernmost tip is **Vestkapp**, where winds blow fiercely. From here, the closest land is the Shetland Isles off the north of Scotland.

INLAND ALONG NORDFJORD

Nordfjord is 100km (60 miles) shorter than Sognefjord. From the fjord you can travel along Oldedalen as far as **Briksdal Glacier** (Briksdalsbreen), where a frozen cascade of ice hangs above the ice floes and green waters of the glacier lake. To avoid the 5km (3 mile) round trip walk from the end of the road to the base of the glacier, rent a "troll car," an electric vehicle that resembles a golf-cart. In season, there are guided visits to the base of the glacier by inflatable dinghy.

Nordfjord divides into Eidsfjord and Isefjord. At **Eid**, which is also connected to the coast by Road 15, is **Firdariket**, the seat of the last Viking chief. The village has traditional white-painted buildings and its church, which dates from 1824, is decorated with beautiful **rose paintings**.

To the south of Eid, Road 1 crosses Utfjord and then runs along

Briksdal Glacier, part of the great Jostedalsbreen.

Gloppenfjord, which ends at **Sandane** ㉞, the main town of Gloppen, the biggest farming district in the county and also a large fur-breeding centre. The **Nordfjord Folk Museum** (Folkemuseum; tel: 57 88 45 40; http://nordfjord.museum.no; mid-June–mid-Sept daily 10am–5pm, mid-Sept–mid-June Mon–Fri 10am–3pm, Sun 11am–3pm) started in 1920 with five turf-roofed houses and now has more than 40 historic buildings, including a mountain *seter*. Moored just outside Sandane is a 100-year-old **sailing barge**, *Holvikjekta*, the last of the traditional freighters that served coast and fjord. There is also a fine adventure centre, Glopen Camping og Fritidssenter (tel: 57 86 62 14; www.gloppen-camping.no), which offers a variety of activities, including riding, canoeing, rafting, mountain- and glacier-walking, boat trips and sightseeing to various beauty spots.

Continuing east along Road 15 from Eid you come to Hornindalsvatnet, then Grodås. Hornindal valley has traditions in handicrafts and folk music, and musicians wear black breeches, or, for women, the long black skirt and green bodice of the area. The most famous artist here was Anders Svor (1864–1929), first a woodcarver and then, after a time at the Copenhagen Academy of Art, a sculptor. The **Anders Svor Museum** (tel: 57 87 97 76; http://web.sfk.museum.no; mid-June–mid-Aug Sat–Sun 9am–4pm, in July also Tue–Fri or by appointment) contains more than 400 sculptures.

FJORD END

Further east you reach inner Nordfjord, where the fjord system ends at **Stryn** ㉟, **Loen** and **Olden**, the start of three lovely valleys stretching up to the northwest edges of the Jostedalsbreen. Three tunnels from the Stryn valley cut through the mountain to spectacular Geirangerfjord to the north. Stryn is famous for summer skiing on the northeast of Strynsvatn, where the ground rises to Tystigbreen. In winter, there are eight prepared slopes on the glacier, a snowboard park, a skiing school and a ski rental shop. Cross-country skiing is another possibility, and the area also attracts many off-piste enthusiasts (guides are available).

⊙ **Fact**

Hornindalsvatnet is Europe's deepest freshwater lake. Following the melting of the ice at the end of the last Ice Age, the Hornindal valley flooded to a depth of 514 metres (1,686ft).

Sturdy fjord horses typical of the region at Stryn.

Seven Sisters Waterfall,
Geirangerfjord.

MØRE OG ROMSDAL

The county of Møre og Romsdal has a bit of everything: a jewel of a fjord, Geirangerfjord; the Art Nouveau town of Ålesund; the peaks of Trollheimen, Home of the Trolls; and delightful islands to spare.

For nearly a century the coastal steamers of the Hurtigruten have called at Ålesund, Molde and Kristiansund along the sea route that leads to Trondheim and the north. Taking into account the circumference of every fjord, bay and inlet, this part of Norway's jagged coastline is 6,000km (3,730 miles) long; more than 10 percent of the county's population lives on islands. It's scarcely surprising that, even today, the sea is still a great provider for Møre og Romsdal, with North Sea oil and gas ever more significant.

Looking at the jumble of coastline, islands and fjord mouths on a map, it is sometimes hard to distinguish where sea and islands end and fjord and mainland begin. Yet move inland and half the area lies above 600 metres (2,000ft). In the southeast, the highest peaks reach more than 1,800 metres (6,000ft). The county is divided into three municipalities: **Sunnmøre**, **Romsdal** and **Nordmøre**, of which the main centres are, respectively, Ålesund, Molde and Kristiansund.

Sea trade has always been important and, from the Middle Ages, the accolade for a settlement was to be given *kaupang* (market) status. At that time there were just two: Borgundkaupangen, 5km (3 miles) east of Ålesund, in Sunnmøre; and Veøykaupangen, in Romsdal. Both were centres for north–south and east–west trade routes on sea and land.

Today, the **Sunnmøre Museum** at Borgundkaupangen, 4km (2.5 miles) east of Ålesund (tel: 70 17 40 00; www.sunnmore.museum.no; May–Sept Mon–Fri 10am–4pm, Sun noon–4pm, in July also Sat 10am–4pm; Oct–Apr Tue–Fri 10am–3pm, Sun noon–4pm), retells the region's history. This open-air museum has over 50 traditional buildings and 40 historic boats. Beside it, in the Medieval Age Museum (Middelaldermuseet; www.sunnmore.museum.no; June–Aug Mon–Fri noon–pm, Sun noon–3pm; free entry with Sunnmore Museum ticket)

Main Attractions

Ålesund
Geirangerfjord
Trolls' ladder and Trolls' wall
Atlantic Road
Kristiansund

Map on page 244

Ålesund.

artefacts and documents revealed by and relating to the Borgundkaupangen trading post are arranged around the excavations themselves.

ART NOUVEAU ÅLESUND

Ålesund ❶, Norway's largest fishing town, is equally well known for its Art Nouveau architecture. The city was rebuilt in 1904 after a great fire destroyed most of the centre, giving rise to the Norwegian saying: "I've never heard anything like it since Ålesund burned down."

First to the rescue came the Norvegophile Kaiser Wilhelm II of Germany, who sent four ships laden with supplies and building materials (the stained-glass windows in the gable end of the **church** were an inauguration gift from the emperor). With help and donations from all over Europe, the people of Ålesund and recently graduated students of architecture, both Norwegian and German, completed the rebuilding of the town by 1907 in the now carefully preserved Art Nouveau style. The **Jugendstil Art Nouveau**

Centre (Jugenstil Senteret; tel: 70 10 49 70; www.jugendstilsenteret.no; Jun–Aug daily 10am–5pm; Sept–May Tue–Sun 11am–4pm) has a dramatic 14-minute multimedia presentation of the reconstruction of Ålesund and displays a rich selection of Art Nouveau ceramics, furniture and textiles.

Towers, turrets and medieval-romantic frontages, often with more than a trace of Nordic mythology, give the town a harmony which extends to the painted wooden warehouses along **Brosundet**, the deep inlet of the inner harbour. Until the 1950s, Ålesund was the centre for fishermen, their boats, and fish (especially *klippfisk*, traditional Norwegian split, dried cod). But as fishing changed so did Ålesund, which expanded into fish processing and fish farming. Many former warehouses are now offices and restaurants, whose fish-oriented menus include *bacalao*, a Mediterranean take on *klippfisk* that's simmered with ingredients such as tomato sauce, olives, onions and garlic, and the more traditional *brennsnute*, a potato and meat stew.

LIFE ON THE SEA

If the climb up the 418 steps of **Aksla** hill that rises from the centre of town doesn't leave you breathless, the view certainly will. From the top, you can see over several islands, all linked by 12km (8 miles) of tunnel.

On the islands, you'll find sea caves, bird cliffs, little harbours, campsites, clean, white beaches and *hytter* (holiday lodges) to rent. For an introduction to the marine fauna of the area, visit the **Atlantic Sea Park** (Atlanterhavsparken; tel: 70 10 70 60; http://atlanterhavsparken. no; June–Aug Sun–Fri 10am–6pm, Sat 10am–4pm, Sept–May Mon–Sat 11am–4pm, Sun 11am–6pm). At Tueneset, a few minutes' drive from Ålesund town centre, it's one of the largest saltwater aquariums in Scandinavia.

BIRD ISLAND OF RUNDE

The island of **Runde ❷**, 67km (42 miles) southwest of Ålesund, is not to be missed. Runde attracts professional and amateur naturalists from all over the world. More than 200 bird species have been recorded, but this small island is best known for breeding birds, which line the cliffs in their hundreds of thousands. When they fly, it looks as if a gigantic swarm of insects has darkened the sky. From the island's small harbour, boats run several times daily to view the best seabird sites, plus an offshore seal colony. As a bonus, in the waters round the island are interesting wrecks; not so long ago divers found a cache of gold from a Dutch ship, *Ackerendam*.

GEIRANGERFJORD

South from Ålesund between Vartdalsfjord and Hjørundfjord, the **Sunnmøre Mountains ❸** plunge straight into the fjord near Ørsta, one of the early targets for the many British climbers who first made Norway's mountains known to the world.

Ålesund is also the main entrance to **Storfjord**, where the cruise ships turn in to reach their goal of **Geirangerfjord ❹**, claimed by many to be Norway's most beautiful fjord. One road (No. 60) to Geiranger goes through Stranda, main town of inner Storfjord, another (No. 655) via Ørsta, both ending at

⊙ Tip

For keen walkers, instead of taking the road down Trollstigen to Åndalsnes it is now possible to follow the well-marked Kløvstien, the old mountain track that was the only way through the mountains before the road.

Looking down on Geirangerfjord.

⊙ Fact

The Rauma Line (Rauma-banen), the 114km (71-mile) long stretch of railway between Dombås and Åndalsnes, is one of the most spectacular in Norway.

Hellesylt. From there you can travel to the inner end of Geirangerfjord by boat or, in summer, there is a path along the fjord's high southern wall.

In this most secret of fjords far from the sea, great waterfalls tumble in such delicate cascades that they are given feminine names – **De Syv Søstre** (The Seven Sisters) and the **Brudesløret** (Bridal Veil). Lofty mountains are reflected in the mirror-still water and, in some places, farms cling to unlikely pockets of green. The spectacle is much too beautiful to miss, and everyone stays on deck until the boat reaches **Geiranger** ❺, which huddles under the half-circle of mountains.

Halfway up the winding road behind the village is the appropriately named Hotel Utsikten, which has one of the best views in Norway, and further on the road passes by **Dalsnibba**, the highest peak in Sunnmøre. To reach the wild valley of **Norangsdalen**, drive from Hellesylt to **Øye**, where you'll find the classic wooden Hotell Union Øye, a car ferry over the fjord and more stunning views.

ALONG THE TROLL ROAD

Heading north once more (along Road 63) towards Åndalsnes, the first stretch, leading to Eidsdal on Norddalsfjord, is known as the **Ørn-eveien** ❻ (Eagle's Road), and it is not difficult to see why as it winds ahead to **Ørnesvingen**, another vantage point. Across the fjord an even more spectacular road leads across the **Gudbrandsjuvet** gorge. Mountains rise into the distance to the west, until you reach the top of the **Trolls' Ladder** or **Trolls' Causeway** ❼ (**Trollstigen**). To the east is Trolltindane, around 1,800 metres (6,000ft) above sea level. From the top, where snow can linger even in July, it's a short, exhilarating 15-minute plunge around 11 sweeping bends hewn out of solid rock into the green valley that leads to Åndalsnes.

Åndalsnes is known as "the village between *fjell* (mountain) and fjord". It sits on a promontory encircled by fjord and mountain, looking up to tops that challenge climbers of every nationality. Only the most skilful and experienced

Trolls' Causeway.

⊙ FIRST TOURIST HOTEL

To cater for all the early mountaineers and sightseers to Romsdal in the 19th century, a local police sergeant, Anders Landmark, opened a simple wooden inn at **Aak** in 1850, which is regarded as Norway's first tourist hotel. Many of Europe's mountain addicts have stayed here to take advantage of the beautiful surroundings, with the Troll Wall (Trollveggen) and Romsdals-hornet close by.

Situated some 5km (3 miles) into the Romsdal valley from Åndalsnes on the E136, Aak is now both a modern hotel with excellent restaurant (mid-June–Aug; book in advance), and a mountain sports centre, offering summer courses in climbing and scrambling and, in winter, instruction in ice climbing and mountain (or Telemark) skiing (tel: 71 22 71 71; www.hotelaak.no).

tackle the **Trolls' Wall** (Trollveggen), part of craggy **Trolltindane ⑧**, which rises almost vertically from Romsdalen to its summit bowl of permanent snow. Trollveggen has more than 1,000 metres (3,300ft) of vertical and overhanging rock, first climbed in 1965. New climbing routes up the face are still being created. By less hazardous paths, the climb up Trolltindane takes four hours and requires boots and strong clothing.

Åndalsnes is the terminus for the Raumabanen railway that runs through **Romsdalen ⑨** to Trondheim. It brings in enough visitors each year to more than double the summertime population. A 19th-century British traveller, Lady Beauclerk, described Romsdalen as "precipitous, grey rocks ending in points apparently as sharp as needles... emerging into the sunniest, and the most lovely little spot... sheltered from every wind by the snow-capped mountains that surrounded it, while a most tempting river ran through the dale". Her words are as true today as when they were written.

FAMOUS CLIMBERS

The pleasant valley was the base camp for early climbers such as William Slingsby and Johannes Vigdal who, in 1881, made the first ascent of **Store Vengetind**. In the same year, another early Danish pioneer, Carl Hall, made the second ascent with two local climbers to the sharp point of **Romdalshornet**. It had first been conquered in 1828 by two local farmers Cristian Smed and Hans Bjermeland. In later years Arne Randers Heen made a name for himself by ascending Romdalshornet no fewer than 233 times – he is said to have built the shelter at the top of the summit, and to have waved the Norwegian flag there during World War II (something forbidden under the German occupation).

Rafting and canoeing are also promising possibilities on the River Rauma , one of Norway's best-known fishing rivers, which runs through the valley. But it is not necessary to be a rock climber to get up high into these mountains. Most have easy

The viewpoint at Åndalsnes.

alternative walking routes, and some have access by road.

THE ROSE TOWN OF MOLDE

Heading back towards the coast and Molde along Road 64, it is worth taking a detour into Langfjord as far as **Nesset**  on Eresfjord, deep in the mountains. Norway's 19th-century writer and patriot Bjørnstjerne Bjørnson, who had a summer home in the area, described the Nesset Mountains: "some standing white, others standing blue, with jagged, competing, agitating peaks, some marching along in ranking row".

The view today from the ferry along the **Eikesdalsvatnet** ⓫ illustrates what he meant. The mountain peaks rise abruptly out of the fjord sides, and you get a glimpse of **Mardalsfossen**, northern Europe's highest waterfall with a fall of 650 metres (2,000ft). In an early example of environmental activism in the 1970s, hundreds of people chained themselves together near the waterfall, to prevent the building of a hydroelectric power

The Atlantic Road.

station. It became a hot political issue and, though they did not win the final battle, the protesters ensured that the summer falls still tumble.

Molde ⓬ is part of an archipelago sheltered from the Norwegian Sea; its mild climate, green vegetation and rose gardens earn it the title "Town of Roses". A statue of the Little Rose Seller stands in the marketplace, where stalls sell everything from fruit and vegetables to clothes and, of course, roses. This modern town was almost entirely rebuilt after German bombing in World War II. A one-hour signed trail leads from town to **Varden**, Molde's best vantage point, overlooking fjord and island to the snow caps of the Sunnmøre Mountains. The view from here is known as the **Molde Panorama** – townspeople claim you can see 222 peaks.

FISHERY AND FOLK ART

Molde has its outdoor museum, the **Romsdalsmuseet** (tel: 71 20 24 60; mid-June–mid-Aug daily 11am–5pm, mid-Aug–mid-June Mon–Fri 11am–3pm, Sat–Sun 11am–4pm) where more than 50 buildings, including barns, farms, storehouses and a reconstructed chapel, have been moved in from the countryside and assembled to form a short street. In July, there are informative guided tours in English.

From Molde, an hourly boat makes the 10-minute journey to the island of Hjertøya and its **Hjertøya Fishery Museum Fishery Museum** (Fiskerimuseet; mid-Jun–early Aug Tue–Sun noon–5pm). With its cod-liver oil factory, fisherfolks' shacks and a substantial collection of boats that formerly plied the sound, it evokes the spartan life of fishing communities from the 1850s until quite recently.

There is little that is traditional about Molde's entertainment. The modern football stadium is located, spectacularly, by the sea and recent results are equally impressive; this small-town club was Norway league champion in 2011, 2012 and 2014, and took the Norwegian Cup in 2013 and 2014. In summer, buskers play in the streets, particularly during the famous **Molde International Jazz Festival** (tel: 71 20 31 50; www.moldejazz.no; mid-July), which pulls in more than 100,000 aficionados each year.

Roads 64 and 664 from Molde lead to the 16th-century coastal village of **Bud**. Here a boat trip goes to the old fishing station of **Bjørnsund**, now only inhabited in summer. Between Molde and Bud, a walk leading from Road 64 takes you to the **Troll Church** ⓭ (Trollkirka) – a cave, some 70 metres (230ft) long, divided into three sections, with a great waterfall tumbling down from the upper opening into a white marble basin in the mountains.

THE ATLANTIC ROAD

From Bud a small coastal road leads back to Road 64 and the simply magnificent **Atlantic Road** (Atlanterhavsveien; www.theatlanticroad.com). Although it's a mere eight kilometre (5 mile) stretch of Road 64, which rambles between Molde and Kristiansund, it will leave you gasping. Waves pound against the piles of the eight, sinuous bridges that buck like sea serpents, connecting the islets below, each exposed to the full force of the ocean.

The route to Kristiansund continues over the island of Averøya, the largest in the area. Archaeologists believe that **Averøya** ⓮ was one of the first places to be settled after the last Ice Age. Their finds are remnants of the early **Fosna Culture** that existed around 7000 BC during the Stone Age. ("Fosna" was the original name of Kristiansund).

Near **Bremsnes** ⓯, on the northeastern tip of Averøya, is the Viking **Stone of Horg** (Horgsteinen), where the victor of the battle of Hafrsfjord, Harald Hårfagre, had his hair cut and washed (and no doubt blow-dried at this windy spot), having fulfilled his vow not to touch it until Norway was united. A tunnel leads from Bremnes to Kristiansund.

KLIPPFISK **AT KRISTIANSUND**

Unlike Ålesund and Molde, **Kristiansund** ⓰ has little protection from the worst of the North Atlantic gales. It is right on the coast, with weather-beaten rocks pounded by the sea. Kristiansund is *Klippfisk* Town, for long the biggest exporter of Norwegian dried cod.

Like most Norwegian towns with "Kristian" in their title, Kristiansund was named after a Danish king, Christian VI, who gave it town status in 1742. A good introduction is by *sundbåtene*, the harbour boats which for more than 100 years have linked the town's islands. **Mellemverftet**, part of the Nordmøre Museum (mid-June–mid-Aug Mon–Fri noon–5pm), once one of four shipyards in Kristiansund, has come to life again as a centre for preserving the craft of shipbuilding, carefully restoring the beautiful lines of traditional Norwegian boats.

While on Averøya, don't miss the fine stave church at Kvernes (mid-June–mid-Aug 11am–5pm). Built in 1300, it has an unusually richly decorated mid-17th century interior in homage to shipping. Next door, the local museum features a collection of buildings from the area.

Altar of Kvernes stave church.

A COUNTRY AFLOAT

Sailing is second nature to Norwegians, a third of whom spend their holidays on the water, while others compete worldwide.

To the world, Norway and seafaring are synonymous; the very word Viking means "Men of the Bays". From the age of sail until after World War II, the Norwegian merchant fleet was one of the world's largest, and Norwegian could be heard in ports worldwide.

Among the country's most popular museums are the Maritime Museum (Sjøfartsmuseum) on the Bygdøy peninsula in Oslo, along with the Viking Ship Museum (Vikingskipshuset), with magnificently preserved longships unearthed from various sites and burial mounds around Norway, the Kon-Tiki Museum, with the rafts used by ethnographic explorer Thor Heyerdahl, and the Fram Museum (Frammuseet), built around the sturdy vessel that carried Fridtjof Nansen and Roald Amundsen on their heroic polar explorations.

Norwegians seem happiest when they are in, on or around the sea. Each year, over a third of the population spend their summer holidays partly or

Sailing is second nature to Norwegians.

completely in craft that range from small dinghies to large motor launches and ocean-going yachts. Even the most conservative estimates place the number of pleasure craft in Norway at 650,000, about one for every seven Norwegians. The sea is a natural part of life.

Geography and topography are the deciding factors. There are thousands upon thousands of islands, and the fjords and coastal archipelagos are a paradise for competitive and recreational sailors, king and commoner alike. Rocky shores and fjord meadows are dotted with colourful holiday huts and a boat of some form moored nearby.

King Olav V, the father of the present King Harald, was, in his day, the country's foremost sailor. He won a gold medal in sailing in the 1928 Olympics, making him the world's only Olympic medallist monarch. He also won medals in the Sailing World Championships in 1971 and 1976.

In founding its first sailing club in 1868 in Tønsberg, then a major merchant fleet port, Norway triggered a long latent urge. In 1883 the Royal Norwegian Sailing Association was formed in the capital, and in 1900 sailing became an Olympic sport. Norwegians were a major force in Olympic and championship sailing worldwide.

In the days of wooden yachts, Norwegian shipyards and naval architects were among the world's best, and one in particular stands out: born in the port of Larvik, Colin Archer (1832–1921) grew up with boats and at an early age started building craft to his own design. Among his best known are the stable, sturdy rescue schooners that bear his name and the three-masted Arctic exploration vessel *Fram*, built in 1892. The tradition of boatbuilding, like that of ski-making, continues to this day, albeit somewhat altered: fibreglass hulls and masts changed the picture completely. Nowadays, Norway exports motor cruisers and imports yachts.

Wherever there's water, there are all manner of motor and sailing craft. Small boat harbours in and near major cities, particularly Oslo, Kristiansund, Ålesund, Stavanger and Bergen, never fail to impress visitors by the number and types of crafts lying there.

From windsurfing in fjords to major regattas, Norwegians love being on the water.

Kristiansund sits on three islands. One of them is **Innlandet**, the oldest preserved part of the town with its first customs house (1660–1748), hospital, school and other restored buildings. Walk to the **Sjursvika** on the east side for a look at the old warehouses.

The small **Nordmøre Museum** (tel: 71 58 70 00; Mon–Fri 10am–2pm) has a few finds from the Fosna culture. Much more impressive is the **Klippfish Museum** (Klippfiskmuseum; mid–June– mid–Aug daily noon–5pm), another element of Nordmore Museum, which recounts the history of *klippfisk* and illustrates how it is processed.

The town's oddest monuments must be the tall pointed natural stones erected as tributes to town dignitaries: Bäckstrøm, who built the reservoirs, Brinchman, the provider of the water supply, Bræin, the musician founder of a musical family, which gave birth to an annual Opera Festival, and Hanson, the polar explorer.

Kristiansund's main church was destroyed by bombing in 1940. The architect responsible for its replacement named his creation "Rock Crystal in Roses", a striking white building known more prosaically as the **Atlantic Ocean Cathedral** (Atlanterhavskatedralen; all year). Its choir wall is a 30-metre (100ft) sweep of 320 stained-glass panels, rising from the lower parts, which symbolise the heavy, dark colours of the earth and soaring up to eternal light.

MIRACLE AT GRIP

An entirely different church stands on the island of **Grip**, northwest from Kristiansund. The island has a long and eventful history of flood and storm, and the islanders often took refuge in the small church. In 1796, a nor'wester tore down and washed away 100 houses. When the same thing happened seven years later, the pastor recorded the piteous prayer: "Almighty God, spare us further destruction and misery." Whether it was that plea or

not, the ancient little red stave church survived, only 8 metres (25ft) above the sea. Once 400 souls lived on Grip, scraping a living from fishing: today people live there only in summer when it becomes a holiday island and makes a popular excursion from Kristiansund.

KULI INSCRIPTION

To the north and northeast of Kristiansund, the last big island is **Smøla** ⑰, at the mouth of the Trondheimfjord, where the county ends in a string of islands which retain something of the life of the old farmer-fishermen.

Sanden is one of several buildings that form Smøla's scattered museum, with the main 18th-century building, warehouses, barn and a storehouse on wooden pillars, just as it was when the last owners left.

A number of these old fishing grounds where cod was split, salted and dried on the rocks are now marinas providing simple accommodation and seafood menus.

The island of **Kuli** off Smøla is rich in relics, the most famous being the **Kuli**

Kristiansund.

Stone. On this stone the name Norway is mentioned for the first time in an inscription which dates to the first years after the coming of Christianity to these parts.

LAND OF THE TROLLS

Inland, the northern part of the county ends in a crisscross of fjords eating into the islands and peninsulas which lead to **Trollheimen**, the "Home of the Trolls", where the mountains reach nearly 1,600 metres (5,000ft). This haunt of climbers and skiers is bounded by two major valleys, **Surnadalen** and **Sunndalen**, with between them the tiny **Todalfjord**. Beside Todalfjord, **Svinvik Arboretum ⑱** (Svinviks Arboret; tel: 71 66 35 80; mid-May–mid-Aug Wed–Sun 11am–4pm) has beautiful gardens with thousands of plants, including rhododendrons and conifers. Despite the northern latitude, plants from other climatic zones thrive at Svinvik.

On the way to Sunndalen along Road 70 from Kristiansund, you come to **Tingvoll ⑲**, which has Nordmøre's oldest church, popularly known as the

Nordmøre Cathedral (Nordmøresdomen; June–Aug). The Tingvoll church is believed to date from the 12th century; it's a well-preserved granite-and-brick structure surrounded by a stone wall with an arched entrance way.

Sunndalen is deep in the Nordmøre wilderness, with narrow valleys between the mountain ranges forming sheltered farming country which supplies grain for most of the county. At the end of the fjord lies the industrial village of Sunndalsøra, once a mecca for British "salmon lords". The **Leikvin Cultural Heritage Park** (tel: 97 47 19 42; mid-June–mid-Aug Tue–Sun noon–5pm) at Grøa tells of their exploits up to the end of the 19th century. The Driva River debouches into the fjord and the surrounding mountains are of breathtaking beauty – a magnificent area for walking and skiing as well as fishing.

Road 70 follows the course of the valley to Oppdal on the third side of Trollheimen. On foot, there are more energetic routes over the mountains, with a mountain centre in Innerdalen and ski lifts as well. The **River Driva** is one of the most famous in a country of good salmon and trout rivers. Between the head of Sunndalen and Grødalen, next door at Åmotan, a spectacular gorge, **Jenstadjuvet ⑳**, is the place where five valleys and their watercourses meet in two furious waterfalls. In Grødalen is **Alfheim**, an incongruous small hunting lodge from 1876 built in Scottish Highland style by a Scot, Lady Arbuthnott, who became something of the "laird" of the valley. It is possible to visit her old farm at **Elverhøy**.

To the north, Surnadal has another good salmon river, the **Surna**; side valleys lead up to the heart of Trollheimen, and to signposted trails leading from mountain hut to mountain hut, in what seems like the top of the world. At valley level, the road through Surnadal is the inland route out of west Norway, straight on to the city of Trondheim, the gateway to the north.

*Waterfall,
Trollstigen Pass.*

De Syv Søstre (Seven Sisters), Geirangerfjord.

Olav Tryggvason monument.

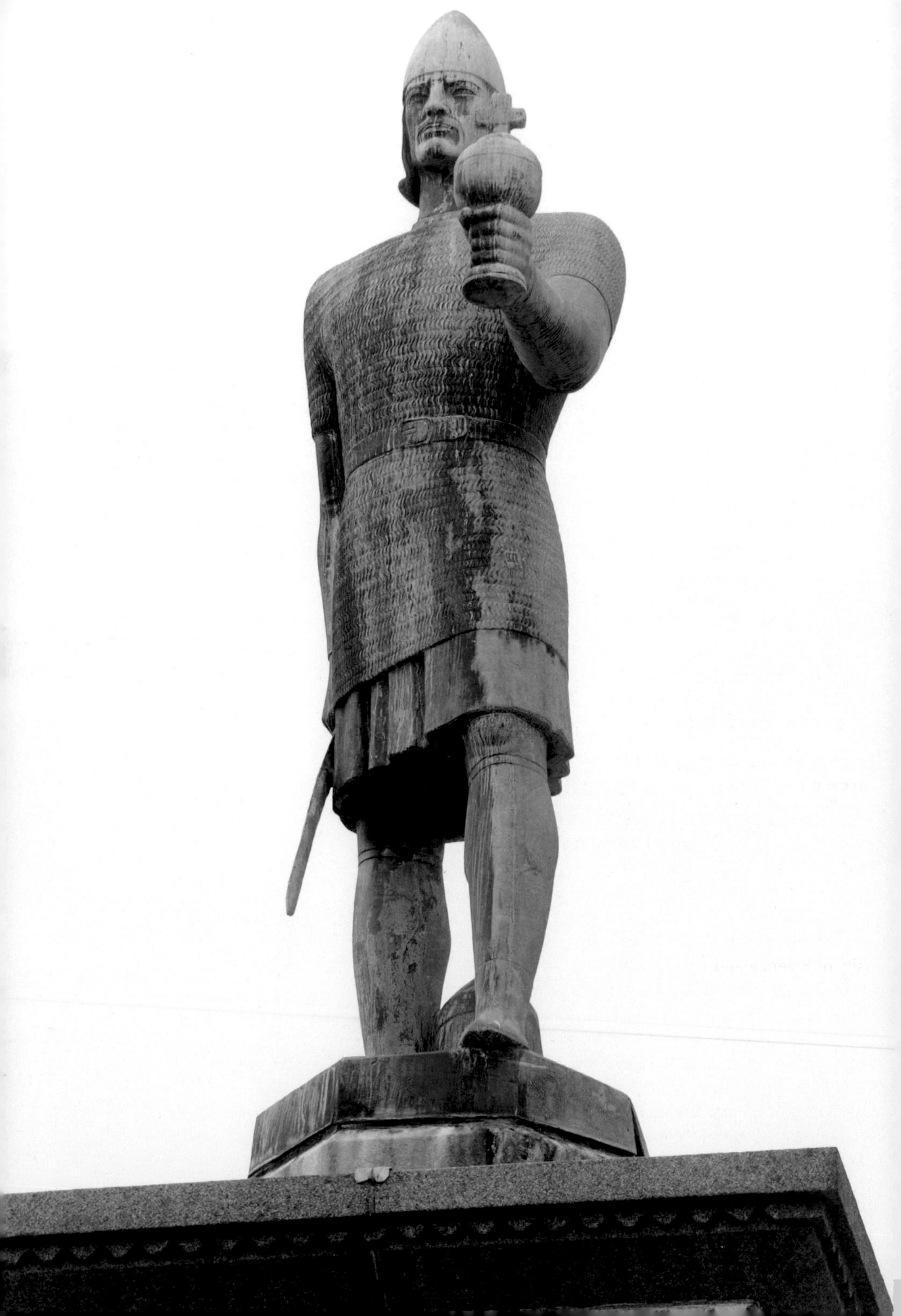

TRONDHEIM

Although Trondheim has lost its political pre-eminence, to many Norwegians the city remains the country's historical, cultural and religious capital, and is host to the annual celebrations of its patron saint, St Olav.

A thousand years ago, Trondheim, then called Nidaros, was the capital of Norway, and the resting place of King Olav Haraldson. The city was founded in 997 by King Olav Tryggvason. A reminder of its early days and of the old harbour is provided by the **wharves**  and the narrow streets (veitene) that run between the wooden buildings. Though they date back only to the 18th century, these coloured warehouses echo the architecture of medieval times, and it is not too difficult to feel what the atmosphere must have been like around that busy harbour when fish and timber dominated the city.

CENTRE OF SCIENTIFIC RESEARCH

Today, Trondheim is the home of SIN-TEF, Scandinavia's largest foundation for scientific and industrial research, and is at the forefront of Norwegian education and church affairs. Situated near SINTEF is the Norwegian University of Science and Technology (NTNU), the country's second-largest university. The city has been a scientific centre since the 18th century – the **University Museum**, from 1760, is Norway's oldest scientific institution – and today both SINTEF and the university attract high-tech businesses to Trondheim, with the advantage of being able to turn to the research establishments for help.

Church of our Lady.

CITY CHARM

Modern though it may be, Trondheim has retained much of the charm of the past, with the heart of the Old City lying on what is virtually an island between the **River Nidelva** and **Trondheimsfjord**, joined only by a narrow neck of land to the west, once the western fort. It's also a city that lives very much in the present, recognised as a centre of science and technology and home to both an architecturally exciting museum of rock music and the **National Museum of Decorative Arts**  (Nordenfjeldske

Main Attractions
Nidaros Cathedral
Archbishop's Palace
Trøndelag Folk museum
Rockheim
Stiklestad

Map on page 256

Kunstindustrimuseum; tel: 73 80 89 50; www.nkim.no; June–late Aug Mon–Sat 10am–4pm, Sun noon–4pm, late Aug–May Tue–Wed and Fri–Sat 10am–3pm, Thu noon–8pm, Sun noon–4pm), which has a superb permanent collection of the best of Scandinavian design.

NIDAROS CATHEDRAL

Though King Olav Tryggvason had attempted to introduce Christianity to Norway in the late 10th century, many Norwegians still clung to their pagan gods, and it was only after the death of his successor, Olav Haraldson, at the Battle of Stiklestad some 30 years later (see page 261) that Christianity acquired a focal point in Norway. Olav's men buried him in sandy ground near the river, but when miracles began to happen he was moved to the town's only church. Then, according to the sagas, a spring began to flow near his first grave and "men were healed of their ills by the waters". The king was declared a saint and martyr in 1164.

Olav's nephew, Olav Kyrre, built a great stone church over the place where the saint's body had lain. This is now the resplendent **Nidaros Cathedral C** (Nidarosdomen; to book tours tel: 73 89 08 00; www.nidarosdomen.no; June–Aug Mon–Fri 9am–6pm, Sat 9am–2pm, Sun 1–5pm; Sept–May times vary; combined tickets including the Archbishop's Palace and crown jewels available), Trondheim's finest building. Once again, the saint's body was moved and the cathedral became a place of pilgrimage. For centuries, pilgrims came from the south of Norway, Sweden and Finland, Iceland, the Faroe Islands and even Greenland to pay homage to St Olav. When the Reformation came to Norway in 1537, the cult of the ancient relic was abolished and pilgrimages ceased. From mid-June to mid-August, a special musical evening mass is held for visitors.

ROYAL TRADITION

Until the Reformation, Nidaros Cathedral was the seat of the archbishop, and the setting for the coronation of Norwegian monarchs, a tradition revived after 1814, when Norway shrugged off its 400 years of Danish rule and united

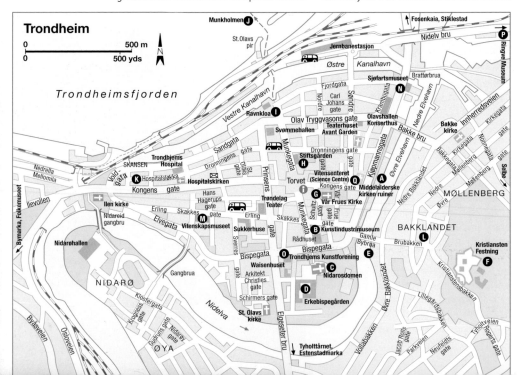

with Sweden. In 1991 King Harald V was crowned in Nidaros Cathedral.

The **great arched nave** is in a Gothic style and, looking back to the west end, the most striking feature is the brilliant stained-glass **rose window** above the main entrance, the work of Gabriel Kjelland in 1930. Both inside and out there are many statues of saints and monarchs; but the beautiful interior lines of the cathedral, built in a green-grey soapstone, are its finest feature.

Next door to the cathedral is Scandinavia's oldest secular building, once the **Archbishop's Palace** **D** (Erkebi-spegården; June–Aug Mon–Fri 10am–5pm, Sat 10am–3pm, Sun noon–4pm; Sept–May times vary). In 1222, Archbishop Guttorm was empowered by King Håkon Håkonsson to mint and circulate coins, a privilege which his successors exercised until 1537 and the Reformation. Their mint was uncovered in the 1990s when the museum was rebuilt after fire and is a highlight. The **crown jewels** are on display in the west wing of the palace and feature royal crowns, sceptres and other regal trappings. The building was at one time a military establishment, and the **National Military Museum** (Rustkammeret; www.forsvarets museer.no/Rustkammeret/Om-Rustkammeret/ English; May–Sept Mon–Sat 10am–4pm, Sun noon–4pm; free) includes exhibits on World War II and the Resistance movement. Nearby is **Waisenhuset**, a beautiful timber building dating from 1772, originally an orphanage.

Around the original medieval city are the remains of fortifications, which were reinforced or built in the late 17th century by a military architect from Luxembourg, General Johan Caspar de Cicignon, after the great fire of 1681 devastated most of medieval Trondheim.

From the cathedral area it is just a short walk to the **Old Town Bridge** **E** (Gamle Bybrua), also erected after 1681 when de Cicignon was constructing **Kristiansten Fort** **F** (Kristiansten Festning) on a hill to the east, at that

time outside the city proper. The first bridge had a sentry box and excise house at either end. The western building still remains and is now used as a kindergarten. The present bridge and gates were built in 1861.

VIEW FROM KRISTIANSTEN FORT

Kristiansten Fort provides one of the best views of Trondheim. From here you can see the old stone walls of the 13th-century **Church of Our Lady** **G** (Vår Frues Kirke; 24 hours a day) and **Stiftsgården** **H** (http://nkim.no/stiftsgarden; June–mid-Aug Mon–Sat 10am–4pm, Sun noon–4pm; visit only by tour, departing on the hour), Scandinavia's largest timber mansion, on **Munkegata**. Stiftsgården was built as a private house in the 1770s and today serves as the official residence of the Norwegian royal family when visiting the city.

Northeast from the bustling harbour of the **Ravnkloa** **I** at the northern end of Munkegata, and past the ornate railway station, is **Fosenkaia**, where sightseeing and other boats tie

Church of Our Lady painting.

Old Town Bridge (Gamle Bybrua) offers good views of the warehouses along Kjøpmannsgate.

Wannabe rockstars at Rockheim.

up. At midday, the Hurtigruten coastal express (see page 229) will be lying at one of the two main quays, giving cruise passengers a half-day to spend in Trondheim before the ship heads north. Returning south on a summer evening, the ship is outlined against the light as its passengers make an excursion to see the midnight sun from the summit of **Mount Storsteinen**.

The remains of Trondheim's old defences, **Skansen**, lie to the west where the city gate once stood. Skansen is now a park. Also near the harbour is a curious warehouse built out on iron stilts over the sea; its shape is explained by the fact that it was a World War II U-boat bunker when German forces occupied the city.

Well out into the fjord is the islet of **Munkholmen** ● (hourly ferry from Ravnkloa; late May–Aug), where Benedictine monks built a monastery very early in the 11th century. This was one of the first two monasteries in Norway. Before the arrival of the Benedictine monks, the site had been Trondheim's execution ground and in 1658 it became a prison fort. You can take a tour of the fort, and the island also offers good sea bathing.

WALKING IN THE OLD TOWN

Trondheim is an easy walking city. Two places best toured on foot are **Hospitalsløkka** ●, the area around the old Trondheim Hospital, and **Bakklandet** ●, on the eastern side of the Nidelva, not far from the Old Town Bridge and opposite the riverside warehouses.

In the grounds of the hospital, which was founded in 1277 and is Scandinavia's oldest surviving hospital, lies the first **octagonal timber church** (1705) to be built in Norway. The surrounding area is full of old timber houses, restored by their present owners. Bakklandet is another area of old wooden houses, and was originally a working-class quarter. It and the Mollenberg and Rosenborg districts have been restored and gentrified.

LOOKING INTO THE PAST

At the **NTNU University Museum** in Erling Skakkes gate ● (Vitenskapsmuseet;

www.ntnu.edu; July–Aug daily 11am–5pm; Sept–June Tue–Fri 10am–4pm, Sat–Sun noon–4pm), the main exhibits trace the history of the area up to the Middle Ages, and the development of church furnishings from the 13th to the 18th century. Also on show are skeletons, a coin collection and a display covering Trøndelag flora and fauna. The **Maritime Museum** Ⓝ (Sjøfartsmuseet; Mon–Fri 9am–2pm, Sun noon–4pm), situated in an old penitentiary from 1725, covers shipping, fishing and whaling.

Trøndelag Folk Museum (Folkemuseet; http://sverresborg.no; tel: 73 89 01 00; bus 8 or 18 from Dronningensgate; June–Aug daily 10am–5pm; Sept–May Tue–Fri 10am–3pm, Sat–Sun noon–4pm) in Sverresborg, on the west side of the city has more than 60 reconstructed buildings from the Trondheim area. They are centred round a market square and include a post office and dentist's surgery. There is a stave church dating from 1170 and an exhibit of *passementerie* (the making of trimmings and lace for women's Sunday best). Within the museum are the remains of King Sverre's palace, **Zion**, from around 1180, and the 18th-century tavern has a good restaurant. There is also a Sami Museum.

DRAMA AND MUSIC-MAKING

Trondheim also has Norway's oldest theatre building, **Trøndelag Teater**, in the centre of the Old Town. Other arts are represented by galleries and institutions such as the **Academy of Art** Ⓞ (Trondhjems Kunstforening; tel: 907 29 133; Fri–Sun noon–4pm), showing and selling contemporary paintings.

The **Ringve Museum of Musical History** Ⓟ (buses 3 and 4 from Munkegaten; tel: 73 87 02 80; www.ringve.no; May–Aug daily 10am–5pm, Sept–Apr Tue–Sun 11am–4pm) occupies an ancient manor. The permanent exhibition is in the former barn. Here, light and sound guide you through various moments and movements in the history of music, such as "the invention of the piano" and "pop and rock".

Since the late 19th century, the house had belonged to the Bachke family. In 1946, the last representative, Christian Anker Bachke, died and his widow, Russian-born "Madame Victoria", worked steadily to build up the couple's collection of musical instruments from all over the world. Her persuasiveness in prising relics from many countries is legendary, and when the museum opened in 1952 the collection had grown substantially. A selection of the instruments are played by the music-student guides during the tour. In addition to the more formal, classical instruments, there are examples of music boxes, old folk instruments such as the *langeleik* – a sort of Norwegian zither – and clay flutes shaped like birds and soldiers.

Just before her death in 1962, Madame Victoria opened the museum's concert hall. Built into the old cowsheds, it is used for formal musical occasions. After the museum, stroll around the **Botanic Gardens** (Ringve

> **⊘ Fact**
>
> Trondheim is the site of the world's first bicycle lift, "Trampe", built on Brubakken hill in 1995. It operates like a ski tow. Cyclists pay using keycards at the bottom and are pulled 130 metres (430ft) to the top.

⊘ THE HOME OF ROCK

Norwegian pop and rock is showcased at **Rockheim** (Brattørkaia 14; tel: 73 60 50 70; www.rockheim.no; Tue–Sun 10am–6pm), housed in an eye-catching modern building just north of Trondheim's central train station (Rockheim means literally "the home of rock"). The permanent exhibition at Rockheim presents Norway's pop and rock heritage with a journey through contemporary Norwegian popular music and culture from the 1950s to today. It includes a mix of sounds, images and videos, as well as artefacts from the various periods represented. Additional temporary exhibitions focus on aspects of music history and contemporary culture, taken from the local, national and international scene.

Visitors will also have the opportunity to get involved, by, for example, learning how to play the guitar with TNT guitarist Ronnie Le Tekro, mixing hip-hop tracks using professional equipment, and experiencing the kick of standing on a stage in front of thousands of virtual fans. The *mediatheque*, which is central to the project, gives the public access to a wealth of rock literature and original footage from the museum's extensive music and video archives. There is a professional stage featuring the latest technology and equipment, and an auditorium accommodating up to 350 people. Check out the latest programme of concerts, as well as seminars and tutorials. There is also a restaurant and shop on site.

⊙ Tip

For a bird's-eye view of the city from the 124-metre (406ft) telecommunications tower, Tyholttårnet (all year), take buses 20 or 60. There's a revolving restaurant at the top of the tower.

Botaniske Hage; daily, free) next door, one of the most northerly botanical gardens in the world.

Families with children might also want to check out the **Science Centre** ⊙ (Vitensenteret, Kongens gate 1; 72 90 90 07; mid-June–mid-Aug Mon–Fri 10am–5pm, Sat–Sun 11am–5pm; rest of year Mon–Fri 10am–6pm, Sat–Sun 11am–6pm), a popular science adventure centre with some 150 interactive exhibits designed to bring the fun back into science.

OUTDOOR LIFE

Trondheim's back garden is **Bymarka** to the west, where Gråkallen (Old Man) at some 520 metres (1,700ft) is the city's favourite skiing area. In summer, it offers great walking. Its counterpart to the east is **Estenstadmarka**. Fishing is good in the River Nidelva, which is renowned for the size of its salmon. The River Gaula to the south is another fine fishing river, while the fjord itself is ideal for sea fishing.

From June to August, the tourist office (tel: 73 80 76 60; www.trondheim.

no) runs two-hour bus tours of Trondheim. It also organises a two-hour walking tour of Trondheim, which takes in a number of sites and museums, departing daily at 1pm from Torget, next to the tourist information office. You can also visit the ancient manor of **Austråtborgen** (May–Aug) at Ørland on Trondheimsfjord. Another idea for a day outing is to take a short leg of the Hurtigruten and return by bus or train. Alternatively, you can travel southeast to the **Norwegian Radio Museum** (Radiomuseet; late May–Aug Sat–Sun 1–5pm) at Selbu, devoted to the history of radio in the years 1890–1980. The museum has a pleasant café that also hosts concerts. Road 705 to Selbu is a particularly scenic route that's marketed as **Ferieveien** ("holiday road").

For most people Trondheim means history and culture. Like the pilgrims of old, visitors come to see the cathedral, the Archbishop's Palace and de Cicignon's 17th-century city, and to participate in historical events such as the annual 10-day **St Olav Festival** (www.olavsfestdagene.no) at the end of July.

Munkholmen.

STIKLESTAD

Thousands of pilgrims flock to Sticklestad every summer to commemorate the battle at which the venerable King Olav died.

Stiklestad is a name that is revered by Norwegians. A momentous battle on this site in 1030, at which King Olav Haraldson died at the hands of King Canute, was a turning point in Norwegian history. For Stiklestad, 100km (60 miles) north of Trondheim, saw the foundation of Norwegian national unity and the adoption of the Christian faith. A church marks the spot where Olav died.

In the 11th century Norway was a country constantly disrupted by disputes between rival chieftains, and Olav's ambition was a united Norway. He also aimed to create a Christian country with Christian laws and churches and clergy.

He was not the first to attempt this. In the previous century Olav Tryggvason (a descendant of Harald Hårfagre) had been converted to Christianity in England and confirmed by the Bishop of Winchester. He returned to his native land in 995 with the express purpose of crushing the chieftains and imposing his new-found faith. But Olav Tryggvason's conversion had not swept away all his Viking instincts, and in his religious zeal he used great cruelty in his attempt to convert the populace. As a result, he fell in the Battle of Svolder in the year 1000, due to the defection of some disenchanted Norwegian chieftains.

Olav Haraldson was also a descendant of Harald Hårfagre and he ascended the throne in 1015. But, like his predecessor, Olav foolishly made too great a use of the sword to establish Christianity. The result was the same: with his eye on the Norwegian throne, King Canute of Denmark and England gave support to discontented factions within the country and in 1028 invaded Norway, forcing King Olav to flee to Russia.

Undaunted, King Olav returned with a few followers, but whatever loyalty he had once inspired had been lost through his ruthless methods. He died on 29 July 1030 at the Battle of Stiklestad. Olav's corpse was taken to the then capital, Nidaros (the Trondheim of today) and buried on the banks of the Nidelva River. According to legend, when the body was disinterred a year later by the bishop, it showed no signs of decay: his face was unchanged and his nails and hair had grown. At that time this was taken as a sign of sanctity.

Following this revelation, Olav was proclaimed a saint and his body placed in a silver shrine in Nidaros Cathedral. Faith in the holiness of King Olav – or St Olav as he now was – spread and, until the Reformation, his shrine became a goal of Christian pilgrims.

Canute's triumph at the Battle of Stiklestad was brief. He ceded the reins of power to his son Sweyn but, as the rumours of Olav's sanctity grew, support for Canute evaporated and Sweyn was exiled to Denmark in 1035.

All the while, St Olav's son, Magnus, had also been living in exile, in Russia. Norway now invited Magnus to return and accept the crown.

Stiklestad has been a place of pilgrimage ever since. People still come at the end of July for a festival to commemorate the battle. There is a beautiful open-air theatre here, and on the anniversary of the battle, a cast of more than 300 actors, choristers, dancers and musicians re-enact the events of July 1030 (for more details, see www.stiklestad.no).

King Olav (1016–28) became St Olav, patron saint of Norway.

INTO THE ARCTIC

North of Trondheim lies a beautiful but often harsh landscape, caught between the sea and the mountains inland. Beyond the imaginary border that cuts across it extends the vast expanse of the Arctic.

⊙ Main Attractions
Stiklestad
Svartisen Glacier
Arctic Circle
Saltstraumen
Torghatten

Map on page 264

The city of Trondheim is the gateway to the north. The first county north of Trondheim, Nord Trøndelag, has wide areas of rich agricultural land with prosperous-looking farms. Running right up the middle of the county is Norway's north–south jugular, the E6 highway, accompanied for long stretches by the Nordland railway. Just north of Trondheim, a branch line (with a companion road) reaches over the border into Sweden. It veers off at the small village of **Hell**, whose station must be one of the most photographed in the country and whose tickets are collectors' items. In September, Hell hosts an annual Blues Festival, which attracts international stars to this otherwise quiet settlement.

For motorists, there is little of interest along this section of the E6 and the inclination is to keep going north; but make time for **Værnes ❶**, which has an interesting church from the Middle Ages with a fine Baroque pulpit. Near the church is **Stjørdal Museum** (tel: 74 82 70 21; www.stjordalmuseum.no; mid-June–mid-Aug Tue–Sat 11am–4pm, Sun noon–4pm; rest of the year Mon–Fri 8am–3.30pm). The **Frostatinghaugen rock carvings** at Frosta are the site of the first Norwegian legislative assembly (AD 600–1000), with rock carvings going back a further 3,500 years.

Some 6km (4 miles) east of Stjørdalshalsen on the E14 is the **Falstad Centre** (tel: 74 02 80 40; http://falstadsenteret. no; May–Aug Mon–Fri 9am–4pm, Sat–Sun noon–5pm, rest of the year shorter hours) at Levanger. Located in the main building of Norway's second-largest SS prison camp during World War II, the memorial includes two execution sites and a cenotaph in the Falstad forest.

About 4km (2.5 miles) further on lies **Hegra Fort** (Hegra Festning; grounds always open; free). Built following independence, it was the site of several battles during World War II as well as a 25-day German siege. The fort has

Svartisen Glacier.

been restored and includes a Resistance Museum.

ST OLAV'S BATTLEGROUND

Just north of Verdalsøra is the road to **Stiklestad ❷**, the battleground where King Olav Haraldson was killed in 1030. The site is revered by Norwegians as the birthplace of Norwegian national unity (see page 261). The Stiklestad **National Cultural Centre** (Stiklestad Nasjonale Kultursenter; tel: 74 04 42 00; www.stiklestad.no; daily July–Aug 9am–8pm, Sept–June 9am–6pm) in Verdal produces an annual open-air play about St Olav (end of July), a spectacular dramatisation of the battle and Olav's death. The centre also has exhibitions about local natural and cultural history, and includes a Resistance Museum, a Folk Museum with 30 buildings and Stiklestad church from 1180.

The first town of any size north of Trondheim is **Steinkjer**, which has been a centre of commerce for more than 1,000 years. Like so many northern Norwegian towns, Steinkjer was all but destroyed in World War II. These sparsely populated northern areas suffered dreadful destruction through the bombing which followed the German invasion.

Nowadays Steinkjer is home to a hard-rock festival in June, and a popular traditional market in August. One of Norway's foremost contemporary artists, Jakob Weidemann (1923–2001), who was a local resident, decorated Steinkjer's church with murals and a beautiful stained-glass window.

REINDEER ROCK CARVING

North of Steinkjer it is worth branching off the E6 onto Road 763, which runs along the eastern side of Snåsavatnet (lake), to take a look at the impressive rock carvings near **Bøla ❸** (May–Oct). Among them, the Bøla Reindeer is recognised as a classic example of a hunting carving from the stone age. For curiosity, it's rivalled by the Bola Man, a carving of a human with, apparently, a pair of skis. The scenery around the lake is remarkably soft and gentle for a latitude between 63 and 64 degrees north. At its northern end is **Snåsa**, the centre of south Sami (Lapp) culture. The village

A rock festival is held in Steinkjer every June.

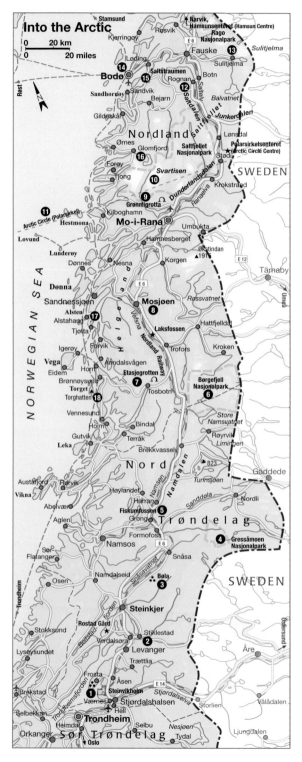

has a Sami cultural centre at Saemien Sijte, which includes a museum (tel: 74 13 80 00; mid-June–mid-Aug Mon–Fri 10am–5pm, Sat–Sun 11am–5pm, rest of the year daily 9am–3pm).

To the east, about 50km (30 miles) away and close to the border with Sweden, the **Gressåmoen National Park** ❹ (Nasjonalpark) is a mix of typically thick Trøndelag forest and mountain landscape.

Dotted throughout Norway – and particularly in the north – are small towns or villages which are essentially transport crossroads. Typical of these is Grong, where the E6 runs north to south and the road and railway to Namsos, on the coast, goes off to the west, while just south of the town the secondary road, No. 74, runs east through wild countryside to the Swedish frontier at Gäddede. It is also the junction of two rivers, the Namsen and the Sanddøla, both popular with anglers. Each river has an impressive waterfall not far from Grong: to the north, **Fiskumfossen** ❺ on the Namsen and to the south, **Formofossen** on the Sandøla. You can learn all there is to know about salmon at the **Namsen Salmon Aquarium** (Laksakvarium; tel: 74 31 27 00; summer daily 11am–4pm, rest of the year shorter hours) at Fiskumfossen. Namsos is also home to the **Nord Trøndelag Art Gallery** (Fylkesgalleri; tel: 74 21 73 30; Mon–Thu 11am–4pm, Fri 11am–3.30pm, Sat 11am–2pm), whose collection includes works by Norwegian and international artists.

TOUCHED BY THE GULF STREAM

From Fiskumfossen, the E6 runs northwards up the long valley of **Namdalen**, while to the northeast is **Røyrvik**, a huge mountainous area which stretches to the Swedish frontier. Half of this region is above the tree line and there are three major lakes: Tunnsjøen, Limingen and Store Namsvatnet. The first has an island peak soaring to 812 metres (2,660ft), and was once a Sami place of sacrifice.

Here the contrast between the east and west of Nord Trøndelag is very marked. The frontier mountains to the east, which bulge into Sweden, have a harsh beauty, but much of the land is desolate and empty. To the west, the coastal scenery is green and fertile. All year round, the Gulf Stream warms the western coast as far as the very north of Norway, making the climate much gentler at the same latitude than it is further inland, and allowing the Hurtigruten to continue sailing throughout winter.

NORDLAND'S COAST AND CAVES

The north end of Namdalen valley marks the border with the county of **Nordland**, the beginning of the real north. This border is straddled by the **Børgefjell National Park** , a district of high mountains, lakes and numerous watercourses – a backpacker's idyll.

Nordland stretches 500km (300 miles) north to Narvik. The Arctic Circle (Polarsirkel) runs through the middle,

and the county includes the long, narrow islands of Vesterålen and the grey peaks of the Lofoten Islands (see page 275). If you take in all the fjords and islands, Nordland has a quarter of Norway's coastline, as well as mountains more than 1,900 metres (6,200ft) high, countless islands and skerries, the second-largest glacier in Norway, Svartisen, and the largest inland lake, Røssvatnet.

Near the Helgeland coast is **Bindalen**, a green, forested valley. At one time, the discovery of gold turned it into a mini-Klondike. Today, it slumbers once more. Close to Bindal is the mountain massif of **Tosenfjellet**, a favourite haunt of potholers and cavers. The biggest cave is **Etasjegrotten** ❼, 1,400 metres (4,600ft) long, where cavers discovered an underground lake.

Between Trofors and Mosjøen on the E6 is the wide but shallow **Laksfossen** (waterfall), which has a 16-metre (50ft) drop. At **Mosjøen** ❽, an industrial town where a splendid location is somewhat marred by a large aluminium works, there is **Dolstad** church, built in

Tip

The best time to see Norwegian waterfalls is in late May, or even June this far north, when summer creeps northwards, melting the snow and ice to swell the rivers.

Vesterålen.

1735 and the oldest octagonal church in north Norway. Look closely at the traces of the old ornamental decor and at a wooden angel beneath the ceiling, which is lowered for use as a baptismal font. **Vefsn Museum** (tel: 75 11 01 00) in Mosjøen has two branches. Near the church is the **Open-Air Museum** (Bygde-samlinga; late June–mid-Aug Mon–Fri 10am–3pm, Sat–Sun 11am–3pm), which brings together 12 buildings from the surrounding district and a collection of some 5,000 objects from the old days of farming, fishing, hunting and domestic life. On Sjøgata, the **Jakobsenbrygge Warehouse** (late June–mid-Aug Mon–Fri 11am–6pm, Sat–Sun 11am–2pm, rest of the year Mon–Fri 10am–3pm, Sat 11am–2pm) is an excellent small museum that illustrates the town's history by means of artefacts, documents and evocative photographic blow-ups.

LAST STOP BEFORE THE ARCTIC

Beyond Mosjøen the scenery changes as farmland gives way to bare mountains (*Fjell*). There are camping sites with tents and cabins on both sides of the road north that offer inexpensive – for Norway – accommodation. **Mo i Rana** is also on a fjord and, like Mosjøen, is dominated by industry – in this case, the former steelworks of Norsk Jernverk, now privatised. These industries in small northern towns may offend the sensibilities of the casual visitor, but they counteract the pull of the more populated south and offer employment that is otherwise scarce hereabouts. Mo i Rana is within reasonable distance of several "must sees" – caves, a glacier and the Arctic Circle (Polarsirkel).

The **Grønnligrotten** ❾ (caves; tel: 75 14 83 12; www.gronligrotta.no; mid-June–mid-Aug, guided tours hourly 10am–6pm, shorter hours rest of the year) lie about 20km (12 miles) north of the town. Guides shepherd parties on 40-minute tours through a glittering underground world of stalactite-hung caverns. At **Setergrotta** (tel: 95 97 44 97; www.setergrotta.no; mid-June–mid-Aug 2-hour guided tours 3pm, plus July 11.30am) the cave calls for care and is more suitable for experienced cavers, with unexplored

The edge of Svartisen Glacier.

caverns, crevices and passages, and interiors of marble and limestone.

From Mo i Rana, it is easy to reach Norway's second-largest glacier, **Svartisen** ⑩ (Black Ice), which covers 370 sq km (140 sq miles) over two separate glaciers, east and west side. It is also one of the lowest-lying glaciers on the European mainland, reaching down to within 170 metres (560ft) of sea level. The road that heads northwest to Svartis Lake leaves the E6, 9km (5.5 miles) north of Mo i Rana. You then cross the water by boat, and walk about 3km (2 miles) to the glacier.

CROSSING INTO THE ARCTIC

From Mo i Rana, the road makes its way through the temperate landscape of Dunderlandsdalen, past Storsforshei iron-ore mine. Then, beyond Krokstrand, the scenery begins to change as the road approaches **Saltfjellet**, a wild region of bare, brooding mountains. Apart from the road, railway line and river, there is little else of note until you come to the monuments that indicate that you've finally reached the **Arctic Circle** ⑪

(Polarsirkel). Alongside the official markers are numerous small stone cairns erected by visitors who felt the need to leave their mark. The tawdry **Arctic Circle Centre** (Polarsirkelsenteret; tel: 75 12 96 96; www.polarsirkelsen teret.no; May–Sept 8am–10pm; free) sells overpriced certificates to confirm that you've crossed the line, plus an eyewatering range of boreal tat. There's a small exhibition of stuffed animals that also includes an audiovisual introduction to the lands of the Arctic.

Outside, two monuments bear witness to the region's darker side in World War II when thousands of prisoners-of-war, mainly Yugoslavs and Russians, were used as slave labour to build the railway and Arctic Highway that you're driving along. Many perished in the bitter winter conditions, and their memorials stands in the wild mountains where they worked and died.

The highest point of the Saltfjell road, is at **Stødi**, 700 metres (2,300ft) above sea level. The watershed generally marks the limit for most temperate flora and fauna. This said, as the road begins

Arctic fox in his summer coat; he is as white as snow in the winter.

Reindeer in the North Cape.

to descend, first you meet the tree-line again at Lønsdal and then, as it races down towards sea level at Rognan, the vegetation becomes lush and abundant, flanked by tall mountains on either side. About halfway down, a detour to the right and a steep climb to **Junkerdalen** takes you to the "silver road", a historic route from Skellefteå, on the Gulf of Bothnia in Sweden, to Bodø. This dramatic mountain scenery also leads to a remarkable botanical phenomenon. A bedrock of mica, which provides exceptional growing conditions, has led to a profusion of rare plants such as cyclamens, usually found only in lowland or more temperate regions. Nowhere else can you find similar growth at this height and nearly 67 degrees north.

Barely 2km (1.5 miles) north of **Rognan** ⑫, the centrepiece of open-air **Saltdal Folk Museum** (tel: 75 50 35 35; mid-June–mid-Aug Tue–Sun 11am–5pm) is a lovely 19th-century farmstead, once the home of a sea captain. In the extensive grounds are 20 or so rural buildings including a cookhouse and tiny school, all of which you can enter. Also

in the grounds is the moving **Blodveimuseet** (Blood Road Museum) dedicated to prisoners-of-war and housed in a former German barracks. Visit is by 30-minute guided tour. The 1,657 Yugoslav, Russian and Polish prisoners who died here in World War II are buried in a cemetery a little further north at **Botn**. Though these prisoners slaved to build a road and not a railway, the result was the same and the stretch between Rognan to Fauske earned the name of the "blood road". In another cemetery nearby 2,700 German soldiers are buried, and a plaque commemorates the 1,932 who died on the battle cruiser *Scharnhorst*, sunk off Nordkapp (North Cape) in 1943.

COPPER, SILVER AND GOLD

Fauske, on the Skjerstadfjord, is another crossroads town. The ever-present E6 goes north to south, while another road (No. 830) heads eastwards for 40km (25 miles) along scenic Langvassdalen. It ends at **Sulitjelma** ⑬, which owes its existence to the discovery of copper by a Sami herder in 1858. The now-defunct mines descend

Saltdal Folk Museum.

to 400 metres (1,300ft) and once produced half a million tonnes of ore a year. Copper pyrites, sphalerite and iron pyrites were extracted from the ore, plus a tidy haul of silver and gold.

For many years, a railway was the only link between Sulitjelma and the outside world, but when that closed today's road was built over the former track-bed. The wild, desolate mountain scenery of this remote area is dominated by the **Sulitjelma Glacier**. Such scenery and the Sulitjelma Mining Museum (Gruvemuseum; tel: 75 50 35 18; mid-June–mid-Aug daily 11am–5pm) at Sulitjelma make a detour worthwhile, and there is tourist accommodation and a camping site.

In this narrow part of Norway – and even more so as the road heads north – you are never far from either the sea or the Swedish border. At Fauske, midway between both, Road 80 and the railway turn west and run along the north of the fjord to Bodø, on the west coast.

END OF THE LINE AT BODØ

Bodø,  like many coastal towns, began as a small community, a safe place for boats and fishermen. It remained small until the 1860s, when three changes brought prosperity: the herring fisheries developed fast, the Sulitjelma mines started production, and the first coastal steamer service began to link the towns of the west coast.

Bodø too was largely laid waste by German forces in May 1940. Today it is a spacious modern town with a population of around 50,000. It is the commercial and administrative centre of the area. It is also a staging post for summer visitors, the end of the Nordland railway line, where the backpackers alight and continue north by bus and coastal express or take a ferry over to the Lofoten Islands.

The midnight sun can be seen in Bodø from 2 June to 10 July. The town is home to the **Norwegian Aviation Museum** (Norsk Luftfartsmuseum; tel: 75 50 78 50; www.luftfartsmuseum.no; June–Aug daily 10am–7pm, rest of the year shorter hours), which includes a U2 spy plane, Spitfires, Mosquitos, a flight simulator and even an old traffic control tower.

Hurtigruten boat moored in Bodø.

Some 40km (25 miles) to the north on the coast is the old trading centre at **Kjerringøy** (late May–Aug). Long overtaken by Bodø, Kjerringøy was one of the richest trading settlements in northern Norway in the 19th century. It has 15 preserved buildings, all with their furnishings, and some typical Nordland boats.

SOUTH, AWAY FROM THE E6

If you've travelled north on the E6, which is almost entirely an inland route, when you reach Bodø again on your return journey, consider taking the incomparably beautiful Kystriksveien (Coastal Road) southwards, being sure to build in time for the several ferry crossings that this entails. Road 17 starts by bridging the **Saltstraumen** **⓯**, where the combination of powerful currents and a narrow channel twice a day creates a vast rush of water, and violent "kettles" or whirlpools. This is the most powerful maelstrom in Scandinavia: some 370 million cubic metres (480 million cubic yards) of water pour through the sound, which is less than 15 metres (50ft) wide, at a rate of up to 28 knots. Saltstraumen is a joy to anglers and seabirds alike, as the current brings an abundance of fish.

The road follows coast and fjord on its way south, and passes **Våg** on the island of Sandhornøy, and **Blixgård** (manor house), which has a memorial to the Norwegian poet Elias Blix.

At **Glomfjord ⓰** you get wonderful views from the top of its chair-lift. From the village, you can also reach an arm of the Svartisen Glacier (Norway's second-largest, see page 267). However, it is better to keep to Road 17, which goes through a major tunnel under the outer edge of the glacier and comes out alongside Nordfjord. From here, take the 10-minute ferry journey across Holandsfjord, then walk the 3km (2 miles) track that leads to the base of the glacier.

ALSTAHAUG'S PARSON-POET

Four ferries later, the road reaches **Sandnessjøen**, on the northern tip of the island of **Alsten**, a trading centre for more than 300 years. **Alstahaug ⓱**

Alstahaug.

on the southern point has a 12th-century church and memorial stone to the parson-poet Petter Dass, who lived there from 1689 until his death in 1707. Dass was so well known that, after his death, most Norwegian ships carried a black patch on their sails as a badge of mourning, a practice that continued for more than 100 years. Today, his life and work are commemorated by a biennial event organised by the striking **Petter Dass Museum** (tel: 75 11 01 50; www.petterdass-museet.no; mid-June–mid-Aug daily 10am–6pm; rest of the year Tue–Fri 10am–3.30pm, Sat–Sun 11am–5pm) at Alstahaug.

A short ferry crossing takes you to the island of **Dønna**, where **Dønna Manor** has been an estate from saga times until the present day. The 13th-century stone church has secret passages cut into the walls which revealed a hoard of coins, some dating back to the time of King Håkon Håkonsson (1204–63).

On the eastern side of Alsten is a mountain range with seven peaks known as **The Seven Sisters** (De Syv Søstre). South of Sandnessjøen is **Tjøtta** which was the home of Hårek, one of the chieftains who killed King Olav at Stiklestad. This area is full of burial mounds and monoliths. There is a cemetery for 7,500 Russian prisoners-of-war. Equally moving is the **Riegel Cemetery**, which has the graves of 1,000 of an estimated 3,000 mainly Russian prisoners of war who died when the *Riegel*, a Norwegian ship under German control was sunk in 1945 outside Tjøtta by Allied aircraft unaware of its human cargo.

THE LEGEND OF TORGHATTEN

Further south near Brønnøysund, and after two more ferry crossings, is the hat-shaped peak of **Torghatten** ⑱, pierced by a great hole that's 160 metres (520ft) long by more than 35 metres (125ft) high. Legend has it that the hole was made by a horseman, thwarted in love, who shot an arrow at his paramour, the Maid of Leka. Just in time, the mountain king of Sømnafjellet saw what was happening and threw his hat in the air to intercept the arrow.

At that very moment the sun rose and all were transformed into stone. The Maid of Leka stands petrified on the island of **Leka**; Torghatten has its hole; and to the north is the island of **Hestmona** to represent the horseman. A more prosaic explanation lies in the action of frost and sea towards the end of the last Ice Age, when the island was lower than it is today. A small road takes you to Torghatten, from where it is a 30-minute scramble up to the hole.

The Brønnøysund area has some of the most fertile land in northern Norway. The island museum of Leka has many curiosities, including boats and fishing equipment. South of Leka is **Vikna**, linked to the mainland by a bridge over the Nærøysund, which, so the old legends relate, was the battleground of giants and trolls. After one more ferry, Road 17 moves inland through Namsos until it joins the E6 just north of Steinkjer.

Brønnøysund.

📷 LAND OF THE MIDNIGHT SUN

Some of Norway's most stunning natural wonders lie above the Arctic Circle and are a prime target for tourists visiting the north in summer.

The phrase "land of the midnight sun" was originally coined by the French American explorer Paul Belloni du Chaillu (c.1831–1903), who published a travelogue by the same title in 1881 after travelling extensively in northern Europe. The name caught on: more than 100 years later, tourists still flock to the North Cape every summer to experience this natural spectacle.

The phenomenon of the midnight sun is due to the inclination of the Earth's axis, and to the fact that the axis points in the same direction during the whole period of the Earth's yearly revolution around the sun. It may be witnessed at any point on the Arctic Circle on 21 June or on the Antarctic Circle on 21 December. Within these circles the length of time the sun is in the sky without setting gradually increases, being 76 days at latitude 70° and 134 days at latitude 80°. For six months, the sun never sets at the poles.

WINTER DARKNESS

Of course, the downside to the phenomenon is that during the winter the sun never appears above the horizon and thus all regions above the polar circles are plunged into darkness as they experience a long polar night.

In Tromsø this period of darkness lasts from 26 November to 15 January, while the midnight sun can be seen from 20 May to 22 July. For the people of the north, the midnight sun is not so much a phenomenon as a way of life.

Near the Arctic Circle the sun stays above the horizon all night from around 21 May to 21 July, as seen here in this composite of 12 exposures taken every 15 minutes on a 5th of July night.

Witnessing the midnight sun from a cruise ship.

The winter sun is a popular draw to the north.

The northern lights above Ersfjorden, Trømso.

The Northern Lights

The northern lights, or aurora borealis, are a huge natural light show, filling the winter sky with patterns of light and colour.

In medieval Europe this remarkable phenomenon was thought to be reflections of heavenly warriors; we now know that it originates from electric particles sent out into space by the sun. These are drawn into the Earth's magnetic field where they collide with other particles in our atmosphere. The resulting electric charges give rise to the greenish patterns of light which dance across the night sky.

The sun has a number of holes in its corona from which high-energy particles stream out. These particles are ejected into the solar system as solar wind that meets the Earth's magnetosphere, compressing it on the daylight side, while drawing out the tail at night.

The solar wind particles accelerate to Earth along the open magnetic fields of the polar regions. When the particles collide with air molecules their energy is transferred into light. These processes occurring simultaneously result in the northern lights.

Kayaking is popular among hardy adventurous types in the fjord region.

Glacier-walking on Briksdal Glacier, an arm of Jostedal.

Enjoying the midnight sun – when the sun remains above the horizon at midnight – in Trømso.

Frozen landscape, Lofoten Islands.

THE FAR NORTH

For many, the aim of travelling this far north is to visit Nordkapp, Europe's northernmost tip; along the way you can go island-hopping in the Lofotens or cross the great expanse of the Finnmarksvidda.

Viewed from the mainland across the broad expanse of Vestfjord, the **Lofoten Islands** present an imposing wall of jagged peaks rising up sheer from the sea. On the west these mountains form a mighty breakwater from the onslaught of the Arctic Ocean. This 112km (70-mile) archipelago stretches from the tiny island of Røst in the south to the waters of the narrow Raftsundet in the north. In winter the coast is one of the stormiest in Europe, while the unsurpassed beauty of the islands makes them one of Norway's major tourist attractions, especially in summer, when the midnight sun is visible from 27 May until 17 July.

Between the mountains, which are composed of some of the oldest rocks in the world, are stretches of fertile farmland, fjords and deep ravines, while the coastline is sprinkled with white sandy beaches, fishing villages and one or two small towns.

A phenomenon peculiar to the Lofotens is the annual cod fishing, which in the past involved up to 6,000 boats and 30,000 fishermen. Between January and March these migrant fishermen lived in simple waterside wooden cabins called *rorbuer*. By 1947 the number of fishermen was declining. Today it is down to 2,000, and this seasonal event has been replaced by a

Small boats and rorbuer (old fishing cottages) in Stamsund.

year-round fishing fleet. In the summer, the cod is left to dry on traditional wooden racks by the harbour.

AROUND THE LOFOTENS

Svolvær , the main town on the island of Austvågøy, has been a trading centre since the 17th century. Surrounded by water, it is flanked by sharp, pointed rocky peaks. The town has its own special mountain, the Svolværgeita ("Svolvær goat"). Svolvær is connected to the mainland by ferry to Skutvik, and by boat (including the coastal express)

Main Attractions
The Lofoten Islands
Tromsø
Hjemmeluft rock carvings
North Cape
Karasjok

Map on page 276

Many of the old rorbuer on the Lofotens have been restored and fitted with modern conveniences and are rented out to summer visitors.

and air to Bodø. It, like the Lofotens as a whole, has attracted many artists and craftsmen, and is now the site of the **North Norwegian Art Centre** (Nordnorsk Kunstnersenter; tel: 76 06 67 70; www.nnks.no; daily 10am–4pm and 6–10pm). Scenes like those described above are captured on canvas by local artist Dagfinn Bakke who owns and runs a gallery here (May–Aug), while at **Kabelvåg ❷** there is an art school and an impressive wooden church which looks old but was in fact built in 1898.

PAYMENT IN FISH

On the outskirts of Kabelvåg is the **Lofoten Museum** (Lofotmuseet; tel: 76 06 97 90; www.museumnord.no; June–mid-Aug daily 10am–6pm; times vary rest of the year), sited where Vågar, the first town north of the Arctic Circle, existed in the Middle Ages. In the 14th century, 80 percent of Norway's national export was stockfish, allowing Vågar a broad market and cultural exchange with Europe. The main museum building was originally in the centre of the thriving fishing community, and one room is furnished as a fish station owner's office from the 1880s. He would own all the *rorbuer*, and the fishermen who rented them would pay in fish from their catches. There is a typical *rorbu* from 1797, with its primitive and crowded living conditions, and a boathouse with three traditional boats of various sizes. Another building is devoted to the development of the Lofoten fishing industry, which in its modernised form plays a vital role in the economy of the islands.

Kabelvåg is also home to the **Lofoten Aquarium** (Lofotakvariet; tel: 76 07 86 65; www.museumnord.no; June–Aug daily 10am–6pm; times vary rest of the year), which is designed as a small fishing village, and includes both salt- and freshwater fish and a seal tank as well.

ISLAND-HOPPING, NORWEGIAN-STYLE

To journey south on the E10 means going from island to island, all of which are linked by impressive bridges. This route must rank as one of the most outstanding in Norway. At every turn the traveller is confronted with another seemingly

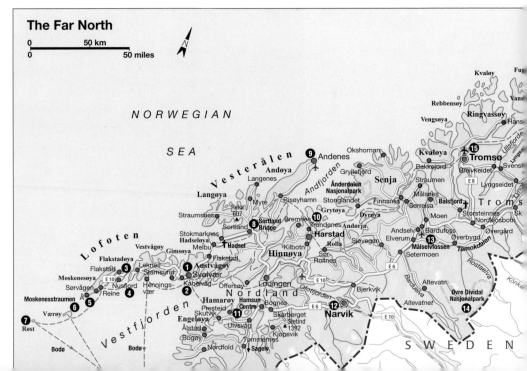

The Far North

0   50 km
0   50 miles

haphazard series of jagged peaks possessing a stark beauty that contrasts with the green scenery at sea level.

On the southern tip of Austvågøy is **Henningsvær**, one of numerous Lofoten fishing villages and home to the Karl Erik Harr Gallery (tel: 91 59 50 83; www.galleri-lofoten.no; June–Aug 9am–7pm, May 10am–7pm; shorter hours rest of the year). The imposing bridge over Gimsøystraumen, 840 metres (2,760ft) long, provides access to the small island of Gimsøya. From here a second bridge takes the road across Sundklakkstraumen to Vestvågøy. **Stamsund**, on a secondary road, is a coastal village and a port of call for the Hurtigruten.

The Lofotr Viking Museum in Borg (tel: 76 08 49 00; www.lofotr.no; June–mid-Aug 10am–7pm; shorter hours rest of the year) includes a reconstruction of an 83-metre (272ft) long Viking chieftain's house (the largest of its kind found in Norway), a smithy and three Viking ships. Guides in period dress demonstrate old crafts, and various activities take place in summer (you can help row the Viking ship, for example). **Leknes** is the main centre of population on the island and a typical small Norwegian town with a long straggling main street.

FLAKSTADØYA HERITAGE SITE

A few kilometres south of Leknes at Lilleeidet there was once a ferry to **Flakstadøya**, which was replaced by a tunnel that goes 50 metres (165ft) below the surface of Nappstraumen.

A surprise of the west coast of Flakstadøya is its scattering of small, **sandy beaches**. On a sunny summer's day, the sight of children paddling belies the fact that it is in the Arctic. The hamlet of **Flakstad ③** has a pretty 18th-century church with an onion dome, while nearby are monuments to those who died in World War II and fishermen whose lives were lost at sea.

Nusfjord ④ and Sund are two other fishing villages on the island. The former is on Unesco's list of preservation-worthy environments because of its unique wooden structures (Nusfjord is considered the best-preserved fishing village in the whole of Norway), while

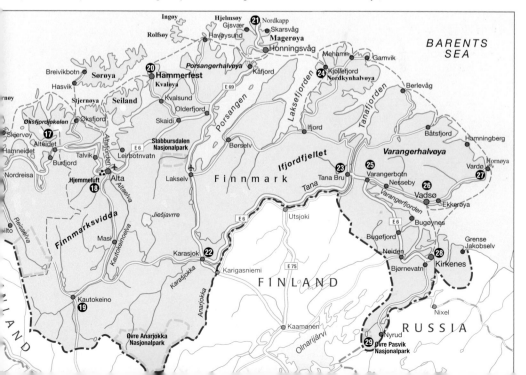

Sund has a small fisheries museum and smithy, famed for its stylishly crafted steel cormorants (June–Aug). Also on the island is **Storbåthallaren**, the oldest known Stone Age settlement in northern Norway, populated 6,000 years ago.

The last bridge takes the road across to the island of Moskenesøya. This also has its quota of fishing villages, of which the most picturesque is **Reine**. Here you can hire a kayak or a bike to explore the area, or visit the excellent Gallery Eva Harr.

ENDING AT Å

The E10 finally runs out at Å ❺ – aptly named, as "Å" is the last letter of the Norwegian alphabet – which marks the end of the line of peaks that make up the **Lofotenveggen** (Lofoten "wall"). It has one of the few trading posts to be preserved in its original condition. There is the small **Norwegian Fishing Village Museum** (Norsk Fiskeværsmuseum; tel: 76 09 14 88; www.museumnord.no; mid-June–Aug 9am–7pm, shorter hours rest of the year; closed weekends Sept–June) in a 19th-century barn. Beyond the tip of

Moskenesøya is the **Moskenesstraumen** ❻, a maelstrom which may not match the Saltstraumen near Bodø but which was once greatly feared by sailors. Even in calm weather it seethes and boils, and was made famous through the works of Edgar Allan Poe and Jules Verne, in his *20,000 Leagues Under the Sea*.

The maelstrom separates Moskenesøya from the small island of **Værøy**, beyond which is the even smaller island of **Røst** ❼. These are the "bird islands", which attract thousands of different species including puffin, auk, eider, guillemot, kittiwake and cormorant. Both islands have small airfields with flights to Bodø, obviating a sea trip which, because of the rapidly changing sea conditions, can be unpleasant. Thanks to the Gulf Stream, Røst and Værøy do not have severe winters, and sheep can graze on the meadows.

VESTERÅLEN: HOME OF THE HURTIGRUTEN

North of Svolvær the views remain splendid but do not quite measure up to those in the south. The road keeps close

The Lofotens in summer.

to the Austnesfjord, beyond which, to the northeast, is Raftsundet and spectacularly narrow **Trollfjord**, visited in summer by the coastal steamer, which scarcely has room to turn around. At Fiskebøl the ferry takes the visitor away from the Lofotens to **Melbu** on the first of the Vesterålen Islands, **Hadseløya,** with its open-air **Norwegian Fishing Industry Museum**(tel: 76 15 40 00; www.museumnord.no; mid-June–mid-Aug Tue–Sun 11am–5pm), on the site of a former herring oil factory and a treat for lovers of industrial archaeology.

Between Melbu and Stokmarknes on the northern side of the island is **Hadsel Kirke** (church; 1824), distinctive in style and with an altarpiece from 1520. **Stokmarknes** is the headquarters of the Vesteraalen Steamship Company, founded by Richard With, sometimes called the father of the coastal steamer. At the **Hurtigruten Museum** (Hurtigrutemuseet; tel: 76 11 81 90; mid-June–mid-Aug daily 10am–6pm; times vary rest of the year), you may buy special Hurtigruten tickets for return trips to Svolvær.

The Hadsel Bridge carries the main road to the island of **Langøya**. Here the principal town is **Sortland**, a commercial centre with a fishing harbour that has a busy, pleasant atmosphere. The western side of the island has imposing mountains, the most unusual being the looming **Reka** at 620 metres (2,000ft), which is popular with climbers.

WHALE SAFARIS

The **Sortland Bridge** ❽, 950 metres (3,150ft) long, is the link to **Hinnøya**, mainland Norway's largest island, which hosts a popular festival every June in Harstad. Away to the northwest is the long island of **Andøya**, which is also connected by bridge and, unlike most other Vesterålen islands, is flat. Much of the land is peat, renowned for its cloudberries.

Andenes ❾, at the northwestern extremity, is a large fishing village with the **Andøy Museum** (Andøymuseet; tel: 76 11 54 32; www.museumnord.no; daily mid-June–late Aug). First a fishing village in the Middle Ages, then a Dutch whaling base in the 17th century,

⊘ Tip

Whale safaris are very popular, so it is worth booking in advance. Trips leave from Andenes, Stø and Nyksund and last 3–5 hours. If you don't spot a whale first time around, repeat the journey for free. Details from the tourist information office in Svolvær, tel: 76 06 98 00; www.whalesafari.no.

Whale-watching in Vesterålen.

today it is one of the starting points for **whale safaris**.

Hinnøya's varied scenery includes farmland along the coastal fringe, green valleys, rugged mountains and fjords. Following the E10 southeast from the Sortland Bridge you come to Lødingen on the eastern coast, with a ferry service to **Bognes** on the mainland and the E6. A little further to the north is **Trondenes** , which has a 13th-century stone church (all year). In the bay below there are Viking burial mounds. Also here are the **Adolf Cannons** (Adolfkanonen; June–Aug), massive long-range guns installed by the Germans during World War II to protect the approaches to Narvik.

A final lengthy bridge carries the E10 over **Tjeldsundet** and onto the mainland, with the road skirting Ofotfjord, which provides deep-water access to Narvik.

TAKING THE E6 NORTH

If you omit Lofoten and Vesterålen islands in your travel northwards, the alternative and more travelled route is by the E6. From Fauske it clings to the

The Lofotens.

side of fjords, going through a succession of tunnels, with the **Rago National Park** away to the east. This is a vast mountainous area with no roads, judged to be the most magnificent but least accessible of all Norway's national parks.

A superb section of highway, which cuts across exciting mountainous country, has been built from Sommarset, where formerly there was a ferry. There are several tunnels, the longest being below the Sildhopfjell.

North of Kråkmo, at **Sagelv**, there are 5,000-year-old rock carvings of reindeer. At Ulvsvåg a road goes off west to **Skutvik** for the ferry to Svolvær. The road continues onto Engeløya island, which was a seat of power many centuries ago, and there are numerous graves and burial mounds, the biggest being at **Sigarshaugen**. At Presteid on the island of Hamarøy you will find the new **Hamsun Centre** , dedicated to Norway's most famous novelist.

Back on the E6, a little north of **Bognes**, are more rock carvings depicting 40 different subjects. To the east of Tysfjord is a mountainous section popular

⊘ HAMSUN CENTRE

The Hamsun Centre (Hamsunsenteret; tel: 75 50 34 50; www.hamsunsenteret.no; June to mid-Aug daily 10am–6pm; rest of the year Tue–Fri 10am–3.30pm, Sat–Sun 11am–5pm, closed Jan), located in Presteid on Hamarøy, west of Narvik, was opened in 2009 to mark the 150th anniversary of the birth of Knut Hamsun (1859–1952), Norway's most famous novelist, considered by many as the father of the modern novel. Hamsun, who received the Nobel Prize for Literature in 1920, was a controversial figure in his homeland, as famous for his writings as for his Nazi sympathies. He was a fervent supporter of the Nazi regime both before and after World War II, and famously mailed his Nobel medal to Joseph Goebbels. His best-known works include *Growth of the Soil*, *Hunger* and *Mysteries*.

with climbers, especially **Stetind**, 1,392 metres (4,567ft) high, sometimes known as "the world's greatest obelisk". There are many caves for those who prefer to go down rather than up, the best known being **Råggejavie**, 620 metres (2,000ft) deep.

NARVIK

Thanks to the deep, ice-free waters of Ofotfjord, **Narvik** ⑫ became a major centre for exporting iron ore mined in northern Sweden. A railway was completed from the mining town of Kiruna to the port in 1883. Narvik is now the end of the Ofotbanen line, the steeply climbing Norwegian railway connecting with the northern Swedish line. In World War II Narvik was the scene of bitter fighting, and German forces occupied it for over five years – portrayed in the **Narvik War Museum** (Narvik Krigsmuseum; tel: 76 94 44 26; https://narviksenteret.no; mid-June–mid-Aug Mon–Fri 10am–7pm, Sat 10am–6pm, Sun noon–6pm, rest of the year times vary). For an overview of Narvik take the cable car (in summer) 650 metres (2,132ft) to the top of Fagernes. From June to August, a "tourist train" takes visitors on a three-hour guided tour between Narvik and the Swedish border, with photo opportunities and a chance to buy Sami souvenirs.

TROMS, A COUNTY OF CONTRASTS

North of Narvik the E6 crosses Rombakfjord over another major bridge, passes the junction with the road to Sweden, and joins with the E10 at Bjerkvik. Then it follows a climb up Gratangseidet county boundary into Troms. Troms has widely contrasting scenery, all typically north Norwegian: rugged mountains with sharp peaks, countless islands and skerries, a softer landscape at sea level and fast-flowing rivers and numerous lakes. The county is split up by a number of major fjords and is also notable for its extensively forested valleys.

Setermoen, just north of Narvik, lies in the heart of a military area and has a large garrison. The military presence is also apparent further north at Bardufoss, with its major airbase. From Bardufoss the E6 follows the Målselv River until it turns abruptly east past Takvatnet, where a new turn-off provides some stunning views of distant mountains. Near **Balsfjord church** (kirke), about 10km (6 miles) from Storsteinnes, are rock carvings which are 2,500 to 4,000 years old. The area around Balsfjord has some of the richest farming land in Troms, where goat-farming is a major activity.

PREDATORS AT ØVRE DIVIDAL NATIONAL PARK

Alternatively, before you get to Bardufoss turn eastwards at Elverum onto Road 857, from which you can reach **Målselvfossen** ⑬ (waterfall). It may only have a drop of 15 metres (50ft), but it extends over 600 metres (2,000ft). There are salmon ladders, and the Målselv River, which is renowned for its salmon, was discovered by English anglers in the 1840s. At Rundhaug a secondary road

◉ Tip

The rock carvings near Balsfjord church (Kirke) are part of the Tennes Heritage Trail, which is one of the many trails included in *Fotefar mot Nord (Trails to the North)* available from tourist offices.

A lynx, one of Norway's major predators.

follows the Målselv River to Øverbygd, then continues along **Tamokdalen** until it rejoins the E6 near Øvergård.

To the south, adjacent to the border with Sweden, lies the **Øvre Dividal National Park** , where all four of Norway's major predators – bear, wolf, lynx and wolverine – have their habitat.

TROMSØ, CITY OF THE ARCTIC

Tromsø occupies most of the island of Tromsøya and overflows onto the adjoining island of Kvaløya. With a population of 64,300 it is the largest city in northern Norway and, until the opening of the first bridge, in 1960, everything had to be ferried across from the mainland.

Today there is a second bridge and an amazing network of road tunnels under the city, including subterranean car parks and roundabouts. The tunnel system links the city centre with Tromsø Langnes International Airport: if you arrive by air the taxi route into town runs through the tunnel system. The town has variously been called the Gateway to the Arctic, the Arctic Ocean City and even the Paris of the North.

Archaeological finds indicate settlements dating back 9,000 years. Tromsø became an ecclesiastical centre in 1252, and much of the subsequent development from 1300 to the 1700s was influenced by the Hanseatic League. Trade restrictions led to strong dependence on Bergen throughout the Middle Ages. In 1794, the town was granted market town *(kaupang)* privileges and the right to independent trade, and became a focal point for the Pomor trade, with Russian ships bringing timber, rape, flour and other items from the White Sea in exchange for fish and goods brought north by the Hanseatic traders.

In the early 19th century Tromsø was the natural starting point for trapping expeditions to the pack ice to the north and east and to the archipelago of Svalbard (Spitsbergen). It has also been the site of a number of sea battles, including the sinking of the German battleship *Tirpitz*, pride of the German fleet, which was destroyed by British bombers while guarding the entrance to Tromsø in 1944.

Tromsø.

POLAR ART AND WORSHIP

Though fishing (for shrimps, herring and other fish) is of prime importance, Tromsø University and a regional teaching hospital are also major employers here. **Tromsø University Museum** (tel: 77 64 50 00; https://uit.no/tmu/tmu; June–Aug daily 9am–6pm; times vary rest of the year) focuses on the cultural and natural history of the north and the Sami, and has a reconstructed Viking longhouse. Polar explorers are the centre of attention at the **Polar Museum** (Polarmuseet; tel: 77 62 33 60; https://uit.no/tmu/tmu; mid-June–early Aug daily 9am–6pm; rest of the year 11am–5pm) in the historic harbour area. Housed in a distinctive building a bit further south on the waterfront, **Polaria** (tel: 77 75 01 00; www.polaria.no; mid-May–Aug daily 10am–7pm; rest of year noon–5pm) is another stop for anyone interested in the Arctic, and includes a museum, an aquarium and a 3D cinema.

The **Art Museum of Northern Norway** (Nordnorsk Kunstmuseum; tel: 77 64 70 20; www.nnkm.no; all year daily 10am–4pm; free) has a good collection of Sami and northern Norwegian art. In the centre of the town is the **Cathedral** (Domkirke; June–Aug Tue–Sun) of the Lutheran Church of Norway, dating from 1861 and one of the country's largest wooden churches.

Situated on the mainland is the striking **Arctic Cathedral** (Ishavskatedralen; June–mid-Aug Mon–Sat 9am–7pm, Sun from 1pm; times vary rest of the year), designed by Jan Inge Hovig and completed in 1965. The cathedral features a huge stained-glass window by Victor Sparre covering the entire east wall, 23 metres (75ft) high, depicting the Second Coming. Nearby is the cable car to the top of the **Storsteinen** (420 metres/1,380ft), from where there are magnificent views over the town and the surrounding area. Tromsø's **Botanical Gardens** specialise in flora from all over the world's cold regions, while the town enjoys a different kind of fame as the site of Europe's northernmost brewery, Mack, established in 1877 and renowned for its Arctic Ale. The brewery is a short walk from the centre, and there is a beer hall on the premises.

The Arctic Cathedral (Ishavskatedralen) in Tromsø represents the shape of a Sami tent and the iciness of a glacier.

WHERE GLACIER AND SEA MEET

To the northwest of Tromsø a number of islands stand guard where the lengthy Ullsfjord and **Lyngenfjord** reach the sea. Between these is a long, wide peninsula. On its eastern side lie the range of mountains known as the **Lyngen Alps** (Lyngsalpene). The full majesty of these snow-capped peaks and glaciers is best seen from the eastern side of Lyngenfjord. For a short cut that avoids the main road and affords fine views of the mountains, take Road 91 just south of Tromsø through the Breivik valley, a ferry across Ullsfjord to Svensby, then drive to Lyngseidet and hop onto a second ferry across Lyngenfjord to Olderdalen to rejoin the E6.

The more obvious route is south along the E8 to where it joins the E6 at Nordkjosbotn and then northeast through Skibotn, keeping along the shore of the Lyngenfjord with its views of the mountains across the water. After continuing east along the side of the Rotsundet, opposite the island of

The Hurtigruten at Ullsfjord.

Uløya, the road swings inland before meeting Reisafjord. There are fine views to the west, which are even better after climbing over the summit of **Kvænangsfjellet**. There is an impressive panorama of islands and mountains before descending to Burfjord. Just past Alteidet, a minor road goes north to the Jøkelfjord where the **Øks-fjordjøkelen** (glacier) calves into the sea, the only one in mainland Norway to do so. To the east is the boundary into Norway's most remote county, Finnmark.

FINNMARK

No one describes Finnmark without a combination of superlatives and impressive statistics. It is Norway's most northerly county and the largest, covering 48,000 sq km (18,500 sq miles), equal to 15 percent of the entire country, yet it has only just over 75,000 inhabitants, less than 2 percent of the population.

Finnmark lies along the same latitude as Alaska, but the Gulf Stream ensures that the harbours do not freeze even in the depths of winter. Inland, the temperature can drop to a

⏱ SCORCHED EARTH

World War II was particularly traumatic for Finnmark. When Soviet liberators crossed Norway's northern border in the autumn of 1944, the German occupation forces began a "scorched earth" policy as they retreated south, burning towns and villages and even individual farms as they went. Whatever fields or forests they encountered were not spared either, and local transportation and communication infrastructure suffered as a result.

The result of this widespread devastation can be seen in **Alta**, the first town across the county border from Troms and the biggest in Finnmark, where some of the architecture is decidedly undistinguished. This is often the case in the towns of northern Norway, which had to rebuild rapidly after the war came to an end.

chilling –50°C (–70°F), while during the short summer it may hit 32°C (90°F). Between mid-May and the end of July the sun never sets – you can read a newspaper outside at midnight – while in winter the sun stays snug below the horizon from the end of November to the end of January.

The scenery is spectacular, with the highest areas in the northwest and a vast mountain plateau, the **Finnmarksvidda**, to the south and southeast. The bare grey rocks of the coast take the full force of the winter storms. It is the vastness of the uninhabited areas that makes the greatest impression: ranges of mountains and *fjell* stretch away to the horizon, seemingly without end.

Much of this wonderful county is now easily accessible by car or public transport on well-surfaced main roads, while there is an extensive network of air services that land at tiny airports dotted all over the area. The Hurtigruten serves towns and villages along the coast.

The people of Finnmark are greatly attached to their part of Norway, which has been inhabited for 10,000 years. They include not only Norwegians and Sami (Lapps) but also many folk of Finnish origin. The Norwegians settled the coast in the 14th century, but major changes in the 18th and 19th centuries brought in people from the south of the country. At the same time came a large migration from Finland and Sweden.

ANCIENT ROCK CARVINGS

On the southern outskirts of **Alta** is an outstanding collection of prehistoric rock carvings at the **Alta Museum** ⑱ (signs from Alta; tel: 41 75 63 30; www. altamuseum.no; mid-June–mid-Aug 8am–8pm, times vary rest of the year). Discovered in 1972 and on Unesco's World Heritage list, there are about 5,000 carvings on four different sites. The biggest concentration is at Hjemmeluft itself. These "stories in pictures" vary from 2,500 to 6,000 years old and depict people, animals (particularly

reindeer), boats and weapons. Traces of these early inhabitants, the Komsa people, were discovered in 1925 on Komsafjell, on Altafjord. The dwelling sites go back some 10,000 years – a reminder of how long humans have lived in this inhospitable region.

SAMI CULTURE

Finnmark has few roads, so it's easy to find your way. Going south from Alta is Road 93 to **Kautokeino** ⑲ and the Finnish frontier. Kautokeino is the largest Sami community in the country, the centre of Sami education with a reindeer-herding school, and possibly the coldest town in Norway. The **Kulturhuset** has the only Sami theatre in Norway, and the open-air **Kautokeino Museum** (all year) presents a complete traditional Sami settlement.

Northwards from Leirbotnvatn (around the fjord from Alta) to the village of **Skaidi** are 45km (28 miles) of sheer emptiness. The E6 takes a lonely course through the wild countryside. Almost the only building is the small **Sami chapel**, dwarfed

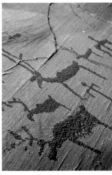

One of the prehistoric carvings at Hjemmeluft.

Camping in Finnmark.

by its surroundings. The only signs of life away from the road are the herds of reindeer. You are constantly aware of how little human activity has impinged on the grandeur of these great empty spaces.

HISTORY OF DISASTERS

Skaidi is a popular base for anglers, hunters and winter-sports enthusiasts. It is also the junction of the E6 and Road 94 to **Hammerfest ⓴**, 56km (35 miles) away on the bare, rocky island of Kvaløya. Hammerfest is the world's most northerly town. Founded in 1789, for centuries it was the best ice-free harbour in northern waters, although storms and hurricanes plus many man-made disasters have repeatedly wrought havoc on the town. In 1825, a hurricane destroyed houses and boats, and an even more ferocious storm in 1882 moved the German kaiser, Queen Victoria and the tsar of Russia to donate money to repair the considerable damage.

In 1890, the town had ambitious plans for a hydroelectric power station,

Hammerfest.

but only a month after work started, fire again destroyed two-thirds of the town. In the following year, nevertheless, Hammerfest became the first European town to have electric lighting when it purchased a generator from Thomas Edison in 1891.

The harbour has always been of importance both commercially and strategically, and ships have long called there. When Norway was invaded in 1940, it was a growing and flourishing community. The retreating Nazis burned down the entire town, and by 10 February 1945 only the **chapel** in the graveyard still stood. Today, Hammerfest is Norway's main trawler port and an increasingly important base for offshore oil and gas activity tied to the Snow White field.

MEASURING THE PLANET

Hammerfest clings to the shoreline, which is backed by a steep escarpment. Its most notable monument is the **Meridian Column** (Meridianstøtta), which was erected by King Oskar II in the late 19th century to mark the first

international measurement of the Earth (1815–52), a joint enterprise by Russia, Norway and Sweden.

On the highest point of a walk from the town up the escarpment is the Midday Pole, topped by a cannonball. When the shadow from the pole points directly to the Meridian Column, the time is 12 noon precisely.

In 1809, after Norway entered the Napoleonic Wars, two British warships attacked Hammerfest. The town fell and the British stayed for a week of plunder and destruction. The cannonball placed on top of the Midday Pole is the permanent reminder of this unhappy event.

To prevent further attack the military built a redoubt or **Skansen** in 1810 with eight guns, which, Hammerfest folk are happy to report, has never been fired in anger. This walk also passes a beacon built by the town's young people in 1882–3 "as they had no other amusements".

More noticeable today is the circular **Polar Bear Hall** (Isbjørnhallen), used for sporting events and exhibitions.

At the other end of town is the equally striking **church** (June–Aug), its form inspired by traditional fish-drying racks. Its altarpiece, a glass mosaic dating from 1632, comes from the town's first church.

In a shrewd move in 1963, Hammerfest created the **Royal and Ancient Polar Bear Society** (Isbjørnklubben), which offers one of the more original souvenirs of its kind. To get a certificate of membership, plus pin and sticker you must apply in person to the society's **museum**, which shares premises with the town tourist office.

ON TOP OF EUROPE

From Skaidi the E6 goes northeast across wild, uninhabited territory before the road descends to the sea at Olderfjord. Here most visitors turn north for **North Cape**  (Nordkapp), Europe's northernmost point. This is for many the end of their pilgrimage by car, motor home, motorbike, bus or even bicycle. The alternative way to reach Honningsvåg is by air or sailing by Hurtigruten or cruise liner.

Watch out for elk crossing.

North Cape (Nordkapp).

Puffins can be found all along the northern coasts.

The road hugs the edge of Porsangenfjord, with rugged country to the landward side, and ends at Kåfjord, where a tunnel connects to **Honningsvåg** on the island of Magerøya. Between Honningsvåg and Nordkapp lie 35km (21 miles) of truly Arctic scenery. It may be bare and treeless, but there is an unusual beauty about the island which, on a sunny day, is emphasised by the clarity of the atmosphere; too often, alas, it is misty. The coastal steamers have provided the biggest impetus to tourist traffic, and by 1920, the wild grandeur of the headland had learned to live with the incongruity of its first building. The road to the Cape from Honningsvåg opened in 1956, as did a centre with the usual souvenir shop, cafeteria and post office.

In 1989, this earlier building gave way to the **North Cape Hall** (Nordkapphallen; tel: 78 47 68 60; mid-May–mid-Aug 11am–1am, times vary rest of the year), with its circular Compass Restaurant and, below, the Super-videograph, a 225-degree screen with wraparound sound which brings the

The Midday Pole at the North Cape.

four seasons of Finnmark to the visitor, whatever the time of year. It also has a chapel for marriage ceremonies. Nordkapp illustrates the seasonal extremes in this area: 24-hour darkness occurs from November to the end of January, while the midnight sun lasts from mid-May to the end of July.

An underground tunnel leads from the new hall and champagne bar, an amphitheatre cut out of the rock and overlooking the Arctic Ocean. Even if you suffer from vertigo, look briefly from the balcony, which provides a spectacular view straight down to the sea far below. Along the tunnel are tableaux depicting historical events at Nordkapp. On what is in danger of becoming a crowded plateau are seven circular, wheel-like sculptures. They are monuments to the children of the world, sculpted in 1988 by seven children from seven lands to celebrate "joy, friendship and working together".

"HADDOCK" ENGLISH

Apart from the main road to Nordkapp itself, there is only one other road on

⊘ A NEW ROUTE TO CHINA

The name North Cape was given to the imposing headland by an Englishman, Captain Richard Chancellor. In 1553, as master of the *Edward Bonaventure*, he was seeking a new route to China when he rounded Europe's most dramatic northern point; but it was not until the 19th century that Nordkapp began to attract visitors.

In 1845, passengers from the *Prinds Gustav* were rowed ashore and then had to struggle up 300 metres (1,000ft) to the plateau at the top. After a visit by the intrepid King Oskar II in 1873, Thomas Cook arranged the first organised tour for 24 Englishmen in 1875. By 1880, a path with primitive railings from Horn Bay to the top had appeared and you can still see the remains of the quay by taking the 11km (7-mile) walk from the plateau.

the island, which leads to the village of **Gjesvær** on the west coast. On the eastern side of Magerøya is the little fishing community of Skarsvåg. Honningsvåg, where the ferry arrives, has been a fishing harbour for many years and an important pilot station. In the old days, trawlers were the most frequent visitors, and up to 4,000 called each year. Most were British and, through their visits, Honningsvåg developed "haddock English", a mixture of sign language and occasional English words. Like other centres in the north, Honningsvåg was burned down during World War II, and by the end of the war, the 1884 church was the only building left standing. There is a small local museum, the **North Cape Museum** (Nordkappmuseet; tel: 78 47 72 00; June–mid-Aug daily 10am–7pm, shorter hours rest of the year), which reopened in new premises in 2017.

Most villages and towns in Finnmark sit along the coast, but the two main Sami communities are the exception: Kautokeino and **Karasjok** ㉒ are deep inland. Returning from Nordkapp,

continue south through Lakselv at the end of Porsangenfjord to get to Karasjok. The town's 1807 **Gamle Kirke** is the oldest church in Finnmark, having survived the war, and the **Sami Museum and Library** (De Samiske Samlinger; mid-June–mid-Aug daily 9am–6pm, times vary rest of the year) has a notable collection of Sami literature. Karasjok is Norwegian Samiland's capital and the seat of the Sami parliament, which sits in a magnificent modern building in the shape of a Sami tent.

Sápmi Park, the Sami theme park (tel: 78 46 88 00; www.visitsapmi.no; mid-June–mid-Aug daily 9am–7pm; rest of year times vary), depicts Sami culture and history through dwellings, food, colourful costumes and handicrafts. At Karasjok the E6 makes a massive U-turn and heads north again, keeping company with the **Tana River** through its every twist and turn, all the way to **Tana Bru** ㉓, the first bridge across the River Tana and a meeting place of four roads. One is the alternative route east from Lakselv (Road 888), which veers away from the E6 at the

Magerøya island.

head of Porsangerfjord. This long road has few communities but an abundance of beautiful scenery, and it rolls ahead across two magnificent inland stretches – from **Børselv** to **Laksefjord** and across the **Ifjordfjellet**.

At Ifjord the road pushes further north to the Nordkyn peninsula and **Kjøllefjord** ㉔, Mehamn and Gamvik, across the very top of the country. About 15km (9 miles) from Kjøllefjord, including a 30-minute ramble along a well-prepared trail, are the remains of the **Oksevåg whaling station**, which was used from 1864–1905. Further walks are marked through the **Slettnes Nature and Heritage Reserve** at Gamvik (all year).

Over the bridge at Tana Bru, the road divides; the E6 winds a long route east towards **Kirkenes**, only 5km (3 miles) from the Russian border, while Road 890 heads north to **Berlevåg** and **Båtsfjord**, crossing the highest pass in Finnmark, the **Oarddojokke** at 400 metres (1,300ft) above sea level. Berlevåg and Båtsfjord are fishing villages, both on the far coast of the Varanger peninsula. Places of interest include

On safari at Kirkenes.

the **Løkvika Fishing Cabin and Partisan Cave** (Fiskehytte og Partisanhule; all year), where locals fought off the Germans in World War II.

VARANGERFJORD

Continuing east on the E6, you come to **Varangerbotn** ㉕. In this part of Norway, where the fjords bite deep into the land, you are rarely far from water. Varangerbotn has a small but interesting Varanger Sami Museum, the **Samiske Museum** (tel: 78 95 99 20; www.varjjat.org; mid-June–mid-Aug daily 10am–6pm; mid-Aug–mid-June Mon–Fri 10am–3pm), and it is worth making a detour along the north coast of the Varangerfjord on Road 98 to **Vadsø** ㉖, the administrative centre of Finnmark. At **Nesseby** you will find a wooden church (1858) and Varanger's oldest log cabin (1700). This remote area is rich in archaeological finds, indicating human occupation as early as 9000 BC.

FINNISH MIGRATION

A monument in Vadsø explains why many inhabitants are of Finnish origin and Finnish-speaking (Kvens), and

the local Vadsø Museum – **Ruija Kven Museum** (tel: 78 94 2890; www.varangermuseum.no; mid-June–mid-Aug Tue–Fri 10am–3pm, Sat–Sun noon–3pm) is housed in two buildings, one a Finnish-style dwelling, Tuomaingården, and the other, Esbensengården, a patrician house from 1840. Vadsø's **church**, built in 1958, is of striking appearance. In front, the King Stone bears the signatures of King Olav V of Norway, President Kekkonen of Finland and King Carl Gustav of Sweden, who all visited the town in 1977 to unveil the **Immigrant Monument** (Innvandrermonumentet) to the Finns who came to find food and work in Finnmark in the 1800s. Another landmark is the **mooring mast** (luftskipsmasta) used by Amundsen's airship, *Norge*, in 1926 and Nobile's airship *Italia*, two years later.

Beyond Vadsø there is only the town of **Vardø** ㉗, Norway's easternmost town and the only one situated in the Arctic climate zone. There have been fortifications at Vardø since around 1300, but the present octagonal star-shaped redoubt was built in 1738. The only remnant of the original fortress is a beam which bears the signature of King Christian IV and is dated 1599, while later monarchs have added their names: King Oskar II (in 1873), King Håkon VII (in 1907) and King Olav V (in 1959); the beam is in the **Vardøhus Fortress** (Festning; tel: 90 92 28 13; mid-Apr–mid-Sept daily 10am–9pm; until 6pm rest of the year).

Along the coast west of Vardø is the abandoned fishing village of **Hamningberg** with its old architecture and church – one of the very few not destroyed in World War II. As you return south again, you come to **Ekkerøya**, Finnmark's only bird rock accessible by car. Beyond Varangerbotn, the E6 follows the coast through another huge uninhabited area to the southeast and some beautiful views across the waters of Varangerfjord. **Bugøynes** is an old fishing village on the coast, which, like Hamningberg, escaped destruction in the war. Further east, **Bugøyfjord** is an old trading centre and birthplace of the Sami artist John Savio.

Only 8km (5 miles) from the Finnish border to the southwest, the little

Fact

The Kirkenes Snow Hotel is built from scratch every year. Tel: 78 97 05 40; www.kirkenessnowhotel.com.

Deep winter in Varangerbotn.

town of **Neiden** has the only Greek Orthodox church in Norway, where the Skollé Lapps worship. Each year since 1965, the church has held a service to bless the waters of the Neiden River to ensure that their reputed healing powers continue. The restored Labahå farm at Neiden, built by Finnish immigrants, is part of the **Sør-Varanger Museum** (www.varangermuseum.no; daily mid-June–Aug 9.30am–5pm, rest of the year until 2pm) at Kirkenes.

This easternmost wedge of Norwegian territory became important with the discovery at Bjørnevatn of iron ore, which from 1906 until 1996 was mined and shipped from the port of **Kirkenes** . The region is also a centre for fishing, farming, forestry and reindeer husbandry. Kirkenes is dominated by the deserted installations of the Sydvaranger Iron Ore Company. Although it now has one smart modern place to stay, the Thon Hotel Kirkenes, the town's somewhat rough-and-ready appearance is explained and easily forgiven when you learn that the 20th century brought no less than four wars

Kirkenes is a long way away...

fought in or near it. Apart from Malta, Kirkenes acquired the unsolicited honour of being the most bombed centre in Europe in World War II. It was liberated by the Russians in 1944, which engendered a rare lack of nervousness of, and sympathy for, the "Russian Bear". Subterranean tunnels used to shelter residents during the war can be visited. Kirkenes is the final point of call for the Hurtigruten coastal express before it returns south to Bergen.

UNUSUAL BORDER POST

The extreme eastern tip of Norway, at **Grense Jakobselv**, has a chapel built on the order of King Oskar II in 1869 as an unusual means of protecting Norwegian interests. The idea of a chapel rather than a fort at this strategic location came about when the Norwegians noticed that the Russians attended their own Orthodox church not far over the border. Faced with a Protestant church, the argument ran, the Russians would realise they had strayed into Norwegian territory. This unusual, non-aggressive approach to maintaining the frontier was highly successful.

In the extreme north of Finnmark, Norway is sometimes only a kilometre or two wide between the border and the sea, and a long pocket of the country hangs south between Russia and Finland. Here the **Øvre Pasvik National Park** (Nasjonalpark) includes the largest virgin forest in the country. This comparatively flat area has pine forests, bare rock, swamps, and two watercourses that are tributaries of the Pasvik River (the official boundary between Norway and Russia). Wildlife in the park includes elk, reindeer, bear and wolverine; there are whooper swans, great grey owls, bean geese, sea eagles, gyr falcons, spotted redshanks and cranes; the whole area is protected from development and pollution to form a peaceful border, 122km (76 miles) long between east and west.

King crab safari in Kirkenes.

Polar bears roam the Arctic.

SVALBARD

Nearly as close to the North Pole as to Norway, the Svalbard Archipelago (with its main island of Spitsbergen) teems with bird, mammal and plant life in the short Arctic summer.

From Tromsø in the north of Norway, the plane drones almost due north for an hour and a half. Far below is a seemingly empty sea, hidden here and there by banks of clouds. Suddenly you become aware that through the clouds, stark, jagged mountain peaks project like huge fangs, and that some of those clouds are in reality snow-covered glaciers. This is Svalbard, the land of the pointed mountains.

The Svalbard Archipelago lies 640km (400 miles) north of the mainland of Norway and has two main islands, Spitsbergen and Nordaustlandet, plus numerous smaller islands that dot the surrounding seas. In winter, the pack ice of the Arctic is all around and only some 950km (600 miles) separate the islands from the North Pole. Only three islands are populated: Spitsbergen, Bjørnøya and Hopen.

LONGYEARBYEN

The airport runway lies on the narrow coastal plain between the mountains of Spitsbergen and the sea of Isfjord. With a minimum of formality, you're out and into a land where the forces of nature are still in control. On the landward side, the mountain slopes darkly up into the clouds, traversed by a row of pylons; now disused, they carried coal from the mines down to the loading jetties. The Svalbard coal mines are rare for Europe

in that the mine shafts do not go down into the ground but are driven horizontally into the mountains. The township of **Longyearbyen** ❶ was built solely to accommodate the people who came north, mainly from Norway, to work at the hard and dangerous job of mining coal from the inside of the mountains.

Coal was first discovered on the island in the early 17th century, but for many years it was used simply as a source of fuel for trappers. Only since around 1900 have serious attempts been made to exploit this resource, and

⊙ **Main Attractions**
Longyearbyen
Svalbard Museum
Spitsbergen Airship
Museum
Skiing and dog-sledging
trips
Boat trips and walking

◉
Map on page 296

Russian church in Barentsburg.

the first to claim mining rights was a Norwegian skipper from Tromsø called Zakariasen. He was followed by others, including John Longyear, an American after whom the village is named.

Around 2,000 hardy people live in Longyearbyen year round and this population that almost doubles during the brief summer. Year-rounders hunker down in modern, well-insulated houses, served by facilities such as shops, a bank, restaurants and bars, a café, a library, and a sports centre with a swimming pool. The population is much younger than on the mainland, and there are three kindergartens and one school in Longyearbyen.

You'll learn a lot about the tough life of whalers, trappers, hunters and, more recently, miners at **Svalbard Museum** (tel: 78 02 64 92; www.svalbard museum.no; daily Feb–Sept 10am–5pm, Oct–Jan noon–5pm), a little gem of a place. Nearby, the **North Pole Expedition Museum** (tel: 91 38 34 67; www. spitsbergenairshipmuseum.com; Apr–Sept daily 9am–5pm, rest of the year shorter hours) recounts, in particular the history

of three airship expeditions that took off from Svalbard, aiming for the North Pole.

As if to remind you that summer, if sweet, is short: in front of most houses you will see a parked skidoo, a motor scooter with rubber tracks and steering "skis", which is the only means of transport in the long winter months when snow lies thick on the ground.

MINERAL RIGHTS

After World War I, Norway was granted sovereignty over the archipelago, though the various countries which agreed to the 1920 treaty reserved the right to exploit minerals. Today, Russia is the only one of the original signatories to the Svalbard Treaty to retain an interest in coal mining, and has a substantial operation at **Barentsburg ❷**, only a few miles further down the fjord from Longyearbyen. Around 500 people, mostly Ukrainians, live in a coal-dusty village on the steep fjordside which, nevertheless, has an indoor farm of dairy cattle and chicken sheds. Kittiwakes scream from their nests on the window ledges and,

Hiking in Svalbard.

on an esplanade below, well-dressed fur-hatted groups sell cheap Russian souvenirs and, now and then, a family "treasure" to cruise-ship passengers.

NATURE IN THE RAW

Svalbard should not, and is unlikely ever to become, a place for mass tourism: the islands cannot support it and, in any case, the appeal is to people who like to find their own wildlife and explore nature in the raw. However, the cruise ships are beginning to threaten the peace. Longyearbyen has three hotels, several guesthouses and even a small campsite for the hardy, and hardly a day goes by in summer without a luxury cruise ship depositing its passengers on the shore for a barbecue or a short trip around the area. For safety reasons, outside the limits of Longyearbyen visitors are normally accompanied by someone with a rifle and are strongly advised not to leave the pre-set routes. Thus, the polar bear takes care that mass tourism never spoils the environment and only a few well-equipped campers go further afield – with a rifle...

The area around Longyearbyen is a pleasant place during the summer, the stark mountains offset by a valley which has meadows spangled with flowers. Here you will find the tiny bells of cassiope mixed with purple saxifrage and, perhaps, a patch of boreal Jacob's ladder, *Polemonium boreale*, an Arctic rarity with beautiful flowers. Near the shores where the glaucous gulls congregate, look for the fleshy-leafed *Mertensia maritima*, or oyster plant.

The polar winter is a different matter. The sun does not rise above the horizon and everything is locked in darkness, lit only by the moon and the multicoloured rays of the **aurora borealis** (northern lights, see page 273). When the sun reappears and gathers strength, the ice pack retreats north, speeded by the warming influence of the Gulf Stream. This warm current flows up the west coast of Spitsbergen and ensures that, in summer, ships can have an ice-free passage. The sun's return is cause for a week-long Sunfestival in March, with concerts and outdoor events.

The small yellow blooms of the Svalbard mohn.

A coal train in Ny-Ålesund.

Spitsbergen is mountainous and glaciated, with around 50 percent of its surface covered in permanent ice. The highest mountain, **Newtontoppen**, reaches over 1,700 metres (5,500ft). Further from the influence of the Gulf Stream, the second-largest island, **Nordaustlandet**, is almost completely covered in ice.

UNKNOWN AND UNEXPLORED

According to old Icelandic annals, in 1194 land was found to lie "four days sailing from Langanes, at the northern end of the sea". They called it Svalbard, but then the islands were forgotten for several hundred years. The next mention was in the journals of the great Dutch explorer, Willem Barents, in 1596. Barents, with two ships under his command, was trying to find a northern route to China when he sighted an island which, from the shape of its mountains, he named Spitsbergen (Dutch for "jagged mountains"). The two ships parted, one to carry news of fjords filled with whales and walrus back to the Netherlands, while the other ship with Barents on board continued eastwards, only to become trapped in the pack ice and forced to spend the winter there, during which Barents and many of his crew died.

STORY OF THE WHALES

By 1612 hunting expeditions had begun to arrive around the coast of Spitsbergen. News of the numbers of whales spread, and soon the Dutch whalers were joined by English, French, Basques and Danes. Inevitably, trouble flared as they disputed rights, violence broke out and occasionally a warship would be dispatched north to defend the claims of its country's whalers.

The English and Dutch at last agreed on a division of hunting territories and a measure of peace was restored. The Dutch set up a shore base on **Amsterdam Island**, which grew to be almost a town, with a fort, church and whale-oil refinery, and a summer population of a couple of thousand. They called it **Smeerenburg ❸**, the "blubber town", and you can still find the outlines of stone buildings and the furnaces built to render the whale blubber into oil. The large numbers of bleached whale bones testify to the growing demands for whale oil, and in some places there is further mute testimony in the graves of men who died in this inhospitable environment. As a result of decades of over-hunting, the whale stock declined, and by around 1720 whaling ceased.

Such intensive whaling was purely a summer activity. In winter the islands were deserted except by accident. In 1630, an English ship was wrecked and the crew managed to cling to life throughout the winter. In 1633, some Dutchmen wintered at Smeerenburg, but the following year those who attempted to stay on all died of scurvy. The English had intended to colonise the archipelago, but even prisoners under sentence of death refused to face the prospect of the Arctic night.

⊙ SVALBARD SEED BANK

In 2008 the Norwegian government opened a seed bank, effectively a "Noah's ark" for the world's most important plant varieties. The Svalbard Global Seed Vault (nicknamed Doomsday Seed Vault) serves as a repository for crucial seeds in the event of global catastrophe, be it nuclear war, natural disasters or gene pollution from genetic modification.

The bank, which is located just outside Longyearbyen, lies inside an abandoned coal mine. At 135 metres (440 feet) above the fjord below, it's safe and protected, should the seas rise as a result of global warming. Carved deep into the permafrost and rock, it remains well below freezing point year round, and the seeds are further protected by metre-thick walls of reinforced concrete, two airlocks and high-security blast-proof doors.

The Svalbard seed bank will be of global importance; local seed banks rely on artificial refrigeration and are prone to local problems – dozens of unique crops were lost during the wars in Iraq and Afghanistan.

Construction of the seed vault, which cost NOK 45 million (US$9 million), was funded entirely by the Norwegian government, and storage of seeds in the vault is free of charge. By September 2016, the seed count at the Svalbard Global Seed Vault had reached 860,000 samples. Each sample can contain up to 500 seeds, so the total number of seeds currently being stored is today nearing 430 million individual seeds.

TOUGH LIFE OF THE TRAPPER

The Russians were made of sterner stuff, however, and in the early part of the 18th century a number of hunting parties built houses on Svalbard and continued to hunt bear, fox, walrus and seals throughout the winter darkness. Not until the late 18th century did Norwegian hunters first arrive. They too overwintered, and today the remains of one or two cabins still lie along the shoreline.

A trapper led a tough and rigorous life. He had to set his traps, mainly for Arctic fox whose beautiful pelts were most valuable in winter, in a hunting territory that covered many square kilometres. He also shot or caught polar bears in baited "fell traps" and hunted seals, not just for food and skins, but for the oil which he extracted from the blubber.

Ever since its discovery, Svalbard has attracted scientific expeditions. The first on record was in 1773 and included no less a personage than Horatio Nelson, then a midshipman. In 1827, the first Norwegian geological expedition took place under Professor B.M. Keilhau, and this was soon followed by expeditions from many nations. Today, the **Norsk Polarinstitut** is the clearing house for all expeditions to this Arctic outpost.

NATURAL LABORATORY

Svalbard offers a splendid environment for the study of ecology and natural history by scientist and amateur alike. Many visitors who make the long journey north come primarily for the wildlife in general and birds in particular, and Svalbard's short Arctic summer offers a rich feast. For though the archipelago is inhospitable for much of the year, in the 24-hour days of summer the tundra slopes between the mountains and near the sea offer enough thin soil to encourage and support a surprising number of plants. These, in turn, support other wildlife such as insects, 36 bird species and a few mammals. The surrounding seas, although cold, are rich in fish and invertebrates, which attract seabirds and sea mammals that use the shores and cliffs for breeding and resting.

Kittiwakes, and glaucous and ivory gulls push north as soon as daylight allows and are soon followed by Arctic terns, all the way from the southern hemisphere. The kittiwake is essentially an ocean bird which feeds almost exclusively at sea. At nesting time they set up huge, noisy colonies on suitable cliffs, or even on window ledges in some places. Another ocean wanderer is the fulmar. Most of the Svalbard fulmars are in the "dark-grey phase" of development and therefore largely confined to Arctic waters, which at first puzzles some bird-watchers from further south. Four species of auks breed in Svalbard: Brünnich's guillemot, the little auk, puffin and black guillemot. While Brünnich's guillemot nests on open but inaccessible ledges, the others seek the safety of crevices or burrows, where predators such as Arctic fox and glaucous gulls have less chance of getting at their eggs or young. There are also some waders.

The large expanses of barren mountain do not offer much in the way of

> **Tip**
>
> Svalbard offers a wide range of activities for the outdoor enthusiast, including dog-sledging and skiing, fossil hunting, camping expeditions, trekking and boat trips. See www.visitsvalbard.com for details.

The Svalbard ptarmigan is the only bird to stay on the archipelago through winter.

food for land birds, but walking along the slopes and valleys, which are often carpeted in dwarf birch and polar willow, you may well find snow buntings foraging for seeds and singing from the rocks. The Svalbard ptarmigan also uses this habitat, and it is the only bird to stay through the winter. Three kinds of geese breed on Svalbard – pink-footed, Brent and barnacle – naturalists who have studied the barnacle geese have discovered that the entire Svalbard population travels to Scotland each year, to spend the winter in the Solway area in the southwest, then returns in spring to breed. When you spot the plentiful flocks of common eider along the shores, look closely because you may be lucky enough to find a few king eiders showing off their plumage, superior to that of their less flashy kin.

ARCTIC MONARCH

There is only one kind of grazing mammal on the islands, and that is the hardy Svalbard reindeer. Smaller than its Samiland counterpart, the Svalbard reindeer is quite tame, living a spartan life in small herds and feeding off plants and lichens in the valley bottoms. The only other land mammals are the Arctic fox and the polar bear. The Arctic fox is a very attractive-looking little animal, with a coat of varying shades of white and grey in summer and pure white in winter. Though it was hunted heavily in the past, it is still remarkably tolerant and curious about humans, and is not too difficult to find on the sea-bird cliffs in summer, where it digs out nests or picks up any young birds that have fallen from the ledges.

The undoubted king of the Arctic, however, is the polar bear. Adult males especially lead a nomadic life on the pack ice for much of the year and live mainly on seals, while young males and females with cubs tend to spend the summer on the islands. Though they were formerly hunted for their skins, polar bears are nowadays protected and can be killed only if they threaten human life. They are not uncommon, especially on favourite breeding islands, such as **Barentsøya** and **Edgeøya**. But climate change is threatening their habitat and hunting grounds – today the polar bear is listed as a threatened species.

The fjords of Svalbard may no longer be "filled with whales and walrus", as they were said to be in the 15th century, but you will certainly find sea mammals around the islands. Though it is now rare to see any of the great whales, species such as the lesser rorqual or minke whales come into the fjord quite often. The beluga or white whale is easiest to identify with its white body and lack of dorsal fin. You might be lucky enough to sight the remarkable narwhal, with its spear-like tusk projecting out in front.

The immense herds of walrus which in days past thronged places like **Moffen Island** have never fully recovered from over-hunting, but sometimes small groups appear at Moffen or on the south of Edgeøya, where they feast on the clam beds or rest on the shore: a hopeful sign in an age when Svalbard is visited for its stark natural beauty and summer wildlife.

Svalbard reindeer are much shorter than other species.

Spitsbergen is mountainous and glaciated.

The road to Nusfjord,
Lofoten Islands.

NORWAY

TRAVEL TIPS

TRANSPORT

By Air

Scandinavia's flagship carrier, **SAS** (Scandinavian Airlines System; www.flysas.com) runs a wide range of flights between Oslo Gardermoen Airport (https://avinor.no) and other world capitals (usually involving a feeder service to and from one of the main European hubs – London, Copenhagen or Frankfurt), with some direct services to Bergen, Oslo, Stavanger, Tromsø and Trondheim.

British Airways (www.britishairways.com), **Lufthansa** (www.lufthansa.com), **Air France** (www.airfrance.com) and **KLM** (www.klm.com) also connect Norway's cities with daily flights to Europe.

Approximate flying times to Oslo are: London, 2 hours; Frankfurt, 1 hour 50 minutes; Paris, 2 hours; Budapest, 3 hours 35 minutes; and Warsaw, 3 hours 25 minutes.

SAS offers daily flights from Heathrow to Oslo, Stavanger and many other Norwegian destinations. It also has flights to/from Birmingham, Manchester and Newcastle. **BA** operates from Heathrow and Manchester to Oslo.

Budget operator Ryanair (http://ryanair.com) offers low-cost flights from London Stansted to Oslo Torp near Sandefjord (in fact 130km/80 miles south of the capital) and Oslo Gardemoen Airport. Ryanair also flies between Oslo Torp and Manchester.

☉ Oslo Gardemoen Airport

The main terminal building at Oslo Gardermoen Airport is the largest laminated wood structure in the world.

Widerøe flies to multiple destinations, big and small, within Norway and has flights to Norway from Aberdeen, Copenhagen and Gothenburg. **Norwegian** operates from 19 airports in Norway to a variety of destinations within and outside the country including London Gatwick.

SAS

In UK
Tel: 0871 226 7760
www.flysas.com
In North America
Tel: 1-800 221 2350
In Norway
Tel (reservations): 05400

British Airways

In UK
Tel: 0844 493 0787
www.britishairways.com
In Norway
Tel: 81 53 31 42

Norwegian

In UK
Tel: +47 21 49 00 15
In Norway
Tel: 81 52 18 15
www.norwegian.com

Widerøe

In Norway
Tel: 67 12 05 51 or 81 00 12 00
www.wideroe.no

Ryanair

In UK
Tel: 0871 246 0000
In Norway
Tel: 82 00 40 02
www.ryanair.com

By Sea

There is currently no ferry service between the UK and Norway. **Color Line** is the main ferry service linking Oslo to mainland Europe, with large cruise-ferries sailing to Kiel

☉ Oslo: Cruise Destination

Oslo is an important port of call for cruise ships heading to both the Baltic and the Norwegian west coast. The main cruising market comes from Germany, the UK, the US and Norway, which together account for well over 50 per cent of cruise passengers visiting the Norwegian capital.

in Germany. Services also sail to the northern tip of Denmark (Hirtshals) from Kristiansand and Larvik and between Sandefjord and Stromstad in Sweden.

Color Line
Tel: 99 56 19 00
www.colorline.com

By Rail

Numerous rail services link Norway with the rest of Scandinavia and Europe. Within mainland Europe, express trains operate to Copenhagen, where inter-Scandinavian trains connect to Oslo. There are train connections in Oslo to other cities in Norway as far north as Bodø. First- and second-class coaches are available on these express trains, plus sleeper coaches on all of the overnight expresses.

Seat reservations are required on all night and long-distance day trains, as well as on express and high-speed "Signatur" services.

The Norwegian State Railway (NSB) is part of the InterRail, Eurailpass and Eurail Youthpass system, which offers various discount tickets (including to students). InterRail: www.interrail.eu, Eurail: www.eurail.com.

There are frequent connections from Copenhagen, Stockholm and Gothenburg to Oslo.

Bergen Airport.

⊘ Tickets and info

For tickets, routes, times and all other queries about public transport, **Ruter** in Oslo offers an information and booking service. Its office is at Jernbanetorvet 1, by Oslo Sentralstasjon (at the bottom of the glass tower at the front of the station). Office: Mon-Fri 7am-8pm, Sat 9am-6pm, Sun 10am-4pm). Tel: 81 50 01 76. Info line: 177 (lines: Mon-Fri 7am-8pm, Sat 9am-6pm, Sun 10am-4pm); https://ruter.no.

There is an additional Ruter at Gardermoen Airport and at Aker Brygge.

You can also get to northern Norway from Stockholm, with Trondheim and Narvik the principal destinations.

International trains arrive and depart from Sentralstasjon (Oslo S). Flytoget, the high-speed rail link to/from Oslo Gardermoen Airport, has a terminal at Oslo S, and trains also run to/from Asker via Nationalteatret station. NSB provides train information and also operates as a travel bureau across Norway:

Norwegian State Railways
Tel: 81 50 08 88
www.nsb.no
Flytoget
Tel: 23 15 90 00
www.flytoget.no

By Road

Most major shipping lines to Norway allow passengers to bring cars.
Norges Automobil Forbund
(NAF or Norwegian Automobile Federation)
Østensjøveien 14, 0609 Oslo
Tel: 23 21 31 00
Emergency tel: 08505
Kongelig Norsk Automobilklub
(KNA or Royal Norwegian Automobile Club)
Nils Hansens vei 2, Oslo
Tel: 21 60 49 00
Emergency tel: 800 31 660 (members only)

GETTING AROUND

Public Transport

There is a generally excellent network of domestic transport services

Although covering great distances can be expensive, Norway offers transport bargains through special tourist cards such as the Fjord Pass, plus some of the pan-European programmes such as InterRail and Eurail. Within larger cities, tourist passes cover urban transport and give free entry to many museums.

From the Airport

Gardermoen Airport is 50km (30 miles) north of Oslo. It is served by the Airport Express Train/Flytoget, which zips to Oslo S (the Central Station) at a record 210kmh (130mph) every 10 minutes, taking only 19–22 minutes. Details at www.flytoget.no. Regional and local trains also connect Oslo and the airport, and are cheaper – they take about 45 minutes; there is normally a train at least every hour. Note that rail passes are not valid on the Flytoget. See also www.nsb.no.

The airport bus departs three or four times an hour from Oslo Busterminal and takes 40 minutes. Tel: 177 or 40 00 11 66; www.flybussen.no.

Nor-Way Flybusekspress. No. F1 also links Majorstuen in west Oslo to Gardermoen with frequent departures throughout the day. Tel: 81 54 44 44; www.nor-way.no.

If you arrive from London Stansted at **Torp Airport** at Sandefjord on the southwest side of the fjord, take the **Torp-Expressen** (www.torpekspressen.no), which meets and greets Ryanair and Wizzair passengers but is available to all. Otherwise, a combination of bus

and train will take up to 2.5 hours to reach the capital, depending on traffic conditions.

Bergen Airport is at Flesland, 19km (12 miles) southwest of the city. The airport bus goes to the bus station via the Radisson SAS Royal Hotel at Bryggen. For details, tel: 177; www.flybussen.no.

All other major city airports are serviced by buses and taxis.

By Air

Norway is exceptionally well served by domestic airlines, with about 50 airports and airfields throughout the country.

The main domestic airlines are SAS, Widerøe and Norwegian. Each offers discount travel passes.
SAS Scandinavian Airlines System
Tel: 05400
Widerøe
Tel: 81 00 12 00 or 67 12 05 51
Norwegian
Tel: 81 52 18 15

By Rail

Rail services are far more extensive in the south than in the north, and tend to fan out from Oslo, so you may have to jump aboard ferries and buses, unless you are travelling in the south or to major towns.

Oslo S (Oslo Sentralstasjon) is Norway's busiest railway station, located in central Oslo at the eastern end of Karl Johansgate on Jernbanetorget. Long-distance, express and local suburban trains arrive and depart here. It is also the terminal for the Oslo Gardermoen Airport high-speed

⊘ Norway in a Nutshell

One of the most pleasurable ways of seeing Norway is to take a **Norway in a Nutshell** journey (see page 214). The trip uses various forms of public transport and takes you from Myrdal to Flåm, Gudvangen and Voss, through some of the country's most beautiful scenery. A selection of packages is on offer. Tel: 55 55 76 60; www.fjordtours.com.

The railway line from Myrdal to Flåm is a masterpiece of engineering. When you have made the 850-metre (2,800ft) descent you are at the head of one of the longest fjords in the world, Sognefjord, and on the brink of another scenic high through Aurlandsfjord and narrow Nærøyfjord.

The trips can be made in either direction and from any of the stations between Oslo and Bergen.

Norway in a Nutshell round trip: train from Oslo to Myrdal/ Flåm, boat to Gudvangen, bus to Voss, train to Oslo.

Norway in a Nutshell one way: train from Oslo to Myrdal/Flåm, boat to Gudvangen, bus to Voss, train to Bergen.

Tickets are sold at the railway stations in Oslo and Bergen or from travel agencies. See www. norwaynutshell.com for more details.

If you plan to take special fast trains, you must book ahead. Ticket sales are from the main hall of the train station (tickets for ordinary trains can usually be bought on board). Watch out for *minipris* tickets on the Norwegian State Railways' website (www.nsb.no) – if you're flexible with dates, and book well in advance, you could snap up a single ticket to any destination in Norway for as little as NOK 199.

For information about timetables, ticket prices and bookings, contact Ruter, Jernbanetorvet 1, by Oslo S; tel: 177.

By Bus/Coach

Where the rail network stops, the bus goes further. Usually it is not necessary to book in advance; just pay the driver on boarding. NOR-WAY Bussekspress has 18 routes covering mainly southern Norway. Children up to the age of 4 travel free, 4 to 16 years pay 75 percent of the adult price.

NOR-WAY Bussekspress AS, Storgata 17, NO-0184 Oslo; tel: 22 31 31 50; www.nor-way.no.

Lavprisekspressen (tel: 67 98 04 80; www.lavprisekspressen.no) runs along the southern coast

rail link, Flytoget (some trains continue under the city to Asker via Nationaltheatret station). The end of the northbound line from Oslo is at Bodø, but the country's most northerly railway station is at Narvik, which is reached through Sweden by train or by bus from Fauske. The Oslo–Bergen line, which celebrated its 100th year in 2009, is one of the world's most spectacular railway journeys.

Trains are modern and efficient. Inter-city express (ICE) trains offer one class only and there is a wide range of special offers.

National rail passes from NSB are valid for 3–8 travel days in any month. The rail pass is sold under the name of Norway Rail Pass (or Eurail Norway Pass) in the US, while in Europe the offer is called Interrail Norway (see www.nsb.no). Visit www.interrail.eu or www. raileurope.com for more information.

The Hurtigruten is the best way to see the Norwegian coastline.

between Oslo and Stavanger and also has a couple of northbound routes that take travellers as far as Trondheim. It tends to be cheaper than its competitors; your best option is to reserve online.

Water Transport

Ferries

Ferries allow short cuts across fjords to eliminate long road journeys; in built-up areas they are crucial to commuters, like the Horten–Moss ferry across Oslofjord between Vestfold and Østfold. Ferries to the fjord islands around Oslo leave from the Vippetangen quay near Akershus Castle.

Almost all town marinas have places for guest boats. A mooring fee is required.

The following company operates the ferries that run between the centre of Oslo and the Bygdøy Peninsula, where many of the main museums are located.

Norway Yacht Charter & Båtservice Sightseeing AS
Rådhusbrygge 3
Tel: 23 35 68 90
www.nyc.no

Long-Distance Ships

Hurtigruten, the Norwegian Coastal Express service, is an important means of water transport for Norwegians and also a superb way for visitors to see Norway's dramatic coast. In summer, boats leave daily, travelling between Bergen and Kirkenes and back in

---

◙ Fjord Tours

Whether you are planning a short break or a long holiday, many companies offer tours of the fjord, coastal and mountain scenery. Two of the main ones are:

Fjord Tours
Møllendalsveien 1A
5009 Bergen
Tel: 55 55 76 60
www.fjordtours.com

Fjord Travel Norway
Østre Nesttunvei 4–6
5221 Nesttun, Bergen
Tel: 55 13 13 10
www.fjordtravel.no

◙ Travel Passes

The Oslo Pass, issued for one, two and three days, with half-price for children, is your ticket to unlimited public transport (including city ferries), free parking, free guided tours, free entry to over 30 museums and many other discounts. If you want a card for travel only in the Oslo and Akershus area, there are several options, including a 24-hour and 7-day Ruter ticket, plus other passes appropriate for longer stays.

12 days and putting in at 34 ports (see page 229).

The ships take cars, and should be booked well in advance. You can travel on shorter stretches too, and special packages are available year-round.

Hurtigruten
Tel: 31 31 73 70
www.hurtigruten.com

Kystopplevelser (Coastal Experiences)
Tel: 56 31 90 04
www.kyst-opplevelser.no (in Norwegian only)

Buses and Trams

Oslo's bus and tram system is comprehensive and punctual; there are detailed timetables at every stop. Ruter can suggest bus or tram routes. There are night buses on some routes and also very early morning buses starting at 4am. Bergen and Trondheim also have tram systems.

Underground

Oslo's underground is called the T-bane and is simple to use. There are five lines that converge under the centre of the city. A circle line links the station of Storo with Carl Berners plass. You can catch a train to any of the far-flung suburbs from any of the stations between Tøyen and Majorstuen. Station entrances are marked with a "T". Ruter (see page 305) has route maps. One of the most scenic routes is T-bane 1 up to Frognerseteren. From there enjoy panoramic views over Oslo.
Ruter
Jernbanetorvet 1

The Oslo Pass may be purchased at the Central Railway Station (Oslo S), Ruter (see page 305), as well as all *Narvesen* kiosks, major hotels, some campsites and tourist offices.

Other cities offer similar tourist travel cards: for example, the Bergen Card, a 24-hour, 48-hour or 72-hour pass available from tourist information offices, the railway station, some hotels and campsites and the Hurtigruten terminal.

Tel: 177
https://ruter.no

Taxis

Taxis are widely available, even in many suburban and rural areas, so you need never risk drink-driving (for which penalties are severe).

In Oslo, telephone 023 23 to be transferred to the nearest taxi rank. Minibuses and taxis (for up to 16 people) can also be booked on 22 38 80 90. You can pick up a taxi from one of the many taxi ranks scattered around the city.

In Oslo, taxis are more expensive at night or if ordered by phone. At night there are two things to watch out for: when everyone leaves the bars and restaurants late, long queues build up at taxi ranks. Also, be wary of "pirate" taxis. These either cruise up out of the blue or a "dummy" comes and asks you if you want a taxi without queuing. Pirate taxis can be something of a risk. If you use one, make sure you agree a price beforehand. They tend to gather at Stortorget, opposite GlasMagasin.

Private Transport

By Car

Norway's roads are good – mercifully so, given the treacherous weather conditions encountered in winter. Be prepared for tunnels as some routes have long lengths of road underground, most notably in the fjords.

EU driving licences are valid in Norway, but drivers from some countries must carry an international driving licence. Driving is on the right.

Traffic regulations are strictly enforced (see page 308).

Winter Driving

In winter, when your car must be equipped with winter tyres, even major roads may be temporarily impassable.

Small roads in the north and in mountainous areas are often closed so the authorities can put all manpower into keeping main roads safe, and even the E6 highway from Oslo to Trondheim has been known to close.

Snow-Tyre Hire

If you are driving in Norway in winter you can hire the appropriate tyres and snow chains by the week. Ask in any petrol station. In the UK contact:

Snowchains Europroducts

Tel: 01732 884408
www.snowchains.co.uk

Breakdown and Accidents

The AA and RAC are affiliated to the AIT (Alliance Internationale de Tourisme), so members receive free assistance (with journey planning as well as backup in case of breakdown or accident) from Norway's NAF (Norges Automobil Forbund). More comprehensive repairs can be carried out at NAF-contracted garages (for which you will have to pay). NAF also patrol Norway's main roads and mountain passes from mid-June to mid-August. They have emergency phones along the mountain passes.

NAF, Østensjøveien 14, 0609 Oslo
Tel: 23 21 31 00
Emergency tel: 08505
www.naf.no

If you are involved in an accident where there are no injuries, telephone **Viking Redningstjeneste AS** on 06000 or 22 08 60 00. Their offices provide a 24-hour service for all Norway.

It is not necessary to call the police for minor accidents, but drivers must exchange names and addresses; leaving the scene without doing so is a crime.

If an emergency, call the **police** (on **112**) or an **ambulance** (on **113**)

Rules of the Road

Some Norwegian driving regulations vary from those in the UK and mainland Europe.

Speed Limits The maximum speed limit is usually 80kmh (50mph),

though 100kmh (62mph) is permitted on a few highways (mainly motorways). The limit is reduced to 40kmh (24mph) in built-up areas, and even 30kmh (18mph) on certain residential roads. On-the-spot fines (which may be as much as NOK 3,500) are given to drivers found speeding. Speed cameras and radar traps are both used.

Giving Way This can be confusing to the visitor. Roads marked at intervals by yellow diamond signs indicate that you have priority. On all other roads, you are required to give way to traffic entering from the right. Additionally, some roads have a series of white triangles painted across them at junctions, which mean stop and give way.

On roundabouts, priority is from the left. Always give way to trams, buses and taxis. Many roads have a right-hand lane exclusively for buses and taxis.

Drinking and Driving The permissible limit is 0.02 per ml, and penalties are severe (imprisonment, a high fine and loss of licence are automatic).

Documentation and Equipment You should always have the following with you in your vehicle: driving licence, car registration documents, European accident statement form, insurance policy and a reflective warning triangle. A snow shovel and tow-rope are also useful in winter. For regularly updated information in the UK, the AA runs a good fact line for just a small charge on tel: 0870 600 0371; www.theaa.com.

Lights It is obligatory to drive with dipped headlights during the daytime, even on the brightest summer day. This rule applies to all vehicles, including motorcycles and mopeds. We recommend you carry spare bulbs. In principle, right-hand-drive cars require black adhesive triangles (often supplied by ferry companies), or clip-on beam deflectors, so you don't dazzle oncoming drivers.

Seat Belts These must be worn, both front and back (there are on-the-spot fines for failing to comply). Motorcycle and moped drivers and their passengers must wear helmets.

Tyres It is obligatory to use winter tyres from October to April. These are either tyres with studs (pig-gdekk) or specially designed tyres

for use in ice and snow. Studded tyres are preferred, but these may soon be prohibited in urban areas for environmental reasons, and in many places (including Oslo) a fee is levied on cars using them.

Caravanning

For information contact:
Norsk Bobil og Caravan Club (NBCC)
PO Box 104, 1921 Sørumsand
Tel: 63 82 99 90
www.nocc.no (in Norwegian only)

Car Hire

Hiring a car in Norway, like everything else, is expensive. Look out for special weekend and low-season prices.

Avis Bilutleie-Liva Bil AS
PO Box 154, N-1361 Billingstad (near Oslo)
Tel: 66 77 10 10
Booking tel: 81 53 30 44
www.avis.no

Europcar
Grini Næringspark 10, PO Box 173, 1332 Østerås
Booking tel: 81 55 18 00/81 57 46 00
www.europcar.no

Hertz Bilutleie
PO Box 331, N-1324 Lysaker/Oslo
Tel: 03700 (in Norway)
Tel: 21 51 37 00 (from abroad)
www.hertz.no

Cycling

Cycling in Norway is generally safe, as there is so little traffic on many minor roads. If you're cycle touring, bear in mind that cyclists are not allowed to go through most longer tunnels because of car fumes. Bicycles are allowed on most trains and buses for a small charge.

Special cycle trains are laid on during the summer. Pick up a free

---

☑ Road Information

Vegmeldingssentralen (The Road User Information Centre) is an office of the *Statens Vegvesen* (www.vegvesen.no; Public Roads Administration). Its main function is to monitor and provide information about roads and road conditions. You may also get information about distances and ferry timetables. 24 hours all year, tel: 175 or 81 54 89 91.

When driving, beware of elks and reindeers.

copy of *Oslo Guide* and a city map at the Oslo Visitor Centre (also at Gardermoen airport and at many hotels) which has suggestions for a *Nordmarka* (Oslo's forest land) route. Tourist offices have details of mountain cycle tours.

The Cycling Association (**Syklistenes Landsforening**) can help plan tours and cycling holidays: Østensjøveien 29, 0661 Oslo. Tel: 22 47 30 30; www.syklistene.no.

Cycle Rental

Norway is a cycle-friendly country and in many towns, both large and small, you can hire bikes from a hotel, campsite, local tourist office or sports shop, as well as small cycle-hire shops.

Both Oslo and Trondheim have municipal bike hire schemes that visitors can join. Sign on to **Oslocitybike** at one of the city's tourist offices and pick up your cycle from any stand. In Trondheim (which has the world's only cycle lift), the scheme is smaller but

equally convenient. For details of both, see www.bysykler.no.

White Water AS
Grensen 3, Oslo
Tel: 23 10 40 50
www.whitewater.no
White Water AS deals in extreme-sports gear. Off-road and mountain bikes are available for hire.

On Foot

There is almost nowhere in Norway you can't go happily on foot; it is a nation of devout walkers, and hiking is one of the most popular outdoor activities at weekends.

The law of access to the natural environment, known as *allemannsretten* or "everyman's right", allows you to walk wherever you want in the wilderness such as seashore, forests, mountains and in other non-cultivated regions. Use paths and roads when walking in agricultural and populated areas.

If you plan to camp wild, the law requires you to pitch your tent at

least 150 metres (160 yards) from the nearest house or hut. Open fires are prohibited from 15 April to 15 September.

Detailed maps are available from the Norwegian Trekking Association (DNT). Membership allows you to use the association's huts. The association's map and guidebook selection is excellent; there is a charge for survey maps of Norway, but sketch maps are free.

The Norwegian Tourist Board has plenty of information on hiking in Norway, including suggested itineraries for mountain walks and details of chalets and where to stay.

Visit Norway
(Norwegian Tourist Board)
PO Box 448 Sentrum, 0158 Oslo
Tel: 22 00 25 00
www.visitnorway.com
Den Norske Turistforening (Norwegian Trekking Association)
Youngstorget 1, Oslo
Tel: 40 00 18 68
www.dnt.no

A

Accommodation

Hotels, like everything else in Norway, come expensive, but, in common with the rest of Scandinavia, they reduce their rates during the summer holiday period, when business visitors are fewer. Weekends (usually Friday and Saturday but sometimes Sunday too) are also usually cheaper. The official visitors' site, www.visitnorway.com, can be a good starting point for tracking down hotels.

Hotels

A very high percentage of Norwegian hotels belong to or are affiliated to local chains. Most offer passes and discount schemes. In return for a modest one-time fee (around NOK 100), you get discounted rates, mostly in the summer and at weekends. Fjord Pass (www.fjordtours.com/fjordpass) is not bound to one chain and offers discounts of up to 50 percent. A breakfast buffet is almost always included in the room rate.
Hotel chains in Norway include:
Best Western Hotels
www.bestwestern.no
Nordic Choice Hotels
www.nordicchoicehotels.no
Radisson Blu Hotels
www.radissonblu.com
Scandic Hotels
www.scandichotels.no
Thon Hotels
www.thonhotels.com
Two splendid associations of quality historic hotels with charm are:
De Historiske
www.dehistoriske.no
A group of over 50 historic hotels, manor houses or timbered lodges, plus almost 20 selected restaurants.

The Great Life Company
www.dvgl.no/en
Seven mostly historic inns and restaurants.

Booking in Oslo/Bergen

In Oslo, the Visitor Centre at Østbanehallen in Jernbanetorget 1, next to the Central Station (tel: 81 53 05 55; www.visitoslo.com), will book accommodation in the capital for those requesting it in person. This service covers private rooms, pensions and hotels.
The tourist office in Bergen offers a similar reservation service for hotels in Bergen and the surrounding area. It is located at Strandkaien 3 on Torget – the Fish Market (tel: 55 55 20 00; www.visitbergen.com). Here too, the service is only available for callers-in.

Chalets (Hytter)

There are abundant holiday *hytter* (cabins or chalets) available for rent. These usually house four to six people. If you want to spend just one night in a chalet and then move on, you can stay in one on a campsite without booking ahead.

Fishermen's Cabins (rorbuer)

On the Lofoten Islands in northern Norway, and at many places elsewhere along the north coast, you can rent a *rorbu*, once a fisherman's cabin. Nearly all have been modernised – and many, in fact, are attractive recent constructions, built in traditional style.
Destination Lofoten AS
Tel: 76 06 98 00
www.lofoten.info

Camping

Norway has more than 1,000 campsites, classified by 1–5 stars, depending on the standard and facilities available. The fixed charge per plot is usually NOK 100–200, with additional charges per person.
Many campsites have cabins that may be booked in advance. Most are small and basic with simply a bunk bed and a single electric ring but some are larger and well equipped.
For further information, log onto www.camping.no.

B&Bs

Look out for signs for *Rom or Husrom* outside houses. *The Norway Bed & Breakfast Book* by Anne Marit Bjorgen has a reasonable listing of choices. The website www.bbnorway.com may also help.

Youth and Family Hostels

Norway has more than 100 youth and family hostels. A night's accommodation in a dorm costs NOK 200–350, and breakfast is usually included. Many hostels also have double or family rooms.
Hostelling International Norway
Tel: 22 15 21 85
www.hihostels.no

Admission Charges

You can expect to pay between NOK 60 and NOK 100 for admission to a museum or gallery, and NOK 110–120 for admission to some of the most popular attractions. Several museums and galleries in Oslo are free, and many museums have a day when they don't charge admission; check individual venues for more information. Family tickets are usually good value for money, so opt for these if you are travelling with children. Some places have discounts for students and senior citizens. The Oslo Pass and Bergen Card offer free entrance to museums and attractions together with free public transport and parking (see page 307).

B

Budgeting for Your Trip

Norway is expensive: the price of a cup of coffee in a smart city café can be exorbitant, and even the smallest of items like toiletries can be double the amount they are elsewhere in Europe. Look out for *lavpris* shops, which offer lower prices. The cost of alcohol is enough to make even heavy drinkers think twice about another bottle of wine; beer is a cheaper alternative and can be bought from supermarkets at good prices. Discount cards on accommodation and public transport are available, plus Norway offers tourists tax-free shopping. The Oslo Youth Information Centre (www.ung-info.oslo.no) publishes a budget guide, *Streetwise*, available from tourist offices.

When budgeting for a stay in Norway, there are a number of ways to save your kroner. Norwegian hotel breakfasts usually offer a large buffet, so if you can have a hearty breakfast as your main meal of the day, and avoid eating a large evening meal in a restaurant, you'll manage to keep to a reasonable budget. The most common street snack is the *pølse* – a long, skinny hot dog served either with *brød* (bread) or rolled in a *lompe* (potato pancake). There are quite a lot of cafés, brasseries and pizzerias where you can get a decent meal that won't break the bank. Full meals can be reasonable, too, as long as you don't order alcohol.

In summer, hotel rates are deeply discounted to make up for the lack of business and conference traffic. In winter, weekend rates can sometimes be attractive outside school and ski-holiday weeks when hotels are crowded and rates rise. Pensions and youth hostels are usually reasonably priced. Camping is another economical option in summer.

A beer: NOK 80
A glass of house wine: NOK 80
A main course in a budget restaurant: NOK 100
A main course in a moderate restaurant: NOK 250
A main course in an expensive restaurant: NOK 350
A double room in a cheap hotel: NOK 900
A double room in a moderate hotel: NOK 1,500

A double room in a deluxe hotel: NOK 2,000
A taxi journey from Gardermoen to Oslo centre: NOK 600–700
A single bus/metro ticket: NOK 33
A one-day travel pass: NOK 90
The Oslo Pass: NOK 395 for 24 hours, NOK 595 for 48 hours and NOK 745 for 72 hours (children and seniors pay less than half-price).

Business Travellers

Like all Scandinavians, Norwegians take their summer holiday very seriously as a time for retreating to a fjord or mountain *hytte* (usually a log cabin). During the common holiday in July, offices and factories empty, and it is virtually impossible to arrange an appointment or do any business.

People take work seriously, but also know how to maintain a pleasantly relaxed business atmosphere. Norwegians dress for business much as they do elsewhere, although in summer dress codes are relaxed slightly.

If you are looking up someone's number in a phone book, you'll find his or her profession listed next to the name. Not only is this a matter of professional pride; it's a real help in a country with a limited number of surnames. Amazingly, you can also find a person's yearly taxable income, the details of which are freely available on government internet sites. Norwegians take freedom of information quite literally.

Liquid lunches are unusual, and the work day often ends at 3.30 or 4pm (even an hour earlier in summer).

C

Children

Norway is a welcoming and safe place for children. Many outdoor activities, from skiing to kayaking, are geared up for youngsters, and it is easy to rent equipment for them too. Train rides will give younger visitors a thrill. The Flåm railway is the most spectacular, but the Rauma and Bergen lines are other exciting options. On both trains and buses, children under four normally travel free, while those aged between four and 15 pay half price.

In and Around Oslo

EKT Riding School and Pet Park (tel: 22 19 97 86; www.rideskole.no). Horse riding on fjord ponies and petting zoo in the Ekeberg forest southeast of the city centre.
International Children's Art Museum (Barnekunstmuseet), Lille Frøens vei 4; tel: 22 69 17 77; www.barnekunst.no (all year). Exhibits and workshops.
Norwegian Museum of Science and Technology (Norsk Teknisk Museum), Kjelsåsveien 143; tel: 22 79 60 00; www.tekniskmuseum.no. Interactive exhibits for children of all ages (all year).
Puppet Theatre Torshovgata 33; tel: 22 34 86 00 (May–Sept).
Tusenfryd Amusement Park, Ås, Akershus; tel: 64 97 64 97; www.tusenfryd.no. Transport by bus 541 from Oslo S or Rådhuset. Attractions include a roller coaster, Spaceshot, flume ride, carousel, magic carpet and climbing wall. Height restrictions apply on some rides (Apr–Sept).

Around Norway

Aquarium (Akvariet), Bergen; tel: 55 55 71 71; www.akvariet.no. Shark tunnel, penguin-feeding and seal show (all year).
Atlantic Sea Park (Atlanterhavsparken) near Ålesund; tel: 70 10 70 60; www.atlanterhavsparken.no. One of the largest saltwater aquariums in Scandinavia (daily).
Hunderfossen Family Park near Lillehammer; tel: 61 27 55 30; www.hunderfossen.no. Attractions include river rafting, fairytale castle, the world's largest troll, fairytale cave, Supervideograph, Photo Adventure, Energy Centre (exhibition centre for oil and gas), Wax

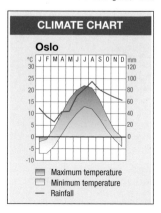

CLIMATE CHART

Oslo

- Maximum temperature
- Minimum temperature
- Rainfall

Museum, Experience Centre for Ice Cream, plus outdoor entertainment (May–Sept).

Kongeparken near Stavanger; tel: 51 61 26 66; www.kongeparken.no. Over 40 attractions, including a giant Gulliver (85 x 7.5 metres/280 x 25ft), riding tracks, bob track, farm, car track, Wild West City, funfair (Apr–Sept).

Kristiansand Dyrepark tel: 97 05 97 00; www.dyreparken.no. Norway's largest wildlife park, with amusement park, water park, leisure park and Kardemomme By, a tiny village from a well-known children's book by the Norwegian author Thorbjørn Egner (all year).

Mikkelparken, Kinsarvik; tel: 53 67 13 13; www.mikkelparken.no). Theme park (May–Aug).

Telemark Sommarland at Bø, Telemark, tel: 35 06 16 00; www.sommar land.no. Norway's biggest water park with various wet and dry attractions, including waterslides, a 26-metre/80ft high water chute, surf wave and a floating river. Plus live entertainment, pony rides, Wild West City and children's playground (June–Aug).

Vilvite, Bergen; tel: 55 59 45 00; www.vilvite.no. Interactive science centre (all year, closed Mon mid-Aug–May).

Vitensenteret, Trondheim; tel: 72 90 90 07; www.vitensenteret.com in Norwegian. Popular science adventure centre; interactive experiments (daily).

Climate

In Oslo the January average daytime high is –2°C (28°F) and the night-time low is –7°C (19°F); Bergen

is less cold (high 3°C/37°F, low –1°C/30°F). Further north sub-zero temperatures can last for months, and a good number of roads are permanently closed over winter due to long-term snow, although on the coast conditions are usually a little milder. February and March are the best skiing months. March and April and sometimes even early May are the wet spring months when skies are grey, and roads are buckled due to thaws and refreezes; during this time the daily high slowly rises from about 4°C (39°F) to 16°C (61°F).

Come summertime and the season of the midnight sun, Oslo can enjoy daily temperatures averaging 20–25°C (68–77°F), while the north has a perfect hiking temperature, hovering around 17°C (63°F). October sees temperatures dip below 10°C (50°F), then continue their slide towards zero. The first snow can be expected any time from mid-October to early December, depending on the location.

The summer months are the most popular with visitors, but May and September are good times to visit too. The Easter ski break is a time of mass exodus from schools and jobs to the slopes and trails. Otherwise, Norwegians mainly holiday from mid-June to early August. The traditional common holiday is in July *(ferietide)*, when some businesses shut down.

What to Bring/Wear

In summer, as Norway is protected by the Gulf Stream it can sometimes be warmer than its southern neighbours. In the south, temperatures

above 25°C (77°F) are not unusual. The average temperature for the country as a whole in July, including the far north, is about 16°C (60°F), 22°C (71°F) in Oslo. Bring swimming gear, as the water in most fjords, except northern Norway, is 20°C+ (68°F+) in midsummer.

Pack the clothes you would normally wear in northern Europe, including jumpers and a raincoat, and bring some strong walking shoes.

The mountains can be cold, so bring some warmer garments. You are not usually required to dress formally for dinner at Norwegian resort hotels. Spring and autumn are rainy (an umbrella is always useful), and nights can be chilly. It is rainy year-round on the west coast.

In winter bring very warm clothing and dress in layers (cotton against the skin and then wool). Woollen mittens or gloves and hats (covering the ears) are strongly advised (and face cover and goggles, if you are skiing). In the far north, temperatures drop to below –20°C (–4°F). In January, the average daytime temperature in Oslo is –2°C (28°F) and –7°C (19°F) at night. Inland areas are generally colder than the coast.

A first-aid kit is recommended if you plan to make any trips to remoter parts. And be sure to include medicines for preventing and treating mosquito bites, as from midsummer into early autumn biting insects are rife, especially in Finnmark.

Crime and Safety

The streets of Oslo are relatively safe compared with the bigger cities of Europe and North America, even though Norwegian tabloids detail muggings, stabbings and other crimes of violence with relish, as do their counterparts everywhere.

Crime against tourists is rare, however. Take the same precautions here as you would anywhere: park safely and hide valuables out of sight. The same applies when out on the town. Simply stick with the happy crowds and avoid the sleazy joints.

Norwegian cities late at night are usually full of young people, some the worse for wear from drink.

In Oslo, most bars have good bouncers, so alert them if you're having trouble. Police patrols are

Beautiful Norway in winter.

now outnumbered by private-sector security personnel and *Nattravene* (Night Ravens, a Guardian Angeltype patrol).

Another potential threat can be drug abusers. However, they are usually placid and in Oslo generally gather around Jernbanetorget (Central Station). There is no strict rule here; a no-go area today could be tomorrow's in place.

Customs Regulations

The following can be brought into Norway by visitors:

Money Notes and coins (Norwegian and foreign) up to NOK 25,000 or equivalent. If you intend to import more, you must fill in a form (available at all entry and exit points) for the customs authorities.

Alcohol and tobacco Permitted imports include 1 litre of spirits (up to 60 percent vol.), 1.5 litres of wine, 2 litres of beer, 200 cigarettes (or 250g of other tobacco goods) and 200 sheets of cigarette paper. The tobacco quota can be exchanged with 1.5 litres of wine or beer. People aged 18 are eligible to bring beer, wine and tobacco products while people over 20 are allowed to bring spirits.

Prohibited goods Narcotics, medicines (except for personal use), spirits over 60 percent volume, endangered animal and plant species, poisons, firearms, ammunition and explosives. Note: the mild narcotic leaf *khat* is illegal in Norway.

D

Disabled Travellers

Visitors in need of assistance should contact **Norges handikapforbund** (the Norwegian Association for the Disabled), Schweigaardsgt 12, 0134 Oslo; tel: 24 10 24 00; www.nhf.no, which is a useful source of Norway-specific advice.

Norway, like the other Scandinavian countries, compares favourably when it comes to accessible travel, and all new buildings are required by law to have wheelchair access.

Hotel listings in accommodation guides have symbols designating disabled access and toilets. At www.visitoslo.com/en/oslo/practical-information/accessibility you'll find useful

accessibility links. Most hotels adapt their furnishings to the needs of people with physical disabilities.

The Norwegian State Railways (NSB) have carriages specially furnished for the disabled, and the newer Hurtigruten ships have lifts and cabins for disabled people.

The **Society for Accessible Travel and Hospitality** (SATH), based in the US, provides information and advice for travellers with disabilities; www.sath.org.

The **Norwegian Association for the Disabled** (Norges Handikapforbund; tel: 24 10 24 00; www.nhf.no) is a useful source of Norway-specific advice.

E

Eating Out

Norwegians eat hearty breakfasts, but light lunches; the size of the evening meal *(middag)* depends on the day of the week and the occasion.

With abundant seafood and what can be gleaned from forest and field, the Norwegian diet has traditionally been healthy and appetising. White bread is rarely purchased as most Norwegians prefer brown bread or dry crackers for breakfast. However, the younger generation tends to eat frozen pizzas and ready-meals.

The hunting season (early autumn) offers some irresistible temptations: pheasant, grouse, elk and reindeer steaks served with peppercorns, berry preserves and coulis, and rich wild mushroom sauces. It is also a good time of year to make the most of seafood (with cod considered best in months with an R in them).

Outside main meals there are many coffee breaks, often served with *bolle* (raisin buns) and *wienerbrød* (lighter pastries with fruit or nuts).

Frokost (breakfast) is more or less a variation of the lunch *Kaldtbord*, a spread including breads (try *grovbrød* and *knekkebrød*), sausage, cheese (try the piquant Gudbrandsost, a delicious burned goats' milk cheese with a dark golden colour), ham, eggs, and coffee and tea. Norwegians seldom eat a warm meal for lunch, preferring something light and cold.

Dinner in someone's home might be mutton stew or a fish ragout. Boiled potatoes, sometimes with parsley, usually accompany a hot main course. Norwegians usually eat their dinner very early (a 4pm start is not unusual in restaurants).

Ice cream is a favourite dessert, as is apple pie. In summer there are all kinds of puddings based on the fresh berries that grow in Norwegian woods. Waffles are also extremely popular, and are usually served with sour cream and strawberry or raspberry jam.

Norwegian Specialities

Norway is not famed for its cuisine, but there are a few specialities that are worth seeking out, particularly around Christmas time, when favourites include:

Pinnekjøtt: Salted, dried and sometimes smoked mutton or lamb ribs which are rehydrated and then steamed, usually over birch twigs *(pinne)*; hence the name.

Ribbe: Roasted pork belly, usually served with sauerkraut and boiled potatoes, Christmas sausage, meatballs and gravy.

Lutefisk: Cod treated in lye and served with bacon bits, green peas, butter sauce and again, boiled potatoes. The fish acquires a jelly-like texture (the more pronounced the longer you cook it).

Other non-Christmas-related specialities include *fårikål*, *rakfisk* and *smalahove*.

Fårikål: Traditionally eaten in the last week of September, *fårikål* literally means "sheep in cabbage", although some Norwegians use lamb instead. Because the cabbage and the meat simmer for hours in the pot, they become so soft that they almost melt in the mouth.

Rakfisk: A speciality from Valdres, in eastern Norway, *rakfisk* is made of fish (usually trout or char) that has been left to ferment in brine for two to three months before being eaten raw, usually on a slice of flat bread with onions, sour cream and boiled potatoes. It's pungent stuff and there is even a Rakfisk Festival, held every year in November, that attracts thousands of *rakfisk*-lovers.

Smalahove: Not for the squeamish: half a head of sheep is salted and smoked, then boiled for a few hours. It makes up in flavour for what it lacks in looks.

Where to Eat

At lunchtime many restaurants offer special fixed-price menus. More casual meals can be had from establishments such as *stovas*, *kros*, *bistros*, *kafés*, *kafeterias* and *gjæst-giveris*. For fast food, pizza places and kebab stalls abound and the hot dog is almost the Norwegian national dish.

Electricity

220 volts AC, 50 cycles. Plugs have two small round pins, so you may need an adaptor for appliances you bring with you.

Embassies and Consulates

Australia (in Denmark; in an emergency, contact the UK embassy)
Dampfærgevej 26, Copenhagen
Tel: +45 70 26 36 76
www.denmark.embassy.gov.au
Canada
Wergelandsveien 7
Tel: 22 99 53 00
www.canadainternational.gc.ca/norway-norvege
Ireland
Haakon VIIs Gate 1
Tel: 22 01 72 00
www.embassyofireland.no
New Zealand (the New Zealand Embassy in the Netherlands handles enquires from Norway)

Eisenhowerlaan 77N, 2517 KK The Hague
Tel: +31 70 346 9324
www.nzembassy.com
South Africa
Drammensveien 88C
Tel: 23 27 32 20
www.dirco.gov.za/oslo
UK
Thomas Heftyesgate 8
Tel: 23 13 27 00
www.gov.uk/world/organisations/british-embassy-oslo
US
Morgedalsvegen 36
Tel: 21 30 85 40
https://no.usembassy.gov

F

Festivals

January

Geilo: Ice Music Festival, where all the musical instruments have been carved from a block of ice.
Tromsø: International Film Festival.

February

Kristiansund: Opera Festival. Two or three opera productions plus church music, ballet and other concerts.
Longyearbyen, Svalbard: Polar Jazz. The world's northernmost jazz festival, 645km (400 miles) from the

North Pole. First held in 1998, this festival is still going strong.
Rorosmartnan: The Roros Fair has been an annual tradition since 1854. Markets, concerts, exhibitions.
Tromsø: Northern Lights Festival. Music ranging from Baroque to contemporary, from jazz to classical.

March

Alta: Borealis Winter Festival, with music, theatre, markets, ski and snowmobile competitions and plenty of fun in the snow.
Narvik: Winter Festival. Church music, jazz, classical music, markets, carnival and sports events.
Voss: Vossajazz. Three days and nights of jazz and folk music with international and Norwegian performers.
Oslo: International Church Music Festival. Concerts in Oslo Cathedral and other churches in the city. Oslo: Inferno Festival, heavy metal.
Kautokeino: Sami Easter Festival, with concerts, art exhibits, reindeer races and snowmobile rallies.

April

Trondheim: Nidaros Blues Festival.
Bergen: Music Festival, including blues, country & western, cajun and rock. Norwegian and international artists perform throughout the city.

May

Constitution Day (17 May). Celebrations and parades all over Norway.
Stavanger: International Jazz Festival (MaiJazz).
Bergen: International Festival. One of Norway's artistic highlights. World-class music, dance and theatre in a beautiful setting. Also Nattjazz – an international jazz festival.
Ål: Norwegian Folk Music Week with concerts, song and dance. Competition between the best fiddlers and dancers in the region.
Bergen: Dragon Boat Festival in the harbour.
Hardanger: Music and culture from the Hardanger fjord area, with chamber, church and folk music.

June

Oslo: Norwegian Wood. Rock music festival with Norwegian and international artists.
Kopervik: Viking Festival, with plays, storytelling, market and Viking camp.

☉ Etiquette – Visiting a Norwegian Home

Norwegians usually eat dinner around 5 or 6pm, but dinner parties usually start later, at around 7.30pm. An invitation for any other time of the day usually means coffee and cake (if in doubt call the host and make certain).

Norway is not a "drop-in" society, so you can expect the food to be well planned and of high quality. Things to bear in mind are:

Norwegians are very punctual and expect others to be. Guests usually arrive exactly on time, jokingly called *Norsk time*, sometimes even early.

When entering a room, shake hands with everybody present, unless a large function makes that impossible. Introduce yourself to those you have not met before; give a friendly greeting to those you do know, but still shake hands.

If it's your first visit to

someone's home it is customary to take a small gift along (usually flowers, a plant or chocolates).

Dinner parties in Norwegian homes follow a fixed pattern and include short speeches even on family occasions. After tapping his glass, the host will always give a welcome speech and then propose a *skål*. It would be discourteous to touch the wine *before* this initial toast (but expect a liberal helping of *skåls*!).

Second helpings *(annen servering)* are so much the rule in Norwegian homes that the host will specifically point out if the dish is only to be passed round once. The secret is not to take too much the first time.

Every meal in Norway is concluded with a *takk for maten* (thank you for the food) and, if it's dinner, a general *skål*.

June/July

Harstad: Arctic Arts Festival, with music, theatre, dance and art exhibitions.
Grimstad: Norwegian Short Film Festival, screening around 80 short and documentary films.

July

Kristiansand. Quart International rock festival. Performers both local and from the US and Europe.
Larvik: Stavernfestivalen music festival at Larvik Golf Arena.
Forde: Norway's largest folk music festival, with more than 250 performers from all over the world.
Molde: International Jazz Festival. Norway's largest jazz festival, with more than 400 performers, many of them world-famous.
Bø: Telemark Festival with traditional folk, blues and jazz music.
Stavanger: Gladmat, the country's largest food festival, a gargantuan scoff all around the harbour.
Lofthus: Cherry Festival.
Åndalsnes: Norway's Mountain Festival.

July/August

Vinstra: Peer Gynt Festival. Art exhibits, music, processions with national costumes, open-air theatre. Performance of Henrik Ibsen's Peer Gynt and Edvard Grieg's music.
Trondheim: St Olav's Festival. Various cultural events commemorating the death of St Olav at the Battle of Stiklestad in 1030.

August

Oslo: Jazz Festival. Over 60 concerts in six days. Øya Music Festival, rock music festival.
Bodø: Nordland Music Festival. Classical, jazz, rock and folk music – with national and international artists. Also church concerts, music theatre, art exhibitions.
Stavanger: International Chamber Music Festival. Renowned soloists and new talents perform chamber music in various ensembles.
Hammerfest: Music and Theatre Festival focusing on culture in northern Norway.
Haugesund: Norwegian International Film Festival. Also Sildajazz, international jazz festival.
Risør: Wooden Boat Festival.
Notodden: Notodden International Blues Festival.
Ålesund: Food Festival (Den Norske Matfestivalen).

⊙ Emergency Numbers

Fire 110
Police 112
Ambulance 113
Emergency at sea 120
Medical problems For emergency medical treatment in Oslo (legevakt), ring 22 93 22 93.
Internal directory enquiries 180
International directory enquiries 1882

September

Oslo: Ultima Contemporary Music Festival. Norway's largest.

October

Lillehammer: Jazz Festival. Mainly Norwegian performers.
Stavanger: Norwegian Youth Chamber Music Festival.

November

Fagernes: Rakfisk Festival: a festival celebrating this local speciality, which consists of salt-cured trout left to ferment in brine for several months, and then eaten uncooked. You can sample this local favourite on the first weekend of the month.

December

Oslo: Parade past the Grand Hotel to honour the winner of the Nobel Peace Prize, plus a Nobel concert in the Oslo Spektrum. Christmas Market at City Hall Square.

H

Health and Medical Care

The are no major health hazards in Norway. No vaccinations are necessary to enter the country and the tap water is reliable. A degree of common sense is required when travelling in remote areas, especially during winter. When hiking/skiing in the mountains always let someone know of your travel intentions, and use guides wherever possible. Mosquitos can be a problem in the north in summer, particularly inland near bogs and swamps. Bring repellent and keep legs and arms well covered.

Treatment

Norway has reciprocal treatment agreements with the UK and many other European countries; your own National Insurance should cover you to receive free treatment at public hospitals. EU citizens should obtain the relevant documentation to entitle them to this (for British citizens an EHIC, European Health Insurance Card, is available from post offices). People from countries without such agreements, and those without an EHIC card, will have to pay a small fee.

If you are concerned whether you need extra insurance cover, check in your own country before you go. The EHIC card only covers emergency treatment and does not include the cost of medicine, so it is advisable to take out additional medical insurance.

You will need to take out extra cover if you are going skiing or doing any other dangerous sports.

Doctors and Hospitals

The standard of health provision in Norway is very high, and even in remote areas you should have no problem getting medical help. Most doctors and nurses speak good English, and if they don't they'll soon find someone who does.

In medical emergencies EU members will receive free treatment at state hospitals, but have to pay towards the non-hospital costs and for prescriptions.

If you are ill, ask your hotel, tourist office or a pharmacy for the address of an English-speaking GP. Private doctors are listed in the directory under Leger (doctors). Make sure you keep receipts if you have medical insurance.

Pharmacies

For minor problems, head for a pharmacy, or Apotek (for opening hours, see page 317). Most larger cities have all-night pharmacies. In other

⊙ Bergen Festival

Bergen's International Festival (Festspillene i Bergen) in late May/early June is one of Scandinavia's largest cultural events, covering music, drama, ballet, opera, jazz and folk arts.

For a festival brochure and further details contact: Bergen International Festival, PO Box 183, 5804 Bergen, tel: 55 21 06 30; www.fib.no.

cities enquire at your hotel, or try the emergency number in the phone book under *Legevakt* (doctor on duty).

Where there is a rota of 24-hour pharmacies in a city, a list will usually be posted on the door of each one.

Oslo
Vitus Apotek, across from *Central Station,* Jernbanetorget 4B. Tel: 23 35 81 00. 24 hours.

Bergen
Vitus Apotek, Strømgata 8. Tel: 55 21 83 84. Mon–Sat 8am–11pm, Sun 1–11pm.

Stavanger
Vitus Apotek Løven, Olav Vs gt. 11. Tel: 51 91 08 80. Daily until 11pm, Christmas, New Year, Easter and Whitsun 9am–8pm.

Trondheim
Vitus Apotek Solsiden, Beddingen 4. Tel: 73 88 37 37. Mon–Sat 8.30am–midnight, Sun 10am–midnight.

Dentists
Emergency dental treatment in Oslo, outside regular dentists' office hours, is available from:
Oslo Kommunale Tannlegevakt, Schweigaardsgate 6, 3rd floor (near Sonia Henies Plass station).
Tel: 22 67 30 00.
Mon–Fri 7–10pm, Sat–Sun and public holidays 11am–2pm and 7–10pm. Please note that emergency treatment is very expensive.

LGBTQ Travellers

In common with the rest of Scandinavia, Norway has a very relaxed attitude to homosexuality. There is very little open hostility to gays and lesbians in general society. The commercial gay scene is relatively small. Tourist offices (see page 318) carry details of the main places and events, including the Gay Pride celebrations in Oslo and Bergen and the annual Oslo Fusion International Film Festival. The main bars and clubs include:
Elsker, Kristian IVs Gate 9, Oslo. Tel: 45 25 60 42
London Pub, Hambros Plass 5, Oslo. Tel: 22 70 87 00; http://londonpub.no.
Fincken Café and Bar, Nygardsgate 2a, Bergen. Tel: 55 32 13 16; www. fincken.no.

For more information:
FRI – the Norwegian Organization for Sexual and Gender Diversity
Tollbugata 24
Tel: 23 10 39 39
Email: post@foreningenfri.no; https://foreningenfri.no (in Norwegian only)
For the gay scene in the capital, go www.visitoslo.com and click on "Gay Oslo".

Maps

For tourist maps, contact the Norwegian Trekking Association:
Den Norske Turistforening
Youngstorget 1, 0181 Oslo
Tel: 40 00 18 68
www.dnt.no

Media

Newspapers
Most larger kiosks (like the *Narvesen* chain) and some bookshops sell English-language newspapers.

Deichmanske Bibliotek, the main public library, is at Henrik Ibsens gate 1 in Oslo; you'll find a selection of international papers and periodicals in its reading rooms, as well as free internet access.

Television
Norway has five main television stations: NRK1, NRK2, NRK3 (public broadcaster), and TV2 and TV Norge (TVN). Cable TV is common here and allows you to pick up a

Newspaper kiosk.

variety of channels, including BBC Prime, BBC World, CNN, Swedish TV1 and TV2, Discovery, MTV, French TV5, Eurosport, TV3 and so on, depending on the distributor. Most hotels have pay channels in addition to the above. English films on Norwegian television are invariably subtitled, not dubbed.

Money

The Norwegian krone (NOK) is divided into 100 øre. Notes come in denominations of NOK 50, 100, 200, 500 and 1,000, and coins are 50 øre and NOK 1, 5, 10 and 20.

You can change currency at post offices, the Oslo S train station, international airports, some hotels and commercial banks. FOREX offices have good rates and no fees. It is always useful to carry a certain amount of cash with you in case of emergency.

Credit Cards/Travellers' Cheques
Use of credit cards is widespread in Norway, with Eurocard, Visa, MasterCard, American Express and Diner's Club the most common. Check with your own credit-card company about acceptability and other services.

ATMs are widely available, and it is possible to pay for even small amounts (such as parking and toll fees) by credit card.

Tipping
Hotels include a service charge and tipping is generally not expected. Restaurants usually have the

service charge included, in which case it's your choice to add anything (5–10 percent is customary). The same applies to taxis. Table service in bars (particularly outdoor tables) requires tipping.

With hairdressers a tip isn't quite as customary, but again 5–10 percent would be appropriate – and appreciated.

Cloakrooms usually have a fixed fee of about NOK 5–10; if not, leave a few crowns for the attendant.

O

Opening Hours

Office hours are 8 or 9am–4pm; lunch is taken early, usually 11.30am–12.30pm, or noon–2pm for a restaurant lunch or lunch meeting, which are always business-like affairs.
Shops Mon–Fri 10am–5pm, Thu until 8pm, Sat 10am–2pm.
Shopping centres Mon–Fri 10am–9pm, Sat 9am–6pm. Shops and shopping centres are closed on Sundays.
Banks Mon–Fri only 8.30am–3pm. To 5pm Thu.
Pharmacies Mon–Fri 9am–5pm, Sat mornings and on a rota basis in larger cities.

P

Postal Services

Post offices in Oslo open Mon–Fri 9am–5pm and Sat 9am–3pm.

Letters and postcards cost the same price to send to the UK and Continental Europe, slightly more to send to North America. Post takes 2–3 days to Europe and 7–10 days to North America.

R

Religious Services

The Lutheran Church is Norway's state Church, with around 86 percent of the population registered as Lutherans. Oslo has many Lutheran places of worship, including one American Lutheran church

(Fritzners gate 15; tel: 22 44 35 84; www.alcoslo.org).

Services are held in English at the **American Lutheran church** and the **Anglican/Episcopalian church** (St Edmund's, Møllergate 30; tel: 22 69 22 14; www.osloanglicans.no).

Minority religious groups are Pentecostalists, Baptists, Seventh Day Adventists, Evangelical Lutherans, Methodists, Catholics, Jews (the **synagogue** is at Bergstein 13, near St Hanshaugen; tel: 22 69 65 70) and Muslims.

S

Shopping

What to Buy

Popular souvenirs from Norway include knitted jumpers, cardigans, gloves and mittens, pewter, silver jewellery and cutlery, hand-painted wooden objects (such as traditional bowls with rose designs), trolls and fjord horses carved out of wood, goat and reindeer skin, enamel jewellery, woven wall designs, furs, handicrafts, glassware and pottery.

Major department stores have a good selection of most of these items. In Oslo, if you want speciality stores there is a detailed "Shopping" section in the *Oslo Guide* (see www.visitoslo.com or pick up a copy of the guide at Oslo City Centre). Karl Johans gate, Grensen and Bogstadveien are all major shopping streets. Away from Oslo, most towns are so compact that it's easy to simply browse and window-shop.

There are several bookshops in Oslo with English-language sections, including: **Tanum Karl Johan** at Karl Johans gate 37, tel: 22 47 87 30, and **Norli**, Universitetsgata

☉ Public Holidays

1 January New Year's Day
March/April Easter: Thursday to Monday inclusive
1 May Labour Day
17 May National Independence Day
May/June Ascension Day
May/June Whit Monday
25 December Christmas Day
26 December 2nd Christmas Day

Norwegian kroner.

20–24, 0162 Oslo, tel: 22 00 43 00, the largest bookshop in Norway.

Fruit and vegetable prices vary considerably according to season. Look out for *lavpris* (low-price) shops offering discounts. The first Saturday of each month is "Super Saturday", when shops in Oslo open longer and offer special discounts. If the krones really count, most bottles (whether plastic or glass) have a returnable deposit of NOK 1 *(pant)*.

In the capital, Glasmagasinet, Stortorvet 9, and Steen & Strøm, Kongensgate 23, are Oslo's largest department stores. Oslo City and By Porten, next to Oslo main train station, and Aker Brygge on the waterfront are three major malls. The largest shopping centre in Norway, with 200 shops over eight floors, is located a few kilometres west of the city centre at Sandvika.

Tax-Free Shopping

If you are a resident of a country other than Norway, Sweden, Denmark or Finland, you are entitled to tax-free shopping on purchases in excess of NOK 315 at any of the 3,000 stores connected to the scheme.

The store issues you with a tax-free voucher for the amount of VAT paid. When you leave Norway, a refund of 11–18 percent (depending on the sale price) will be refunded on presentation of the goods, the tax-free voucher and your passport, on condition that the item has not been used while in Norway.

Glaciers are awe-inspiring.

Student Travellers

There are numerous opportunities for reduced student rates, especially for travel; contact the following for more information:
Ung Info (Young info)
Møllergata 3
Tel: 24 14 98 20
Email: post@ung.info
www.unginfo.oslo.no

T

Telephones

Calls abroad can be made from hotels – but usually with a hefty surcharge – or from phone booths or the main telegraph office at Kongensgate 21 (entrance Prinsensgate), Oslo.

Norwegian payphones take 1, 5, 10 and 20 kroner pieces. Phonecards, which can be used in the green phone booths, can be bought in *Narvesen* kiosks and at post offices. Credit cards are accepted in card phones.

The prefix when calling from Norway to foreign countries is 00. Cheapest calling times (between 5pm and 8am) are outside business hours:. Extra-cheap international calling cards, such as Eurocity, can be purchased from a variety of kiosks and corner shops in most major towns.

Telephone directories have a page of instructions in English in the index. When looking up names, remember the vowels æ, ø, and å come at the end of the alphabet, in that order.

Some US phone companies have their own international access numbers, to allow US citizens cheaper calls, as follows:
Sprint 800-19 877
AT&T 800-19 011

Tourist Information

There are around 350 local tourist offices around Norway, as well as 18 regional tourist offices.

For general information contact:
The Norwegian Tourist Board
PO Box 448 Sentrum, N-0158 Oslo
Tel: 22 00 25 00
www.visitnorway.com

For business-related information contact:
Innovation Norway (Trade Council)
(Innovasjon Norge)
PO Box 448 Sentrum, Aksersgata 13, N-0104 Oslo
Tel: 22 00 25 00
www.innovasjonnorge.no

Regional Information

Oslo/Oslofjord
The Oslo Visitor Centre is located by the Central Station, at Jernbanetorget 1.
Visit Oslo
Tel: 81 53 05 55
Email: info@visitoslo.com
www.visitoslo.com
Østfold Visit Oslofjord
Kirkegaten 31B, 1621 Gamle Fredrikstad
Tel: 69 30 46 00
www.visitoslofjord.no
Visit Vestfold
Torpveien 130, N-3241 Sandefjord
Tel: 33 46 05 90
www.visitvestfold.com

South Norway
Kristiansand Tourist Office
Radhusgate 18,
NO-4611 Kristiansand
Tel: 38 07 50 00
Email: turistinformasjon@kristiansand.kommune.no
Visit Telemark
Uniongata 18, Kunnskapsverkstedet, NO-3732 Skien
Tel: 35 90 00 20
Email: info@visittelemark.no
www.visittelemark.com

Fjord Norway
Bergen
Tourist Information in Bergen
Strandkaien 3
NO-5014 Bergen
Tel: 55 55 20 00
Email: mail@visitbergen.com
www.visitbergen.com
Fjord Norge AS
Torggaten 3
NO-5014 Bergen
Tel: 55 30 26 40
Email: info@fjordnorway.com
www.fjordnorway.com
Hardangerfjord – Destination Hardanger Fjord
Sandvenvegen 40
NO-5600 Norheimsund
Tel: 56 55 38 70
Email: info@hardangerfjord.com
www.hardangerfjord.com
Flåm AS
PO Box 42, 5742 Flåm
Tel: 57 63 14 00
Email: info@visitflam.com
www.visitflam.com
Region Stavanger
Vågsgte 22, NO-4306 Sandnes
Tel: 51 85 92 00
Email: info@regionstavanger.com
www.regionstavanger-ryfylke.com
Visit Sognefjord
Trolladalen 30, 6856 Sogndal
Email: info@sognefjord.no
www.sognefjord.no
Visit Nordmøre & Romsdal AS
Torget 4, NO-6413 Molde
Tel: 70 23 88 00
Email: info@visitnorthwest.no
www.visitnorway.com

⊙ Tourist Info Abroad

Wherever you're living, the website to consult is www.visit norway.com
Australia
The Norwegian embassy deals with tourist information.
17 Hunter Street, Yarralumla, Canberra act 2600
Tel: 2 6273 34444
UK
Innovation Norway
West End House
11 Hills Place
London W1F 7SE
Tel: 020 7389 8800
US/Canada
Norwegian Tourist Board
Scandinavian Tourism Inc.
655 Third Avenue, Suite 1810
New York, NY 10017-911
Tel: 212 885 9700

Central Norway
Hallingdal Reiseliv AS
Gamlevegen 6, NO-3550 Gol
Tel: 32 02 99 26
Email: info@fjellandfjord.com
www.fjellandfjord.com
Lillehammer
Visit Lillehammer AS
Jernbanetorget 2
NO-2609 Lillehammer
Tel: 61 28 98 00
Email: info@lillehammer.com
www.lillehammer.com
Trøndelag Reiseliv AS
Nordre gate 11, 7011 Trondheim
Tel: 73 84 24 40
Email: touristinfo@trondelag.com
www.trondelag.com
Visit Trondheim AS
Nordre gate 11, 7011 Trondheim
Tel: 73 80 76 60
Email: post@visittrondheim.no
https://trondheim.com
Northern Norway Tourist Board – Bodø
Tollbugata 13, PO Box 434, N-8001 Bodø
Tel: 90 17 75 00
www.nordnorge.com
Lofoten Islands – Destination Lofoten
PO Box 210, NO-8301 Solvær
Tel: 76 06 98 00
Email: post@lofoten.info
www.lofoten.info
See also www.lofoten.com
Visit Tromsø
Kirkegate 2, PO Box 311
NO-9253 Tromsø
Tel: 77 61 00 00
Email: info@visittromso.no
www.visittromso.no

North Norway
Northern Norway Tourist Board – Finnmark
Markedsgata 3, PO Box 1163
NO-9504 Alta
Tel: 90 17 75 00
www.nordnorge.com

⊘ Weights and Measures

Norway uses the metric system. Distances are given in kilometres (km). Norwegians sometimes refer to a *mil* which is 10km (thus 10 mil = 100km). When talking about land area you will often hear the word *mål*. This old measure of 984.34 sq metres has been rounded up to 1,000 sq metres (or 1 decare).

Visit Svalbard
PO Box 323, N-9171 Longyearbyen
Tel: 79 02 55 50
Email: info@visitsvalbard.com
www.visitsvalbard.com

Websites
Norway's official travel website
State tourism officials compile this portal offering information on everything from attractions to special events to accommodation, with links to regional sites all over the country. www.visitnorway.com
Oslo's official travel website
The capital's visitors' bureau compiles this site full of information about what's happening in Oslo, accommodation and tourist tips. www.visitoslo.com
The Norwegian Trekking Association (DNT)
This organisation manages hiking and skiing trails all over the country, runs lodges and cabins in the mountains and other scenic areas, and its staff are experts on hiking and outdoor life. www.dnt.no
Foundation Norwegian Heritage (Norsk Kulturarv)
The foundation seeks to preserve Norway's history through "historical vitality", that is, opening historic farms and other sites to the public. It offers listings of historic sites, lodging and attractions around the country, using the St Olav's Rose as its symbol for quality. www.kulturarv.no.
De Historiske
Characterful hotels in historical buildings throughout Norway, the perfect alternative to chain hotels. www.dehistoriske.com.
Hurtigruten
Norway's famous coastal voyage from Bergen in the south to Kirkenes in the north, and back. One of the most beautiful cruises anywhere in the world. www.hurtigruten.com.

Tour Operators
Specialist Tour Operators in the UK
Norway Specialists
Hurtigruten in the UK
Tel: 0203 553 1681
www.hurtigruten.co.uk
Norsc Holidays
The Court, The Street, Charmouth, Dorset, DT6 6PE
Tel: 01297 560 033
www.norsc.co.uk

⊘ Time Zone

Central European Time, 1 hour ahead of Greenwich Mean Time, 6 hours ahead of Eastern Standard Time. The clock is set forward an hour to summer time at the end of March, and back an hour at the end of September.

Scandinavia Only
PO Box 176, Tofts House, Tofts Road, Cleckheaton, West Yorkshire, BD19 3WX
Tel: 01274 875 199
www.scandinaviaonly.co.uk

Arctic Voyages
Arcturus
Tel: 01837 840640
www.arcturusexpeditions.co.uk
Discover the World
Tel: 01737 214 250
www.discover-the-world.co.uk

Activity Holidays
Crystal Holidays
Tel: 020 8939 0726
www.crystalholidays.co.uk
Exodus Travels
Tel: 0203 811 5440
www.exodus.co.uk
Explore Worldwide
Tel: 01252 883 758
www.explore.co.uk
Inntravel
Tel: 01653 617 001
www.inntravel.co.uk
ScanAdventures
Tel: 0207 529 8759
www.scanadventures.co.uk

V

Visas and Passports

A valid passport is all that is necessary for citizens of most countries to enter Norway. Norway is a member of the Schengen agreement, allowing citizens of other Schengen countries to enter without passports. If you enter from another Nordic country (Denmark, Finland, Iceland, or Sweden), you won't get a new entry stamp. Tourists are generally limited to a three-month visit; it is possible to stay longer, but you must apply for a visa after the initial three months or if you plan to work in Norway.

LANGUAGE

INTRODUCTION

Germanic in origin, Norwegian is one of the three Scandinavian languages, and is closely related to Danish and Swedish. There are two official forms of Norwegian, *bokmål* and *nynorsk*. The former reflects Norway's 400 years of Danish domination, while *nynorsk* is built on native Norwegian dialects. The Sami population (Lapps) in north Norway speak Sami. English is widely understood and spoken throughout the country.

USEFUL WORDS AND PHRASES

Yes *Ja*
No *Nei*
Good morning *God morgen*
Good afternoon *God ettermiddag*
Good evening *God kveld*
Today *I dag*
Tomorrow *I morgen*
Yesterday *I går*
Hello *Hei*
How do you do? *Hvordan står det til?*
Goodbye *Adjø/Ha det bra/Hadet*
Thank you *Takk*
How much is this? *Hvor mye koster det?*
It costs *Det koster...*
How do I get to...? *Hvordan kommer jeg til...?*
Where is...? *Hvor er...?*
Right *Høyre*
To the right *Til høyre*
Left *Venstre*
To the left *Til venstre*
Straight on *Rett frem*
Money *Penger*
Can I order please? *Kan jeg få bestille?*
Could I have the bill please? *Kan jeg få regningen?*

What time is it? *Hvor mye er klokken?*
It is (The time is...) *Den er (Klokken er...)*
When? *Når*
Where? *Hvor?*
Could I have your name please? *Hva er navnet ditt?*
My name is *Mitt navn er...*
Do you have English newspapers? *Har du engelske aviser?*
Do you speak English? *Snakker du engelsk?*
I only speak English *Jeg snakker bare engelsk*
May I help you? *Kan jeg hjelpe deg?*
I do not understand *Jeg forstår ikke*
I do not know *Jeg vet ikke*
It has disappeared *Den har forsvunnet*
Chemist *Apotek*
Hospital *Sykehus*
Doctor *Lege*
Police station *Politistasjion*
Parking *Parkering*
Department store *Hus/Stormagasin*
Toilet *Toalett/WC*
Gentlemen *Herrer*
Ladies *Damer*
Vacant *Ledig*
Engaged *Opptatt*
Entrance *Inngang*
Exit *Utgang*
No entry *Ingen adgang*
Open *Åpent*
Closed *Stengt*
Push *Skyv*
Pull *Trekk*
No smoking *Røyking forbudt*
Breakfast *Frokost*
Lunch *Lunsj*
Dinner *Middag*
Eat *Spise*
Drink *Drikke*
Cheers! *Skål!*
Hot *Varm*
Cold *Kald*
Aircraft *Flymaskin*

Car *Bil*
Train *Tog*
Ticket *Billet*
Single/return *En vei/tur-retur*
To rent *Leie*
Free *Ledig*
Room to rent *Rom til leie*
Chalet *Hytte*
Can we camp here? *Kan vi telte her?*
No camping *Camping forbudt*
Grocery store (in countryside) *Landhandel*
Shop *Butikk*
Food *Mat/kost*
To buy *Kjøpe*
Sauna *Badstue*
Off licence/liquor store *Vinmonopol*
Clothes *Klær*
Overcoat *Frakk*
Jacket *Jakke*
Suit *Dress*
Shoes *Sko*
Skirt *Skjørt*
Blouse *Bluse*

DAYS AND MONTHS

Sunday *søndag*
Monday *mondag*
Tuesday *tirsdag*
Wednesday *onsdag*
Thursday *torsdag*
Friday *fredag*
Saturday *lørdag*
January *januar*
February *februar*
March *mars*
April *april*
May *mai*
June *juni*
July *juli*
August *august*
September *september*
October *oktober*
November *november*
December *desember*

FICTION

Classics

Knut Hamsun: Norway's best-known novelist. His works *Hunger* and *Growth of the Soil* are his most famous, although *Mysteries* is a more accessible title for novices.

Henrik Ibsen: Norway's most famous playwright, whose works have been performed the world over. Try *A Doll's House* or *Peer Gynt*, two of his most famous plays.

Snorri Sturluson: Any of the Icelandic historian, politician and poet's sagas are worth reading, but *The Prose Edda* and *Heimskringla, History of the Kings of Norway*, are a good place to start.

Sigrid Undset: The only female Norwegian author to receive the Nobel Prize for Literature (1928), for her trilogy *Kristin Lavransdatter*.

Other

Knut Faldbakken: Faldbakken's novels often focus on the changing role of men in society. *Sleeping Prince, Honeymoon* and *Insect Summer* are among those that have been translated into English.

Jostein Gaarder: *Sophie's World*, a novel about the history of philosophy, has sold millions of copies, and been translated into over 50 languages. It's an unusual introduction to Western philosophy as seen from the eyes of a teenage girl.

Garrison Keillor: Lake Wobegon series: a fun account of life in a fictional small farm town populated by Norwegian immigrants in the American Midwest.

Erlend Loe: One of the most exciting literary talents to come out of Norway in recent years. Only one of his novels, *Naiv.Super*, has so far been translated into English, but look out for more.

Per Petterson: *Out Stealing Horses* is a touching novel by one of Norway's best authors. The book won several literary prizes in both Norway and abroad.

Lars Saabye Christensen: Award-winning writer, two of his most famous titles are *Beatles* and *Half-Brother*, both about growing up in 1960s Oslo.

Crime

Karin Fossum: The Norwegian queen of crime has enjoyed huge success at home and abroad. Her most popular books include *Don't Look Back, Calling Out for You* and *The Whisperer*.

Jo Nesbø: Crime is a popular genre in Norway and Jo Nesbø, with titles such as *The Redbreast, The Snowman* and *The Thirst*, has established a solid reputation.

Gunnar Staalesen: The man behind the private investigator Varg Veum series, whose adventures have been adapted for TV in Norway. *Where Roses Never Die* is his latest title in English, but you could also try *The Writing on the Wall* or *Yours Until Death*.

Comic Strip

Nemi, by Lise Myhre. A comic strip character that maybe appeals more to women than men. She made her appearance in the UK in the *Metro* newspaper, but three book versions are also available for dedicated fans.

◉ Send Us Your Thoughts

We do our best to ensure the information in our books is as accurate and up-to-date as possible. The books are updated on a regular basis using local contacts, who painstakingly add, amend and correct as required. However, some details (such as telephone numbers and opening times) are liable to change, and we are ultimately reliant on our readers to put us in the picture.

We welcome your feedback, especially your experience of using the book "on the road". Maybe you came across a great bar or new attraction we missed. We will acknowledge all contributions, and we'll offer an Insight Guide to the best letters received.

Please write to us at:
Insight Guides
PO Box 7910
London SE1 1WE

Or email us at:
hello@insightguides.com

NON-FICTION

Art

Edvard Munch: Behind the Scream, by Sue Prideaux, is an interesting account of Munch's life, and how it shaped Norway's most famous artist. **They Painted Norway**, by Arvid Bryne, is a great introduction to Norwegian art with high-quality reproductions.

Cookery Books

Kitchen of Light, by Andreas Viestad, one of Norway's most famous chefs. A mix of recipes, essays and photos based on the *New Scandinavian Cooking* TV series he co-hosted.

Famous Explorers

Farthest North, in which Fridtjof Nansen recounts his epic polar exploration, is a classic of the genre.

The South Pole: An Account of the Norwegian Antarctic Exploration in the Fram, 1910–1912, by Roald Amundsen, is a riveting first-person account of the race to the South Pole.

Kon Tiki: Across the Pacific by Raft, in which Thor Heyerdahl recounts the journey that made him a household name in Norway, was a bestseller, and casts light on one of modern times' most daring exploration expeditions.

OTHER INSIGHT GUIDES

Insight Guides in this part of Europe include: *Finland, Iceland, Sweden* and *Scandinavia*.

Insight Guides Explores are route-based self-guided books produced by local writers. Titles include *Copenhagen* and *Stockholm*.

Insight Pocket Guides are compact, practical books. Titles include: *Copenhagen, Oslo* and *Stockholm*.

CREDITS

PHOTO CREDITS

COVER CREDITS

INSIGHT GUIDE CREDITS

Distribution
UK, Ireland and Europe
Apa Publications (UK) Ltd;
sales@insightguides.com
United States and Canada
Ingram Publisher Services;
ips@ingramcontent.com
Australia and New Zealand
Woodslane; info@woodslane.com.au
Southeast Asia
Apa Publications (SN) Pte;
singaporeoffice@insightguides.com
Worldwide
Apa Publications (UK) Ltd;
sales@insightguides.com
Special Sales, Content Licensing and CoPublishing
Insight Guides can be purchased in bulk quantities at discounted prices. We can create special editions, personalised jackets and corporate imprints tailored to your needs.
sales@insightguides.com
www.insightguides.biz

Printed in China by CTPS

All Rights Reserved
© 2018 Apa Digital (CH) AG and
Apa Publications (UK) Ltd

First Edition 1991
Sixth Edition 2018

Every effort has been made to provide accurate information in this publication, but changes are inevitable. The publisher cannot be responsible for any resulting loss, inconvenience or injury. We would appreciate it if readers would call our attention to any errors or outdated information. We also welcome your suggestions; please contact us at:
hello@insightguides.com

www.insightguides.com

Editor: Carine Tracanelli
Authors: Marie Peyre, Doreen Taylor-Wilkie
Updater: Magdalena Helsztyńska-Stadnik
Head of Production: Rebeka Davies
Update Production: Apa Digital
Picture Editor: Tom Smyth
Cartography: original cartography Lovell Johns Ltd, updated by Carte

CONTRIBUTORS

This fully revised edition was managed by **Carine Tracanelli** and updated by **Magdalena Helsztyńska-Stadnik**.
It builds on the excellent foundations created by the writers of previous editions, notably **Marie Peyre**. A journalist and editor, Peyre moved to Norway in 2007 and has been there ever since. She has travelled extensively around Scandinavia in general, and Norway in particular, and covers this region for

a number of publishers in the UK and the US. She speaks (almost) fluent Norwegian, and when she's not working she loves cross-country skiing, hiking and taking photographs.
This edition builds on the work of the late **Doreen Taylor-Wilkie**.
Past contributors also include **Rowlinson Carter**, **Inga Wallerius**, **Bobby Tulloch**, **Jim Hardy**, **Karen Fossli** and **Anita Peltonen**.

ABOUT INSIGHT GUIDES

Insight Guides have more than 45 years' experience of publishing high-quality, visual travel guides. We produce 400 full-colour titles, in both print and digital form, covering more than 200 destinations across the globe, in a variety of formats to meet your different needs.
Insight Guides are written by local authors, whose expertise is evident in the extensive historical and cultural

background features. Each destination is carefully researched by regional experts to ensure our guides provide the very latest information. All the reviews in **Insight Guides** are independent; we strive to maintain an impartial view. Our reviews are carefully selected to guide you to the best places to eat, go out and shop, so you can be confident that when we say a place is special, we really mean it.

Legend

City maps

	Freeway/Highway/Motorway
	Divided Highway
	Main Roads
	Minor Roads
	Pedestrian Roads
	Steps
	Footpath
	Railway
	Funicular Railway
	Cable Car
	Tunnel
	City Wall
	Important Building
	Built Up Area
	Other Land
	Transport Hub
	Park
	Pedestrian Area
	Bus Station
	Tourist Information
	Main Post Office
	Cathedral/Church
	Mosque
	Synagogue
	Statue/Monument
	Beach
	Airport

Regional maps

	Freeway/Highway/Motorway (with junction)
	Freeway/Highway/Motorway (under construction)
	Divided Highway
	Main Road
	Secondary Road
	Minor Road
	Track
	Footpath
	International Boundary
	State/Province Boundary
	National Park/Reserve
	Marine Park
	Ferry Route
	Marshland/Swamp
	Glacier Salt Lake
	Airport/Airfield
	Ancient Site
	Border Control
	Cable Car
	Castle/Castle Ruins
	Cave
	Chateau/Stately Home
	Church/Church Ruins
	Crater
	Lighthouse
	Mountain Peak
	Place of Interest
	Viewpoint

INDEX

MAIN REFERENCES ARE IN BOLD TYPE

INSIGHT ⊙ GUIDES

OFF THE SHELF

Since 1970, INSIGHT GUIDES has provided a unique perspective on the world's best travel destinations by using specially commissioned photography and illuminating text written by local authors.

Whether you're planning a city break, a walking tour or the journey of a lifetime, our superb range of guidebooks and phrasebooks will inspire you to discover more about your chosen destination.

INSIGHT GUIDES

offer a unique combination of stunning photos, absorbing narrative and detailed maps, providing all the inspiration and information you need.

PHRASEBOOKS & DICTIONARIES

help users to feel at home, when away. Pocket-sized with a free app to download, they go where you do.

CITY GUIDES

pack hundreds of great photos into a smaller format with detailed practical information, so you can navigate the world's top cities with confidence.

EXPLORE GUIDES

feature easy-to-follow walks and itineraries in the world's most exciting destinations, with our choice of the best places to eat and drink along the way.

POCKET GUIDES

combine concise information on where to go and what to do in a handy compact format, ideal on the ground. Includes a full-colour, fold-out map.

EXPERIENCE GUIDES

feature offbeat perspectives and secret gems for experienced travellers, with a collection of over 100 ideas for a memorable stay in a city.

www.insightguides.com

Oslo

Inset map (top left):

Strømsdammen Lake
Tryvannstårnet
Øvresetertjern
Frognerseteren
Lillevann
Voksenkollen
500
Skogen
Uttveien
Borgen
Holmenkollveien
Tårnveien
Voksenkollveien
Voksenlia
Tilfeldtsmveien
Sørkedalsveien
Bogstad camping-plass
Holmenkollen kapell
Holmenkollen bakken
Midtstuen
Holmenkollen
Besserud
Bogstad Manor
Ankerveien
Oslo
N

Main map:

Grefsen, Holmenkollen
Fysikk
Diakonhjemmet
Barnekunstmuseet
Fjernsynshuset
N.R.K.
GRAV
BLINDERN
Lille Frøens vei
Apalveien
Kringkastingen
Wilhelm Wedels vei
Holmenkollveien
Borgenveien
Diakonveien
Slemdalsveien
Frøen
Gydas vei
Gardeveien
Suhms gate
Kirkeveien
Majorstuen
Aalls gate
Suhms gate
Faberborggata
VESTRE GRAVLUND
Thurlows vei
Trudvangveien
Hammerstads gate
Schønings gate
Sporveismuseet
Misjons-kirken
Valkyrie
Ole Vigs gate
Hammerstads gate
Industrigata
Vibes gate
Rosenborggata
Fritjof Nansens vei
Colosseum senter
Bogstadveien
Jacob
Gørstads gate
168
Colosseum kino
Essendrops gate
Majorstuen
Ole Vigs gate
Industrigata
Bogstadveien
VIGELANDS-PARKEN
Middelthuns gate
Frogner stadion
MAJORSTUEN
Majorstuveien
Giørstads gate
HEGDEHAU
Monolitten
Professor Dahls gate
Jacob Aalls gate
St Dominikus
Underhaugsveien
Hegdehaugsveien
FROGNERPARKEN
Fugelhauggata
Prof. Dahls gate
HOMANSBYEN
Frogner
Munthes gate
Briskeby
Uranienborgveien
Oscars gate
Oslo Bymuseet
Professor Dahls gate
Josefines
Damveien
Fron
Gyldenløves gate
Eckersborgs gate
Industrigata
Uranienborgveien
Vigeland-museet
Nordraaks gate
Tidemands gate
BRISKEBY
Sundts
Eilert
Rottegata
Josefines gate
FROGNER
Kirkeveien
Frognerveien
Løvenskiolds gate
Arno Bergs plass
President Harbitz gate
Briskebyveien
Skovveien
Uranienborg
Camilla Colletts vei
Kristinelundveien
Nobels
Eckersbergs gate
Oscars gate
Halvdan Svartes gate
Solheimgata
Thomas Heftyes gate
Gimleveien
Odins
Ridderrvolds plass
Skovveien
Inkognitogata
Drammensveien
Olav Kyrres plass
Bygdøy allé
Niels Juels gate
Ridderrvolds gate
Parkveien
SLOTTSPA
Nobels
Elisenbergveien
Meltzers gate
Frøyas gate
Det Kongelige (Royal Pala
Bygdøy allé
Olav Kyrres g.
Drammensveien
Thomas
Frogner
Gimle kino
Frognerveien
DRONNINGS-PARKEN
E18
Frøyas gate
American Lutheran Church
Mogens Thorsens gate
Oslo Energi
Drammensveien
Båthavn
Sophus Lies gate
Bygdøy allé
Gabels gate
Niels Juels gate
Skovveien
Colbjørnsens gate
Hydro
Inkognitogata
Parkveien
Thomas Heftyes gate
Frederik Stangs gate
Bygdøy allé
Parkveien
Observatoriepata
RUSELØKKA
B y g d ø y
Wedels vei
Gabels gate
Niels Juels gate
Drammensveien
Universitets-biblioteket
Solligata
Cort Adelers gate
Huitfeldts gate
Løkkeveien
Ruseløkka
Observatorie terrasse
Hansteens gate
Oscarshall slott
Frognerkilen
SKILLEBEKK
Frammseveien
Rikstrygdeverket
Reichweins gate
AKER BRYGGE
Oscarshallveien
Munkedamsveien
Observatoriegata
Site of r
National Muse
(to open in 2
Båthavn
Munkedamsveien
Drønninghavnveien
Kongen
Ferry port!
Hjørtneskaia
Filipstadveien
E18
Munkedamsveien
Båthavn
Tjuvholmen
Meltbyedalen
Holocaust Center
Dronningen
Filipstadkaia
FILIPSTAD
Filipstadkaia
Langviksveien
Hukveien
Astrup-Fearnley-museet
Huk
Christian Benneches vei
Filipstadutstikker
Kon-Tiki Museet
Filipstadutstikker
Langviksbukta
Frammuseet
Norsk Sjøfartsmuseum
O s l o f j o r d
500 m
500 yds
Denmark, Germany
Hellviktangen Manor, Nesoddtangen
N

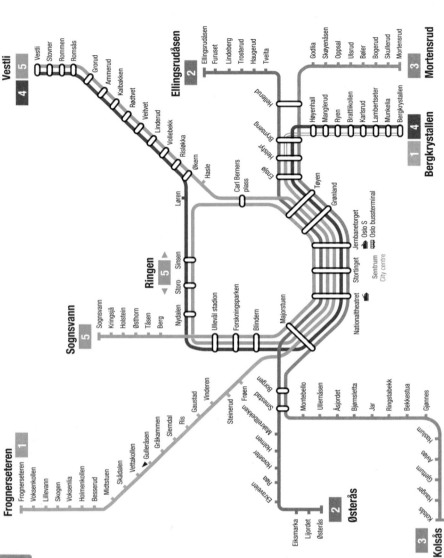